1-2-3® Release 2.2 QuickStart

2nd Edition

Developed by Que® Corporation

Text and graphics pages developed by
David P. Ewing and Katherine Murray

Revised for 2nd Edition by
Joyce J. Nielsen and Kathie-Jo Arnoff

CORPORATION
LEADING COMPUTER KNOWLEDGE
CARMEL, INDIANA

Trademark Acknowledgments

Publishing Director

David Paul Ewing

Acquisitions Editor

Terrie Lynn Solomon

Product Director

Kathie-Jo Arnoff

Production Editor

Nancy E. Sixsmith

Technical Editors

Robert Walker
Jerry Ellis

Book Design and Production

Jill D. Bomaster
Don Clemons
Tom Emrick
Denny Hager
William Hartman
Tami Hughes
Betty Kish
Bob LaRoche
Sarah R. Leatherman
Joe Ramon
Bruce D. Steed
Mary Beth Wakefield

Indexer

Sharon Hilgenberg

Composed in Garamond by

Hartman Publishing

Page Design by

William Hartman
Hartman Publishing

Acknowledgments

Que Corporation thanks the following individuals for their contributions to the 2nd edition of this book:

Dave Ewing, for lending his support and encouragement to the 2nd edition authors who restructured and modified his original text.

Bill Hartman, of Hartman Publishing, for his creative thinking and patience during the development of the new QuickStart design, and for his excellent design and layout of the pages and illustrations in this book.

Kathie-Jo Arnoff, for her ongoing work on the development of the new QuickStart approach, and for restructuring the *1-2-3 Release 2.2 QuickStart* material into the new format.

Joyce Nielsen, for enhancing and further developing the material from the last edition, and for making the text both an exceptional teaching tool and reference book for beginners.

Nancy Sixsmith, for editing the manuscript, and for her outstanding organizational skills in keeping track of the project from the original manuscript through the production process.

Robert Walker and Jerry Ellis, for their careful scrutiny of the text and illustrations in this book, and for their dedication to ensuring the book's technical accuracy.

Contents at a Glance

Contents

Introduction

If you are new to Lotus 1-2-3 and have access to Release 2.2 or an earlier version of the program, this book is for you. *1-2-3 Release 2.2 QuickStart*, 2nd Edition, will allow you to grasp the basics of using 1-2-3—enabling you to begin creating your own worksheets (or modify existing worksheets created by others) with a minimum of effort. You don't even need to be familiar with computers—keyboard basics are covered, as well as how to install 1-2-3 if it is not already installed on your computer.

1-2-3 Release 2.2 QuickStart, 2nd Edition, is a step forward in the evolution of how a book can be organized and structured. The book uses a tutorial approach, taking you through important concepts step-by-step, describing all the fundamentals you need to know about the program. The text supplies essential information and provides comments on what you see. Many illustrations help guide you through procedures or clarify difficult concepts.

Learning any new program can be an intimidating experience. *1-2-3 Release 2.2 QuickStart*, 2nd Edition, is designed to help shorten your learning curve by allowing you to learn basic concepts quickly. Whether you are new to 1-2-3 or have tried unsuccessfully to learn the program, you will find *1-2-3 Release 2.2 QuickStart*, 2nd Edition, a quick way to learn the fundamentals of 1-2-3.

What Does This Book Contain?

The chapters in *1-2-3 Release 2.2 QuickStart*, 2nd Edition, are organized to take you from basic information to more sophisticated tasks, including printing reports and creating graphs.

Chapter 1, "An Overview of 1-2-3," shows you the wide range of 1-2-3's capabilities. You explore how 1-2-3 can be used for spreadsheet, graphics, and database applications.

Chapter 2, "Getting Started," explains how to start and leave 1-2-3, and teaches you the basics about the keyboard, the screen, and 1-2-3's help features.

Chapter 3, "Introducing Worksheet Basics," teaches you about the fundamental tasks of using a spreadsheet. In that chapter, you learn how 1-2-3 fits into the realm of integrated software. You also discover how to enter and edit data, move around in the worksheet, select commands from menus, and save and retrieve files.

Chapters 4, 5, and 6 cover all the basic tasks you need to create a worksheet. Chapter 4, "Working with Ranges," teaches you how to use ranges and the range commands, and shows you step-by-step how to perform formatting tasks. Chapter 5, "Building a Worksheet," shows you how to use each of the worksheet commands to enhance the appearance of your worksheets. And Chapter 6, "Modifying a Worksheet," explains how to modify your worksheet by moving and copying cell contents, and finding and replacing the contents of cells.

Chapter 7, "Using Functions," introduces you to 1-2-3's selection of built-in functions for performing a variety of calculations. Among the functions illustrated are those for performing mathematical, statistical, and logical calculations.

Chapter 8, "Printing Reports," shows you how to set print specifications and organize your data for printing. You also learn to hide columns and rows, control paper movement, enhance a report by adding headers and footers, and change the page layout.

In Chapter 9, "Printing with Allways," you learn about the add-in feature Allways (provided only with Release 2.2), which makes available such presentation-quality printing techniques as using different fonts, including graphs along with data in your printed output, and shading, outlining, or underlining selected ranges.

Chapter 10, "Managing Files," describes how to use passwords to protect your worksheets, how to save and retrieve parts of files, and how to link cells between different files. This chapter also explains how to delete and list your files, as well as how to import files from other software programs into 1-2-3.

Chapter 11, "Creating Graphs," teaches you how to produce graphs with 1-2-3. That chapter takes you from selecting graph types to adding titles and legends. In addition, the chapter teaches you to set and change print specifications and save graphs before printing.

Chapter 12, "Printing Graphs," shows you how to use Lotus PrintGraph, the program for printing graphs that you created in 1-2-3. You also learn how to preview graphs before they are printed.

Chapter 13, "Managing Data," explains how to use 1-2-3 for data management. You learn to create and modify a database, and sort and search for specific records.

Chapter 14, "Understanding Macros," gives you an introduction to the concept of simple keystroke macros. That chapter teaches you to plan, position, create, name, and edit simple macros. The chapter includes macros you can use to start your own macro library.

The book concludes with two appendixes and an index. Appendix A shows you how to install 1-2-3. Appendix B provides a reference to 1-2-3's commands.

As you notice from the index, each topic is referenced in only one or two places. This apparent "lack" of cross-referencing actually means that this book does its job well; most information about a particular topic is contained in one section—or chapter—of this book.

Who Should Use This Book?

1-2-3 Release 2.2 QuickStart, 2nd Edition, is designed to be a quick guide for new 1-2-3 users. Whether you are sitting down with 1-2-3 for the first time or are trying—for the umpteenth time—to learn enough about 1-2-3 to use it efficiently, *1-2-3 Release 2.2 QuickStart*, 2nd Edition, gives you enough information to get you going quickly. The book highlights important concepts and takes you through important information by providing steps and explanations interwoven with examples and illustrations.

3

What Do You Need To Run 1-2-3 Release 2.2?

There are no prerequisites to using this book, or, for that matter, to using 1-2-3. This text assumes, of course, that you have the software, the hardware, and a desire to learn to use the program.

The following hardware is required to run 1-2-3 Release 2.2:

- An IBM PC or compatible computer with a hard disk drive and a single floppy disk drive, *or* two floppy disk drives.
- DOS version 2.0 or later.
- At least 512K of RAM.
- A monochrome or color monitor (a graphics card is necessary for using 1-2-3's graphing features).
- A printer (optional).

What Is New in 1-2-3 Release 2.2?

This book discusses new features available with Release 2.2 of 1-2-3. This version of 1-2-3 has been enhanced with such additional options as the following:

- An Undo feature, which allows you to reverse the last command or action taken. Not only can you undo a mistake, but you can also try unfamiliar commands freely, knowing that you can undo many unsatisfactory results.
- File linking, which lets you use formulas to link the cell(s) of one worksheet to the cells in other worksheets. When one of the linked worksheets is retrieved, it is automatically updated.
- Minimal recalculation, which requires no special action on your part; only relevant formulas are recalculated when you make changes to the worksheet. This feature results in faster, more responsive worksheets.
- Settings sheets, full-screen presentations of current settings, which are displayed automatically when you use print, graph, and database commands.

- Search and replace, which lets you search for the occurrence of any string in a selected range and gives you the option of replacing some or all instances with a different string.
- Group options in /Worksheet and /Graph commands that simplify multiple column-width changes and graph-range definitions.
- Enhanced graph images that make line, bar, and stacked-bar graphs easier to read. Grid lines appear behind bars.
- Macro names can be descriptive names up to 15 characters long, increasing readability and tracking.
- The Allways add-in, a presentation-quality printing package that lets you use different fonts, underlining, outlining, and shading on selected ranges. You can combine text and graphics on printed output. A what-you-see-is-what-you-get (WYSIWYG) image is shown on your screen before you print.

Often there are slight differences between Release 2.2 and previous 1-2-3 versions (Releases 2.0 and 2.01) with regard to the wording of prompts in menus. When these differences are minimal (for example, one version prompts `Create a Table`, another says `Create Table`), the Release 2.2 version is shown in the screen figure, with no comment. When major differences occur, either both screens are presented or the difference is noted in the text.

Where To Find More Help

After you learn the fundamentals presented in this book, you may want to learn more advanced applications of 1-2-3. Que Corporation has a full line of 1-2-3 books you can use. Among these are *Using 1-2-3 Release 2.2*, Special Edition; *1-2-3 Release 2.2 Quick Reference*; *1-2-3 Release 2.2 Workbook and Disk*; and *1-2-3 Tips, Tricks, and Traps*, 3rd Edition. For more information on how to use DOS commands, new computer users can also benefit from reading Que's *MS-DOS QuickStart*, 2nd Edition.

You can use 1-2-3's Help feature to answer some of your questions while working with 1-2-3. Using Help is explained and illustrated in Chapter 2, "Getting Started."

Should all else fail, contact your computer dealer, or Lotus Product Support at 1-617-253-9150. In Canada, contact Lotus Product Support at 1-416-979-9412.

Conventions Used in This Book

A number of conventions are used in *1-2-3 Release 2.2 Quickstart*, 2nd Edition, to help you learn the program. One example of each convention is provided to help you distinguish among the different elements in 1-2-3.

References to keys are as they appear on the keyboard of the IBM Personal Computer and most compatibles. The function keys, F1 through F10, are used for special situations in 1-2-3. In the text, the key name is usually followed by the number in parentheses: Graph (F10).

Direct quotations of words that appear on the screen are spelled as they appear on the screen and are printed in a special typeface. Information you are asked to type is printed in **boldface**. The first letter in each command from the 1-2-3 menu system also appears in boldface: /**R**ange **F**ormat **C**urrency.

Elements printed in uppercase include range names (SALES), functions (@PMT), modes (READY), and cell references (A1..G5).

Conventions that pertain to macros deserve special mention here:

1. Single-character macro names (Alt-character combinations) appear with the backslash (\) and single-character name in lowercase: \a. In this example, the \ indicates that you press the Alt key and hold it down while you also press the A key.

2. 1-2-3 menu keystrokes in a macro line appear in lowercase: /rnc.

3. Range names within macros appear in uppercase: /rncTEST.

4. In macros, representations of direction keys, such as {DOWN}; function keys, such as {CALC}; and editing keys, such as {DEL}, appear in uppercase letters and are surrounded by braces.

5. Enter is represented by the tilde (~).

When two keys appear together, for example Ctrl-Break, you press and hold down the first key as you also press the second key. Other key combinations, such as Alt-F10, are pressed in the same manner.

Within the step-by-step instructions, keys appear similar to those on the keyboard. Blue lines emphasize the most important areas of the illustrations.

An Overview of 1-2-3

1

Before you put your fingers on the keyboard to start using 1-2-3, you need to know the range of capabilities of this software package. If you are inheriting a spreadsheet created by someone else, coming up to speed with 1-2-3 may require little more of you than simply entering data. If, on the other hand, someone has handed you the 1-2-3 package and said, "Prepare a sales forecast for product A," your task may seem a bit intimidating. Whether you are an experienced or a new spreadsheet user, this chapter shows you some of the many features of 1-2-3 and describes how they can fit into your day-to-day tasks.

As you read through this chapter, ask yourself which of the 1-2-3 features you'll be using most often. Will you be maintaining an accounts receivable spreadsheet? Perhaps your department is in charge of setting up a database to track inventory. Will you be responsible for printing reports and graphs? Whatever the application, read the appropriate overview sections closely, and look for chapter references at the ends of these sections for the chapters in the book that deal more specifically with that topic.

Learning how 1-2-3 functions as a spreadsheet

Understanding basic spreadsheet concepts

Discovering the graphics capabilities of 1-2-3

Knowing how 1-2-3 handles data management tasks

Introducing macros as timesaving shortcuts

1

Key Terms in This Chapter

Electronic spreadsheet	The 1-2-3 spreadsheet (or *worksheet*) is known as the electronic replacement for the accountant's pad.
Direction keys	The keys that allow movement within the 1-2-3 worksheet—including PgUp, PgDn, Home, End, Tab, and the arrow keys.
Cell	The intersection of a row and a column in the 1-2-3 worksheet.
Cell pointer	The highlighted bar that allows you to enter data within the worksheet area.
Formula	An action performed on a specified cell or group of cells. For example, +A1+B1 sums the contents of cells A1 and B1.
Function	A shorthand method of using formulas. For example, instead of typing the formula +A1+B1+C1+D1+E1, you can use the @SUM function @SUM(A1..E1).
Command	A menu selection used to carry out an operation within the worksheet.

Whether you are an experienced computer user who is new to the 1-2-3 program or you are using a computer for the first time, you will find that the fundamentals of 1-2-3 can be quickly grasped. If you start by learning the most basic concepts of 1-2-3 and then gradually build on your knowledge and experience, you'll be amazed by how easily you'll learn the program. If, however, you jump right in and start using string functions or macros right away, you may find yourself running into snags. This book uses an easy, step-by-step approach to demonstrate the fundamental tasks you can perform with 1-2-3.

What Is a Spreadsheet?

Sometimes known as a ledger sheet or accountant's pad, a *spreadsheet* is a specialized piece of paper on which information is recorded in columns and rows. Spreadsheets usually contain a mix of descriptive text and accompanying numbers and calculations. Typical business applications include balance sheets, income statements, inventory sheets, and sales reports.

Although you may be unfamiliar with business applications for spreadsheets, you already use a rudimentary spreadsheet if you keep a checkbook. Similar to an accountant's pad, a checkbook register is a paper grid divided by lines into rows and columns. Within this grid, you record the check number, the date, a transaction description, the check amount, any deposits, and a running balance.

NUMBER	DATE	DESCRIPTION OF TRANSACTION	PAYMENT/DEBT (-)	✓	FEE (IF ANY) (-)	DEPOSIT/CREDIT (+)	BALANCE $1000 00	
1001	9/3/89	Department Store Credit	51 03				948	97
1002	9/13/89	Electric	95 12				853	85
1003	9/14/89	Grocery	74 25				779	60
1004	9/15/89	Class Supplies	354 57				425	03
	9/16/89	Deposit				250 00	675	03
1005	9/21/89	Telephone	49 43				625	60

A manual checkbook register.

What happens when you make an invalid entry in your checkbook register or when you have to void an entry? Such procedures are messy because you have to erase or cross out entries, rewrite them, and recalculate everything. The limitations of manual spreadsheets are apparent even with this simple example of a checkbook register.

For complex business applications, the dynamic quality of an electronic spreadsheet such as 1-2-3 is indispensable. You can change one number and recalculate the entire spreadsheet in an instant. Entering new values is nearly effortless. Performing calculations on a column or row of numbers is accomplished with formulas—usually the same type of formulas that calculators use.

Compare the manual checkbook register to the following electronic one. Notice that the electronic checkbook register is set up with columns and rows. Columns are marked by letters across the top of the spreadsheet; rows are numbered along the side. Each transaction is recorded in a row, the same way you record data in a manual checkbook.

1

```
F8: (,2) [W11] +F7-D8+E8                                    READY

      A       B          C              D       E        F
 1 CHECK #   DATE     DESCRIPTION     PAYMENT DEPOSIT   BALANCE
 2
 3          01-Apr-90 Beginning balance       $1,000.00 $1,000.00
 4   1001   03-Apr-90 Department store credit  51.03      948.97
 5   1002   13-Apr-90 Electric                 95.12      853.85
 6   1003   14-Apr-90 Grocery                  74.25      779.60
 7   1004   15-Apr-90 Class supplies          354.57      425.03
 8          16-Apr-90 Deposit                         250.00  675.03
 9   1005   21-Apr-90 Telephone                49.43      625.60
10   1006   23-Apr-90 Clothing store           62.35      563.25
11 ***************APRIL TOTALS      $686.75 $1,250.00 ***********
12   1007   02-May-90 Grocery                  65.83      497.42
13          07-May-90 Deposit                         275.00  772.42
14   1008   10-May-90 Department store credit  50.00      722.42
15   1009   10-May-90 Electric                 75.34      647.08
16   1010   15-May-90 Bookstore                95.24      551.84
17   1011   21-May-90 Hardware store           31.24      520.60
18          21-May-90 Deposit                         250.00  770.60
19   1012   24-May-90 Grocery                  85.21      685.39
20 ***************MAY TOTALS       $402.86   $525.00 ***********
24-May-90  09:44 AM
```

An "electronic" checkbook register.

Assigning column letters and row numbers lends itself well to creating *formulas*. Note the following formula in the upper left corner of the electronic checkbook:

+F7–D8+E8

These instructions to 1-2-3 translate to

Previous BALANCE minus PAYMENT plus DEPOSIT

As you can see from this simple example, formulas let you establish mathematical relationships between values stored in certain places on your spreadsheet. Formulas let you easily make changes to a spreadsheet, and you can quickly see the results. In the electronic checkbook, if you delete an entire transaction (row), the spreadsheet automatically recalculates itself. You can also change an amount and not worry about recalculating your figures, because the electronic spreadsheet updates all balances.

If you forget to record a check or deposit, 1-2-3 lets you insert a new row at the location of the omitted transaction and enter the information. Subsequent entries are moved down one row, and the new balance is automatically calculated. Inserting new columns is just as easy. Indicate where you want the new column to go, and 1-2-3 inserts a blank column at that point, moving existing information to the right of that column.

What if you want to know how much you have spent at the local department store since the beginning of the year? With a manual checkbook, you have to look for each check written to the store and total the amounts. Not only does

1

this task take considerable time, but you may overlook some of the checks. An electronic checkbook can sort your checks by description so that all similar transactions are together. You then create a formula that totals all the checks written to the department store, for example.

This simple checkbook example demonstrates how valuable an electronic spreadsheet is for maintaining financial data. Although you may choose not to use 1-2-3 to balance your personal checkbook, an electronic spreadsheet is an indispensible tool in today's modern office.

The 1-2-3 Electronic Spreadsheet

1-2-3 has a number of capabilities, but the foundation of the program is the electronic spreadsheet. The framework of this spreadsheet contains the graphics and data management elements of the program. Graphics are produced through the use of spreadsheet commands. Data management occurs in the standard row and column spreadsheet layout.

The importance of the spreadsheet as the basis for 1-2-3 cannot be over-emphasized. All the commands for the related features of 1-2-3 are initiated from the same main menu as the spreadsheet commands, and all the commands have the same format. For example, all the commands for graphics display refer to data in the spreadsheet, and they use this data to draw graphs on the screen. For easy data management, the database is composed of records that are actually rows of cell entries in a spreadsheet.

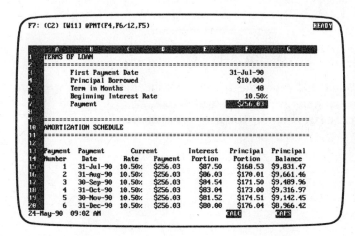

1-2-3's integrated electronic spreadsheet replaces traditional financial modeling tools, reducing the time and effort needed to perform sophisticated accounting tasks.

11

1

With 1-2-3's graphics capabilities, you can create five different types of graphs.

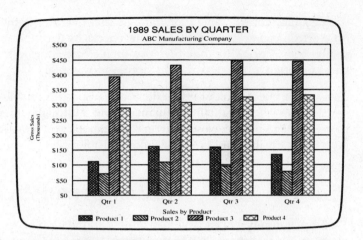

1-2-3's database commands and statistical functions help to manage and manipulate data.

The Size of 1-2-3's Spreadsheet

With 256 columns and 8,192 rows, the 1-2-3 spreadsheet contains more than 2,000,000 cells. The columns are lettered from A to Z, AA to AZ, BA to BZ, and so on, to IV for the last column. The rows are sequentially numbered from 1 to 8192.

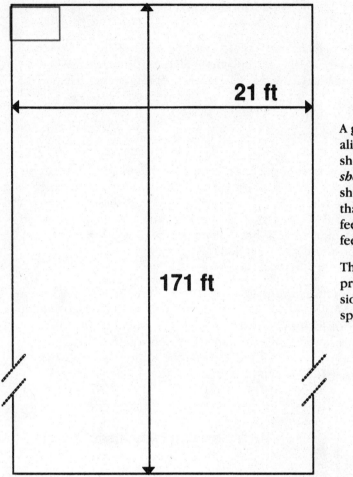

A good way to visualize the spreadsheet (or *worksheet*) is as a giant sheet of grid paper that is about 21 feet wide and 171 feet high.

These are the approximate dimensions of 1-2-3's spreadsheet.

Although the 1-2-3 worksheet contains so many columns and rows, there are some limitations to using the entire sheet. If you imagine storing just one character in each of the 2,097,152 available cells, you end up with a worksheet that is far larger than the 640K maximum random-access memory (RAM) of an IBM PC.

For 1-2-3 Releases 2.0 and 2.01, the program alone requires 215K of RAM. 1-2-3 needs this amount of RAM because the program keeps in its memory all

1

cell formats, worksheet and command ranges, print options, and graph settings.

1-2-3 Release 2.2, which has many additional features, requires at least 320K of RAM. If you want to use the Allways add-in feature (provided with 1-2-3 Release 2.2), you must have a hard disk on your computer and at least 512K of RAM.

The Worksheet Window

Because the 1-2-3 grid is so large, you cannot view the entire worksheet on the screen at one time. The screen thus serves as a *window* onto a small section of the worksheet. To view other parts of the worksheet, you can use the *direction keys* (Tab, PgUp, PgDn, Home, End, and arrow keys) to move the cell pointer around the worksheet. When the cell pointer reaches the edge of the current window, the window shifts to follow the cell pointer across and up (or down) the worksheet.

To illustrate the window concept, imagine cutting a one-inch square hole in a piece of cardboard. If you place the cardboard over this page, you will be able to see only a one-inch square piece of text. The rest of the text is still on the page; the data is simply hidden from view. When you move the cardboard around the page (the same way that the window moves when the direction keys are used), different parts of the page become visible.

The default 1-2-3 worksheet displays 8 columns (each 9 characters wide) and 20 rows.

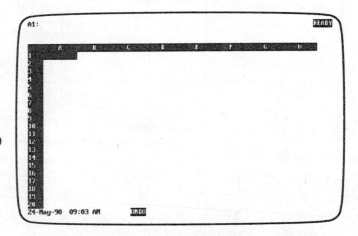

1

You can change the default number of columns that are displayed by narrowing or widening one or more of the columns.

Cells

Each row in a 1-2-3 worksheet is assigned a number; each column is assigned a letter. The intersections of the rows and columns are called *cells*. Cells are identified by their row and column coordinates. The cell located at the intersection of column A and row 15, for example, is called A15. The cell at the intersection of column X and row 55 is named X55. Cells can be filled with two types of information: labels, which are text entries; or values, which consist of numbers and/or formulas.

A *cell pointer* allows you to enter information into the current cell. In 1-2-3, as in most spreadsheets, the cell pointer looks like a highlighted rectangle on the computer's screen. The cell pointer typically is one row high and one column wide.

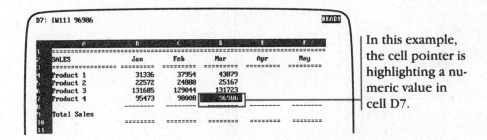

In this example, the cell pointer is highlighting a numeric value in cell D7.

Formulas

Electronic spreadsheets allow mathematical relationships to be created between cells. Suppose, for example, that the cell named C1 contains the formula

    +A1+B1

Cell C1 then displays the sum of the contents of cells A1 and B1. (The + sign before A1 tells 1-2-3 that what you have entered into this cell is a formula, not text.) The cell references serve as variables in the equation. Each time

1

you modify the contents of cell A1 and/or B1, the sum in cell C1 auto-matically reflects these changes.

You now know that only a portion of the entire 1-2-3 worksheet is visible at one time. Although you see only values in the cells, 1-2-3 stores all the data, formulas, and formats in memory. A simple 1-2-3 worksheet displays values, not the formulas "behind" them.

In this example, the cell pointer is positioned on C1, and its formula is displayed at the top left of the screen.

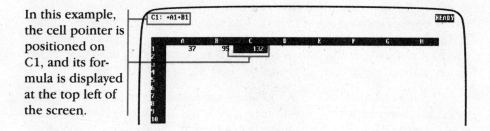

"What If" Analysis

1-2-3 allows you to play "what if" with your model. After you have built a set of formulas into 1-2-3's worksheet, you can modify and recalculate the worksheet with amazing speed, using several sets of assumptions. If you use only paper, a pencil, and a calculator to build your model, every change requires recalculation of each correlation. If the model has 100 formulas and you change the first one, you must make 100 manual calculations so that the change flows through the entire model. If you use a 1-2-3 worksheet, however, the same change requires pressing only a few keys—the program does the rest. This capability permits you to perform extensive "what if" analyses.

Suppose, for example, that you want to forecast sales for two products over the next six months and to recalculate the revenue totals for different discounts.

1

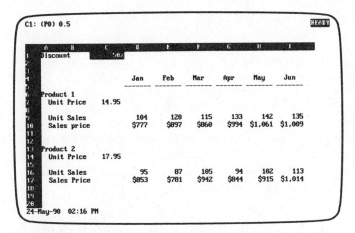

If you enter 50% into C1 as the discount rate, 1-2-3 calculates the sales price figures.

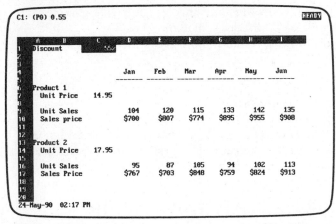

If you change the discount rate from 50% to 55%, 1-2-3 automatically recalculates the new sales price figures.

With 1-2-3's Undo feature, you have even greater flexibility in playing the "what if" game with your worksheet. By inserting a new value, you can see the implications throughout the worksheet. If the results are unsatisfactory, simply use the Undo feature (press Alt-F4), and the worksheet returns to its previous condition. (The Undo feature, which is unavailable in 1-2-3 versions prior to Release 2.2, is explained in greater detail in Chapter 3.)

1

Functions

You can create simple formulas, involving only a few cells, when you refer to the cell addresses and use the appropriate operators (+, −, /, and *). Each formula is stored in memory, and only its value appears in the cell.

You can create complex formulas when you use 1-2-3's functions. These *functions* are shortcuts to help you make common mathematical computations with a minimum of typing. Functions are like abbreviations for long and cumbersome formulas. The @ symbol signals 1-2-3 that an expression is a function. For instance, you can use the shorter @SUM function @SUM(A1..E1) instead of typing the formula +A1+B1+C1+D1+E1.

Building applications would be difficult without 1-2-3's capacity for calculating mathematical, statistical, logical, financial, and other types of formulas. 1-2-3 comes with many functions that let you create complex formulas for a wide range of applications, including business, scientific, and engineering applications. (You learn more about 1-2-3's functions in Chapter 7.)

Commands

1-2-3 has many commands that help you perform a number of tasks in the worksheet. You use these commands at every phase of building and using a worksheet application. Commands are activated by pressing the slash (/) key. This action displays a menu of commands from which you choose the command you want.

Commands are available to format the worksheet; name ranges; erase, copy, and move data; perform calculations; store files; protect worksheet cells; protect files with passwords; use add-in programs; print the worksheets; and do much more, such as create graphs and retrieve files. (Chapter 3 tells you how commands are selected, and Chapter 4 begins a discussion of specific commands.)

1-2-3 Graphics

The spreadsheet alone makes 1-2-3 a powerful program with all the functions many users need. The addition of graphics features, which accompany the spreadsheet, makes 1-2-3 a tool you can use to present data visually and to conduct graphic "what if" analyses. As originally conceived by creator Mitch Kapor, the graphics capability was planned as a significant feature of 1-2-3; and Kapor's background in graphics software design is evident in the program.

1-2-3 has five basic graph types: bar, stacked bar, line, pie, and XY (scatter). You have an exceptional amount of flexibility in your choices of graph formats, colors, shading, labels, titles, and subtitles.

You can represent up to six ranges of data on a single graph (except for pie graphs and scatter diagrams). You can create, for example, a line graph with six different lines.

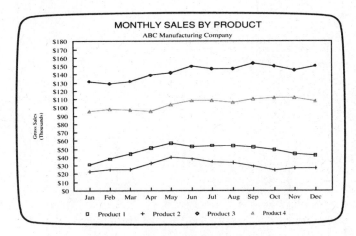

The line graph is the default graph type for 1-2-3. That is, if you do not specify a particular type, 1-2-3 displays the data as a line graph.

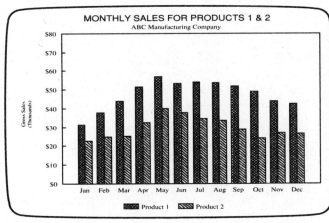

The bar graph, typically used to show the trend of numeric data across time, often compares two or more data items.

1

The XY (scatter) graph compares one numeric data series to another, determining whether one set of values appears to depend on the other.

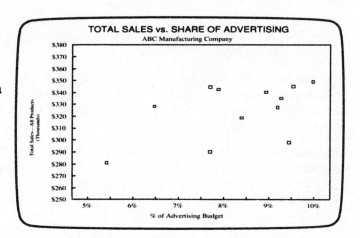

The stacked-bar graph includes two or more data series that total 100 percent of a specific category.

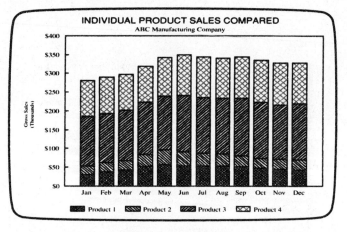

The pie graph shows only one data series, in which the parts total 100 percent of a specific numeric category.

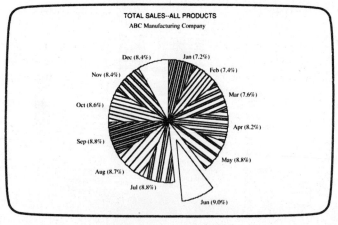

1-2-3 Database Management

1

The row and column structure that is used to store data in a spreadsheet program is similar to the structure of a relational database. When you use 1-2-3's true database management commands and functions, you can sort, query, extract, and perform statistical analyses on data in up to 8,191 records (with up to 256 fields of information).

One important advantage of a 1-2-3 database over independent database programs is that its database commands are similar to others used in the 1-2-3 program. This similarity allows you to learn the use of the 1-2-3 database manager along with the rest of the 1-2-3 program.

A row in 1-2-3 is equal to a record in a conventional database. In that record, you might store a client's name, address, and phone number.

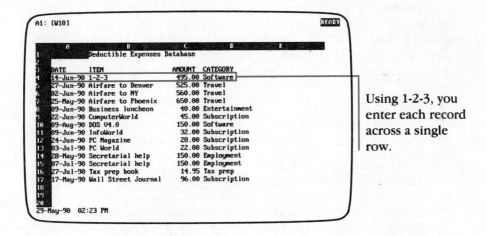

Using 1-2-3, you enter each record across a single row.

1-2-3 has sophisticated facilities for performing sort and search operations. You can sort the database on any number of items and by numerous criteria, and you can find a particular record with a few simple keystrokes.

1   Macros and the Advanced Macro Commands

Two other features help to make 1-2-3 the most powerful and popular integrated spreadsheet, graphics, and database program. When you use 1-2-3's macros and advanced macro commands, you can automate and customize 1-2-3 for your particular applications.

By using 1-2-3 macros, you can reduce multiple keystrokes to a two-keystroke operation. Simply press two keys, and 1-2-3 does the rest—whether you're formatting a range, creating a graph, or printing a worksheet.

You can create a macro, for example, to move the cell pointer to a specific part of the worksheet. Suppose that you've positioned a database section in the range R23..Z100. Because 1-2-3 is first displayed with the cell pointer at A1, you have to use several keystrokes to get to cell R23 when you want to work with the database. You can create a macro that records the keystrokes you need to get to cell R23. After you assign a name and save the macro, you can access that part of the worksheet simply by typing the macro name.

A number of enhancements in Release 2.2 make the macro capability even more powerful and easier to use than in earlier releases of 1-2-3. These enhancements include the following:

- You can use descriptive words (up to 15 characters)—instead of single letters—to name macros.
- The Learn feature allows you to record keystrokes to build macros automatically.
- STEP mode provides an echo of each command at the bottom of the screen while you run the macro—to help you find macro errors.
- The Macro Library Manager add-in lets you create an external file of macros available for all worksheets.

(Macros and the advanced macro commands are covered in Chapter 14.)

Think of simple keystroke macros as the building blocks for advanced macro command programs. When you begin to add advanced macro commands to simple keystroke macros, you control and automate many of the actions required to build, modify, and update 1-2-3 models. At the most sophisticated level, 1-2-3's advanced macro commands are used as a full-fledged programming language for developing custom business applications.

When you use 1-2-3's advanced macro commands, you see what kind of power is available for your 1-2-3 applications. For the applications developer, the set of advanced macro commands is much like a programming language (such as BASIC), but the programming process is significantly simplified by all the powerful features of 1-2-3's spreadsheet, database, and graphics commands. 1-2-3 offers 50 "invisible" commands—the advanced macro commands—that give you a greater range of control over your 1-2-3 applications.

Summary

In this overview chapter, you saw how one of the simplest examples of a spreadsheet—a checkbook register—becomes easier to use in electronic form. You were introduced to the features of 1-2-3's spreadsheet, such as its size, window, and cells. You learned how 1-2-3 worksheets are designated and can be recalculated for "what if" analyses. And you learned about 1-2-3's powerful commands and functions, with which you can build formulas for a wide variety of applications.

The chapter gave you a glimpse of 1-2-3's flexible graphics capabilities. You had a quick view of 1-2-3's database and its power for managing and reporting on stored data. The chapter touched on macros and the advanced macro commands, which allow you to automate and customize your use of 1-2-3 and its graphics and database capabilities.

Specifically, you learned the following key information about 1-2-3:

- The 1-2-3 worksheet contains 8,192 rows and 256 columns. All rows on the 1-2-3 worksheet are assigned numbers. All columns on the 1-2-3 worksheet are assigned letters.
- A *cell* is the intersection of a column and a row. Cells are identified by their column and row coordinates (A2, B4, and G10, for example).
- The *cell pointer* is the highlighted rectangle that allows you to enter data into the worksheet.

1

■ Formulas can be used in 1-2-3 to create mathematical relationships between cells.

■ 1-2-3's *functions* are built-in formulas that automatically perform complex operations.

■ Commands are initiated by pressing the slash (/) key to display a command menu. Using 1-2-3's menu system, you can perform many common worksheet tasks.

■ 1-2-3's graphics capability lets you create five types of graphs from worksheet data. Many options are available for enhancing the appearance of these graphs.

■ Each row of a 1-2-3 database corresponds to a database record. With the database features available in 1-2-3, you can perform complex operations, such as sorting and searching records.

■ Macros and the advanced macro commands deliver exceptional power to 1-2-3 by automating both simple and complex tasks into two-keystroke operations.

The power of 1-2-3 is best realized by actually using the program. The next chapter shows you how to get started.

Getting Started

This chapter will help you get started using 1-2-3. Before you begin, be sure that 1-2-3 is installed on your computer system. Follow the instructions in Appendix A to complete the installation. Even if you have already installed 1-2-3, you may want to check the appendix to make sure that you haven't overlooked any important details.

The information in this chapter will be useful if you have little familiarity with computers or with 1-2-3. If you find this introductory material too basic and want to begin using the 1-2-3 worksheet immediately, you can skip to Chapter 3.

Starting and exiting
1-2-3

Learning the
computer keyboard

Understanding the
1-2-3 screen

Accessing the 1-2-3
help system and
tutorial

2

Key Terms in This Chapter

1-2-3 Access System	The 1-2-3 menu system that links all of 1-2-3's different programs. It includes the main 1-2-3 program as well as programs for printing graphs, translating non-1-2-3 files, installing 1-2-3, and accessing the 1-2-3 tutorial in Release 2.01.
Alphanumeric keys	The keys in the center section of the computer keyboard. Most of these keys resemble those on a typewriter keyboard.
Numeric keypad	The keys on the right side of the IBM PC, the Personal Computer AT, and enhanced keyboards. This keypad is used for entering and calculating numbers, and for moving the cell pointer in the worksheet area or the cursor and menu pointer in the control panel.
Function keys	The 10 keys on the left side of the PC and Personal Computer AT keyboards or the 12 keys at the top of the enhanced keyboard. These keys are used for special 1-2-3 functions, such as accessing help, editing cells, and recalculating the worksheet.
Control panel	The area above the reverse-video border of the 1-2-3 worksheet. The control panel contains three lines that display important information about the contents of a cell, command options and explanations, and special prompts or messages.

Starting 1-2-3

Getting into 1-2-3 is quite easy, particularly if the program is installed on a hard disk. Starting from DOS, you can go directly to a fresh worksheet, or you can enter 1-2-3 by way of the 1-2-3 Access System, which provides several menu options. The following discussion shows you both ways to begin.

26

2

Directions are given for both hard disk systems and for systems having only floppy disk drives.

Starting 1-2-3 from DOS

Starting 1-2-3 from DOS is a shortcut and requires less memory than using the 1-2-3 Access System. In the following instructions, the assumption is that the 1-2-3 program is on drive C of your hard disk, in a subdirectory named 123.

To start 1-2-3 on a hard disk system, follow these steps:

1. With the C> system prompt displayed on your screen, change to the 123 directory by typing **cd \123** and pressing ⏎Enter

2. Start 1-2-3 by typing **123** and pressing ⏎Enter.

If you have a system with only floppy and/or microfloppy disk drives, the start-up procedure is slightly different. (Note that this book uses the term *microfloppy* to refer to 3 1/2-inch diskettes that are used by the newer IBM computers, laptop computers, and some IBM-compatible computers.)

To start 1-2-3 on a floppy disk system, follow these steps:

1. After booting your computer with your DOS diskette (by simultaneously pressing the Ctrl, Alt, and Del keys), remove the DOS diskette and place the 1-2-3 System diskette into drive A.

2. If the A> prompt is not displayed, type **a:** and press ⏎Enter.

3. Start 1-2-3 by typing **123** at the A> prompt and pressing ⏎Enter.

After a few seconds, the 1-2-3 logo appears. The logo remains on-screen for a few seconds. Then the worksheet is displayed, and you're ready to use 1-2-3.

Starting 1-2-3 from the 1-2-3 Access System

Lotus devised the 1-2-3 Access System as a way to link all of 1-2-3's functions. This system is useful for moving quickly between the programs in the 1-2-3 package. The 1-2-3 Access System also has a series of menus that enable you to translate between 1-2-3 and other programs, such as dBASE, Symphony, Multiplan, and VisiCalc.

2

To start the 1-2-3 Access System on a hard disk system, follow these steps:

1. With the C> system prompt displayed on your screen, change to the 123 directory by typing **cd \123** and pressing ⏎Enter .
2. Start the 1-2-3 Access System by typing **lotus** and pressing ⏎Enter .

To start the 1-2-3 Access System on a floppy disk system, follow these steps:

1. Place the 1-2-3 System diskette into drive A.
2. If the A> prompt is not displayed, type **a:** and press ⏎Enter .
3. Start the 1-2-3 Access System by typing **lotus** and pressing ⏎Enter .

The 1-2-3 Access System screen appears.

Each of the options in the Access System's menu bar is explained in the text that follows.

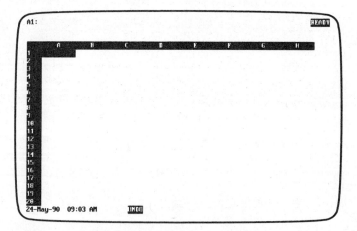

The **1-2-3** option, logically enough, starts 1-2-3. Be sure that you have the 1-2-3 System diskette in drive A if you are using a floppy disk system.

28

2

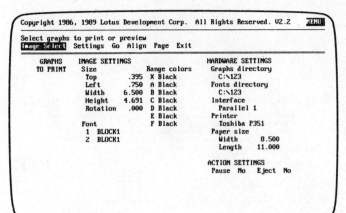

The **PrintGraph** option begins the 1-2-3 PrintGraph program for graph printing. For more about this topic, see Chapter 12.

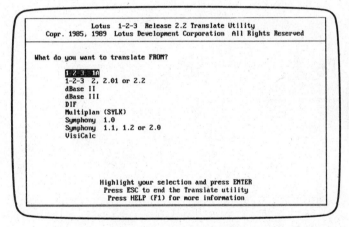

The **Translate** option accesses the 1-2-3 Translate utility, which allows you to translate files between 1-2-3 and other popular programs.

The Translate utility provides links among different versions of 1-2-3, and also between 1-2-3 and other software programs, such as dBASE, Symphony, Multiplan, and VisiCalc. For more information, refer to the Lotus documentation or Que's *Using 1-2-3 Release 2.2*, Special Edition.

2

The Install option accesses the 1-2-3 Install program, which modifies the options set during installation. For more information and complete installation instructions, see Appendix A.

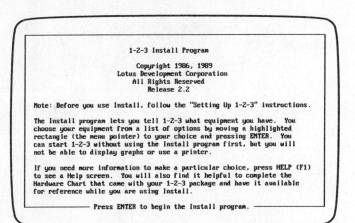

Release 2.01 (and earlier versions) includes a View option, which takes you through the 1-2-3 tutorial, "A View of 1-2-3."

Exit quits the 1-2-3 program and returns you to DOS.

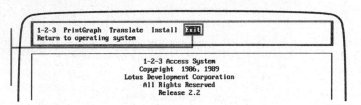

Exiting 1-2-3

There are two ways to leave the 1-2-3 program to return to DOS: by using the /System command or the /Quit command. Both commands are accessible from the 1-2-3 main menu. To access the main menu, press the slash (/) key. The System and Quit commands are listed among the options on this menu.

Using /System To Leave 1-2-3 Temporarily

The /System command returns you to the DOS system prompt, but you do not exit the 1-2-3 program. Your departure is only temporary.

2

To leave 1-2-3 temporarily, follow these steps:

1. Press ⃞/

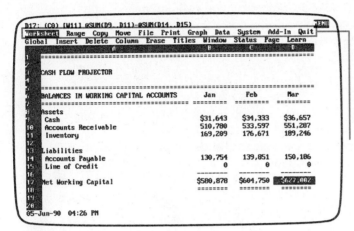

The 1-2-3 main menu is displayed.

2. To select the System command, press ⃞S, or highlight the command and then press ⃞⏎Enter.

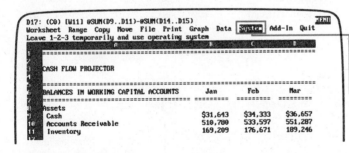

Here, the System command is highlighted.

After you issue the System Command, the DOS prompt is displayed.

2

3. While at the DOS level, perform the desired system operation (such as changing drives and/or directories, copying files, or accessing other programs).

4. To return to the 1-2-3 worksheet, type **exit** and press ⏎Enter. You return to the current worksheet, in the exact place where you issued the /System command.

The Advantages of Using /System

/System is a useful command when you need to check the amount of memory you have on disk before you copy a file to it, or when you want to see how much memory a particular worksheet uses before you load the worksheet. /System saves you the trouble of having to quit the 1-2-3 program, issue the appropriate DOS commands, and then get back into the worksheet.

The /System command is particularly useful for giving you access to your system's file-handling commands. For example, if you want to save your worksheet, but your data diskette is full, you can use the /System command to suspend 1-2-3 processing while you prepare a new diskette using the DOS FORMAT command. After you return to 1-2-3 by typing **exit** and pressing Enter, you can save your worksheet to the new diskette with /File Save.

The Limitations of Using /System

You should be aware of two potential problems in using the /System command. First, if you have a large worksheet that takes up most of memory, the /System command may fail because there is not enough memory to run another program. If the /System command fails, 1-2-3 displays the error message Cannot Invoke DOS, and the ERROR indicator appears in the upper right corner of the screen.

The second problem is that certain programs you run from 1-2-3 by using the /System command may cause 1-2-3 to abort when you try to return by typing **exit** and pressing Enter. You can safely invoke from 1-2-3 the DOS file-management commands—such as FORMAT, COPY, DELETE, DIRECTORY, and DISKCOPY—and most business-application programs. Starting one of the many memory-resident utility programs, however, causes 1-2-3 to abort when you type **exit** and press Enter. Before trying to use the /System command during an important 1-2-3 session, take a few minutes to experiment with the programs you want to use.

Using /Quit To Exit 1-2-3

The /Quit command from the 1-2-3 main menu allows you to exit both the worksheet and the 1-2-3 program. You are asked to verify this choice before you exit 1-2-3, because your data will be lost if you quit 1-2-3 without saving your file.

To exit 1-2-3, follow these steps:

1. Call up the 1-2-3 menu by pressing ⌐/⌐.

   Note: If you haven't saved your file, do so now by pressing ⌐F⌐ and then ⌐S⌐ (for **File Save**). Next, enter the file name. If the file name already exists, press ⌐R⌐ (for **Replace**) to update the current file. Then press ⌐/⌐ again before proceeding with the next step. The process of saving files is explained in more detail in the next chapter.

2. Select **Quit** by pressing ⌐Q⌐, or highlight the command and then press ⌐↵Enter⌐.

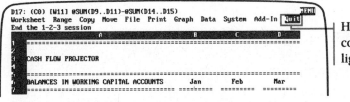

Here, the Quit command is highlighted.

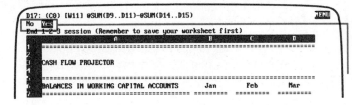

You are asked to verify that you want to exit.

2

3. Select **Yes** by pressing Ⓨ, or highlight the selection and then press ↵Enter.

If you have made changes in your current worksheet but have not saved them with /File Save, 1-2-3 beeps and displays a reminder when you try to exit.

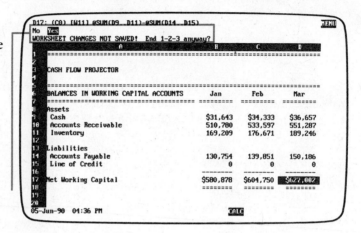

```
D12: (CO) [W11] @SUM(D9..D11)-@SUM(D14..D15)                              MENU
No  Yes
WORKSHEET CHANGES NOT SAVED!  End 1-2-3 anyway?
             A                         B          C          D
1  ===================================================================
2
3  CASH FLOW PROJECTOR
4
5  ===================================================================
6  BALANCES IN WORKING CAPITAL ACCOUNTS   Jan        Feb        Mar
7  =========                            =========  =========  =========
8  Assets
9    Cash                                $31,643    $34,333    $36,657
10   Accounts Receivable                 510,780    533,597    551,287
11   Inventory                           169,209    176,671    189,246
12
13 Liabilities
14   Accounts Payable                    130,754    139,851    150,186
15   Line of Credit                            0          0          0
16                                       --------   --------   --------
17 Net Working Capital                  $580,878   $604,750   $627,002
18                                       ========   ========   ========
19
20
05-Jun-90  04:36 PM                                        CALC
```

4. If you have already made changes to the file since it was last saved and you want to abandon these changes, press Ⓨ (or highlight **Yes** and press ↵Enter) to override the warning message and exit from 1-2-3. (This warning is unavailable in 1-2-3 versions prior to Release 2.2).

   Otherwise, if you need to save the file before exiting 1-2-3, press Ⓝ (or highlight **No** and press ↵Enter). Then use /File Save to save your file before you exit 1-2-3.

Note: If you started 1-2-3 from the 1-2-3 Access System, you are returned to the Access System when you select /Quit. To exit the 1-2-3 Access System and return to the operating system, press **E**, or use the arrow keys to highlight **Exit** and press Enter.

Learning the Keyboard

Before you begin learning 1-2-3, you need to get to know your keyboard. Each of the three most popular keyboards consists of these sections: the alphanumeric keys in the center, the numeric keypad with direction keys on the right, and the function-key section on the left or across the top. The enhanced keyboard, the standard keyboard for all new IBM personal computers and most compatibles, also has a separate grouping of direction keys.

The original IBM PC keyboard

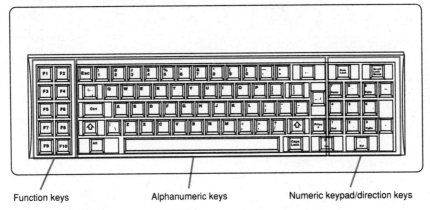

Function keys   Alphanumeric keys   Numeric keypad/direction keys

The original IBM Personal Computer AT keyboard

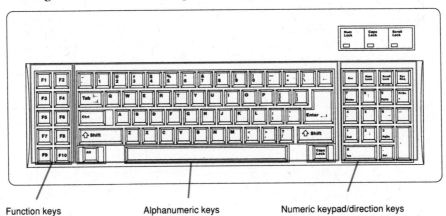

Function keys   Alphanumeric keys   Numeric keypad/direction keys

2

The IBM Enhanced Keyboard   Function keys

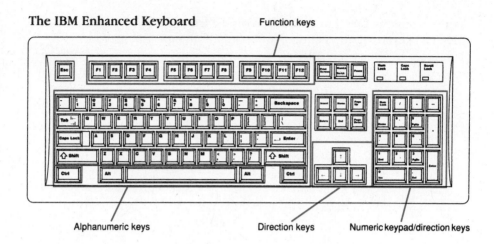

Alphanumeric keys   Direction keys   Numeric keypad/direction keys

The Alphanumeric Keys

Most of the alphanumeric keys on the computer keyboard perform the same actions as those on a typewriter. In 1-2-3 several of the keys have special functions. For example, the slash (/) key accesses the 1-2-3 menu, and the period (.) key defines a range of cells. Table 2.1 highlights each of these important keys.

Table 2.1
The Special Keys

Key	Action
[Esc]	Returns to the previous menu; erases the current entry during editing, or the range or command specification; returns from a help screen; clears error messages from the screen.
[Tab⇄]	Moves the cell pointer one screen to the right. [⇧Shift][Tab⇄] moves the cell pointer one screen to the left.
[Caps Lock]	Activates capitalization of all alphabetic characters when keys for those characters are pressed. Displays the CAPS indicator in the status line when active. Remains in effect until you press this key again (acts as a toggle).

2

Table 2.1—(continued)

Key	Action
(⇧Shift)	Changes lowercase letters and characters to uppercase. When not in Num Lock mode, allows typing of numbers on the numeric keypad.
(Ctrl)	When used with the left- or right-arrow key, moves the cell pointer one screen to the left or right in READY mode, or moves the cursor five characters to the left or right in EDIT mode; when used with Break, returns 1-2-3 to READY mode or halts execution of a macro.
(Alt)	When used with other keys, invokes macros, activates Learn mode, performs an Undo, or executes other commands.
Space bar	Inserts a space within a cell entry; moves the highlighter one item to the right when selecting commands from a menu.
(⬅Backspace)	Erases the previous character in a cell during cell definition; erases the character to the left of the cursor during editing.
(↵Enter)	Accepts an entry into a cell or selects a highlighted menu command.
(.)	Defines a range of cells or anchors a cell address during pointing. Also used as a decimal point.
(/)	Calls up the 1-2-3 main menu; also functions as a division sign.
(Scroll Lock)	Scrolls the entire screen one row or column when the cell pointer is moved. Displays the SCROLL indicator in the status line when active. Acts as a toggle.
(Num Lock)	Activates the numeric representation of keys in the numeric keypad. Displays the NUM indicator in the status line when active. Acts as a toggle.
(Ins)	Changes 1-2-3 from insert mode to overtype mode during editing. When pressed, causes the OVR indicator to be displayed in the status line and enables new characters to overwrite existing text. Acts as a toggle.
(Del)	Deletes the character above the cursor during the editing process.

2

The Numeric Keypad and Direction Keys

The keys in the numeric keypad are used mainly for data entry and for moving the cell pointer or cursor. The enhanced keyboard has separate direction keys for this movement function.

When you want to use the numeric keypad to enter numbers rather than to position the cell pointer or cursor, you can either press Num Lock before and after you enter the numbers and *then* move to the next cell, or hold down Shift when you press the number keys.

Neither way is ideal, because you have to switch between functions. If you have an enhanced keyboard, you don't have this problem because your keyboard has a special set of direction keys that have no other purpose. If you don't have an enhanced keyboard, you can create a simple macro that lets you enter numbers and move to the next cell without having to press Shift or Num Lock.

The Function Keys

You use the function keys F1 through F10 for special tasks, such as accessing Help, editing cells, and recalculating the worksheet. Although the enhanced keyboards have 12 function keys (F1 through F12), 1-2-3 uses only the first 10 of these. A plastic function-key template that describes each key's function on the enhanced keyboard is provided with the Lotus software. Another version of the template is provided for users with PC, AT, or compatible keyboards. Table 2.2 explains the operations of the function keys.

Table 2.2
The Function Keys

Key	Action
F1	**(Help)** Accesses 1-2-3's on-line help facility.
F2	**(Edit)** Shifts 1-2-3 to EDIT mode.
F3	**(Name)** Displays a list of named ranges in the control panel in POINT and VALUE modes. Pressing F3 a second time switches to a full-screen display. Displays a full screen of file names in /File commands.

Table 2.2— (continued)

Key	Action
F4	**(Abs)** Changes a relative cell address into an absolute or a mixed cell address during cell definition.
F5	**(GoTo)** Moves the cell pointer to the cell coordinates (or range name) provided.
F6	**(Window)** Moves the cell pointer to the other side of a split screen. In MENU mode, toggles between a display of the worksheet and a settings sheet.
F7	**(Query)** Repeats the most recent /Data Query operation.
F8	**(Table)** Repeats the most recent /Data Table operation.
F9	**(Calc)** Recalculates all formulas in the worksheet.
F10	**(Graph)** Displays the current graph on-screen.

Understanding the 1-2-3 Screen

The main 1-2-3 display is divided into three parts: the control panel at the top of the screen, the worksheet area, and the status line at the bottom of the screen. A reverse-video border separates the control panel from the worksheet area. This border contains the letters and numbers that mark the columns and rows of the worksheet area. The sections that follow describe each of these areas in more detail.

The Control Panel

The control panel, the area above the reverse-video border, contains three lines of information about the current cell as well as the menu commands.

2

The first line of the control panel shows information about the current cell (the cell highlighted by the cell pointer).

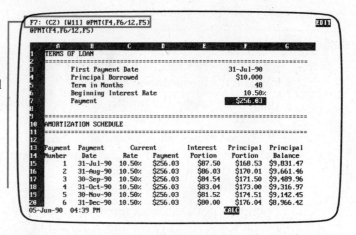

In this example, the control panel shows the following:

F7: (C2) [W11] @PMT(F4,F6/12,F5)

This line displays the address of the cell (F7), followed by the display format chosen (C2 for Currency, 2 decimal places), the column width (11 characters), and the content of the cell (in this case, a formula). This line may also show the protection status of the cell. The upper right corner of the first line always displays the mode indicator, such as EDIT in this example. Mode indicators are explained in detail later in this chapter.

The second line of the control panel contains any characters that are being entered or edited, or displays the options in a menu. The preceding example shows a formula to be edited.

This example shows the main menu with the Worksheet menu option highlighted.

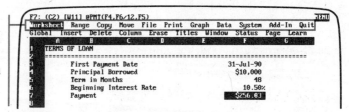

The third line of the control panel displays the menu options or description of the command that is now highlighted.

The Worksheet Area

The largest part of the 1-2-3 screen is composed of the worksheet area. As described in Chapter 1, the 1-2-3 worksheet consists of 256 lettered columns and 8,192 numbered rows, yet only a portion of the worksheet is displayed on the screen at any time. All information entered into the worksheet is stored in a cell—the intersection of a column and a row.

The Status Line

The status line is the bottom line of the 1-2-3 screen. This line normally displays the current date and time, but you can change it to reflect the current file name or to display neither the date and time or file name. The current date and time can be displayed in the status line in two different formats. When certain types of errors occur, the status line displays the appropriate error messages. This line also contains any status or key indicators, described in the following sections.

The 1-2-3 Indicators

The 1-2-3 screen may display three different types of indicators. The mode indicators appear in the upper right corner of the control panel. The status indicators appear within the status line along the bottom of the screen. And the key indicators appear within the status line in the lower right corner. The 1-2-3 indicators are summarized in table 2.3. The next few sections explain each of these types of indicators.

Table 2.3
The 1-2-3 Indicators

Indicator	Description
The Mode Indicators	
READY	1-2-3 is waiting for a command or cell entry.
VALUE	A number or formula is being entered.
LABEL	A label is being entered.
EDIT	A cell entry is being edited.
POINT	A range is being pointed to.

2

Table 2.3— (continued)

Indicator	Description
FILES	1-2-3 is waiting for you to select a file name from the list of file names.
NAMES	1-2-3 is waiting for you to select a range from the list of range names.
MENU	A list of command choices is being displayed.
HELP	1-2-3 is displaying a help screen.
ERROR	An error has occurred, and 1-2-3 is waiting for you to press [Esc] or [↵Enter] to show the error; or to press [F1] to discover information about the cause and possible correction.
WAIT	1-2-3 is in the middle of a command and cannot respond to other commands. WAIT flashes on and off.
FIND	1-2-3 is in the middle of a /Data Query operation and cannot respond to commands.

The Status Indicators

Indicator	Description
STAT	1-2-3 is displaying the status of your worksheet.
CALC	The worksheet has not been recalculated since the last change to the worksheet.
CIRC	A circular reference (a formula that refers to itself) has been found.
MEM	Random-access memory is almost exhausted. MEM flashes on and off.
CMD	A 1-2-3 macro is executing.
SST	A macro is in single-step execution.
STEP	[Alt][F2] has been pressed, and you are now "stepping through" a macro one character or command at a time.
LEARN	You have pressed [Alt][F5], and 1-2-3 is now recording all your keystrokes in a Learn range that you defined with /Worksheet Learn. (Not available in 1-2-3 versions prior to Release 2.2.)
UNDO	The ability to undo a command by pressing [Alt][F4] is enabled. (Not available in 1-2-3 versions prior to Release 2.2.)

Table 2.3—(continued)

Indicator	Description
The Key Indicators	
OVR	The (Ins) key has been pressed, and 1-2-3 is in overtype mode.
NUM	(Num Lock) has been pressed and is active.
CAPS	(Caps Lock) has been pressed and is active.
SCROLL	(Scroll Lock) has been pressed and is active.
END	The (End) key has been pressed and is active.

The Mode Indicators

One of 1-2-3's modes is always in effect, depending on what you are doing. The mode indicator is shown in reverse video in the upper right corner of the screen, within the control panel. For example, READY is shown whenever data can be entered into the worksheet or whenever the menu can be invoked. VALUE is displayed as the mode indicator when you enter numbers or formulas; and LABEL appears when you enter letters, as in a title or label. You see the EDIT indicator after you press Edit (F2) in order to edit a formula or label in the control panel.

The Status Indicators

Other indicators report the status of the worksheet. They include general message indicators, such as CALC and OVR, and warnings, such as CIRC and MEM. These indicators appear in reverse video along the bottom line of the screen. Note that when an error occurs, 1-2-3 displays a message in the lower left corner. To clear the error and get back to READY mode, press Esc or Enter.

2

The Key Indicators

The key indicators NUM, CAPS, and SCROLL represent the keyboard's Num Lock, Caps Lock, and Scroll Lock keys, respectively. These keys are "lock" keys because they can temporarily lock the keyboard into a certain function. When a lock key is active, 1-2-3 displays the key's indicator in reverse video in the lower right corner of the screen. Many keyboards also use different lights that show when a particular lock key is active. Each lock key is a *toggle*, which means that pressing the key repeatedly turns its function alternately on and off. Therefore, to turn off a lock key that is on, you simply press it again.

Two other key indicators used within 1-2-3 are OVR for the Ins key and END for the End key. When OVR appears in reverse video at the bottom of the screen, you know that 1-2-3 is in overtype mode. That is, whatever you type replaces existing characters, numerals, or symbols.

Accessing the 1-2-3 Help System and Tutorial

One of the biggest selling points of 1-2-3 is its user-friendliness. Lotus went to a great deal of trouble to ensure that the spreadsheet program is easy to learn and use. The program offers you two basic kinds of assistance: a context-sensitive help system and a tutorial.

The 1-2-3 Help System

1-2-3 has a context-sensitive help system. In other words, when you need clarification on a particular topic, you can press Help (F1) and select the topic you need from the list that is displayed.

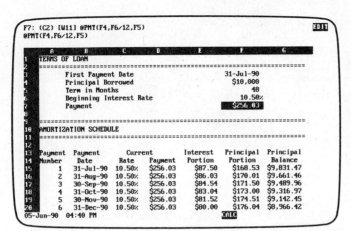

If you need to access the help screen for financial functions, for example, you can display the help screen directly from your worksheet.

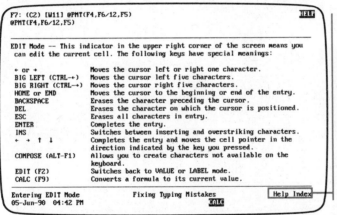

While in EDIT mode, press Help (F1) to display a context-sensitive screen about how to use EDIT. To access the Help Index, highlight Help Index at the bottom of the screen and press Enter.

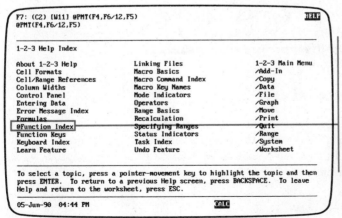

From the Help Index, you can choose many different topics. To access the help screen for functions, select @Function Index.

45

From the second of two screens that list all functions, choose @PMT to learn more about that function.

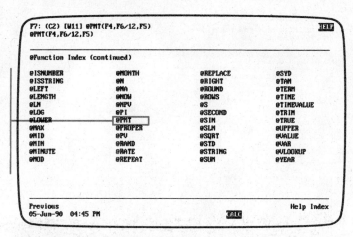

Within the alphabetical list of function descriptions, you find information about the one you chose.

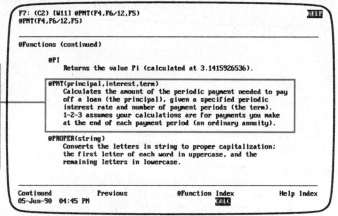

By pressing the Backspace key, you can again look at the preceding screen. The repeated use of Backspace takes you back to previous help screens. Press Esc at any time to return to your worksheet.

The 1-2-3 Tutorial

1-2-3 Release 2.2 offers a set of tutorial files and a tutorial section within the manual. The 180-page section in the manual is divided into chapters—each with several different lessons—that use the tutorial files. The chapters, which cover a variety of topics, are titled "Building a 1-2-3 Worksheet," "Graphing

Your Worksheet Data," "Linking Files," "Managing a Database," and "Automating Your Work with Macros."

Release 2.01 has an on-line tutorial, "A View of 1-2-3," available through the View option of the 1-2-3 Access Menu. This tutorial provides easy-to-follow instructions that guide you through the various stages of the tutorial on-screen.

2

Summary

In this chapter, you learned that you can enter 1-2-3 directly from the DOS prompt or through the 1-2-3 Access System. You can leave 1-2-3 temporarily to perform DOS commands, or exit 1-2-3 entirely after verifying your intention to leave the program.

You were introduced to the different sections of the keyboard and learned how various keys of these sections are important to 1-2-3. The chapter also called attention to the parts of 1-2-3's screen. Information about each indicator was provided in a table, which you can refer to as you learn more about 1-2-3.

Finally, the chapter acquainted you with two features designed especially to make 1-2-3 user-friendly: the help system and the 1-2-3 tutorial.

Specifically, you learned the following key information about 1-2-3:

- If you have 1-2-3 on a hard disk system, you can start the program directly from DOS by typing **123** and pressing Enter from the 123 directory. If you have a floppy disk system, you can start 1-2-3 directly by placing the 1-2-3 System diskette into drive A, typing **123** and pressing Enter from the A> prompt (after booting the computer with a DOS diskette).

- To start 1-2-3 from the 1-2-3 Access System, which allows entry into other 1-2-3 programs such as PrintGraph and Translate, type **lotus** (instead of **123**) and press Enter from the appropriate drive and directory.

- The /System command enables you to leave 1-2-3 temporarily so that you can perform DOS commands. To return to the current 1-2-3 worksheet, type **exit** and press Enter from DOS.

2

■ Use the /Quit command to exit the worksheet and the 1-2-3 program. 1-2-3 allows you the option of canceling this choice when changes are made to the worksheet since it was last saved.

■ Most keyboards contain alphanumeric keys in the center of the keyboard, a numeric keypad and direction keys on the right side, and function keys on the left side or across the top.

■ The 1-2-3 screen consists of three different areas: the control panel (three lines at the top of the screen), the worksheet area (the major portion of the screen), and the status line (one line at the bottom of the screen).

■ The mode indicator is always displayed in the top right corner of the screen. The status and key indicators are displayed at different times in the status line at the bottom of the screen.

■ 1-2-3 provides a context-sensitive help system that you can access by pressing Help (F1) during a 1-2-3 session. You can also access an index that provides several options from which you can choose a particular topic.

■ Release 2.2 users are provided with a comprehensive tutorial section in the Lotus manual that is accompanied by tutorial files on disk. Release 2.01 users can use an on-line tutorial by selecting View from the 1-2-3 Access System.

Now that you are familiar with the 1-2-3 environment, you are ready to begin using 1-2-3 by entering data and formulas.

Introducing Worksheet Basics

3

In a previous chapter, you learned that 1-2-3 is an integrated program that can do much more than make spreadsheet calculations. Depending on your business needs or assigned tasks, you can use 1-2-3 to create worksheets, generate reports, develop simple or complex databases, and produce graphics that illustrate worksheet data.

This chapter explores some of the most elementary operations in 1-2-3: moving around the worksheet; selecting commands from menus; entering and editing data; using formulas and functions; and naming, saving, and retrieving files. If you have used other spreadsheet programs, you may be familiar with some of the procedures that are discussed in this chapter. If this is your first experience with spreadsheets, however, you'll find the basics discussed in this chapter informative and helpful.

3

Key Terms in This Chapter

Cursor	The blinking underscore that appears inside the cell pointer or within the control panel in EDIT mode.
Range name	An alphanumeric name given to a cell or a rectangular group of cells.
Menu pointer	The rectangular bar that highlights menu commands.
Data	Labels or values that are entered into a worksheet cell.
Label	A text entry that is entered in the worksheet.
Value	A number or formula that is entered in the worksheet.
Label prefix	A single character that is typed before a label for purposes of alignment.
Operator	A mathematical or logical symbol that specifies an action to be performed on data.
Order of precedence	The order in which an equation or formula is executed; determines which operators are acted on first.
Wild card	A character, such as an asterisk or question mark, that represents any other character(s) that may appear in the same place.

Moving around the Worksheet

After you start entering data in your worksheet, you need some easy ways to move the cell pointer quickly and accurately. Remember that the 1-2-3 worksheet is immense—it contains 8,192 rows, 256 columns, and more than 2,000,000 cells. You may have many blocks of data of various sizes in widely separated parts of the worksheet. The program provides several ways to quickly move the cell pointer to any location in the worksheet.

Remember that the cell pointer and the cursor are not the same. The *cell pointer* is the bright rectangle that highlights an entire cell in the worksheet area. The *cursor* is the blinking underscore that is sometimes inside the cell pointer and sometimes in the control panel. The cursor indicates the position on the screen where keyboard activity takes effect; the cell pointer indicates the cell that is affected. Whenever you move the cell pointer, the cursor—inside the pointer—moves with it.

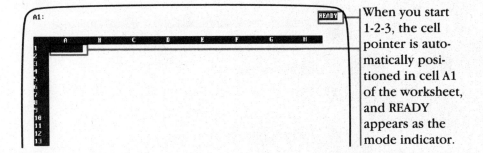

When you start 1-2-3, the cell pointer is automatically positioned in cell A1 of the worksheet, and READY appears as the mode indicator.

When 1-2-3 is in READY mode, the program is ready for you to enter data into the highlighted cell. To enter data in a different cell, first move the cell pointer to the desired location by using the direction keys.

When you begin to enter data, the READY mode indicator changes to LABEL or VALUE, depending on whether you are entering text or numbers. The blinking cursor disappears from the cell pointer and appears in the control panel—where the action is taking place.

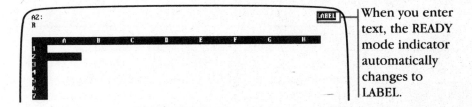

When you enter text, the READY mode indicator automatically changes to LABEL.

The POINT mode indicator signifies that the cell pointer can be positioned and/or expanded to highlight a range in your worksheet.

51

When 1-2-3 is in
POINT mode, the
direction keys
are used to point
out a range.

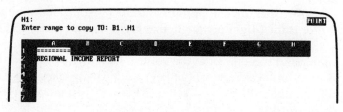

3

The direction
keys either can-
not be used at all
or have different
actions when you
are editing in
EDIT mode,
making a cell en-
try, or entering a
1-2-3 command.

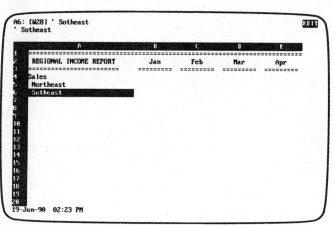

To edit a label or value in EDIT mode, use the Home, End, and left- and
right-arrow keys to move the cursor in the control panel. The actions of the
direction keys are described in table 3.1.

Table 3.1
Direction Keys

Key	Action
←	Moves the cell pointer one column to the left in the worksheet. In the control panel, moves the cursor one character to the left in EDIT mode or the menu pointer one item to the left in MENU mode.
→	Moves the cell pointer one column to the right in the worksheet. In the control panel, moves the cursor one character to the right in EDIT mode or the menu pointer one item to the right in MENU mode.

52

Table 3.1— (continued)

Key	Action
↑	Moves the cell pointer up one row.
↓	Moves the cell pointer down one row.
Tab⇄ or Ctrl→	Moves the cell pointer one screen to the right in the worksheet. In the control panel, moves the cursor five characters to the right in EDIT mode.
⇧Shift Tab⇄ or Ctrl←	Moves the cell pointer one screen to the left in the worksheet. In the control panel, moves the cursor five characters to the left in EDIT mode.
PgUp	Moves the cell pointer up one screen.
PgDn	Moves the cell pointer down one screen.
Home	Returns the cell pointer to cell A1 from any location in the worksheet. When used after the End key, positions the pointer at the lower right corner of the current worksheet.
End	When used before any arrow key, moves the cell pointer (in the direction of the arrow key) to the next boundary between a blank cell and a cell containing data.
F5 (GoTo)	Moves the cell pointer to the cell coordinates (or range name) you specify.

Using the Basic Direction Keys

The arrow keys on the numeric keypad (or on the separate pad of the enhanced keyboard) are the basic keys for moving the cell pointer. The cell pointer moves in the direction of the arrow on the key as long as you hold down the key. When you reach the edge of the screen, the worksheet continues scrolling in the direction of the arrow.

Scrolling the Worksheet

You can scroll the worksheet—one screen at a time—to the right by pressing the Tab key, and to the left with Shift-Tab (hold down the Shift key while you press Tab). You can also scroll the worksheet by holding down the Ctrl key and pressing the right- or left-arrow key. To get the same effect up or down, use the PgUp and PgDn keys—instead of the up- and down-arrow keys—to move up or down one screen at a time. These scrolling methods provide quick ways of paging through the worksheet.

3

In this income worksheet, the cell pointer is positioned at cell A1.

| A1: [W28] \= | | | | | READY |

	A	B	C	D	E
1					
2	REGIONAL INCOME REPORT	Jan	Feb	Mar	Apr
3					
4	Sales				
5	Northeast	$30,336	$33,370	$36,707	$40,377
6	Southeast	20,572	22,629	24,892	27,381
7	Central	131,685	144,854	159,339	175,273
8	Northwest	94,473	103,920	114,312	125,744
9	Southwest	126,739	139,413	153,354	168,690
10					
11	Total Sales	$403,805	$444,186	$488,604	$537,464
12					
13	Cost of Goods Sold				
14	Northeast	$10,341	$11,272	$12,286	$13,392
15	Southeast	6,546	7,135	7,777	8,477
16	Central	65,843	71,769	78,228	85,269
17	Northwest	63,967	69,724	75,999	82,839
18	Southwest	72,314	78,822	85,916	93,649
19					
20	Total Cost of Goods Sold	$219,011	$238,722	$260,207	$283,626

19-Jun-90 02:27 PM

When you press Tab, the worksheet scrolls one screen to the right. The cell pointer now appears in cell F1, and columns F through K are displayed.

| F1: [W11] \= | | | | | READY |

	F	G	H	I	J	K
1						
2	May	Jun	Jul	Aug	Sep	Oct
3						
4						
5	$44,415	$48,856	$53,742	$59,116	$65,028	$71,531
6	30,119	33,131	36,445	40,089	44,098	48,508
7	192,800	212,080	233,288	256,617	282,278	310,506
8	138,318	152,150	167,365	184,101	202,511	222,762
9	185,559	204,114	224,526	246,978	271,676	298,844
10						
11	$591,211	$650,332	$715,365	$786,902	$865,592	$952,151
12						
13						
14	$14,597	$15,911	$17,343	$18,904	$20,605	$22,460
15	9,240	10,072	10,978	11,966	13,043	14,217
16	92,943	101,308	110,425	120,364	131,196	143,004
17	90,295	98,421	107,279	116,934	127,458	138,929
18	102,077	111,264	121,278	132,193	144,090	157,058
19						
20	$309,152	$336,976	$367,303	$400,361	$436,393	$475,669

19-Jun-90 02:28 PM

If you then press Shift-Tab, the worksheet scrolls one screen to the left. In this example, the cell pointer returns to its original location at cell A1.

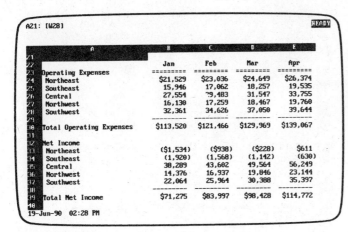

```
A21: [W28]                                                    READY

      |          A           |  B   |  C   |  D   |  E   |
  21  |
  22  |                          Jan    Feb    Mar    Apr
  23  |Operating Expenses    ========= ========= ========= =========
  24  |  Northeast             $21,529  $23,036  $24,649  $26,374
  25  |  Southeast              15,946   17,062   18,257   19,535
  26  |  Central                27,554   29,483   31,547   33,755
  27  |  Northwest              16,130   17,259   18,467   19,760
  28  |  Southwest              32,361   34,626   37,050   39,644
  29  |                        -------- -------- -------- --------
  30  |Total Operating Expenses $113,520 $121,466 $129,969 $139,067
  31  |
  32  |Net Income
  33  |  Northeast             ($1,534)  ($938)  ($228)   $611
  34  |  Southeast              (1,920)  (1,568)  (1,142)  (630)
  35  |  Central                38,289   43,602   49,564   56,249
  36  |  Northwest              14,376   16,937   19,846   23,144
  37  |  Southwest              22,064   25,964   30,388   35,397
  38  |                        -------- -------- -------- --------
  39  |Total Net Income         $71,275  $83,997  $98,428  $114,772
  40  |
  19-Jun-90  02:28 PM
```

When you press PgDn, the worksheet scrolls down one screen. The cell pointer now appears in cell A21, and rows 21 through 40 are displayed.

When you then press PgUp, the worksheet scrolls up one screen, and the cell pointer returns to its original location at cell A1.

Pressing the Scroll Lock key to activate the scroll function makes the worksheet appear to move in the opposite direction of the arrow key you press—no matter where the cell pointer is positioned on the screen. Learning 1-2-3 is usually easier with the scroll function deactivated.

```
A1: [W28] \=                                                  READY

      |          A           |  B   |  C   |  D   |  E   |
   1  |
   2  |REGIONAL INCOME REPORT    Jan    Feb    Mar    Apr
   3  |========================= ========= ========= ========= =========
   4  |Sales
   5  |  Northeast             $30,336  $33,370  $36,707  $40,377
   6  |  Southeast              20,572   22,629   24,892   27,381
   7  |  Central               131,685  144,854  159,339  175,273
   8  |  Northwest              94,473  103,920  114,312  125,744
   9  |  Southwest             126,739  139,413  153,354  168,690
  10  |                        -------- -------- -------- --------
  11  |Total Sales             $403,805 $444,186 $488,604 $537,464
  12  |
  13  |Cost of Goods Sold
  14  |  Northeast             $10,341  $11,272  $12,286  $13,392
  15  |  Southeast               6,546    7,135    7,777    8,477
  16  |  Central                65,843   71,769   78,228   85,269
  17  |  Northwest              63,967   69,724   75,999   82,839
  18  |  Southwest              72,314   78,822   85,916   93,649
  19  |                        -------- -------- -------- --------
  20  |Total Cost of Goods Sold $219,011 $238,722 $260,207 $283,626
  19-Jun-90  02:33 PM                                          SCROLL
```

With the cell pointer positioned at cell A1, press the Scroll Lock key. The SCROLL indicator appears in the lower right corner of the screen.

3

When you press the right-arrow key with Scroll Lock enabled, the entire worksheet, not just the cell pointer, moves one column to the right.

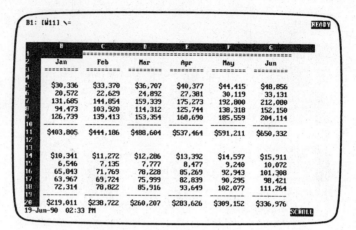

Using the Home and End Keys

The Home key provides a quick way to return to the beginning of the worksheet when 1-2-3 is in READY or POINT mode. Pressing Home makes the cell pointer return to cell A1 from anywhere in the worksheet. Pressing the Home key in POINT mode is a handy way to quickly highlight a range of data you plan to move or copy.

Note: As you'll learn later in this chapter, some keys, such as Home and End, have different actions in EDIT mode. For example, in EDIT mode, the Home key moves the cursor in the control panel.

When you press Home in READY mode, the cell pointer moves to cell A1.

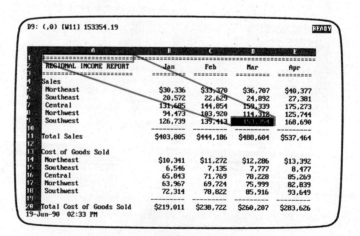

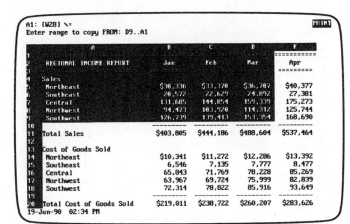

When you press Home in POINT mode, the cell pointer high-lights a rectangle with one corner at A1 and the op-posite corner at the original posi-tion of the cell pointer.

3

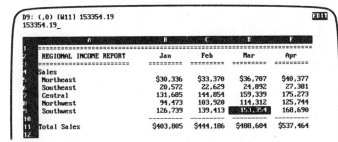

When you press Edit (F2), the cursor is posi-tioned in the control panel after the last character of your cell entry.

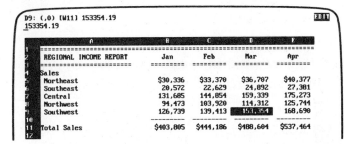

When you press Home in EDIT mode, the cursor moves to the first character in the cell entry.

1-2-3 uses the End key in a unique way. When you press an arrow key after you have pressed and released the End key, the cell pointer moves in the direction of the arrow key to the next boundary between a blank cell and a cell containing data. Remember that if there are gaps (blank lines) in the blocks of data, this End key procedure will be less useful, because the cell pointer moves to the boundaries of each gap.

As the following example illustrates, you can use the End key with the arrow keys to quickly reach the borders of the worksheet area in a new (blank) worksheet.

To learn how the End key works with the arrow keys, start with a blank worksheet and follow these steps:

3

1. If the cell pointer is not in cell A1, press the Home key.

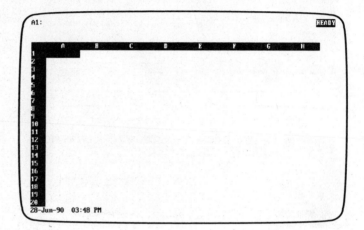

A blank worksheet with the cell pointer in cell A1.

2. Press End, and then press →.

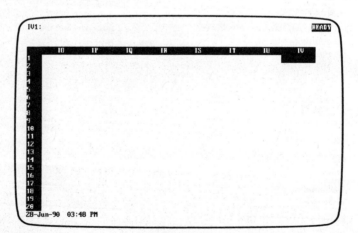

The cell pointer jumps to the upper right boundary of the worksheet, to cell IV1.

3. Press (End), and then press (↓).

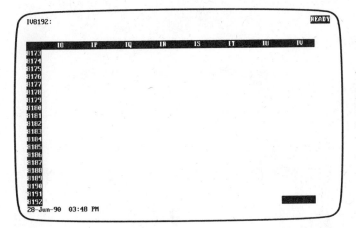

The cell pointer jumps to the bottom right boundary of the worksheet, to cell IV8192.

4. Press (End), and then press (←).

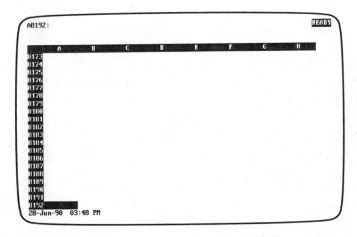

The cell pointer jumps to the bottom left boundary of the worksheet, to cell A8192.

From cell A8192, if you press the End key followed by the up-arrow key, the cell pointer returns to cell A1. You can also use the Home key to perform the same operation.

You can use the End key followed by the Home key to move the cell pointer from any position on the worksheet to the lower right corner of the worksheet. Notice that the End-Home key combination has the opposite effect from that of the Home key used alone.

Using the GoTo (F5) Key

The GoTo (F5) key gives you a way to jump directly to a cell location. To move the cell pointer to any cell on the worksheet, just press the F5 function key.

When you press GoTo (F5), 1-2-3 prompts you for the new cell address.

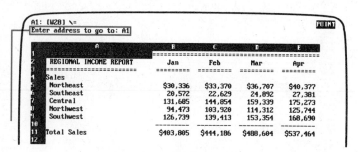

In response to the prompt, type the desired cell address. When you work on a large worksheet, you might forget the cell addresses for specific parts of the worksheet and therefore have difficulty using the GoTo (F5) key. You can, however, use range names with the GoTo (F5) key so that you don't have to remember cell addresses.

You can assign a range name to a cell or a rectangular group of cells. Then you can press the GoTo (F5) key and type the range name instead of the cell address. When the range name refers to more than one cell, the cell pointer moves to the upper left corner of the range. (Ranges and range names are discussed in detail in Chapter 4.)

In this example, JANSALES (a range that begins in cell B5) is specified as the location to go to.

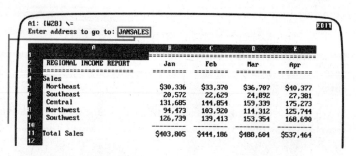

Selecting Commands from Menus

If commands are the tools for performing 1-2-3 tasks, menus are the toolboxes. The menus display the commands available for use. If you select the wrong command, you can press Esc at any time to return to the preceding menu. In 1-2-3, the menus are especially helpful for several reasons.

First, you can access the main menu easily. When you want to display the main menu to select a command, make certain that 1-2-3 is in READY mode and press the slash (/) key.

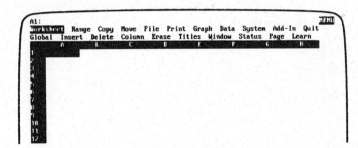 As soon as you press slash (/), the mode indicator changes to MENU and the main menu appears on the second line of the control panel.

The *menu pointer*, the rectangular bar used to highlight menu selections, is positioned on the Worksheet menu option.

A second convenient feature of the menu system is found in the third line of the control panel: either a brief explanation of the highlighted command or the menu that results from choosing the highlighted command. As you point to different commands by moving the menu pointer across the menu, a new explanation (or menu) appears as each command is highlighted. This handy assistance is displayed at all levels of menus.

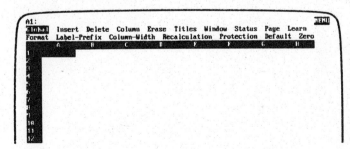 Here, the third line of the control panel displays a list of the choices in the next menu level for the highlighted command.

A third helpful aspect of menus is the ease of starting commands. You can either point to the option you want and press Enter, or you can just type the first letter of the command name. To point to a command on the menu, use the left- and right-arrow keys on the right side of the keyboard. The space bar can be used interchangeably with the right-arrow key to highlight menu commands with the menu pointer. After you highlight the command you want, press Enter.

If you move the menu pointer to the last command of a menu and press the right-arrow key again, the menu pointer reappears on the first command of the menu. Similarly, if the menu pointer is on the first command of a menu, press the left-arrow key to move to the last command. Note that you can also move the menu pointer to the end of the command line by pressing the End key or to the beginning of the line by pressing the Home key.

The other way to select a command is to enter its first letter. When you become familiar with the commands in 1-2-3's various menus, you will probably prefer to use the typing method because it is faster than the pointing method. *Throughout the remainder of this book, all examples emphasize the typing method of selecting commands.*

To select a command, you can use either the pointing method or the typing method:

Pointing Method

    1. Call up the 1-2-3 menu by pressing ⌐/⌐.

    2. Use ⟵ or ⟶ to move the menu pointer to the desired command.

In this example, the cell pointer highlights the Copy command.

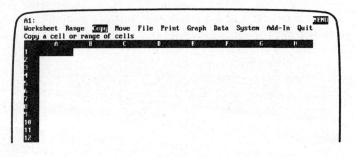

    3. Press ⏎Enter.

62

Typing Method

1. Call up the 1-2-3 menu by pressing ⌐/⌐.
2. Select the desired command by typing the first letter of the command.

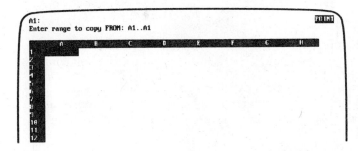

In this example, pressing Ⓒ selects the Copy command from 1-2-3's main menu and takes you directly to a prompt.

If you make the wrong command selection, you can press Esc at any time to return to the previous menu. For instance, if you realize that you should have selected Insert, not Delete, from the Worksheet menu, press Esc to return to the Worksheet menu. You can press Esc as many times as necessary to return to any location in the series of menus or to leave MENU mode completely.

Entering Data into the Worksheet

You can enter data into a cell by highlighting the cell with the cell pointer and typing the entry. To complete the entry, press Enter or any of the direction keys discussed in this chapter.

If you enter data into a cell that already contains information, the new data replaces the earlier information. This is one way to change data in a cell; another involves the Edit (F2) key, and is explained in this chapter's "Editing Data in the Worksheet" section.

There are two types of cell entries: labels and values. Labels are text entries, and values can be either numbers or formulas (including functions, which 1-2-3 treats as built-in formulas). The type of entry can be determined from the first character you enter. Your entry is treated as a value (a number or a formula) when you start with one of the following characters:

0 1 2 3 4 5 6 7 8 9 + − . (@ # $

63

When you begin your entry with a character other than one of the preceding, 1-2-3 treats your entry as a label.

A value—whether a number, formula, or function—can be used for computation purposes. A label is a collection of characters and would not logically be used in a calculation.

3

Entering Labels

Labels are commonly used in 1-2-3 for row and column headings, and they play an important role in worksheet development. Without labels on a worksheet, *you* might know that column H is January data and row 11 is Inventory Assets, but how would someone else who is not familiar with the worksheet know?

Labels make values more evident in a worksheet and help you find information quickly.

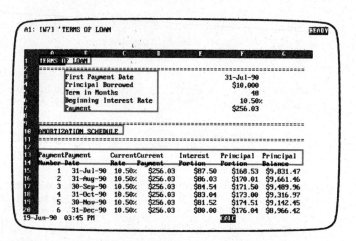

A label can be up to 240 characters long and can contain any string of characters and numbers. A label that is too long for the width of a cell continues (for display purposes) across the cells to the right, as long as the neighboring cells contain no other entries.

When you make an entry into a cell and the first character does not indicate a value entry, the assumption is that you are entering a label. After you type the first character, 1-2-3 shifts to LABEL mode.

You can control how labels are displayed in the cell. By preceding a text entry with a label prefix, you can tell 1-2-3 to left-justify ('), center (^), right-justify ("), or repeat a (\) label when it is displayed.

Because the default position for displaying labels is left-justified, you don't have to type the label prefix when entering most labels—1-2-3 automatically supplies it for you. When you enter numbers followed by text (as in addresses), you must use a label prefix before 1-2-3 will accept the entry into a cell.

When you enter a number as a label—for example, the year **1990**—the assumption is that you are entering a value. You need some way to signal that you intend this numeric entry to be treated as text. You can indicate this by using one of the label prefixes. In this case, you can enter 1990 as a centered label by typing ^**1990**.

Aligning Labels

To align labels as you enter them into the worksheet, you must first type a label prefix. The following label prefixes are used for label alignment:

' Left-justifies

" Right-justifies

^ Centers

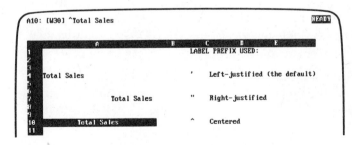

Label prefixes can be used to align labels three different ways within a single cell.

3

Repeating Label Characters

An additional label prefix is available for repeating one or more characters in a single cell. For example, you can use the repeat character—a backslash (\)—to create a separator line that fills an entire cell.

To repeat characters within a single cell, follow these steps:

1. Highlight the cell that will contain the repeating label.

   For example, highlight cell A2 to use the repeat character that creates a separator line.

2. Press ⬚\⬚, the repeat character, and then press the character(s) to be repeated within the highlighted cell.

   In this example, press ⬚\⬚⬚=⬚ to fill cell A2 with equal signs.

3. Press ⬚↵Enter⬚ to enter the label into the highlighted cell.

Cell A2 is now filled with equal signs. Repeat these steps in adjoining cells to form the remainder of the separator line.

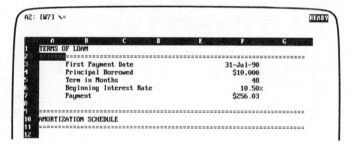

Controlling Label Prefixes

You can control label prefixes in several different ways. If you want to change the alignment of a range of labels *after* the labels are entered, you can use the /Range Label command or the Edit (F2) key (to edit individual cells).

For example, suppose that you enter two rows of labels and then decide that you want the labels to be centered. You can change the alignment of a range of existing labels by using the /Range Label command. (You will learn more about ranges in Chapter 4.)

To align a range of labels, follow these steps:

1. Call up the 1-2-3 menu by pressing ⬚/⬚.

2. Select **Range** by pressing R.

3. Select **Label** by pressing L.

4. Select one of the following alignment choices: **Left**, **Right**, or **Center** (by pressing L, R, or C, respectively).

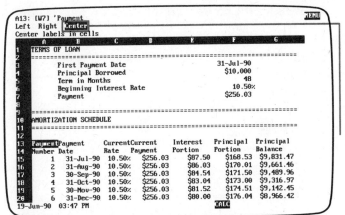

In this example, select Center by pressing C.

5. Specify the range of cells to be aligned by pointing or typing, and then press ⏎Enter. The range is now aligned properly, with label prefixes inserted at the beginning of each label.

In this example, type **A13. .G14** and press ⏎Enter.

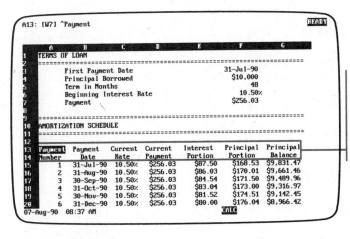

The cells are now displayed as centered, and each label in the range is preceded by a caret (ˆ).

3

If you want to set the alignment of an entire worksheet to the left, right, or center *before* you enter labels, you can use the /Worksheet Global Label-Prefix command. This command will not change the alignment of existing labels, however. The alignment of existing labels can be changed by using the /Range Label command or Edit (F2).

To set the alignment of labels for the entire worksheet, follow these steps:

1. Call up the 1-2-3 menu by pressing ⌤.
2. Select Worksheet by pressing Ⓦ.
3. Select Global by pressing Ⓖ.

1-2-3 displays the Global Settings sheet, described in detail in Chapter 5.

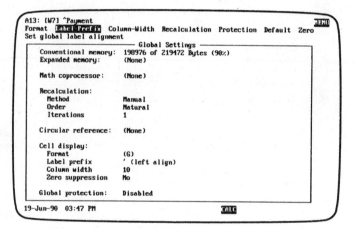

4. Select Label-Prefix by pressing Ⓛ.
5. Select one of the following alignment choices: **Left**, **Right**, or Center (by pressing Ⓛ, Ⓡ, or Ⓒ, respectively).

You can use /Worksheet Global to check the current alignment settings for the worksheet. This information is displayed near the bottom of the Global Settings sheet.

Entering Numbers

As you know, values in 1-2-3 consist of numbers and formulas. Numbers are used frequently in 1-2-3 worksheets for many different types of applications—especially those that involve data entry tasks.

The rules for entering numbers are the following:

- A number cannot begin with any character except the numerals 0 through 9, a decimal point, a minus sign (–), or a dollar sign ($). Numbers can begin with a plus sign (+) or can be entered in parentheses, but the + and the ( ) will not appear in the cell.
- You can end a number with a percent sign (%), which causes 1-2-3 to divide the number preceding the sign by 100.
- A number cannot have more than one decimal point.
- You can enter a number in scientific notation, which is called Scientific format in 1-2-3 (for example, 1.234E+06).
- You cannot enter spaces after numbers.
- Do not start a number entry with a space(s). If you do, 1-2-3 treats the entry as a label. This does not cause an immediate error, but 1-2-3 treats the cell contents as zero the next time the number is used in a formula.

If you do not follow these rules, 1-2-3 beeps when you press Enter and automatically shifts to EDIT mode as if Edit (F2) were pressed.

Entering Formulas

In addition to simple numbers, you can enter formulas into cells. Enter formulas either by *typing* the formula into the cell or by *pointing*, which entails moving the cell pointer so that 1-2-3 enters the cell addresses for you.

Suppose that you want to create a formula which adds a row of numbers. For example, you want to add the amounts in cells C4, C5, C6, and C7, and place the result in cell C9. To do this by *typing*, you type **+C4+C5+C6+C7** into cell C9. The + sign at the beginning of the formula indicates that a formula, not a label, is to be entered. 1-2-3 then switches to VALUE mode, the appropriate mode for entering numbers and formulas.

To enter a formula with cell addresses by using the *pointing* method, follow these steps:

1. Begin with the cell pointer highlighting the cell that will hold the formula, and then press ⊞.

In this example, highlight cell C9 and press ⊞.

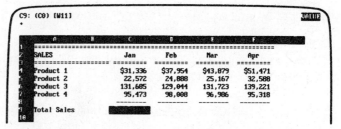

2. Highlight the first cell address of the formula and press ⊞.

In this example, highlight cell C4 and press ⊞.

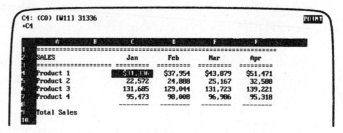

The mode indicator in the upper right corner of the screen shifts from VALUE to POINT as you move the cell pointer to cell C4. Notice that the address for the cell appears after the plus sign in the second line of the control panel—in this case, +C4.

When you press ⊞ again, the cell pointer moves immediately from cell C4 back to the previous cell—in this example, to cell C9. The mode indicator also shifts back to VALUE.

3. Highlight the next cell address of the formula and press ⊞.

In this example, highlight cell C5 and press ⊞.

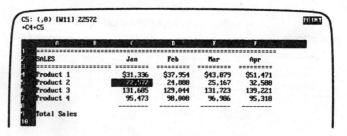

70

4. Continue this sequence of pointing and entering plus signs until the formula is complete.

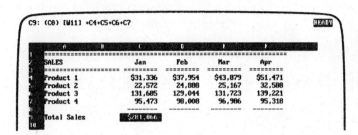

In this example, highlight cell C6 and press ⊕; then highlight cell C7.

5. Press ↵Enter to complete the operation.

Remember that you can use a combination of typing and pointing to enter a formula that contains one or more cell addresses. Use the method that works best for you. The easiest method is to point when cells are close to the one you are defining and to type references to distant cells. You get the same results with either method, and you can mix and match the two techniques within the same formula.

Using Mathematical Operators in Formulas

Operators are symbols that indicate arithmetic operations in formulas, and they are either logical or mathematical. Logical operators are discussed in Chapter 13, "Managing Data." The mathematical operators are the following:

Operator	Meaning
^	Exponentiation
+, −	Positive, negative
*, /	Multiplication, division
+, −	Addition, subtraction

This list indicates, from the top down, the *order of precedence*—that is, the order in which these operators are evaluated. For example, exponentiation takes place before multiplication, and division occurs before subtraction. Operations inside a set of parentheses are always evaluated first. Operators at the same level of precedence are evaluated in order from left to right.

Consider the following formula:

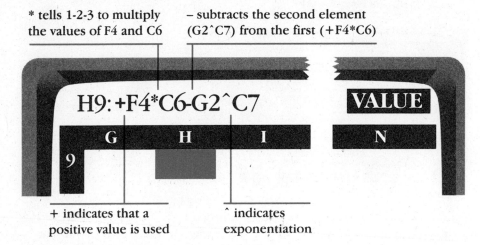

* tells 1-2-3 to multiply the values of F4 and C6

− subtracts the second element (G2ˆC7) from the first (+F4*C6)

H9: +F4*C6-G2ˆC7   VALUE

+ indicates that a positive value is used

ˆ indicates exponentiation

The first operator to be evaluated in a formula is exponentiation—the power of a number. In the formula 8+2ˆ3, for example, 2ˆ3 (2 to the power of 3) is evaluated before the addition. The answer is 16 (8+8), not 1000 (10 to the power of 3).

The next set of operators to be evaluated indicates the sign of a value (whether it is positive or negative). Notice the difference between a + or − sign that indicates a positive or negative value and a + or − sign that indicates addition or subtraction. When used as signs, these operators are evaluated before multiplication and division; when used as indicators of addition and subtraction, they are evaluated after multiplication and division. For example, 5+4/−2 is evaluated as 5+(−2), with 3 as the answer. The − sign indicates that 2 is negative, then 4 is divided by −2, and finally 5 is added to −2, resulting in the answer of 3.

Parentheses can always be used to override the order of precedence. Consider the order of precedence in the following formulas, in which cell B3 contains the value 2, C3 contains the value 3, and D3 contains the value 4. Notice how parentheses affect the order of precedence and the results in the first two formulas.

Formula	Evaluation	Result
+C3–D3/B3	3–(4/2)	1
(C3–D3)/B3	(3–4)/2	–0.5
+D3*C3–B3^C3	(4*3)–(2^3)	4
+D3*C3*B3/B3^C3–25/5	((4*3*2)/(2^3)–(25/5))	–2

Correcting Errors in Formulas

It is easy to make errors when you enter formulas. The more complex the formula, the more likely you are to confirm the saying, "Whatever can go wrong, will." 1-2-3 provides ways to help you discover and correct these sometimes inevitable errors.

If you try to enter a formula that contains a logical or mathematical error, the program will beep, change to EDIT mode, and move the cursor to the section of the formula where the problem most likely exists. You can then correct the error and continue.

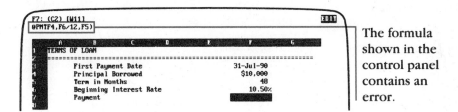

The formula shown in the control panel contains an error.

If you don't know what the problem is, you can give yourself some time to think by converting the formula to a label. While in EDIT mode, follow these steps:

1. To convert a formula to a label from EDIT mode, press (Home), (')
(apostrophe), and (↵Enter).

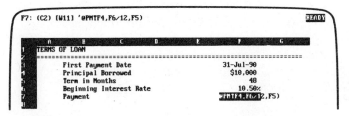

The formula shown in the control panel has been converted to a label.

73

2. After you correct the formula, delete the apostrophe by pressing
   Home followed by Del (while in EDIT mode), and then press
   ⏎Enter

3

The corrected
formula is shown
in the control
panel.

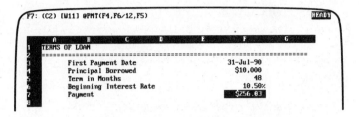

If your formula is long and complex, break it down into logical segments and
test each segment separately. Using smaller segments helps to debug the
formula. Also, because 1-2-3 limits individual cell entries to 240 characters,
the reduced size may be necessary for the program to accept the formula.

Common errors include open parentheses and commas that are missing
from built-in formulas (functions). What appears to be a logical error may be
only a missing punctuation mark. When 1-2-3 beeps to indicate a formula
error, check the formula for a missing parenthesis or comma near the cursor.

Formulas that contain embedded or trailing spaces will result in errors. To
find a trailing space, press the END key while in EDIT mode. If the cursor is
more than one character beyond the end of a formula, you can delete the
trailing spaces with the Backspace key.

1-2-3 provides two commands to help you examine and analyze your
formulas. The **/Print** Printer Options Other Cell-Formulas command
(discussed in Chapter 8) prints a list of all the formulas in your worksheet.
The **/R**ange Format Text command (discussed in Chapter 4) displays existing
formulas in their worksheet locations.

Using Functions in Formulas

Like most electronic spreadsheets, 1-2-3 includes built-in functions. These
functions fall into eight basic categories: (1) mathematical and trigonometric,
(2) date and time, (3) financial , (4) statistical, (5) database, (6) logical, (7)
string, and (8) special. Some of 1-2-3's functions are described in the text
that follows. You can learn more about 1-2-3's functions in Chapter 7.

The *mathematical* and *trigonometric* functions perform standard arithmetic operations such as computing absolute value (@ABS) or square root (@SQRT), rounding numbers (@ROUND), and computing the sine (@SIN), cosine (@COS), and tangent (@TAN).

The *date* and *time* functions, such as @DATE and @TIME, convert dates and times to serial numbers. The serial numbers allow you to perform date and time arithmetic or to document your worksheets and reports.

The *financial* functions calculate returns on investments (@IRR and @RATE), loan payments (@PMT), present values (@NPV and @PV), future values (@FV), and compound growth periods (@TERM and @CTERM).

The *statistical* functions perform standard calculations on lists, such as summing values (@SUM), calculating averages (@AVG), finding minimum and maximum values (@MIN and @MAX), and computing standard deviations and variances (@STD and @VAR).

The *database* functions perform statistical calculations on a field of a database, based on certain criteria. These functions, such as @DSUM and @DAVG, have names and uses similar to the *statistical* functions.

The *logical* functions, such as @IF, @TRUE, and @FALSE, let you perform conditional tests. You can use these functions to test whether a condition is true or false.

The *string* functions help you manipulate text. You can use string functions to repeat text characters (@REPEAT), to convert letters to uppercase or lowercase (@UPPER or @LOWER), and to change strings to numbers and numbers to strings (@VALUE and @STRING).

The *special* functions perform a variety of tasks. For example, @CELL and @CELLPOINTER can return up to 10 different characteristics of a cell, including its width, format, type of address, and prefix.

Entering a 1-2-3 Function

As noted earlier, 1-2-3 has a variety of functions that perform many different tasks—from simple arithmetic to complex statistical analysis and depreciation calculations. Functions consist of three parts: the @ sign, a function name, and an argument or range. Note that *range* refers to the range of the cells that will be used by the function.

3

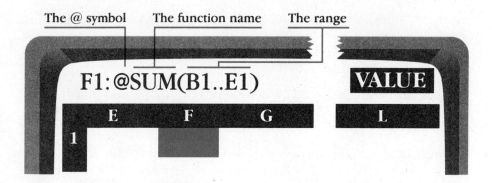

The @ symbol   The function name   The range

F1: @SUM(B1..E1)   VALUE

In the preceding example, the function in cell F1 computes the total of the range of four cells from B1 through E1. The @ sign signals that the entry is a function. SUM is the name of the function being used. Function names can be entered with upper- or lowercase letters; this book uses uppercase letters to denote 1-2-3 functions. The statement (B1..E1) is the argument (in this case, a range). A function's arguments, always enclosed in parentheses, specify the cell or range of cells on which the function will act. This function tells 1-2-3 to compute the sum of the numbers in cells B1, C1, D1, and E1, and to display the result in cell F1.

Some functions can be quite complex. For example, several functions can be combined in a single cell by having one function use other functions as its arguments. The length of an argument, however, is limited—functions, like formulas, can contain only 240 characters per cell.

Entering Formulas Containing Functions

When you enter a formula containing a function that requires a cell address, you can enter the address by typing or pointing.

To enter the formula @SUM(C7..C4), for example, follow this procedure:

1. Move the cell pointer to the cell that will contain the formula, and type @SUM(.

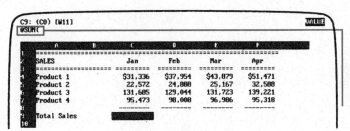

The @ sign, function name, and opening parenthesis are typed.

2. Move the cell pointer to C7 and press [.].

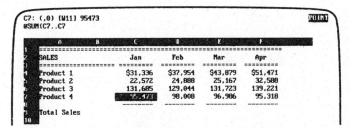

The cell pointer is anchored at C7.

3. Press [↑] three times.

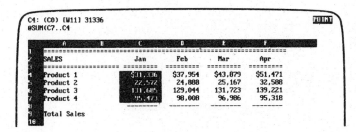

The range of cells between C7 and C4 is highlighted.

4. Type the closing [)] and press [↵Enter].

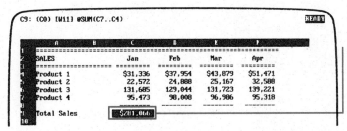

1-2-3 enters the sum of C7..C4 into cell C9.

3

Editing Data in the Worksheet

One of the first things you need to be able to do is to modify the contents of cells without retyping the complete entry. This is quite easy to do in 1-2-3. Begin by moving the cell pointer to the appropriate cell and pressing the Edit (F2) key.

After you press Edit (F2), the mode indicator in the upper right corner of the screen changes to EDIT. The contents of the cell are duplicated in the second line of the control panel (the edit line), the cursor appears at the end of the entry, and you are ready for editing.

When you first press Edit (F2), 1-2-3 is in *insert mode*. Any new characters you type are inserted at the cursor, and any characters on the right side of the cursor are pushed one position to the right. If you activate *overtype mode* by pressing the Ins key on the numeric keypad, any new character you type replaces the character directly above the cursor, and the cursor moves one position to the right. When 1-2-3 is in overtype mode, the indicator OVR appears at the bottom of the screen. Pressing the Ins key again switches 1-2-3 back to insert mode.

To edit the contents of a cell, follow these steps:

1. Highlight the appropriate cell and press [F2] (Edit).

   Notice that the mode indicator changes to EDIT.

In this example, highlight cell A12 and press [F2] (Edit).

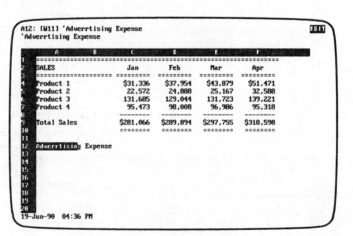

2. With the contents of the cell displayed in the second line of the control panel, move the cursor to the part of the entry you want to edit (by pressing ⬅ or ➡).

   In this example, use ⬅ to move the cursor to the second "r".

3. Use one or more of the editing keys, described in table 3.2, to modify the cell's contents.

   In this example, press Del to delete the character above the cursor.

4. Press ⏎Enter (or type any new characters and then press ⏎Enter) to complete the edit and return the worksheet to READY mode.

You can also use EDIT mode when you are entering data into a cell for the first time. If you make a mistake while you are entering the data, you can correct the error without retyping the entire entry.

Table 3.2
Key Actions in Edit Mode

Key	Action
⬅	Moves the cursor one position to the left.
➡	Moves the cursor one position to the right.
Tab (or Ctrl➡)	Moves the cursor five characters to the right.
⬆Shift Tab (or Ctrl⬅)	Moves the cursor five characters to the left.
Home	Moves the cursor to the first character in the entry.
End	Moves the cursor one position to the right of the last character in the entry.
⬅Backspace	Deletes the character to the left of the cursor.
Ins	Toggles between insert and overtype modes.
Del	Deletes the character above the cursor.
Esc	Clears the edit line. When pressed again, abandons changes and leaves EDIT mode.

Using the Undo Feature

When you use electronic spreadsheet packages, you can destroy hours of work by using the wrong commands. It is easy to confuse the command to delete rows or columns (/Worksheet Delete) with the command to erase a range (/Range Erase) and delete a row or column while intending merely to erase data. The results can be difficult to recover from—particularly when formulas depend on those deleted rows or columns.

The Undo feature, which is activated by pressing the key combination Alt-F4 (hold down the Alt key and press F4), returns the worksheet to its previous appearance and condition. You can undo only the last command, and if you change your mind about what was just undone, you can again use Undo (Alt-F4) to "reverse the undo."

Accidentally deleting a row with cells that are referenced by formulas can cause many cells in the worksheet to display ERR.

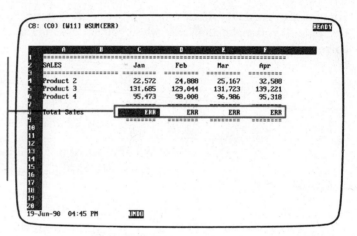

Press Undo (Alt-F4) to undo the last command and return the original contents to the deleted row of cells.

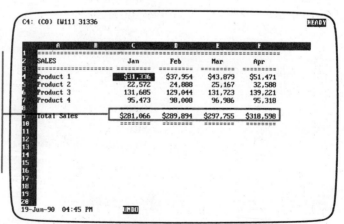

80

Using the command that resets (clears) *all* range names (**/Range Name Reset**), instead of the command that deletes *individual* range names (**/Range Name Delete**), is another common mistake that can create much frustration—especially when many range names are used in a worksheet. Undo is a quick solution for recovering the lost range names. You must, however, catch errors immediately because there is no way to reverse any command except the last one.

The Undo feature also has other uses. Every user is sometimes apprehensive about using certain commands because of the possibility of unexpected results or potential disasters. With Undo you can proceed with a command, having confidence that if you don't like the results you can reverse them.

Activating and Deactivating Undo

When you enter 1-2-3, the Undo feature is automatically activated and available for use. You know that it is activated when you see the UNDO indicator at the bottom of the screen. The UNDO feature of 1-2-3 can be used only when the UNDO indicator is displayed in the status line.

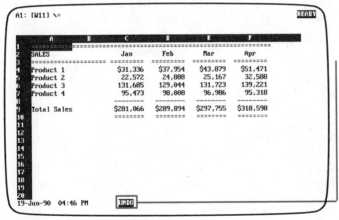

When the Undo feature is available, the UNDO indicator is present when 1-2-3 is in READY mode.

In order for the Undo feature to work, 1-2-3 creates a temporary backup copy of the entire worksheet whenever you start a command or cell entry. This information is stored in your computer's temporary memory (RAM).

81

3

Storing this data takes up space and limits the worksheet size you can build with 1-2-3.

As a worksheet grows in size, the amount of memory reserved for holding a backup copy of the last worksheet image becomes exhausted, and you may not be able to use the Undo feature. Under these circumstances, you can use the /Worksheet Global Default Other Undo Disable command to deactivate the Undo feature temporarily.

To disable the Undo feature temporarily, follow these steps:

1. Call up the 1-2-3 menu by pressing ⟦/⟧.
2. Select Worksheet by pressing ⟦W⟧.
3. Select Global by pressing ⟦G⟧.
4. Select Default by pressing ⟦D⟧.
5. Select Other by pressing ⟦O⟧.
6. Select Undo by pressing ⟦U⟧.
7. Select Disable by pressing ⟦D⟧.

This command makes the Undo feature unavailable, but it creates more room for your worksheet to grow. If you later start to work on another worksheet (before exiting 1-2-3), you can reactivate the Undo feature with the command /Worksheet Global Default Other Undo Enable.

If you become accustomed to the Undo feature and rely on it heavily for security, you must avoid building worksheets so large that they prevent your use of Undo.

What Can't Be Undone?

There is no way to undo some commands. You cannot "unerase," "unsave," or "unextract" a disk file; neither can you "unprint" your last printed output.

You can undo most other commands, however, including the entire sequence of commands associated with creating graphs, setting up ranges for data query commands, and all "undo-able" steps embedded within a macro.

Naming, Saving, and Retrieving Files

The sections that follow explain file operations that beginning 1-2-3 users need most often—naming, saving, and retrieving files. For more information about other file operations, including deleting and listing files; specialized operations such as protecting files with passwords; combining, linking, and transferring files; and using the Translate Utility, see Chapter 10.

3

Naming Files

1-2-3 file names can be up to eight characters long with a three-character extension.

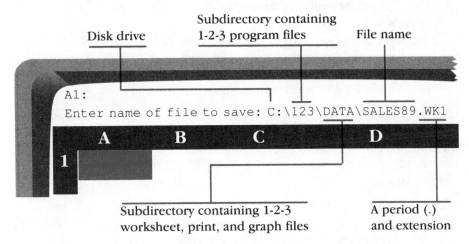

Disk drive | Subdirectory containing 1-2-3 program files | File name

```
A1:
Enter name of file to save: C:\123\DATA\SALES89.WK1
     A        B        C        D
  1
```

Subdirectory containing 1-2-3 worksheet, print, and graph files | A period (.) and extension

The basic rules for naming files are the following:

- File names may include the characters A through Z, 0 through 9, and the underscore (_). Depending on your system, you may be able to use other special characters, but 1-2-3 will not accept the characters <, >, or *. Although 1-2-3 separates the file name from the three-letter extension with a period (.), the program does not accept the period *within* the file name. Therefore, the following file names are illegal:

  CH<15>.WK1

  TOM*BBS.PRN

  SALES.89.WK1

83

- File names may not contain blank spaces. For example, SALES RPT.WK1 is not a valid file name.
- 1-2-3 automatically converts lowercase letters to uppercase letters in file names.

Although you determine the eight-character file name, 1-2-3 automatically creates the extension based on its type of file format. The three basic file extensions are the following:

- WK1 is the extension automatically added to names of worksheet files saved with the /File Save command.
- PRN is the extension automatically added to names of 1-2-3 files that you save in print (ASCII) format with the /Print File command. PRN files can be printed or imported into 1-2-3 and other programs.
- PIC is the extension automatically added to names of graph files saved with the /Graph Save command. You must issue this command *after* creating the file within 1-2-3 and *before* printing the graph from 1-2-3's PrintGraph program.

Note: The different versions of Release 2 can read older 1-2-3 worksheets with WKS extensions, but 1-2-3 writes the new files with WK1 extensions when you save the worksheet. If you want to run WK1 files with earlier versions of 1-2-3, you need to use the Translate Utility (discussed in Chapter 10.)

In addition to creating files with the WK1, PRN, and PIC extensions, Release 2 and later versions let you supply your own extension. Simply enter the file name according to the previously listed rules, enter a period, and add an extension of one to three characters. Note that 1-2-3 will not display any file name with your own extension in the lists of WK1, PIC, or PRN files. The /File Retrieve command, for example, will display all worksheet (WK1) files except for those with your special extensions. To retrieve your special file, type the file name, including the period and extension, after the `Name of file to retrieve:` prompt.

Remember to be descriptive when you think of a name for the new file. Choose a file name that relates something about the file's contents. This will prevent confusion once you have created several different files and need to access a particular file quickly. The following list provides some good examples of file names:

File name	Description
INV_JUN	Inventory worksheet for June
PRO_REST	*Pro forma* worksheet for a planned restaurant
EMPLSTDP	Employee list for the Data Processing Department

3

If you work with many different worksheets containing basically the same information, you should use similar names without, of course, using the same names. In a previous example, the name SALES89 was given to a sales worksheet for the year 1989. Following this naming scheme, you can name the sales worksheets for 1990 and 1991 SALES90 and SALES91, respectively. This naming technique will help you recall file names later.

Saving Files

Computerized spreadsheets have one danger that is not as common in the paper-and-pencil world. If you keep track of your business accounts manually, you can simply get up from your desk and walk away when you decide to quit working. There's nothing to "exit," nothing to turn off (except, perhaps, a calculator), and *usually* nothing that might cause your work to vanish from your desk. Unless they are misplaced or accidentally thrown away, the materials you use in a manual accounting system remain safely on your desk until morning.

With electronic spreadsheets—and with computer files in general—the risks of power outages or human errors can be costly in terms of data and time loss. If you exit 1-2-3 without saving your file, any work that you have done since the last time you saved the file is lost. You can recover the data only by retyping it into the worksheet. You should make an effort, therefore, to save your files frequently—at least once every half hour to one hour (depending on how many changes are made).

To save a new or existing file, follow these steps:

1. Call up the 1-2-3 menu by pressing ⟮/⟯.
2. Select File by pressing ⟮F⟯.
3. Select Save by pressing ⟮S⟯.

When you save a new worksheet file, 1-2-3 automatically supplies a list of the worksheet files on the current drive and directory.

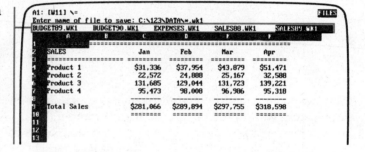

Press ⟮F3⟯ (Name) to view a full-screen list of worksheet file names.

When you save an existing file, 1-2-3 displays the current file name. Press ⟮Esc⟯ followed by ⟮F3⟯ (Name) to view a full-screen list of all worksheet files on the current drive and directory.

4. Either highlight one of the displayed worksheet file names or type a new or existing file name.

Remember to choose descriptive file names that identify the files for ease in locating them later.

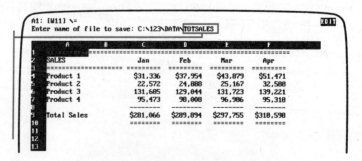

5. Press ⏎Enter. 1-2-3 automatically supplies a WK1 extension for a new file and saves the file on disk.

   If you are saving an existing file, another menu appears with the options Cancel, Replace, and Backup. To update the current file on disk, select **R**eplace by pressing R.

3

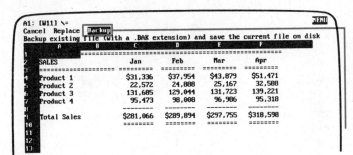

Choose the Backup option if you want to save the latest changes made to an existing file.

Backup is an alternative to the **C**ancel and **R**eplace options of /**F**ile **S**ave. (This option is not available in 1-2-3 versions prior to Release 2.2.) Backup renames the older version of your file—using the same file name—and adds BAK as the file extension. The current version of your file is then saved with the WK1 extension. This process allows you always to have available your two most recent worksheet versions.

Saving on the Hard Disk and also on a Floppy Diskette

If you use a hard disk system, you may want to save your worksheets on the hard disk as well as on a floppy diskette. To do this, follow these steps:

1. To save your worksheet on the hard disk, select /**F**ile **S**ave by pressing / F S , type the file name after the hard disk drive and directory prompt, and press ⏎Enter.

   Note: If you are saving a file that has been previously saved, highlight (or type) the file name, press ⏎Enter, and press R for **R**eplace.

2. To save your worksheet on a floppy diskette, select /File Save by pressing ⃞/⃞F⃞S, and press the ⃞Esc key one or more times—until the prompt Enter name of file to save: is all that remains.

3. Type the disk drive designation (for example A:), followed by the file name, and press ⃞↵Enter.

For example, type **A:SALES89** and press ⃞↵Enter.

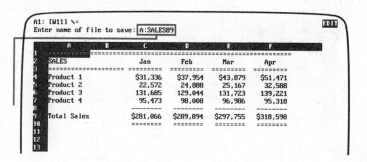

Checking Disk Space before Saving

As you use 1-2-3, you will soon have several worksheet files that take up significant disk space. Although hard disk users generally don't have to worry about running out of disk space when saving, floppy disk users need to check the amount of disk space periodically. You need to monitor the amount of disk space your files use, however, no matter what type of system you use. Nothing is worse than getting the message Disk full after you have worked on an important worksheet and are attempting to save it.

You can avoid this problem by using 1-2-3's /System command. Whenever you press /S from READY mode, 1-2-3 steps aside and displays the DOS prompt. (Even though the DOS prompt is displayed, 1-2-3 and your worksheet are still in memory.)

At the DOS prompt, type **CHKDSK** and press Enter to see how much space is available on your disk.

```
(Type EXIT and press ENTER to return to 1-2-3)


The IBM Personal Computer DOS
Version 3.30 (C)Copyright International Business Machines Corp 1981, 1987
           (C)Copyright Microsoft Corp 1981, 1986


Date: Tue  6-19-1990    Time: 17:37:23.88

[C:\123] CHKDSK A:

   1213952 bytes total disk space
   1160192 bytes in 16 user files
     53760 bytes available on disk

    655360 bytes total memory
    208032 bytes free


Date: Tue  6-19-1990    Time: 17:37:31.02

[C:\123]
```

To check a floppy diskette, you must follow the CHKDSK command with the disk drive designation, such as **CHKDSK A:**.

3

You also can use the FORMAT command within DOS to format a new diskette if you need one (see your DOS manual).

If you are using a hard disk system, and your hard disk is almost full, you can erase some of the old files before saving the new files. (First make sure that you have a proper backup of the old files.)

When you finish the DOS operations, type **exit** and press Enter to return to the 1-2-3 worksheet. Now you can save the working model.

One point to remember: When you use /System to exit to DOS, do *not* start any program from DOS that will alter memory, such as a memory-resident program. If you do, you won't be able to return to the 1-2-3 worksheet, and you will lose any work you have not saved.

Retrieving Files

To call a file back into memory from disk, use the /File Retrieve command. This command replaces the current file with the new file. If you are just starting 1-2-3, this command brings a new file into memory.

To retrieve a file, follow these steps:

1. Call up the 1-2-3 menu by pressing ⌐/⌐.
2. Select **File** by pressing ⌐F⌐.
3. Select **Retrieve** by pressing ⌐R⌐.

1-2-3 displays a partial list of files in the current drive and directory .

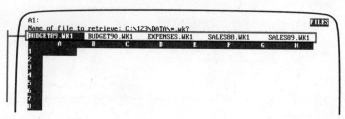

The files have the WK1 extension. Any WKS files from older versions of 1-2-3 are also listed.

4. If you don't see the file name you want, press F3 (Name).

1-2-3 displays a full-screen list of file names in the current drive and directory.

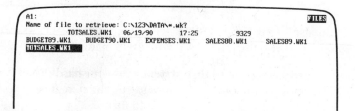

When you highlight a file name, you also see the date and time the file was created, as well as its size.

5. Select the desired file name by highlighting or typing it, and then press ↵Enter.

Using Wild Cards for File Retrieval

When you are retrieving files, you can use wild cards with 1-2-3. Wild cards—the asterisk (*) and the question mark (?)—are helpful when you need to limit the number of files that are displayed on-screen, or when you are unsure of the exact spelling of a file you want to retrieve.

If you want to display only those file names that begin or end with a certain character or characters, use the asterisk (*). For example, you could type **S*** followed by Enter at the Name of file to retrieve: prompt.

All the file names that begin with the letter S are displayed.

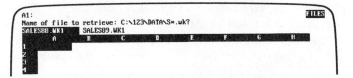

You can use the asterisk (*) wild card in place of any combination of characters; the question mark (?) wild card stands for any one character. The asterisk can be used by itself or following other characters. According to these rules, SALES*.WK1 is acceptable, but *89.WK1 is not. The question mark wild card, on the other hand, can be used in any character position. Therefore, instead of the incorrect retrieval name *89.WK1, you can enter **?????89.WK1**.

Retrieving Files from Subdirectories

1-2-3 keeps track of subdirectory names as well as file names. When you issue the /File Retrieve command, for example, subdirectories of the current directory are displayed with the file names.

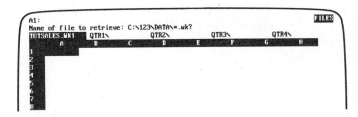

The backslash (\) symbol following a name (within a list of file names) indicates a subdirectory name.

When you point to a subdirectory name and press Enter, 1-2-3 displays the list of files in that subdirectory.

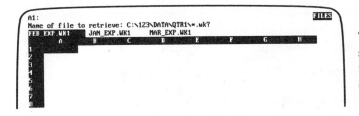

This screen shows the files in the QTR1 subdirectory.

After the prompt is the path 1-2-3 follows to retrieve the specified files.

3

When you need to access a file that is on a different drive—or one that is in a directory that is not a subdirectory of the current directory—use the Esc key or the Backspace key after selecting /File **R**etrieve. When you press the Esc key while the default path name shows on the control panel, 1-2-3 changes to EDIT mode. You can then edit the file specification just as you would any label entry. When you press the Esc key a second time, 1-2-3 erases the current drive and directory specification. You can then enter the specification for the drive and directory you want.

You can use the Backspace key to erase the path name, one entire directory at a time. To reverse the process, select a subdirectory name from the list of files and press Enter.

Some valid file names, with their drive and directory specifications, are the following:

File name	Description
B:\SAMPLE1.WK1	Worksheet file on drive B
C:\123\SAMPLE1.WK1	Worksheet file in subdirectory 123 on drive C
C:\123\DATA*.PIC	List of all PIC files in subdirectory DATA of subdirectory 123 on drive C. 1-2-3 displays the list and waits for you to select a specific file name.
A:*.*	List of all files on drive A. 1-2-3 displays all file names and waits for you to select a specific file name.

Summary

This chapter on 1-2-3 basics covered many important concepts that are essential for beginning 1-2-3 users. You learned about moving the cell pointer around the worksheet; selecting commands from menus; entering and editing data, formulas, and labels; using the Undo feature; and naming, saving, and retrieving 1-2-3 files.

Specifically, you learned the following key information about 1-2-3:

■ The arrow keys move the cell pointer horizontally and vertically, one cell at a time. When used with the End key, however, they can move the cell pointer quickly—even to the remote borders of 1-2-3's large worksheet.

■ The PgUp, PgDn, Tab, and Shift-Tab keys help you move around the worksheet one screen at a time (up, down, right, and left, respectively).

■ The Home key moves the cell pointer to the upper left corner of a worksheet—to cell A1. When you specify a cell address for the GoTo (F5) function key, you make the cell pointer jump almost instantly to any cell in the worksheet.

■ Commands are selected from 1-2-3's menu system by pressing slash (/) and either *pointing* to the desired command and pressing Enter or directly selecting the command by *typing* the first letter of the menu command. The typing method is preferred because it is faster.

■ Two types of data can be entered into a 1-2-3 worksheet: labels and values. Labels are text entries, and values include numbers, formulas, and functions.

■ Label prefixes are used to affect how text data is displayed in individual cells. The label prefixes include ' (left-justify), " (right-justify), ˆ (center), and \ (repeat label). The /Range Label command aligns labels in a *range* of cells, and the /Worksheet Global Label-Prefix command changes the alignment of labels for the *entire* worksheet.

■ A strength of 1-2-3 is its capability to accept and compute complex numerical data, formulas, and functions. 1-2-3's functions, always identified by the @ symbol preceding the function's name, are used within formulas to provide exceptional power in your worksheets.

■ The Edit (F2) key is used to modify any data that has been entered (or is currently being entered) into the worksheet. The direction keys are used to move the cursor in the control panel while editing a cell entry.

■ The Undo feature, which is activated by pressing Alt-F4, allows you to "undo" the previous command before the next command is executed. Many potentially disastrous mistakes can be easily reversed with this convenient feature. To release the memory required by Undo, you can temporarily deactivate the Undo feature with the /Worksheet Global Default Other Undo Disable command. (This feature is not available in 1-2-3 versions prior to Release 2.2.)

3

93

3

■ File names used in 1-2-3 can be eight characters in length, followed by a period (.) and a three-character extension. File extensions used in 1-2-3 include WK1 for worksheet files (WKS for older versions of 1-2-3), PRN for ASCII print files, and PIC for graph files.

■ The /File Save command is used to save the current worksheet file. If the file name already exists, 1-2-3 prompts you to Replace the existing file or Cancel the command. The Backup option, which is unavailable in 1-2-3 versions prior to Release 2.2, ensures that the previous version of the worksheet will always be available.

■ The /File Retrieve command is used to call an existing file into memory. 1-2-3 provides a list of worksheet files (and sub-directories) located in the current directory. The wild-card characters, * and ?, are used to limit the files displayed with the /File Retrieve command.

The 1-2-3 basics provided in this chapter will enable you to begin working with ranges, which are discussed in the next chapter.

Working with Ranges

This chapter (and the next two chapters) teaches you the principles of using commands and shows you how to use some of the fundamental 1-2-3 commands that are needed to build worksheets. Although most of the commands discussed in this chapter are from the Range menu, some options from the Worksheet menu are also included. Chapters 4, 5, and 6 discuss the commands you use to create a worksheet.

To make sense of the command structure, you first need to understand the concept of ranges. While some commands affect the entire worksheet, others affect only certain cells or groups of cells. 1-2-3 uses the term *range* for a rectangular block of cells, and many useful actions in 1-2-3 are built around the range concept. This chapter tells you what ranges are and how to manipulate them with specific commands.

Ranges offer many advantages that can make your work less tedious and more efficient. When you use ranges, you can execute commands that affect all the cells in a group rather than one individual cell. For example, you can format a block of cells to be displayed as currency by executing a single command on the specified range of cells.

4

Key Terms in This Chapter

Range   A rectangular group of cells that is used in a worksheet
                     operation. For example, the rectangular area A10. .D10
                     is a *range*.

Range   Commands used to manipulate cells in ranges.
commands   You can access the /Range commands through the
                     Range option on the 1-2-3 main menu.

Range name   A list of all range names and their corresponding cell
table   addresses. This list is produced with the /Range Name
                     Table command.

Formatting   The process of changing the way data is displayed in the
                     worksheet. Formatting is accomplished with the /Range
                     Format or /Worksheet Global Format commands.

When you use range names instead of cell addresses, you can quickly process
blocks of cells in commands and formulas. A descriptive range name will
help you and others recognize the nature of the data that the range contains.
You can use the name with the GoTo (F5) command to move the cell pointer
quickly to that range in the worksheet.

What Is a Range?

1-2-3's definition of a range is *a rectangular block of adjacent cells*. The
smallest possible range is one cell, and the largest is the entire worksheet.
Remember that ranges are specified by the cells in the upper left and lower
right corners of the range.

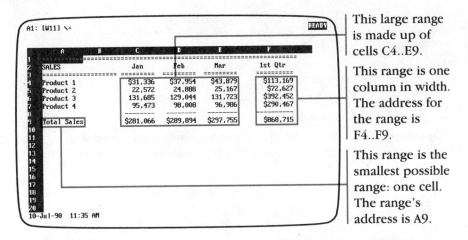

This large range is made up of cells C4..E9.

This range is one column in width. The address for the range is F4..F9.

This range is the smallest possible range: one cell. The range's address is A9.

4

You access the /Range commands by selecting **Range** from the main menu. You then see the following menu of commands:

Format Label Erase Name Justify Prot Unprot Input Value Trans Search

Table 4.1 provides a brief description of the actions of each of these commands.

Table 4.1
The Range Commands and Their Actions

Command	Action
Format	Changes the display of values or formula results in a cell or range of cells.
Label	Aligns text labels in a cell or range of cells.
Erase	Deletes the contents of a cell or range of cells.
Name	Assigns, modifies, or deletes a name associated with a cell or range of cells.
Justify	Fits text within a desired range by wrapping words to form complete paragraphs with lines of approximately the same length.
Prot (Protect)	Prevents changes to cell ranges when /Worksheet Global Protection is enabled.

97

Table 4.1—(continued)

Command	Action
Unprot (Unprotect)	When /Worksheet Global Protection is enabled, allows changes to a range of cells and identifies (through increases in intensity or changes of color) which cells' contents can be changed.
Input	When /Worksheet Global Protection is enabled, restricts cell-pointer movement to unprotected cells in a range.
Value	Copies formulas in a range to their values in another specified range (or the same range).
Trans (Transpose)	Reorders columns of data into rows, or rows of data into columns.
Search	Finds or replaces a string of data within a specified range. (Not available in versions prior to Release 2.2.)

Designating a Range

Many commands act on ranges. For example, the /Range Erase command prompts you for the range to erase. You can respond to a prompt for a range in the following three ways:

- Type the addresses of the upper left and lower right cells in the range.
- Use the cell pointer to highlight the cells in the range.
- Type the range name, or press Name (F3) to display a list of range names and point to the range name you want.

Each method is covered in the following sections.

Typing Range Addresses

Using the typing method, you specify a range by typing the address of the upper left and lower right corners. Be sure to separate the two addresses with one or two periods. 1-2-3 always stores a range with two periods, but you have to type only one period.

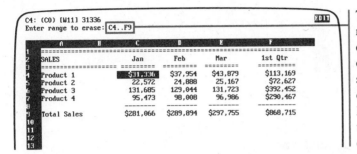

To specify the range C4..F9, you can type **C4..F9** or **C4.F9**. 1-2-3 stores the range containing C4, F4, C9, and F9 as the four corners of the range.

You can type cell addresses to specify a range in several situations: when the range does not have a range name, when the range you want to specify is far from the current cell, and when you know the addresses of the range. Experienced 1-2-3 users rarely type cell addresses; they highlight a range in POINT mode or use range names instead.

Highlighting a Range

The second method, that of highlighting the cells in the range in POINT mode, is used most often. You can point to and highlight a range in commands and functions just as you can point to a single cell in a formula.

Following the prompt to enter a range, 1-2-3 displays in the control panel the address of the cell pointer. This single cell, shown as a one-cell range, is *anchored*. The default range with most /**Range** commands is an anchored one-cell range. When the cell is anchored, you highlight a range as you move the cell pointer.

When a range is highlighted, the cells of the range appear in reverse video. The reverse video allows ranges to be specified easily, with little chance for error. As you move the cell pointer, the reverse-video rectangle expands until you finish specifying the range.

Suppose, for example, that you select the /**Range Erase** command. 1-2-3 displays the prompt Enter range to erase:.

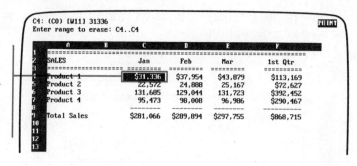

The location of the cell pointer marks the beginning of the range, which is anchored.

4

You can press Esc or Backspace to clear an incorrectly highlighted range. The highlight collapses to the anchored cell only, and the anchor is removed—allowing you to move the cell pointer to the correct location at the beginning of the range.

You can use the End key with the direction keys to quickly highlight large ranges. The End key can be used to move the cell pointer to the boundaries of contiguous data ranges.

After you press End-down arrow and End-right arrow, the range C4..F9 is highlighted and the address appears in the control panel.

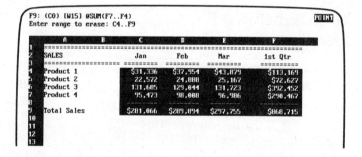

When you press Enter, 1-2-3 executes the command using the highlighted range, and the cell pointer returns to the originating cell.

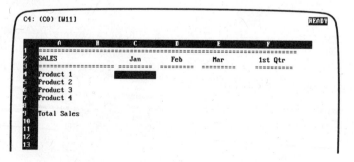

100

Pointing (or highlighting) is faster and easier than typing the range addresses. You also make fewer errors by pointing than by typing because you can see the range as you specify it.

Typing a Range Name

Another way to specify a range is to type an existing range name at the prompt. Range names, which should be descriptive, can contain as many as 15 characters and can be used in formulas and commands.

The use of range names is advantageous for several reasons. Range names are easier to remember than cell addresses, and it can be faster to use a name rather than point to a range in another part of the worksheet. Range names also make formulas easier to understand. For example, when you see the range name NOV_SALES_R1 (rather than the cell address) in a formula, you have a better chance of remembering that the entry represents "November Sales for Region 1."

The process of assigning names to ranges is described in the following section.

Naming Ranges

Range names can contain as many as 15 characters and should describe the range's contents. The advantage of naming ranges is that they are easier to understand than cell addresses, and thus they allow you to work more efficiently. For example, the phrase SALES_MODEL25 is a more understandable way of describing the sales for Model #25 than its cell coordinates. (Note that the underscore is part of the range name.)

Range names can be useful tools for processing commands and generating formulas. Whenever you must designate a range that has been named, you can respond with the range name instead of entering cell addresses or pointing to cell locations. 1-2-3's /Range Name command lets you tag a specific range of the worksheet with any name you choose. After naming the range, you can type the name and press Enter, instead of typing the cell addresses that indicate the range's boundaries.

4

The /Range Name command, for example, lets you give the name SALES1 to the cells in the range C4..E4.

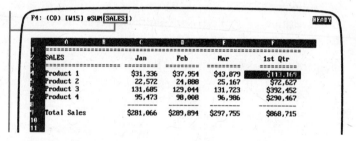

The simplest way to compute the sum of this range would be to use the function @SUM(SALES1). In a similar way, you can use the function @MAX(SALES1) to determine the maximum value in the range. In functions and formulas, you can always use range names in place of cell addresses.

When you name the range, you can use it in a formula or in response to a command prompt that asks for a range.

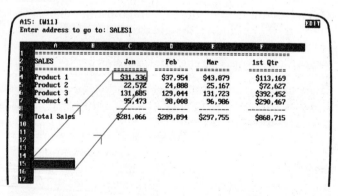

You can also use a range name to jump from one part of the worksheet to another.

Type **SALES1** after pressing GoTo (F5), and the cell pointer moves to cell C4—the first cell (upper left corner) of the range named SALES1.

Once you establish a range name, 1-2-3 automatically uses that name, in place of cell addresses, throughout the worksheet. For example, any

102

formulas in the worksheet that refer to a named range include that name within the formula (rather than the cell addresses of the range).

You can also designate the ranges of cells to be printed or to be extracted and saved to another worksheet. If you set up special names corresponding to different areas and you want to print, or extract and save these areas to another worksheet, you can enter a predefined range name rather than actual cell addresses. For example, if you want to print a portion of a worksheet, you can use the command /**Print Printer Range**. Then you can enter an existing range name, such as PART_1 or PART-5, in response to the prompt for entering a print range.

Ranges are named in one of two ways. You can either issue the /**Range Name Create** command to create a new range name, or you can select /**Range Name Labels** to use a label already on the worksheet as a name for a range. When you create a name, you assign a name to one or more cells. When you use the **Labels** option, you pick up a label from the worksheet and make it the range name of a one-cell range above, below, to the left, or to the right of the label. You can assign more than one label at a time, but each label applies only to one adjacent cell.

Naming a Group of Cells

/**Range Name Create** is ideal when you need to give a name to a multicell range. To use /**Range Name Create** to specify a name for any range, even one cell, follow these steps:

1. Call up the 1-2-3 menu by pressing /.

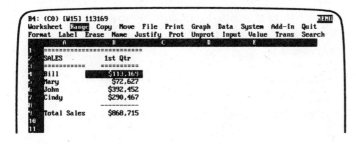

1-2-3 displays the main menu.

103

2. Select **Range** by pressing Ⓡ.

1-2-3 displays a menu of **Range** commands.

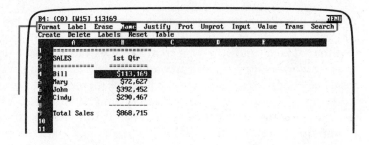

3. Select **Name** by pressing Ⓝ.

The first option on this menu lets you assign a range name.

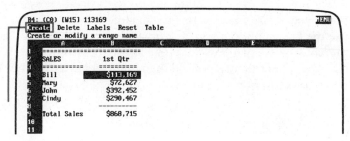

4. Select **Create** by pressing Ⓒ.

5. At the Enter name: prompt, type the range name you want, and then press ⏎Enter. Do not use a name that can be confused with a cell address.

   For this example, type **QTR1** and press ⏎Enter.

6. At the Enter range: prompt, select the range you want to name by typing the cell addresses, pointing to the range, or typing an existing range name; then press ⏎Enter.

For this example, select B4..B9 as the range to name, and press ⏎Enter.

104

Naming a Single Cell

If you need to assign names to a series of one-cell entries with adjacent labels, or to a series of columns or rows with headings, use the /Range Name Labels command. The /Range Name Labels command is similar to /Range Name Create except that the names for ranges are taken directly from adjacent label entries. These names must be text entries (labels); numeric entries and blank cells cannot be used to name adjacent cells with the /Range Name Labels command.

To use /Range Name Labels to assign names to single-cell entries, follow these steps:

1. Position the cell pointer on the first label you want to use as a range name. Remember that you can use this command only on adjacent cells.

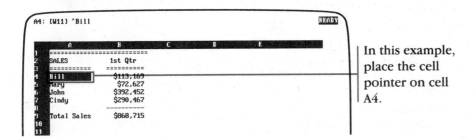

In this example, place the cell pointer on cell A4.

2. Call up the 1-2-3 menu by pressing ⌿.
3. Select **Range** by pressing Ⓡ.
4. Select **Name** by pressing Ⓝ.
5. Select **Labels** by pressing Ⓛ.
6. Select the appropriate option, depending on the location of the individual cells to be named.

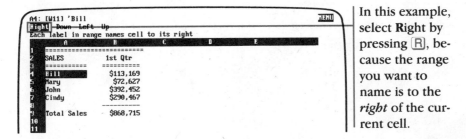

In this example, select **Right** by pressing Ⓡ, because the range you want to name is to the *right* of the current cell.

7. At the prompt Enter label range:, highlight the cells containing the labels you want to use as range names; then press ⏎Enter.

In this example, highlight the range A4..A7; then press ⏎Enter.

Deleting Range Names

You can delete range names individually or all at once. The **/Range Name Delete** command allows you to delete a single range name, and the **/Range Name Reset** command causes all range names to be deleted. The second command is powerful; use it with caution.

To delete a single range name, follow these steps:

1. Call up the 1-2-3 menu by pressing ⌿.
2. Select **Range** by pressing Ⓡ.
3. Select **Name** by pressing Ⓝ.
4. Select **Delete** by pressing Ⓓ.
5. When 1-2-3 displays a list of range names, either highlight or type the range name you want to delete, and then press ⏎Enter.

In this example, the range name QTR1 is highlighted. Press ⏎Enter to delete the highlighted range name.

```
A1: [W11] \=                                                    NAMES
Enter name to delete:
FEB           JAN          MAR              QTR1        SALES1
        A        B        C         D         E         F
1
2  SALES                 Jan       Feb       Mar      1st Qtr
3  ===================== ========= ========= ========= =========
4  Product 1             $31,336   $37,954   $43,879   $113,169
5  Product 2             22,572    24,888    25,167    $72,627
6  Product 3             131,685   129,044   131,723   $392,452
7  Product 4             95,473    98,008    96,986    $290,467
8                        --------  --------  --------  --------
9  Total Sales           $281,066  $289,894  $297,755  $868,715
10
11
```

To delete all the range names in a worksheet, follow these steps:

1. Call up the 1-2-3 menu by pressing ⌿.
2. Select **Range** by pressing Ⓡ.
3. Select **Name** by pressing Ⓝ.
4. Select **Reset** by pressing Ⓡ.

Note: Use this command with caution. 1-2-3 will delete all range names as soon as you enter the command, without giving you a chance to verify your selection.

If you delete a range name, 1-2-3 no longer uses that name and reverts to using the range's cell address. For example, @SUM(SALES1) returns to @SUM(C4..E4). The contents of the cells within the range, however, remain intact. To erase the contents of ranges, use the /**R**ange **E**rase command, which is explained in the next section.

Erasing Ranges

With the /**R**ange **E**rase command, you can erase sections of the worksheet. You can use this command on ranges as small as a single cell or as large as the entire worksheet.

To erase a range, follow these steps:

1. Call up the 1-2-3 menu by pressing [/].
2. Select **R**ange by pressing [R].
3. Select **E**rase by pressing [E].
4. When 1-2-3 prompts you to supply a range, highlight the range you want to erase.

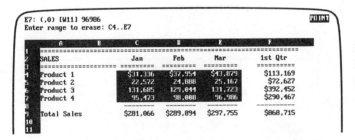

In this example, highlight the range C4..E7.

    Although you can denote a range to be erased by typing the cell addresses of the range or by entering a range name, pointing to the range allows you to see the boundaries of the range you want to erase before 1-2-3 erases the range. Pointing thereby helps to prevent accidental erasure of important data.

5. Press [↵Enter].

107

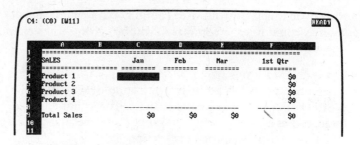

1-2-3 immediately erases the range.

4

After you erase a range, you cannot recover it unless the Undo feature of Release 2.2 is enabled (immediately press Alt-F4 to "undo" the /**R**ange Erase command). Otherwise, if the Undo feature is unavailable, you have to reenter all the data in order to restore the range.

Listing Range Names

Suppose that you select the /**R**ange Erase command and then you can't remember the name of the range you want to erase. You can use the Name (F3) function key to produce a list of the range names in the current worksheet.

To display a list of the range names in the current worksheet, follow these steps:

1. Make sure that the worksheet is in POINT mode, and then press F3 (Name).

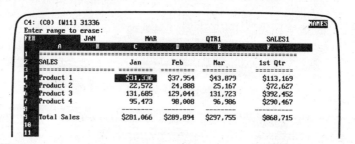

In this example, F3 was pressed in POINT mode.

108

2. If the range names extend beyond the right edge of the control panel, use the arrow keys to display the additional names.

3. To display a full-screen list of range names, press [F3] a second time.

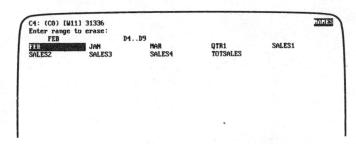

1-2-3 displays the entire list (or as much of it as the screen can hold).

4. Move the cell pointer to the name you want to use and press [↵Enter]. 1-2-3 then returns you to the worksheet.

You can use the space bar, the arrow keys, and the Home and End keys to select the name of the range you want to use. You can also press Tab or Shift-Tab to move right or left one screen (or line) at a time.

Note: If you want to print the displayed list of range names, hold down the Shift key and press the PrtSc key. If you have an enhanced keyboard, just press the Print Screen key. Using Shift-PrtSc or Print Screen while your printer is turned on will print whatever appears on the screen.

To move the cell pointer to a certain range, use the Name (F3) key with the GoTo (F5) key to select the range name. When you press GoTo (F5) and then Name (F3), 1-2-3 displays an alphabetical list of your worksheet's range names in the control panel. To designate the range you want to go to, highlight a name from the list by using the space bar, arrow keys, Home and End keys, and Tab or Shift-Tab. When you press Enter, the list disappears, and the cell pointer is positioned at the beginning of the selected range.

Creating a Table of Range Names

If you have created several range names in your worksheet, you can document them in a table in the worksheet. 1-2-3 provides the /**R**ange Name Table command to perform this task.

109

To create a range name table, follow these steps:

1. Move the cell pointer to the location where you want the upper left corner of the table to appear.

   For example, move the cell pointer to cell C12, a few rows below the data in the worksheet.

2. Call up the 1-2-3 menu by pressing ⌿

3. Select **Range** by pressing Ⓡ

4. Select **Name** by pressing Ⓝ

5. Select **Table** by pressing Ⓣ

1-2-3 asks for the location of the table.

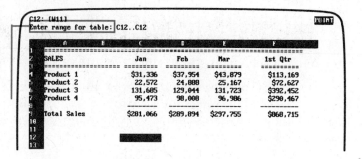

6. Press ↵Enter

1-2-3 produces a table with all the range names in a column and with the referenced ranges to the immediate right.

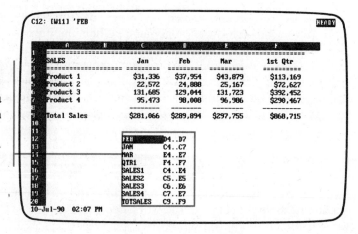

110

Note: Creating a table of range names is simple, but you must exercise care in your placement of the table. Make certain that the table will not write over an important part of the worksheet. The range name table includes range names and addresses at the time the table is created. This list is not automatically updated when you create, delete, or move ranges. For an up-to-date table, you must re-create the table with the /Range Name Table command.

Formatting Cell Contents

You now know that 1-2-3 expects you to enter data in a certain way. If, for example, you try to enter **1,234**, the program beeps, switches to EDIT mode, and waits for you to remove the comma. You get the same result if you try to enter **10:08 AM**—in this case, the colon and the AM are the offenders. If you try to enter **$9.23**, the program accepts the entry, but removes the **$**.

1-2-3 would have limited usefulness if you could not change the way data is displayed on the screen. You can, however, control not only the display of data with commas, time, and currency, but also with a variety of other formats. You determine formats with one of the options of the /Range Format or /Worksheet Global Format commands. The /Worksheet commands are discussed in the next chapter.

Table 4.2 provides examples of the formats that are available in 1-2-3. These formats primarily affect the way numeric values are displayed in a worksheet. Notice that Text format causes a formula to appear in a cell as a formula rather than a value, and Hidden format affects the display of every kind of entry.

Cell formats specified with /Range Format are automatically displayed within parentheses in the first line of the control panel. The worksheet's default cell format, however, does not appear in the control panel. You can use the /Worksheet Status command to view the current default worksheet format.

4

Table 4.2
1-2-3 Format Options

Format	Description	Examples	
		Data entered	Data displayed (when formatted with no decimal places)
Fixed	Controls the number of decimal places displayed.	15.56	16
Sci (Scientific)	Displays large or small numbers, using scientific (exponential) notation.	−21	−2E+01
Currency	Displays currency symbols and commas.	234567.75	$234,568
, (Comma)	Inserts commas to mark thousands and multiples of thousands.	1234567	1,234,567
General	Displays values with up to 10 decimal points or uses scientific notation; the default format in a new worksheet.	26.003	26.003
+/−	Creates horizontal bar graphs or time-duration graphs; useful for computers that cannot display graphs.	4.1 −3	++++ ──
Percent	Displays a decimal number as a whole number with a % sign.	0.25	25%
Date	Displays serial-date numbers. /Range Format Date Time sets time formats.	@DATE(89,8,1) @NOW	01-Aug-89 07:48 AM
Text	Displays formulas as as text, not the computed values that 1-2-3 normally displays.	+B5+B6 @SUM(C4..C8)	+B5+B6 @SUM(C4..C8)

112

Table 4.2—(continued)

Format	Description	Data entered	Data displayed (when formatted with no decimal places)
		Examples	
Hidden	Hides contents from the display and does not print them; hidden contents are still evaluated.	289	
Reset	Returns the format to the current /Worksheet Global format.		

Setting Range and Worksheet Global Formats

Although you will frequently use the /Range Format command to format individual ranges in your worksheet, you can also change the default format for the entire worksheet. The /Worksheet Global Format command controls the format of all cells in the worksheet, and the /Range Format command controls specific ranges.

Generally, you use the /Worksheet Global Format command when you are just starting to enter data in a worksheet. Be sure to choose a format that the majority of cells will use. After you set all the cells to that format, you can use the /Range Format command to override the Global format setting for specific cell ranges.

The /Range Format command takes precedence over the /Worksheet Global Format command. This means that whenever you change the global format, all the affected numbers and formulas will change automatically unless they were previously formatted with the /Range Format command. In turn, when you format a range, the format for that range will override any already set by /Worksheet Global Format.

Although the /Range Format command is generally used on cells that contain data, you may choose to select a format for cells that are now blank but will

113

eventually contain data. Any information put into these cells later will be displayed according to the format you chose with /**Range** Format.

To change the format of a cell or range of cells, follow these steps:

1. Call up the 1-2-3 menu by pressing ⃞/⃞.

2. Select **Range** by pressing ⃞R⃞.

3. Select **Format** by pressing ⃞F⃞.

4. Select the type of format you want to set by pressing the first character (or symbol) of the option.

In this example, select Currency by pressing ⃞C⃞.

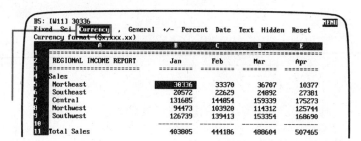

5. If you are prompted to enter the number of decimal places, type a new number and press ⃞↵Enter⃞, or press ⃞↵Enter⃞ to accept the default number.

In this example, type ⃞0⃞ for zero decimal places and press ⃞↵Enter⃞.

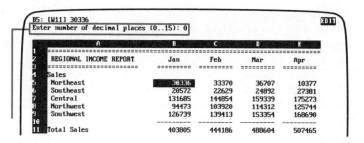

6. Highlight the range you want to format.

114

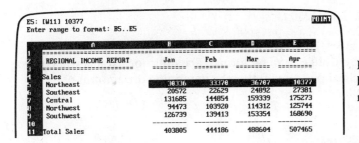

In this example, highlight the range B5. .E5.

7. Press ⏎Enter to complete the command.

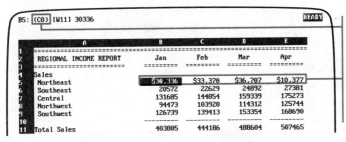

The cell pointer is located on the first cell of the formatted range; the control panel indicates the designated format.

General Format

General format is the default format for all new worksheets. When numbers are displayed in General format, commas that separate thousands and multiples of thousands are not displayed. Trailing zeros to the right of the decimal point are also suppressed. If numbers are too large or too small to be displayed normally, scientific notation is used.

Fixed Format

1-2-3's Fixed format is similar to General format in that it does not display commas or dollar signs. The difference is that Fixed format lets you choose the number of decimal places to be displayed (up to 15).

115

Scientific (Sci) Format

Scientific format causes 1-2-3 to display numbers in exponential form (scientific notation). Unlike **General** format, **Scientific** format lets you control the number of decimal places; you thereby determine the amount of precision that will be displayed.

Currency Format

Currency format displays numbers in cells with a dollar sign ($) before each entry, and with commas to separate thousands and multiples of thousands. Negative values appear in parentheses ( ). Although the dollar sign is the default, other symbols can be used as currency indicators. Currency format also gives you the option of controlling the number of decimal places.

Comma (,) Format

The , (Comma) format is similar to **Currency** format, except that no dollar signs appear when the numbers are displayed. Commas separate hundreds from thousands, hundreds of thousands from millions, and so on. Parentheses ( ) identify negative numbers. After the , (Comma) format has been chosen, you can specify the number of decimal places you want.

Only in **Currency** and , (Comma) formats are negative values displayed within parentheses. In other formats, negative values are preceded by a minus sign.

By using the /Worksheet Global Default Other International Negative command, you can choose either parentheses or minus signs to indicate negative values, for example, (12,300) or –12,300, ($12,300) or –$12,300. This command applies only to **Currency** and , (Comma) formats.

The +/– Format

The +/– format creates a horizontal bar "graph" of plus or minus signs within the cell, depending on the value of the number you enter in the cell. Asterisks are displayed if the size of the bar graph exceeds the column width. If zero is entered in a cell, a period (.) is displayed on the graph and left-justified in the cell.

116

You can use this format to mark a value in a long column of numbers. As you scan the column, the +'s and –'s stand out and are easy to locate.

Percent Format

The **Percent** format is used to display percentages; when you select this format, you also select the number of decimal places. The values displayed in the worksheet are the values you enter, multiplied by 100 and followed by a percent sign. When you use the **Percent** format, remember to enter numbers with the correct decimal point. To display 12%, for example, you must enter **.12**, not **12**.

Date and Time Formats

1-2-3 represents any given date internally as an integer equal to the number of days from December 31, 1899, to the given date. For example, January 1, 1900, is represented by the number 1; December 31, 2099 (the last date in 1-2-3's calendar), is represented by 73050. To enter a date into the worksheet, use one of the three date functions: @DATE, @DATEVALUE, or @NOW.

1-2-3 calculates a period of hours as a fraction expressed in decimals. The calculations are based on a 24-hour clock (military time). Use one of the time functions (@TIME, @TIMEVALUE, or @NOW) to enter a time into the worksheet. You can specify nine date and time formats with the /Range Format Date and /Worksheet Global Format Date commands.

Text Format

Text format displays formulas as they are entered in the command line, not the computed values that 1-2-3 normally displays. Numbers that are entered with this format are displayed as in General format.

The two most important applications of this format are setting up table ranges for /Data Table commands and debugging. Because you can display all the formulas on the screen with the Text format, finding and correcting problems is a relatively easy task. You may, however, have to widen the cell width to see your complete formulas when you use this technique.

4

Hidden Format

The /Range Format Hidden command suppresses the cell contents for any given range. If you want to hide all the cells in a column or range of columns, instead use the /Worksheet Column Hide command, discussed in the next chapter.

Although a cell with Hidden format appears as a blank cell on the screen, its contents are displayed in the control panel when you highlight the cell, and the contents are still available for calculations or formulas. All formulas and values can be calculated and readjusted when values are changed. The contents of hidden cells within a range to be printed will not appear on your printed copy.

Reset Format

The /Range Format Reset command resets the format of the indicated range to the global default setting. When the format of a range is reset, the format indicator for any cell within the range disappears from the control panel. The Reset option does not appear on the /Worksheet Global Format menu.

Controlling the International Formats

1-2-3 allows you to control the punctuation and currency sign displayed by , (Comma) and Currency formats, and to control the way the date and time are displayed when you use the special international Date and Time formats. To control these settings globally for the worksheet, use the /Worksheet Global Default Other International command. This command allows you to choose the format 1-2-3 uses for displaying the date and time, currency symbols, negative values (with a minus sign or parentheses), and punctuation.

Summary

This chapter showed you how to create worksheets by making use of many of the /Range commands. You learned how to use the /Range commands to create and name ranges, delete range names and erase ranges, move quickly to a named range, and display existing range names in the control panel or

118

on the full screen. You also learned how to format a cell or a range of cells to determine how values and formula results appear on-screen.

Specifically, you learned the following key information about 1-2-3:

■ A range in 1-2-3 is defined as a rectangular block of adjacent cells. Ranges are specified by the cell addresses of their upper left and lower right corners, separated by one or two periods. An example of a range is C4..G17.

■ The /Range Name Create and /Range Name Labels commands are used to name ranges of cells within the worksheet. The Create option is commonly used to name new multicell ranges. The Labels option is useful for naming a series of one-cell entries with adjacent labels, or a series of columns or rows with headings.

■ The /Range Name Delete and /Range Name Reset commands are used to delete one or all range names, respectively. The Reset option must be used with caution, because all range names are deleted immediately upon its selection—no verification of this command is provided.

■ The /Range Erase command is used to erase single-cell or multicell ranges. You can denote a range to be erased by typing the cell addresses of the range, entering a range name, or pointing to the range. Pointing is the preferred method because it allows you to see the boundaries of the range you want to erase before 1-2-3 erases the range.

■ To list all ranges that have been named in the current worksheet, press Name (F3) while in POINT mode (when 1-2-3 prompts for a range with the /Range commands).

■ You can use the Name (F3) key with the GoTo (F5) key to select the name of a range to which you want to move the cell pointer. If you press GoTo (F5) and then press Name (F3), 1-2-3 displays an alphabetical list of your worksheet's range names in the control panel.

■ The /Range Name Table command is used to list all range names and their corresponding locations within the worksheet. You should execute this command in a remote portion of the worksheet in order to avoid overwriting your worksheet data.

4

119

■ The /Range Format command is used to change the way data is displayed within the worksheet. Some available formatting options within 1-2-3 include Currency, Fixed, Percent, Text, Hidden, and , (Comma).

The next chapter discusses the various tasks that can be performed with the /Worksheet commands, such as setting column widths, creating windows, freezing titles, inserting and deleting rows and columns, and protecting the worksheet.

4

Building a Worksheet

5

After you enter and format some data, you can use commands from 1-2-3's Worksheet menu to control the way your data is displayed and organized. In the last chapter, you learned how to manipulate data in specified ranges. This chapter shows you how to use commands that affect the entire worksheet at once.

In this chapter you learn how to establish global settings for your worksheet, change the widths of the columns, insert and delete columns and rows, recalculate the formulas, protect certain areas of your worksheet, and perform other tasks. You will learn in the next chapter how to modify your worksheet by making more dramatic changes.

Key Terms in This Chapter

/Worksheet commands	Commands that affect the entire worksheet or certain defined areas of the worksheet. The /Worksheet command is found on the 1-2-3 main menu.
Global Settings sheet	A full-screen display that appears when you select /Worksheet Global commands; indicates the current global worksheet settings.
Windows	Two separate screens that appear, either horizontally or vertically, after you execute the /Worksheet Window command. Windows allow you to view different parts of the worksheet at the same time.
Automatic recalculation	A default 1-2-3 setting indicating that the worksheet is calculated each time a cell's content changes.

Using Worksheet Commands

1-2-3 offers a group of commands that perform some tasks that are similar to the /Range commands, but affect the entire worksheet or preset segments of the worksheet. With /Range commands, you define the range of cells that is affected by the commands. You do not have the same freedom with the /Worksheet commands; they affect the whole worksheet or entire columns or rows.

Worksheet is the first command option on the 1-2-3 main menu. When you select Worksheet, 1-2-3 offers the following group of commands:

Global Insert Delete Column Erase Titles Window Status Page Learn

Table 5.1 provides a brief description of the actions of each of these commands.

Table 5.1
The Worksheet Commands and Their Actions

Command	Action
Global	Sets formats that affect the entire worksheet.
Insert	Inserts blank columns and rows in the worksheet.
Delete	Deletes entire columns and rows from the worksheet.
Column	Sets column widths and the display of columns.
Erase	Clears the entire worksheet from memory.
Titles	Freezes or unfreezes the display of titles.
Window	Splits the screen into two windows or restores the original screen.
Status	Displays the current status of global worksheet settings.
Page	Creates a page break in a printed worksheet.
Learn	Records keystrokes used in macros (see Chapter 14).

Understanding the Global Settings Sheet

When you use the /Worksheet Global commands, a full-screen display of all the global settings of the worksheet is presented.

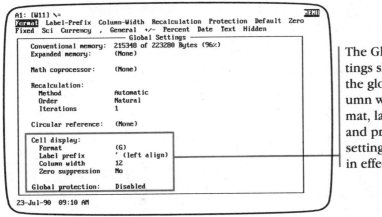

The Global Settings sheet shows the global column width, format, label prefix, and protection settings that are in effect.

If you would rather see the body of your worksheet instead of the Global Settings sheet, you can suppress this settings sheet (and other settings sheets) by pressing the Windows (F6) key. This key acts as a toggle; when you press it again, you see the settings sheet again.

Note: Settings sheets, such as the Global Settings sheet, are not displayed in 1-2-3 versions prior to Release 2.2. You can, however, view the global settings in all releases of 1-2-3 with the /Worksheet Status command described later in this chapter.

Erasing the Worksheet

The /Worksheet Erase command clears the current worksheet from the screen and memory, and replaces it with a blank worksheet. The effect is the same as if you quit 1-2-3 and restarted it from the operating system. You can use this command to create a new worksheet—with no data and the default worksheet settings. This command does not erase the worksheet file stored on disk.

Be sure that you understand the difference between the /Worksheet Erase command and the /Range Erase command. The /Range Erase command can remove the contents of every cell in the worksheet, except those that are protected. The /Range Erase command will not, however, alter any of the global settings, such as column widths, cell formats, and print settings. After you issue the /Worksheet Erase command, the worksheet is exactly as it was when you loaded 1-2-3.

To erase a worksheet from the screen and the computer's memory, follow these steps:

1. Call up the 1-2-3 menu by pressing ⌷.
2. Select **Worksheet** by pressing Ⓦ.

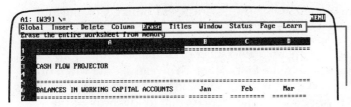

1-2-3 displays the menu of Worksheet commands.

3. Select **Erase** by pressing Ⓔ.

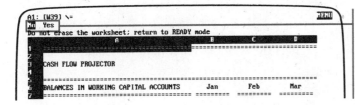

Because this is a potentially destructive command, 1-2-3 prompts you for verification.

4. To erase the worksheet, select **Yes** by pressing Ⓨ.

Or

If you change your mind or need to save your file before erasing the worksheet, press ↵Enter to select the default of **No**.

Note: Once a worksheet has been erased with /Worksheet Erase, you cannot recover it—unless the Undo feature (not available in versions prior to Release 2.2) is active, and Alt-F4 is pressed before you issue the next command. You should always save worksheets you want to keep before you clear the worksheet with this command.

Setting Column Widths

You can control the widths of columns in the worksheet in order to accommodate data entries that are too wide for the default column width. You can also reduce column widths to give the worksheet a better appearance when a column contains narrow entries. With 1-2-3, you have three options for setting column widths: you can set widths one column at a time (with the /Worksheet Column Set-Width command), you can set the widths of all the columns in the worksheet at once (with the /Worksheet Global Column-Width command), or you can set the widths of a number of contiguous columns at once (with the /Worksheet Column Column-Range Set-Width command).

Suppose that you are setting up a worksheet of cash flow projections and want to display long labels in the first column. You can set the width of the first column of your worksheet individually, and then set the other columns to any smaller width you choose. The sections that follow provide the necessary steps to carry out the commands for changing column widths.

Setting the Width of a Single Column

To change the width of a single column, use the /Worksheet Column Set-Width command. To change the width of column A, for example, follow these steps:

1. Position the cell pointer within the column whose width you want to change.

   For example, position the cell pointer in any row of column A.

2. Call up the 1-2-3 menu by pressing ⌐/⌐.

3. Select Worksheet by pressing ⌐W⌐.

4. Select Column by pressing ⌐C⌐.

The options for changing widths appear.

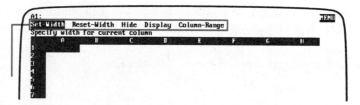

5. Select Set-Width by pressing ⌐S⌐.

6. When the prompt Enter column width: appears, either type a width between 1 and 240, or press ⌐←⌐ or ⌐→⌐ until the desired column width is displayed.

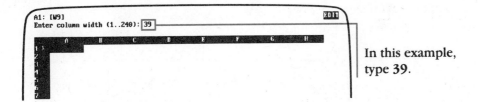

In this example, type **39**.

The advantage of the left- and right-arrow keys is that the column width expands and contracts each time you press a key. To get a good idea of what the width requirements are, experiment when you enter the command.

7. Press <kbd>←Enter</kbd> to complete the command.

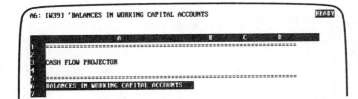

After changing column widths, you can continue entering data into your worksheet.

Note: The /Worksheet Column Reset-Width command returns the width of a single column to the default width of nine characters. The **Hide** and **Display** options allow you to remove a column temporarily from your screen display and redisplay it when needed (see this chapter's "Hiding Columns" section).

Setting the Widths of All Columns at Once

You can set all the column widths in the worksheet at one time with the command /Worksheet Global Column-Width. This command is normally used in the early stages of worksheet creation. Many of the /Worksheet Global commands have corresponding /Range commands that affect only certain areas of the worksheet; in this case, the corresponding commands that affect parts of the worksheet are the /Worksheet Column Set-Width and /Worksheet Column Column-Range Set-Width commands.

To change the widths of all columns in the worksheet at one time, follow these steps:

1. Call up the 1-2-3 menu by pressing ⬚.

2. Select **Worksheet** by pressing 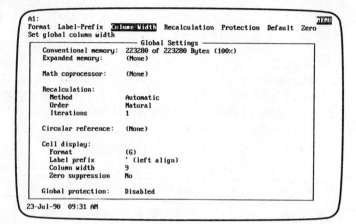W.

3. Select **Global** by pressing G.

1-2-3 displays a menu and the Global Settings sheet.

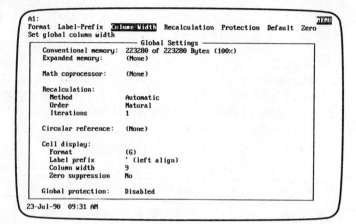

4. Select **Column-Width** by pressing C.

5. When the prompt `Enter global column width:` appears, either type a width between 1 and 240, or press ← or → until the desired column width is displayed.

In this example, type **12**.

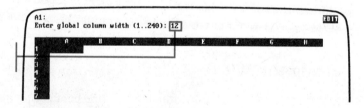

6. Press ⏎Enter to complete the command. Each column in the worksheet now has a width of 12 characters instead of the original default, 9.

In this example, fewer columns are now displayed on-screen.

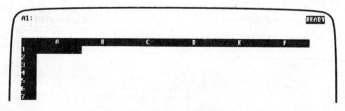

128

Note: The /Worksheet Global Column-Width command will not alter the width of columns already set with either the /Worksheet Column Set-Width or /Worksheet Column Column-Range commands.

Setting the Width of Contiguous Columns

If you want to set a group of adjacent columns to the same width, use the /Worksheet Column Column-Range Set-Width command. This command, which is not available in versions of 1-2-3 prior to Release 2.2, keeps you from having to set each adjacent column individually.

To change the widths of contiguous columns, follow these steps:

1. Position the cell pointer on the first or last column in the range of columns whose widths you want to change.
2. Call up the 1-2-3 menu by pressing /.
3. Select Worksheet by pressing W.
4. Select Column by pressing C.
5. From the options for changing widths, select Column-Range by pressing C.
6. Select Set-Width by pressing S.
7. When the prompt `Enter range for column width change:` appears, highlight cells in the range of columns you want to change. Then press ⏎Enter.

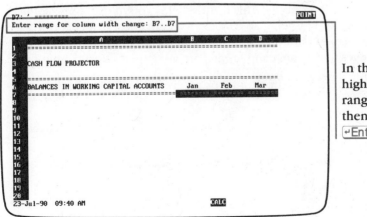

In this example, highlight the range B7..D7; then press ⏎Enter

8. When the prompt `Select a width for range of columns:` appears, either type a width between 1 and 240, or press ← or → until the desired column width is displayed. Then press ⏎Enter .

In this example, type **11**; then press ⏎Enter .

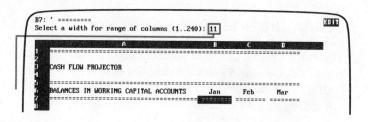

Note: The **Reset-Width** option, on the same menu as **Set-Width**, does not prompt you for a specific width, but returns the widths of all selected columns to the default column-width setting.

To verify what the global column-width setting is, use the command /**Worksheet Status**. Refer to the section "Checking the Status of Global Settings" later in this chapter.

Splitting the Screen

Sometimes the size of a 1-2-3 worksheet can be unwieldy. For example, if you want to compare data in column A with data in column N, you need to be able to "fold" the worksheet so that you can see both parts at the same time. To do this, you can split the 1-2-3 screen display into two windows, either horizontally or vertically. This feature helps you to overcome some of the inconvenience of not being able to see the entire worksheet at one time. By splitting the screen with the /**Worksheet Window** command, you can make the changes in one area and immediately see their effects in the other.

To split the screen into two horizontal or two vertical windows, follow these steps:

1. Position the cell pointer at the location where you want to split the screen.

130

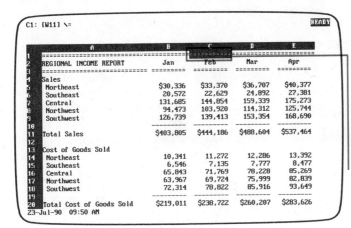

```
C1: [W11] \=                                                    READY
              A              B         C         D         E
1 ========================== ========= ========= ========= =========
2 REGIONAL INCOME REPORT     Jan       Feb       Mar       Apr
3 ========================== ========= ========= ========= =========
4 Sales
5   Northeast                $30,336   $33,370   $36,707   $40,377
6   Southeast                 20,572    22,629    24,892    27,381
7   Central                  131,685   144,854   159,339   175,273
8   Northwest                 94,473   103,920   114,312   125,744
9   Southwest                126,739   139,413   153,354   168,690
10                           --------  --------  --------  --------
11 Total Sales               $403,805  $444,186  $488,604  $537,464
12
13 Cost of Goods Sold
14   Northeast                10,341    11,272    12,286    13,392
15   Southeast                 6,546     7,135     7,777     8,477
16   Central                  65,843    71,769    78,228    85,269
17   Northwest                63,967    69,724    75,999    82,839
18   Southwest                72,314    78,822    85,916    93,649
19                           --------  --------  --------  --------
20 Total Cost of Goods Sold  $219,011  $238,722  $260,207  $283,626
23-Jul-90  09:50 AM
```

In this example, position the cell pointer in any row of column C to split the screen vertically.

2. Call up the 1-2-3 menu by pressing ⃞/.

3. Select Worksheet by pressing Ⓦ.

4. Select Window by pressing Ⓦ.

5. Select either Horizontal by pressing Ⓗ, or Vertical by pressing Ⓥ.

```
C1: [W11] \=                                                    MENU
Horizontal Vertical Sync Unsync Clear
Split the screen vertically at the current column
              A              B         C         D         E
1 ========================== ========= ========= ========= =========
2 REGIONAL INCOME REPORT     Jan       Feb       Mar       Apr
3 ========================== ========= ========= ========= =========
4 Sales
5   Northeast                $30,336   $33,370   $36,707   $40,377
6   Southeast                 20,572    22,629    24,892    27,381
7   Central                  131,685   144,854   159,339   175,273
8   Northwest                 94,473   103,920   114,312   125,744
9   Southwest                126,739   139,413   153,354   168,690
10                           --------  --------  --------  --------
11 Total Sales               $403,805  $444,186  $488,604  $537,464
12
13 Cost of Goods Sold
14   Northeast                10,341    11,272    12,286    13,392
15   Southeast                 6,546     7,135     7,777     8,477
16   Central                  65,843    71,769    78,228    85,269
17   Northwest                63,967    69,724    75,999    82,839
18   Southwest                72,314    78,822    85,916    93,649
19                           --------  --------  --------  --------
20 Total Cost of Goods Sold  $219,011  $238,722  $260,207  $283,626
23-Jul-90  09:55 AM
```

In this example, to compare two columns that cannot be seen together on the 1-2-3 screen, select Vertical by pressing Ⓥ.

6. Press ⏎Enter to complete the command and split the screen.

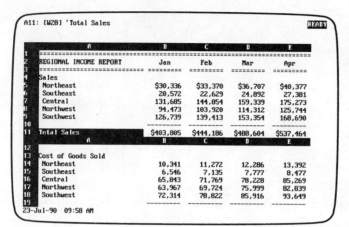

This is an example of a screen split horizontally into two windows with the /Worksheet Window Horizontal command.

5

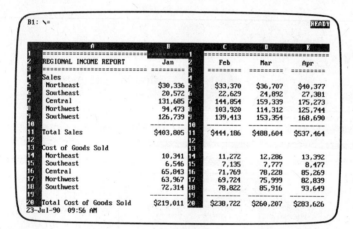

In this example, the screen is split vertically into two windows.

The Horizontal and Vertical options of the /Worksheet Window menu split the screen in the manner indicated by their names. The screen will split at the point at which the cell pointer is positioned when you select the command Horizontal or Vertical. In other words, you don't have to split the screen exactly in half. Remember that the dividing line will require specifying either one row or one column, depending on whether you split the screen horizontally or vertically.

After you use the Horizontal option to split the screen, the cell pointer appears in the top window. When you create a vertical division, the cell pointer appears in the left window. To jump the division between the windows, use the Window (F6) function key.

132

After the screen is split, you can change the screen display so that the windows scroll independently rather than together (the default mode). To scroll the windows independently, select /Worksheet Window Unsync. This command can be reversed by selecting the command /Worksheet Window Sync.

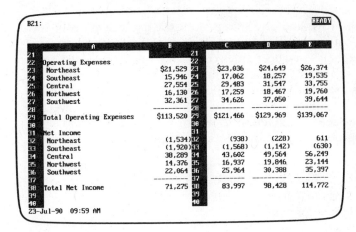

In Sync (synchronized) screen mode, when you scroll one window, the other window automatically scrolls too.

Horizontally split screens keep the same columns in view, and vertically split screens keep the same rows in view.

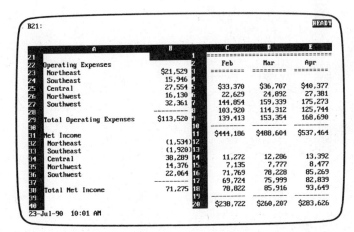

In Unsync (unsynchronized) screen mode, windows are controlled independently of each other in all directions. You can even display the same cells in the two different windows.

To return to the single-window screen, select /Worksheet Window Clear. When you use the Clear option, the single window takes on the settings of the top or left window, depending on how the screen was split.

Freezing Titles on the Screen

If you need to freeze rows and/or columns along the top and left edges of the worksheet so that they remain in view as you scroll to different parts of the worksheet, use the /Worksheet Titles command. The /Worksheet Titles command is similar to the /Worksheet Window command. With both commands, you can see one area of a worksheet while you work on another area. The unique function of the /Worksheet Titles command, however, is that it freezes all the cells to the left or above (or both to the left and above) of the cell pointer's position so that those cells cannot move off the screen.

Because the default screen, without any special column widths, shows 20 rows by 8 columns, you have to shift the screen if your data is outside of this screen area. In fact, you may have to scroll the screen several times in order to enter or view all the information.

Suppose that you want to keep on-screen the headings in rows 1–14, and the payment numbers and dates in columns A and B.

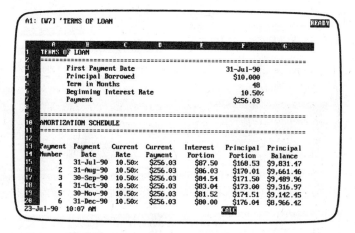

To freeze worksheet titles on the screen, follow these steps:

1. Position the cell pointer one cell below and to the right of the rows and/or columns you want to freeze.

In this example, position the cell pointer in cell C15 to freeze columns A and B, and rows 1–14.

2. Call up the 1-2-3 menu by pressing ⌷/⌷.

3. Select **W**orksheet by pressing ⌷W⌷.

4. Select **T**itles by pressing ⌷T⌷.

5. Select **B**oth, **H**orizontal, or **V**ertical by pressing ⌷B⌷, ⌷H⌷, or ⌷V⌷, respectively. The **B**oth option allows you to freeze rows and columns above and to the left of the cell pointer.

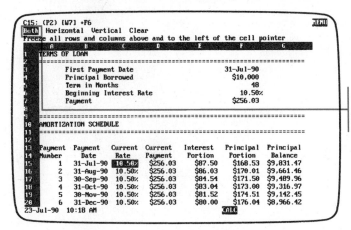

In this example, select **B**oth by pressing ⌷B⌷.

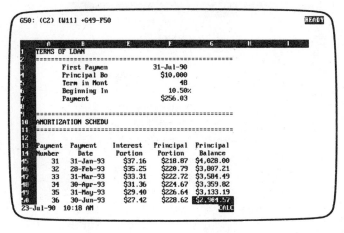

Now, no matter where you move the cell pointer, rows 1–14 and columns A and B are always displayed.

5

135

When you freeze columns and/or rows, you cannot move the cell pointer into the frozen area while 1-2-3 is in READY mode. If you try to move the cell pointer into the frozen area, 1-2-3 beeps. Similarly, the Home key will move the cell pointer only to the upper left cell in the unfrozen area. Normally, the Home key moves the cell pointer to cell A1. You can avoid this restriction, however, by using the GoTo (F5) key to move the cell pointer to the titles area.

Here /Worksheet Titles Horizontal was used to keep the row(s) above the cell pointer frozen on-screen. Rows 9–14 remain at the top of the screen when you scroll up and down.

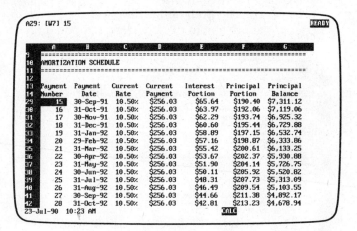

Here, /Worksheet Titles Vertical was used to keep the column(s) to the left of the cell pointer frozen on-screen. Columns A and B remain on the left side of the screen when you scroll left and right.

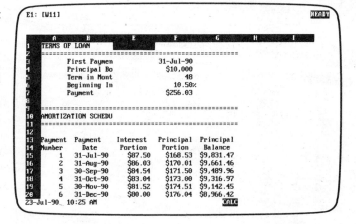

To unlock the frozen worksheet titles, use the /Worksheet Titles Clear command. Now you can move the cell pointer freely throughout the worksheet.

Inserting Columns and Rows

Suppose that you are finished creating a worksheet, but you want to enhance its general appearance. You can improve it by inserting blank columns and rows in strategic places to highlight headings and other important items. Whether you want to insert additional data or to add blank rows or columns to separate sections of your worksheet, you can use the /Worksheet Insert command to insert columns or rows. You can insert multiple adjacent columns and rows each time you invoke this command.

To insert a new column or row into the worksheet, follow these steps:

1. Position the cell pointer at the location of the new column or row to be inserted.

   For example, position the cell pointer in column D to add a new column of data.

2. Call up the 1-2-3 menu by pressing [/].

3. Select **Worksheet** by pressing [W].

4. Select **Insert** by pressing [I].

5. Select **Column** by pressing [C], or **Row** by pressing [R].

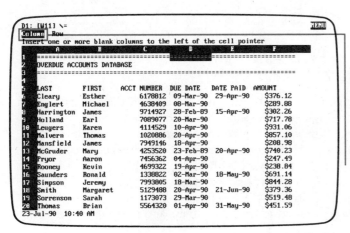

In this example, select **Column** by pressing [C] to insert a new column in the worksheet.

6. In response to the prompt, designate the range where you want the new column(s) or row(s) to be inserted. If you want to insert more than one column or row, press [→] to highlight multiple columns or [↓] to highlight multiple rows to insert.

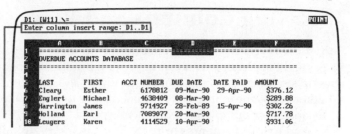

In this example, be sure that the cell pointer is positioned in column D to insert a single column.

7. Press ↵Enter to complete the command. Existing worksheet data is moved to the right of the cell pointer if you are inserting a column, or below the cell pointer if you are inserting a row.

5

In this example, when you press ↵Enter, a blank column is displayed, ready for you to enter new data to the database.

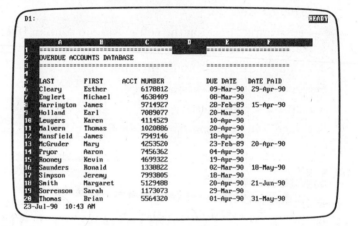

If you issue the /Worksheet Insert Column command and specify an insert range of A10..A10, a single blank column is inserted at column A. 1-2-3 automatically shifts all the values over one column and modifies all the cell formulas for the change. If you then repeat the command, but specify the Row option and a range of A10..A10, 1-2-3 inserts one blank row at row 10. The values that are contained in rows 10 and below are automatically shifted down one row, and any formulas are modified. 1-2-3 does not have the capability of inserting or deleting partial columns and rows.

Deleting Columns and Rows

You can delete single or multiple columns or rows with the /Worksheet Delete command. After you select this command, you then choose Column or Row from the menu that appears on the screen. If you choose Row, 1-2-3 asks you to specify a range of rows to be deleted; the range you specify needs to include only one cell from each row to be deleted.

To delete existing columns or rows from the worksheet, follow these steps:

1. Position the cell pointer at the location of the first row or column to be deleted.

   For example, position the cell pointer in row 6.

2. Call up the 1-2-3 menu by pressing ⌐/⌐.

3. Select **W**orksheet by pressing ⌐W⌐.

4. Select **D**elete by pressing ⌐D⌐.

5. Select **C**olumn by pressing ⌐C⌐ or **R**ow by pressing ⌐R⌐.

   For example, select **R**ow by pressing ⌐R⌐ to delete rows from the worksheet.

6. In response to the prompt, designate the range where you want the column(s) or row(s) deleted.

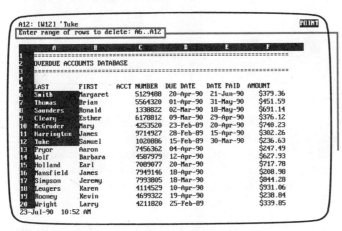

In this example, highlight rows 6 through 12 (in any column).

7. Press ⌐⏎Enter⌐ to complete the command.

5

In this example, when you press ⏎Enter, the original data in rows 6 through 12 is removed from the worksheet, and the data that originally appeared below these rows moves up.

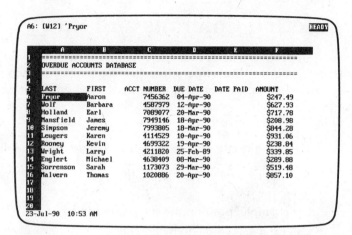

Remember that /Worksheet Delete is different from /Range Erase. /Range Erase simply erases data from a cell or range of cells—not entire columns or rows of data.

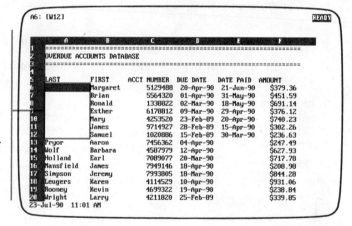

If you plan to use the command /Worksheet Delete to delete a column or row containing values, keep in mind that all formulas in the worksheet that refer to these cells will result in ERR. Also remember that when you use the /Worksheet Delete command, the columns or rows you delete may be gone forever. This command deletes entire columns or rows, not just the range of cells you specify in those columns or rows.

If the Undo feature (not available in versions prior to Release 2.2) is enabled, you can undo the deletion by pressing Undo (Alt-F4) before executing another command. Otherwise, the only remedies are to re-create the missing data or retrieve the worksheet file again. This latter approach works only if you have saved a copy of your worksheet that contains the missing data.

Hiding Columns

With the /Worksheet Column Hide command, you can suppress the display of any single column or adjacent columns in the worksheet. One important use of this command is to suppress the display of unwanted columns when you are printing reports. When you hide intervening columns, a report can display data from two or more separated columns on a single page. Other uses of the /Worksheet Column Hide command include suppressing the display of sensitive information (such as financial statements), hiding the display of columns of cells that have a numeric value of zero, and fitting noncontiguous columns on-screen.

To hide one or more worksheet columns, follow these steps:

1. Call up the 1-2-3 menu by pressing ⌷/⌷.
2. Select **Worksheet** by pressing ⌷W⌷.
3. Select **Column** by pressing ⌷C⌷.
4. Select **Hide** by pressing ⌷H⌷.
5. Specify the columns to hide by either typing or highlighting the range.

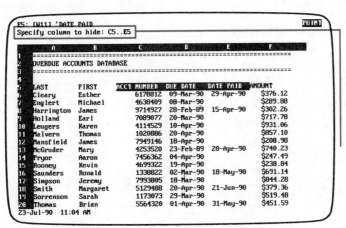

In this example, columns C through E are specified.

6. Press ⏎Enter, and the specified columns are hidden from view.

In this example, columns C through E are now hidden.

```
F5: [W11] 'AMOUNT                                                    READY
          A            B            F      G      H      I      J
1    ====================================================
2    OVERDUE ACCOUNTS DATABASE
3    ====================================================
4
5    LAST         FIRST        AMOUNT
6    Cleary       Esther       $376.12
7    Englert      Michael      $289.88
8    Harrington   James        $302.26
9    Holland      Earl         $717.78
10   Leugers      Karen        $931.06
11   Malvern      Thomas       $857.10
12   Mansfield    James        $208.98
13   McGruder     Mary         $740.23
14   Pryor        Aaron        $247.49
15   Rooney       Kevin        $238.84
16   Saunders     Ronald       $691.14
17   Simpson      Jeremy       $844.28
18   Smith        Margaret     $379.36
19   Sorrenson    Sarah        $519.48
20   Thomas       Brian        $451.59
     23-Jul-90  11:04 AM
```

Although the hidden columns do not appear on the display, numbers and formulas in hidden columns are still present, and cell references to cells in hidden columns continue to work properly. You can tell which columns are missing only by noting the break in column letters at the top of the display. The hidden columns are temporarily redisplayed, however, when you use certain commands, such as /Copy or /Move; the hidden columns are marked with an asterisk (such as C*) during this temporary display.

This screen shows how hidden columns are temporarily displayed when using /Copy.

```
F5: [W11] 'AMOUNT                                                    POINT
Enter range to copy FROM: F5..F5
          A          B          C*          D*          E*          F
1    ====================================================
2    OVERDUE ACCOUNTS DATABASE
3    ====================================================
4
5    LAST       FIRST      ACCT NUMBER  DUE DATE    DATE PAID   AMOUNT
6    Cleary     Esther     6178812      09-Mar-90   29-Apr-90   $376.12
7    Englert    Michael    4638409      08-Mar-90               $289.88
8    Harrington James      9714927      28-Feb-89   15-Apr-90   $302.26
9    Holland    Earl       7089077      20-Mar-90               $717.78
10   Leugers    Karen      4114529      10-Apr-90               $931.06
11   Malvern    Thomas     1020886      20-Apr-90               $857.10
12   Mansfield  James      7949146      18-Apr-90               $208.98
13   McGruder   Mary       4253520      23-Feb-89   20-Apr-90   $740.23
14   Pryor      Aaron      7456362      04-Apr-90               $247.49
15   Rooney     Kevin      4699322      19-Apr-90               $238.84
16   Saunders   Ronald     1338822      02-Mar-90   18-May-90   $691.14
17   Simpson    Jeremy     7993805      18-Mar-90               $844.28
18   Smith      Margaret   5129488      20-Apr-90   21-Jun-90   $379.36
19   Sorrenson  Sarah      1173073      29-Mar-90               $519.48
20   Thomas     Brian      5564320      01-Apr-90   31-May-90   $451.59
     23-Jul-90  11:04 AM
```

142

When the screen display is split, the /Worksheet Column Hide command affects only the current screen.

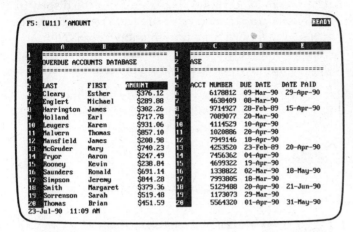

Here, even though columns C through E are hidden in the first window, they are visible in the adjacent window.

5

To redisplay hidden columns, use the /Worksheet Column Display command by following these steps:

1. Call up the 1-2-3 menu by pressing /.

2. Select Worksheet by pressing W.

3. Select Column by pressing C.

4. Select Display by pressing D.

5. In response to the prompt `Specify hidden columns to redisplay:`, enter the range of columns to redisplay.

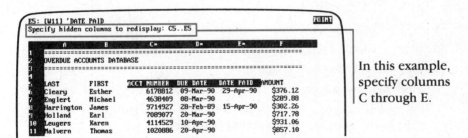

In this example, specify columns C through E.

6. Press ↵Enter, and the hidden columns are redisplayed.

143

Suppressing the Display of Zeros

The /Worksheet Global Zero command allows you to suppress the display in the worksheet of all cells that have a numeric value of zero. For example, this technique is useful for preparing reports for a presentation where cells showing $0.00 would look odd. As an alternative, you may choose to have a label (such as *No Charge*), instead of a blank, displayed in zero-value cells.

You can enter formulas and values for all the items in the report, including the zero items, and then display the results with all the zeros removed or replaced by a label. The actual formula or value is displayed in the control panel when the cell pointer highlights a cell that contains a zero, or a formula that evaluates to zero.

Suppose that you have a worksheet that lists product codes and their associated costs. In some cases, the costs are $0.00, perhaps entered in error.

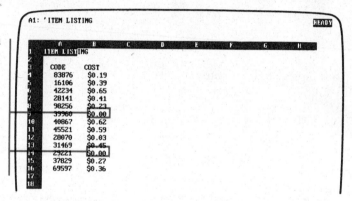

To suppress the display of zeros or to substitute a label for zero entries, follow these steps:

1. Call up the 1-2-3 menu by pressing ⌸
2. Select Worksheet by pressing Ⓦ
3. Select Global by pressing Ⓖ
4. Select Zero by pressing Ⓩ
5. If you want to suppress the display of zeros by substituting a blank, select No by pressing Ⓝ to complete this procedure.

   Or

   If you want to suppress the display of zeros by substituting a label, select Label by pressing Ⓛ and continue with the next step.

144

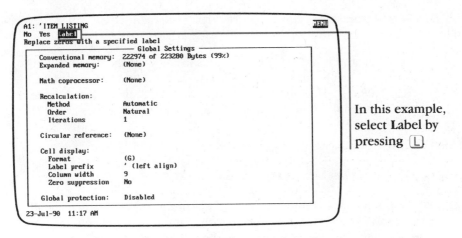

In this example, select **Label** by pressing L

6. When 1-2-3 prompts you to enter the text for the label to appear in every zero-value cell, type the text and press ⏎Enter.

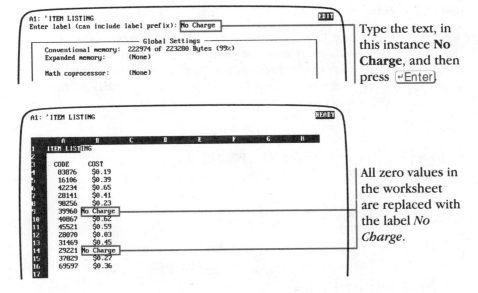

Type the text, in this instance **No Charge**, and then press ⏎Enter.

All zero values in the worksheet are replaced with the label *No Charge*.

If you want the zeros visible again, use the command /Worksheet Global **Zero Yes**. When you use the /File **Save** command to save your worksheet, the zero suppression or label substitution features of this command are not

145

saved with the worksheet. These features are not present when you retrieve a file.

Note: This command is not selective; all cells in the worksheet with a zero value are affected by the substitution. A cell with the value .004 would be displayed as 0.00 if a 2-decimal place format were used. Because the value is not truly zero, it would therefore not be changed by the /Worksheet Global Zero command.

Recalculating the Worksheet

One of the primary functions of a spreadsheet program is to recalculate all the cells in a worksheet when a value or formula in one of the cells changes. 1-2-3 provides two basic recalculation methods: *automatic recalculation* and *manual recalculation*. Using automatic recalculation, the default, 1-2-3 recalculates the worksheet whenever any cell in the worksheet changes. In manual recalculation, the worksheet is recalculated only when the user requests it, either from the keyboard with the Calc (F9) key or from a macro.

1-2-3 also provides three orders of recalculation: the *natural order* and two linear orders, either *columnwise* or *rowwise*. Natural order is the default, but you can choose any of the three orders. You also can choose the number of times the worksheet is recalculated. You select the recalculation options by using the /Worksheet Global Recalculation command.

To select a recalculation setting, follow these steps:

1. Call up the 1-2-3 menu by pressing /.
2. Select **W**orksheet by pressing W.
3. Select **G**lobal by pressing G.
4. Select **R**ecalculation by pressing R.

From the resulting menu, you can choose from six recalculation options, described in table 5.2.

```
A1: [W7] 'TERMS OF LOAN                                        MENU
Format Label-Prefix Column-Width Recalculation Protection Default Zero
Natural Columnwise Rowwise Automatic Manual Iteration
                      Global Settings
     Conventional memory:  202784 of 223280 Bytes (90%)
     Expanded memory:      (None)

     Math coprocessor:     (None)

     Recalculation:
        Method             Automatic
        Order              Natural
        Iterations         1
```

146

Table 5.2
Recalculation Options

Option	Description
Order of Recalculation	
Natural	1-2-3 does not recalculate any cell until the cells that it depends on have been recalculated. This is the default setting.
Columnwise	Recalculation begins at cell A1 and continues down column A, then goes to cell B1 and down column B, and so forth.
Rowwise	Recalculation begins at cell A1 and proceeds across row 1, then goes across row 2, and so forth.
Method of Recalculation	
Automatic	The worksheet is recalculated whenever a cell changes. This is the default setting.
Manual	The worksheet is recalculated only when you press Calc (F9).
Number of Recalculations	
Iteration	The worksheet is recalculated a specified number of times when you change cell contents in automatic recalculation, or press Calc (F9) in manual recalculation. The default is one iteration per recalculation.

As a beginning 1-2-3 user, you may not need to change the recalculation settings at all. 1-2-3's default settings are Automatic recalculation (meaning that the program recalculates cells each time a cell's content changes), and Natural order (meaning that 1-2-3 does not recalculate any given cell until after the cells that it depends on have been recalculated). To save processing time, you can switch to Manual recalculation so that 1-2-3 recalculates the worksheet only when you press Calc (F9).

For more specialized applications, the Columnwise or Rowwise recalculation method can be used. Be extremely careful when you use these orders of recalculation, however; if they are used improperly, they can produce erroneous values on the worksheet.

For more information on automatic, manual, and iterative recalculation, and natural, columnwise, and rowwise orders of recalculation, refer to Que's *Using 1-2-3 Release 2.2*, Special Edition. You'll find in-depth discussions and step-by-step examples on using each of these recalculation options.

Protecting the Worksheet

1-2-3 has special features that protect areas of a worksheet from possible destruction. Using a series of commands, you can set up ranges of cells that cannot be changed without special effort. In fact, columns and rows that contain protected cells cannot be deleted from the worksheet. These commands are particularly beneficial when you are setting up worksheets in which data will be entered by people who are not familiar with 1-2-3.

Protecting the Entire Worksheet

When you first create a worksheet, the global protection feature is not active, enabling you to make changes and add data.

The /Worksheet Global Protection Enable command turns on the worksheet's protection system.

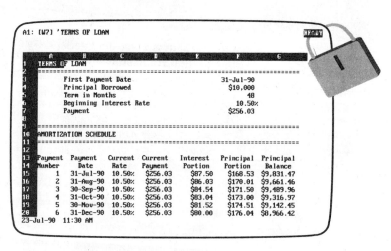

This protection system may be thought of as a series of barriers set up around all the cells in the worksheet. The barriers go down when the worksheet is first loaded, and all the cells in the worksheet can be modified. This arrangement is appropriate because you want to have access to everything in the worksheet when you first begin entering data.

148

After you finish making all your entries in the worksheet, you may want to make sure that certain areas are not modified, or you may want to set up areas with forms for data input and not allow the cell pointer to move anywhere else. To accomplish either of these tasks, you must first enable the protection feature with the /Worksheet Global Protection Enable command. After this command is issued, all the cells in the worksheet are protected. In other words, this command restores all the barriers in the worksheet.

To turn on protection for the whole worksheet, follow these steps:

1. Call up the 1-2-3 menu by pressing /
2. Select **W**orksheet by pressing W
3. Select **G**lobal by pressing G
4. Select **P**rotection by pressing P
5. Select **E**nable by pressing E

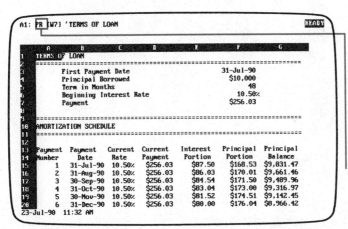

All cells in the worksheet are protected as indicated by the PR in the first line of the control panel.

Turning Off Protection in a Range

You can selectively unprotect certain ranges with the /Range Unprot command. In effect, you "tear down the barriers" that surround these individual cells or ranges of cells. You can reprotect these cells at any time by issuing the /Range Prot command.

To turn off protection for a cell or range of cells in your worksheet, follow these steps:

1. Call up the 1-2-3 menu by pressing ⌧.
2. Select **R**ange by pressing ⓇR.
3. Select **U**nprot by pressing ⓊU.
4. Enter the range of cells where you want to add or change data by typing the cell address (or range name), or by highlighting the desired range.

5

In this example, highlight the range F3..F7.

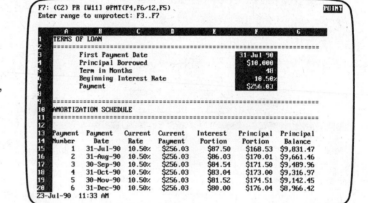

5. Press ⏎Enter to complete the command.

Unprotected cells are identified by a Ⓤ in the control panel.

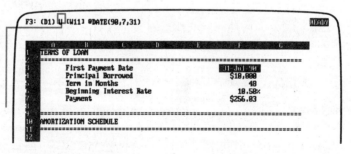

Suppose that you create a worksheet that includes a number of long and important formulas. You may want to protect these formulas against accidental deletion by using 1-2-3's protection capability. But what if you

150

need to make a change in several of these formulas? You can move around the worksheet, unprotecting cells, changing the formulas, and then protecting the cells again. Or you can use the /**Worksheet Global Protection Disable** command to lower the barriers around all the cells. After making the necessary changes, you can restore protection to all the cells by using the /**Worksheet Global Protection Enable** command again.

Restricting Movement to a Particular Range

For even more protection, you can limit the movement of the cell pointer by using the /**Range Input** command. You must use this command, which allows movement to only cells unprotected with the /**Range Unprot** command, to set up special data input areas.

For example, suppose that you create a simple worksheet in which every cell is protected except for those in the range F3..F7, whose cells were unprotected with the /**Range Unprot** command.

To restrict input to unprotected cells in the worksheet, follow these steps:

1. Call up the 1-2-3 menu by pressing ⁄ .
2. Select **Range** by pressing R .
3. Select **Input** by pressing I .
4. Highlight the range of cells that includes the unprotected cells in the data input area; then press ↵Enter .

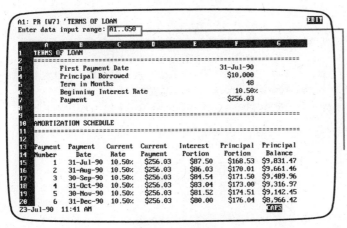

In this example, specify the range A1..G50; then press ↵Enter .

5

Note: You should include the entire data input area (including protected areas) when specifying a range for the /Range Input command. This range should include all cells that are unprotected with /Range Unprot.

5. After the range is entered, the first cell of the data input area moves to the upper left corner of the screen, and the cell pointer jumps immediately to the first unprotected cell in the range.

In this example, the cell pointer jumps to cell F3; only cells in the range F3..F7 can be accessed with the cell pointer.

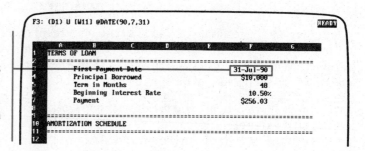

You can now begin to enter or edit data in the unprotected cells. To move the cell pointer to the next unprotected cell after completing an entry, use the arrow keys.

The /Range Input command remains in effect until you press either the Enter key or the Esc key. The cell pointer then returns to the upper left corner of the data input range, and the worksheet returns to the same position on the screen as before the /Range Input command was issued.

Checking the Status of Global Settings

Use the /Worksheet Status command to check the status of all global settings for the worksheet. This command gives you an easy way to view the worksheet settings without having to experiment to find the settings.

To display the global settings of the current worksheet, follow these steps:

1. Call up the 1-2-3 menu by pressing ⁄.

2. Select **W**orksheet by pressing ⬚W⬚.

3. Select **S**tatus by pressing ⬚S⬚.

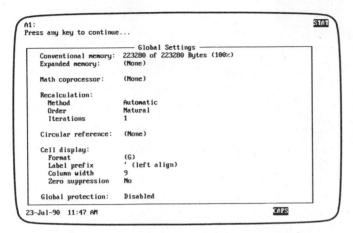

The current settings for the worksheet are displayed.

4. To return to the worksheet, press any key.

The information on the /**W**orksheet **S**tatus screen indicates the available memory as well as the global settings that are active in the current worksheet. In this example, all settings shown are the original default settings for a 1-2-3 worksheet. These settings indicate the following:

- The recalculation method is automatic, with natural order and one iteration per recalculation.
- The cell display format is (G) for **G**eneral (covered in Chapter 4).
- The label prefix is ' for left-justification (covered in Chapter 3).
- The column width is nine characters.
- Zero suppression is off.
- Global protection is disabled.

Entering a Page-Break Character

The /**W**orksheet **P**age command inserts a blank row at the current location of the cell pointer.

153

```
A40: [W28] |::                                                    READY

        A                        B          C          D          E
31  Net Income
32     Northeast                ($1,534)   ($938)     ($228)     $611
33     Southeast                 (1,920)   (1,568)    (1,142)    (630)
34     Central                   38,289    43,602     49,564     56,249
35     Northwest                 14,376    16,937     19,846     23,144
36     Southwest                 22,064    25,964     30,388     35,397
37                              ---------  ---------  ---------  ---------
38  Total Net Income            $71,275   $83,997    $98,428    $114,772
39
40  ::
41
42  ===================================================================
43  REGIONAL RATIO ANALYSIS       Jan       Feb        Mar        Apr
44  ===================================================================
45  Gross Profit on Sales
46     Northeast                 65.9%     66.2%      66.5%      66.8%
47     Southeast                 68.2%     68.5%      68.8%      69.0%
48     Central                   50.0%     50.5%      50.9%      51.4%
49     Northwest                 32.3%     32.9%      33.5%      34.1%
50     Southwest                 42.9%     43.5%      44.0%      44.5%
23-Jul-90  11:52 AM
```

A page-break character (::) is inserted in the cell at which the cell pointer was originally positioned.

The vertical bar (|) that precedes the page-break character (visible in the control panel only) tells 1-2-3 not to print the row. (This symbol is discussed in detail in Chapter 8.) The /Worksheet Page command is similar to the /Worksheet Insert Row command that inserts a row(s) at the row specified by the cell pointer.

To enter a page-break character into a worksheet, follow these steps:

1. Position the cell pointer in the first column of the range to be printed, at the row location where you want a new page to begin.
2. Call up the 1-2-3 menu by pressing ⌐/⌐.
3. Select Worksheet by pressing ⌐W⌐.
4. Select Page by pressing ⌐P⌐.

The page-break character is used when printing a range from the worksheet. Although printing is not covered in detail until Chapter 8, the best time to insert page-break characters is while you are building the worksheet. As you become more experienced in building worksheets and printing reports based on them, you will learn to think of printed pages as you build. Thinking ahead will save time and minimize confusion when you're ready to print.

The page break is effective only when positioned at the left edge of the range being printed. If you add contents to cells in the page-break row, the contents of those cells are not printed when the page break is in effect.

154

Summary

This chapter showed you how the versatile /Worksheet commands can be used to erase an entire worksheet, set column widths (individually or globally), split the screen into horizontal or vertical windows, and freeze titles for scrolling. You also learned how to insert and delete columns and rows, hide columns, suppress the display of zeros, recalculate and protect the worksheet, check the status of the global settings, and insert page breaks in a printed report.

Specifically, you learned the following key information about 1-2-3:

- The Global Settings sheet appears when you select any of the /Worksheet Global commands. This screen indicates the settings of the current worksheet, such as recalculation, formatting, and column width.

- The /Worksheet Erase command erases the current worksheet from memory, but does not erase the file on disk.

- The /Worksheet Column Set-Width command changes the width of a single column. To reset the column to its original default, use /Worksheet Column Reset-Width.

- The /Worksheet Global Column-Width command changes the column width of all columns in the worksheet, except for those already changed.

- The /Worksheet Column Column-Range Set-Width command sets the width of contiguous columns. To reset these columns to the default, select /Worksheet Column Column-Range Reset-Width.

- The /Worksheet Window command splits the screen so that two different parts of the worksheet can be viewed at the same time. Worksheets can be split with the Horizontal or Vertical options. Use /Worksheet Window Clear to return to a single worksheet.

- The /Worksheet Titles command freezes titles along the top and/or left borders of the worksheet so that the titles remain in view when scrolling the worksheet. The /Worksheet Titles Clear command unfreezes the titles.

- The /Worksheet Insert command can be used to insert one or more columns and rows into the worksheet. To delete one or more columns or rows, use /Worksheet Delete.

■ The /Worksheet Column Hide command temporarily removes columns of data from the screen. Hidden columns also do not print when included in a print range. These columns can be restored with the /Worksheet Column Display command.

■ The /Worksheet Global Zero command suppresses the display of zeros in the worksheet. Blank cells or labels, instead of zeros, are displayed on-screen. The actual value (or formula) is displayed in the control panel when a zero-valued cell is highlighted.

■ The /Worksheet Global Recalculation command changes the method, order, and/or number of iterations used in worksheet recalculation.

■ The /Worksheet Global Protection command allows you to turn protection on or off in a worksheet. /Range Unprot can then be used to unprotect individual cells or ranges in the worksheet, to allow entry only in those cells.

■ The /Range Input command restricts input to only unprotected cells in a protected data-input range. The cell pointer moves only among the unprotected cells.

■ The /Worksheet Status command displays a list of the worksheet's current global settings. These settings can be modified with the /Worksheet Global commands.

■ The /Worksheet Page command inserts a blank row that contains a page-break character (::). This character indicates where a new page should begin when a worksheet is printed.

The next chapter will show you how to use the /Copy and /Move commands to modify your worksheet data. You will also learn how to use 1-2-3's search and replace feature.

Modifying a Worksheet

As you begin to create your own worksheets using the basic concepts and commands described in earlier chapters, you need to modify your worksheets by moving and copying data from one location to another. 1-2-3 provides the capability to move and copy data— saving you hours of work when building and modifying your worksheets.

This chapter shows you how to improve your worksheets by moving and copying data effectively. You also learn how to search for and replace a specific string of data in a range of cells in the worksheet.

Moving the contents of cells

Copying the contents of cells

Searching for and replacing cell contents

Key Terms in This Chapter

Relative cell address	A cell reference that adjusts for a new location when used in a formula that is copied to that location.
Absolute cell address	A cell reference that does not adjust for a new location when used in a formula that is copied to that location.
Mixed cell address	A cell reference that combines both relative and absolute cell addressing; used when copying a formula to a new location.
Search string	A set of characters that is used with the /Range Search command to find specified text within a range of cells.

6

Moving the Contents of Cells

In the days of manual spreadsheets, the process of moving data around on the page was called *cutting and pasting* because scissors and glue were used to move sections of the spreadsheet. 1-2-3 lets you cut and paste sections of the worksheet automatically.

With the /Move and /Copy commands, you can move and copy the contents of cells and ranges of cells from one part of the worksheet to another. The difference between moving and copying is that data that is *moved* from one cell to another disappears from the first cell; data that is *copied* appears in both cells.

Suppose that you want to move the contents of the range C2..D3 to the range E2..F3 on your worksheet. To move a range, follow these steps:

1. Call up the 1-2-3 menu by pressing ⌐/⌐.
2. Select Move by pressing Ⓜ.
3. When the prompt Enter range to move FROM: appears, specify the range you want to move by highlighting the range with the cell pointer (or typing the cell addresses), and then press ⌐↵Enter⌐.

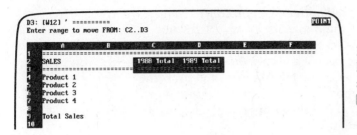

In this example, highlight C2..D3, and then press ⏎Enter.

4. When the prompt Enter range to move TO: appears, move the cell pointer to (or type the cell address of) the upper left cell of the new location, and then press ⏎Enter. Highlighting the entire TO range is not necessary.

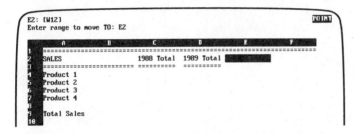

In this example, move the cell pointer to cell E2, and then press ⏎Enter.

6

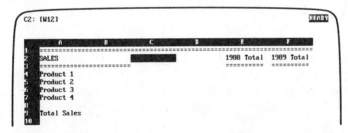

1-2-3 moves the specified range to the new location.

The cell pointer returns immediately to where it was when you initiated the /Move command. Remember that the cell pointer does not have to be positioned at the beginning of the FROM or TO range when you start the /Move command, because you can always press Esc to free the cell pointer.

Note: When you move a range of cells, the TO range is completely over-written by the FROM range that is moved, and any cell contents are lost. If there are cells with formulas that depend on the cell addresses in the TO range, the cells containing these formulas evaluate to ERR.

Use the expanding cell pointer for pointing to ranges. When you select /Move and are prompted to enter a range, 1-2-3 automatically makes the current cell one corner of the range. If you do not want that cell to be a part of the FROM range, press Esc, move the cell pointer to the cell you want as the upper left corner of the FROM range, and press the period (.) key. Use the arrow keys to move the cell pointer over and down. Notice that the cell pointer "expands" so that the entire range is highlighted. When the FROM range is highlighted, press Enter.

Use the End key for pointing to large ranges. Suppose that you want to move the contents of the range A1..E15 to the range that begins at cell A20. When the range prompt A1..A1 appears, press the End key and then the down-arrow key. The cell pointer jumps to cell A15, and the prompt reads A1..A15. Now move the cell pointer by pressing the End key and then the right-arrow key. The prompt now reads A1..E15. This process takes 18 keystrokes if you use only the arrow keys. Instead, using the End key reduces the number of required keystrokes to 4. The difference is even more dramatic when you work with larger ranges.

Remember that when you press an arrow key after the End key, the cell pointer moves in the direction of the arrow key to the next boundary between a blank cell and a cell that contains data. If there are gaps (blank cells) within the blocks of data, however, the End key procedure will be less useful because the cell pointer will go to the boundaries of each gap.

Copying the Contents of Cells

You will often want to copy the contents of cells to other locations in a worksheet. In this section, you'll look at the four different ways in which you can copy data in 1-2-3:

- Copy the contents of one cell to another cell.
- Copy the contents of one cell to every cell in a range.
- Copy from one range to another range of equal size.
- Copy from one range to a larger range.

The procedure used for each copy operation is basically the same. To copy a range, follow these steps:

1. Call up the 1-2-3 menu by pressing ⌷/⌷.
2. Select Copy by pressing ⌷C⌷.

160

3. When the prompt `Enter range to copy FROM:` appears, specify the FROM range.

4. When the prompt `Enter range to copy TO:` appears, specify the TO range.

The only elements that change are the dimensions and locations of the FROM and TO ranges. Remember that you can either type the coordinates of the FROM and TO ranges from the keyboard, or highlight (point to) the ranges in POINT mode.

The four methods of copying data are described in the text that follows.

Method 1: Copying from one cell to another cell

1. Call up the 1-2-3 menu by pressing ⃞/.

2. Select Copy by pressing ⃞C.

3. When the prompt `Enter range to copy FROM:` appears, move the cell pointer to the cell whose contents you want to copy, and then press ⃞←Enter. If the cell pointer is located on the cell to be copied, just press ⃞←Enter.

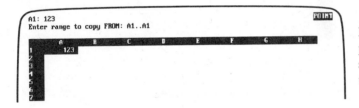

In this example, press ⃞←Enter to select cell A1 as the FROM range.

4. When the prompt `Enter range to copy TO:` appears, move the cell pointer to the cell where you want the data copied, and then press ⃞←Enter.

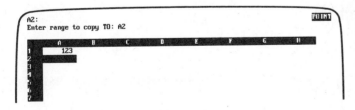

In this example, specify the TO range by moving the cell pointer to cell A2 and pressing ⃞←Enter.

161

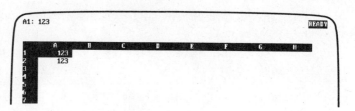

In this copy operation, the contents of cell A1 have been copied to cell A2.

Method 2: Copying from one cell to a range of cells

1. Call up the 1-2-3 menu by pressing ⌐/⌐.
2. Select Copy by pressing ⌐C⌐.
3. When the prompt `Enter range to copy FROM:` appears, move the cell pointer to the cell whose contents you want to copy, and then press ⌐Enter⌐. If the cell pointer is located on the cell to be copied, just press ⌐Enter⌐.

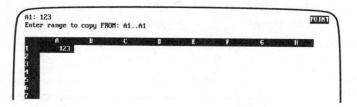

In this example, press ⌐Enter⌐ to select cell A1 as the FROM range.

4. When the prompt `Enter range to copy TO:` appears, highlight the range of cells where you want the data copied, and then press ⌐Enter⌐.

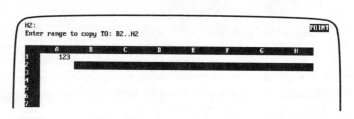

In this example, specify the TO range by highlighting B2..H2 and pressing ⌐Enter⌐.

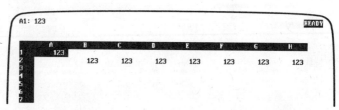

The contents of cell A1 have been copied to each cell in the range B2..H2.

Method 3: Copying from one range to another range of equal size

1. Call up the 1-2-3 menu by pressing ⌐/⌐.

2. Select Copy by pressing ⌐C⌐.

3. When the prompt `Enter range to copy FROM:` appears,
   highlight the range of cells whose contents you want to copy, and
   then press ⌐⏎Enter⌐.

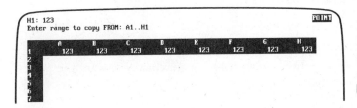

In this example,
highlight the
range A1..H1,
and then press
⌐⏎Enter⌐.

4. When the prompt `Enter range to copy TO:` appears, move the
   cell pointer to the first cell of the range where you want the data
   copied, and then press ⌐⏎Enter⌐. Highlighting the entire TO range is
   not necessary.

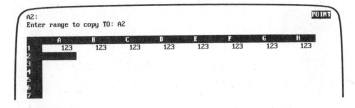

In this example,
specify the TO
range by moving
the cell pointer
to cell A2 and
pressing ⌐⏎Enter⌐.

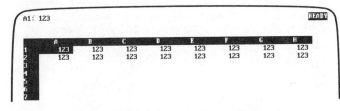

The range A1..H1
has been copied
to the range
A2..H2.

Method 4: Copying from one range to a larger range

1. Call up the 1-2-3 menu by pressing ⌐/⌐.

2. Select Copy by pressing ⌐C⌐.

3. When the prompt `Enter range to copy FROM:` appears, highlight the range of cells whose contents you want to copy, and then press `↵Enter`.

In this example, highlight the range A1..F1, and then press `↵Enter`.

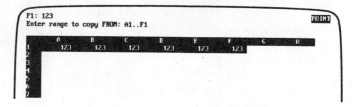

4. When the prompt `Enter range to copy TO:` appears, highlight only the first cells in the rows or columns to which you want the data copied, and then press `↵Enter`.

In this example, to copy the data in row 1 (cells A1..F1) to rows 2 through 20 (cells A2..F20), specify the TO range by highlighting the first cells in rows 2 through 20 (cells A2..A20), and then press `↵Enter`.

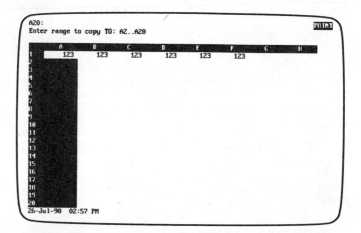

The range A1..F1 has been copied to the larger range A2..F20.

164

Think of this type of copying as an extension of the previous type. The results of this copy operation could have been reached by repeating the copy command 19 times and specifying 19 different single-row TO ranges. The first TO range would be A2, the second would be A3, the third A4, and so on. The results are the same for either method, but you can save a great deal of time by copying to the A2..A20 range, as shown.

The best way to learn how to use different FROM and TO ranges is to experiment on your own. After a while, the rules of copying become second nature to you.

Addressing Cells

Although the connection may not be readily obvious, the way you address cells is tied closely to copy operations. Two different methods of addressing cells can be used when copying: relative and absolute. These two methods of referencing cells are important for building formulas. The type of addressing you use when you reference cells in formulas can affect the results that are produced by these formulas when you copy them to different locations in the worksheet. The following sections cover relative and absolute addressing as well as the combination of both methods—known as *mixed addressing*.

Referencing Cells with Relative Addressing

Relative addressing, 1-2-3's default for referencing cells, means that when you copy a formula, unless you specify otherwise, the addresses of the cells in the formula will be adjusted automatically to fit the new location. Suppose that you have summed the contents of one column, and you need to sum the contents of several adjacent columns, but you don't want to enter the @SUM function over and over again.

To copy a formula with a relative address, follow these steps:

1. Call up the 1-2-3 menu by pressing `/`.
2. Select Copy by pressing `C`.
3. When the prompt `Enter range to copy FROM:` appears, move the cell pointer to the cell containing the formula to be copied, and then press `Enter`.

In this example, move the cell pointer to cell B11, and then press ⏎Enter.

```
B11: (C0) [W13] @SUM(B5..B9)                                    POINT
Enter range to copy FROM: B11..B11
        A           B          C          D          E
 1 ==================================================================
 2 INCOME REPORT    January   February    March     1st Quarter
 3 ==================================================================
 4 Sales
 5    Northeast     $30,336    $33,370    $36,707    $100,412
 6    Southeast      20,572     22,629     24,892     $68,093
 7    Central       131,685    144,854    159,339    $435,877
 8    Northwest      94,473    103,920    114,312    $312,706
 9    Southwest     126,739    139,413    153,354    $419,506
10                  --------
11 Total Sales      $403,805
12
```

4. When the prompt Enter range to copy TO: appears, highlight the range of cells where you want the formula copied, and then press ⏎Enter.

In this example, specify the TO range by highlighting C11..E11 and pressing ⏎Enter.

```
E11: [W13]                                                     POINT
Enter range to copy TO: C11..E11
        A           B          C          D          E
 1 ==================================================================
 2 INCOME REPORT    January   February    March     1st Quarter
 3 ========================== ========== ========== ============
 4 Sales
 5    Northeast     $30,336    $33,370    $36,707    $100,412
 6    Southeast      20,572     22,629     24,892     $68,093
 7    Central       131,685    144,854    159,339    $435,877
 8    Northwest      94,473    103,920    114,312    $312,706
 9    Southwest     126,739    139,413    153,354    $419,506
10                  --------
11 Total Sales      $403,805
12
```

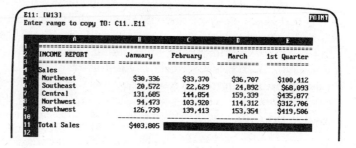

1-2-3 copies the @SUM function to all the cells in the specified TO range, C11..E11.

```
B11: (T) [W13] @SUM(B5..B9)                                    READY
        A           B          C          D          E
 1 ==================================================================
 2 INCOME REPORT    January   February    March     1st Quarter
 3 ========================== ========== ========== ============
 4 Sales
 5    Northeast     $30,336    $33,370    $36,707    $100,412
 6    Southeast      20,572     22,629     24,892     $68,093
 7    Central       131,685    144,854    159,339    $435,877
 8    Northwest      94,473    103,920    114,312    $312,706
 9    Southwest     126,739    139,413    153,354    $419,506
10
11 Total Sales     @SUM(B5..B9) @SUM(C5..C9) @SUM(D5..D9) @SUM(E5..E9)
12
```

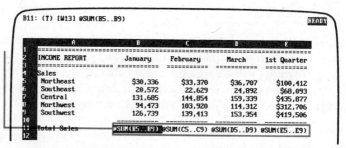

In the preceding example, the range of formulas is displayed in text format to show how each copied formula is adjusted to its new location.

Referencing Cells with Absolute Addressing

In some cases, a formula has an important address that should not be changed when the formula is copied. To keep an address absolute, enter a $

before the cell's column letter and before the cell's row number. For example, $E$11 is an absolute address.

Now that you have summed the contents of several columns of sales, you want to calculate the percentage of sales represented by each month of the quarter. In the example, the best way to do this is to copy a formula that contains an absolute address. When you create the formula in cell B13, place a $ before the E and before the 11 in the second part of the formula.

To copy a formula with an absolute address, follow these steps:

1. Call up the 1-2-3 menu by pressing ⌿.

2. Select Copy by pressing Ⓒ.

3. When the prompt `Enter range to copy FROM:` appears, move the cell pointer to the cell containing the formula with an absolute address to be copied, and then press ↵Enter.

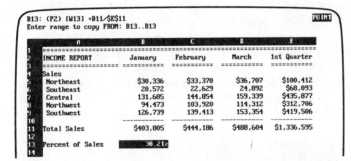

In this example, move the cell pointer to cell B13 and press ↵Enter. Note that cell B13 contains an absolute address in the formula +B11/$E$11.

4. When the prompt `Enter range to copy TO:` appears, highlight the range of cells where you want the formula with the absolute address to be copied, and then press ↵Enter.

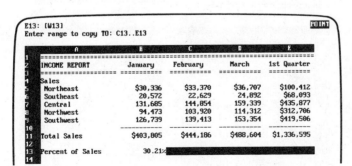

In this example, specify the TO range by highlighting C13..E13 and pressing ↵Enter.

6

167

The range of formulas in row 13 is displayed in text format to show how each copied formula is adjusted to its new location.

```
B13: (T) [W13] +B11/$E$11                                              READY

        A                B            C            D            E
1
2  INCOME REPORT       January     February      March      1st Quarter
3  =================== =========== ============ =========== ===========
4  Sales
5    Northeast          $30,336     $33,370     $36,707      $100,412
6    Southeast           20,572      22,629      24,892       $68,093
7    Central            131,685     144,854     159,339      $435,877
8    Northwest           94,473     103,920     114,312      $312,706
9    Southwest          126,739     139,413     153,354      $419,506
10                      ----------  ----------  ----------   ----------
11 Total Sales         $403,805    $444,186    $488,604    $1,336,595
12
13 Percent of Sales  +B11/$E$11  +C11/$E$11  +D11/$E$11  +E11/$E$11
14
```

Note that the first address of each formula varies, but the second address remains absolute as $E$11 in all four formulas.

Mixing Relative and Absolute Addressing

In some cases, a formula has an important address that cannot be changed as the formula is copied. The last section discussed absolute addresses, which do not change at all when the address is copied. You also can create a mixed address, which can sometimes change, depending on the direction of the copy operation. Mixed addressing refers to a combination of relative and absolute addressing. Because a cell address has two components—a column and a row—it is possible to fix (make absolute) either portion, while leaving the other part unfixed (relative).

If you plan to copy cells that have absolute addresses, you must prepare the cells to be copied by preceding them with dollar signs in both their column and row designations. The dollar signs tell 1-2-3 that the cells have been changed to absolute addresses.

If you want to copy the formula from cell D10 to cell D17, the formula in D10 must contain one mixed address, one absolute address, and one relative address.

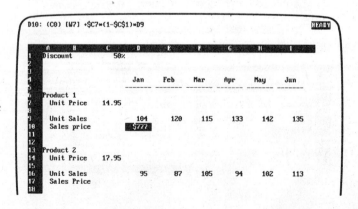

168

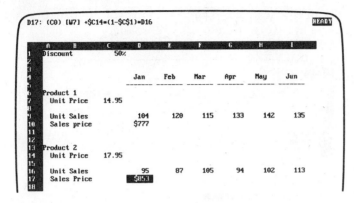

When the formula in D10 is copied to D17, a mixed address ($C14) is used at the beginning of the formula.

Each mixed address refers to the respective unit price of each product. In this example, column C is absolute and row 17 is relative. Also contained in the formula is an absolute address ($C$1) which refers to the discount percentage, and a relative address (D16), which refers to the monthly unit sales for each product.

Using the Abs (F4) Key To Change a Cell Address

There are two ways to enter dollar signs for absolute or mixed addresses in a formula. You can type the dollar signs as you create the formula, or you can later modify the formula by using the Abs (F4) key to have 1-2-3 enter the dollar signs for you. Use the Abs (F4) key in POINT or EDIT mode to make a cell address absolute, mixed, or relative. The F4 key is a four-way toggle. Simply press the F4 key repeatedly until you get the kind of cell reference you want.

To change a cell address with the Abs (F4) key, follow these steps:

1. Highlight the formula you want to change, and then press F2 (Edit).

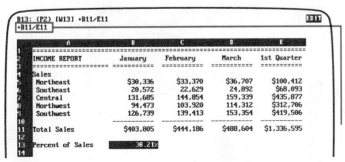

In this example, highlight cell B13 and press F2 (Edit).

169

2. With the cursor located beneath a cell address in the control panel, press F4 (Abs) once to change the address to absolute.

In this example, move the cursor under the second cell address, and then press F4 (Abs) to change E11 to $E$11.

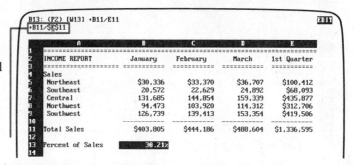

3. Press F4 a second time and the address remains mixed—with the column relative and the row absolute.

In this example, $E$11 changes to E$11.

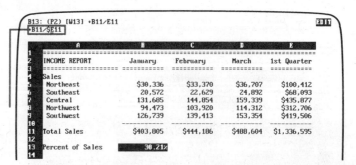

4. Press F4 a third time and the address remains mixed—with the column absolute and the row relative.

In this example, E$11 changes to $E11.

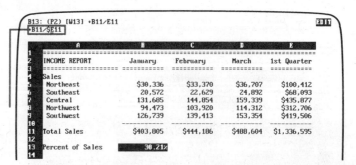

170

5. Press F4 a fourth time and the address changes from mixed back to relative (the default).

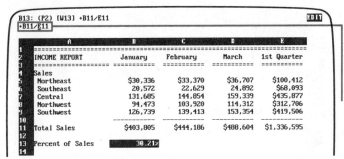

In this example, $E11 changes to E11.

Transposing Rows and Columns

For copy operations that are difficult to perform with 1-2-3's normal copy commands, 1-2-3 has two specialized copy commands: /Range Trans and /Range Value. The /Range Trans command copies columns into rows and rows into columns. The /Range Value command, which is explained in the next section, copies the values (but not the formulas) from one range to another. The /Range Trans command copies each row of the FROM range into the corresponding column of the TO range, or each column of the FROM range into the corresponding row of the TO range. The result is a transposed copy of the FROM range.

Suppose that you want to transpose the data in three rows to columnar format. To transpose the data, follow these steps:

1. Call up the 1-2-3 menu by pressing /.

2. Select **R**ange by pressing R.

3. Select **T**rans (Transpose) by pressing T.

4. When the prompt Enter range to copy FROM: appears, highlight the range of cells you want to transpose, and then press ↵Enter.

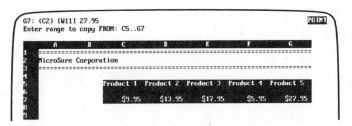

In this example, highlight the range C5..G7 and press ↵Enter.

171

5. When the prompt Enter range to copy TO: appears, highlight the columns to which you want the data copied.

In this example, highlight the range A9..C9. Three columns must be highlighted because the original data covers three rows.

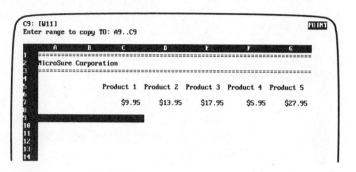

The data appears in its original location as well as transposed in the new location.

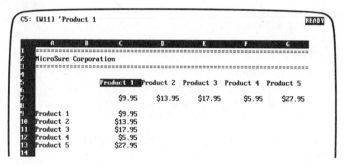

The /Range Trans command can be used to copy data from row to column format (as in this example) and also from column to row format.

When copying formulas, the /Range Trans command behaves just like the /Copy command. When a range is transposed, cell references in the transposed range are adjusted, just as references are adjusted in a normal /Copy command. This adjustment of cell references can lead to serious trouble when you use the /Range Trans command to transpose a range containing formulas. The transposed formulas will be incorrect; the values, however, will remain in the same order. Because the cell references are not transposed, the relative and mixed cell references in the transposed range will refer to incorrect locations after the transposition.

You can avoid the problem of incorrect cell references in transposed ranges by converting the formulas in the FROM range to values before transposing.

Using the /**R**ange **Value** command, discussed in the following section, is a convenient way to convert a range of formulas to values.

Converting Formulas to Values

The /**R**ange **Value** command lets you copy only the *values* of the cells in one range to another range. This command is useful whenever you want to preserve the current formula values of a range of cells instead of having only the changed values after the worksheet has been updated. An important function of the /**R**ange **Value** command is its capability for conversion of formulas to values. You don't have to worry, therefore, about formulas that depend on cell references (when using /**R**ange **Trans**, for example).

To convert formulas to values when copying, follow these steps:

1. Call up the 1-2-3 menu by pressing ⟨/⟩.
2. Select **R**ange by pressing ⟨R⟩.
3. Select **V**alue by pressing ⟨V⟩.
4. When the prompt `Enter range to copy FROM:` appears, highlight the range of formulas to be copied, and then press ⟨↵Enter⟩.

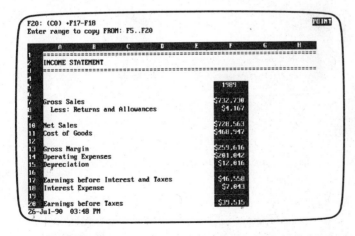

In this example, highlight the range F5..F20, and then press ⟨↵Enter⟩.

5. When the prompt `Enter range to copy TO:` appears, move the cell pointer to the first cell in the range where you want the values copied, and then press ⟨↵Enter⟩.

173

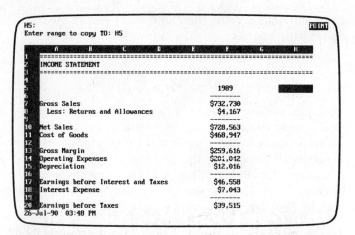

In this example, move the cell pointer to cell H5 and press ↵Enter.

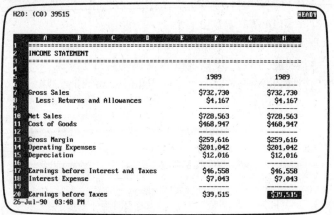

Notice that the formula in cell F20 has become a value in cell H20.

Tips for Copying

Remember the following tips whenever you intend to copy data within the worksheet:

- When you copy a cell, 1-2-3 automatically copies the format of the cell with it. This automatic format-copying feature saves you from having to set the format for an entire range of cells before (or after) copying to them.

- Sometimes the FROM and TO ranges will overlap when you copy. The general rule is to avoid overlapping the end points of the FROM and TO ranges to prevent problems with the copy operation.

If you do overlap them, you may get mixed results. You can, however, overlap ranges without error when the FROM and TO ranges have the same upper left boundary (such as when using /Range Value to copy formulas onto themselves).

- Note particularly the finality of the /Copy command when you disable the Undo feature, and in all versions prior to Release 2.2. If you copy over the contents of a cell, you have no way to retrieve the contents. Make sure that you have properly designated your ranges before you complete the command. You can retrieve the worksheet again if it has already been saved, but all changes made since the last save will be lost.

Searching for and Replacing Cell Contents

6

Looking for a word or string of characters in a large worksheet can be time-consuming and tedious. 1-2-3 offers a feature (not available in versions prior to Release 2.2) that allows you to search for text easily. If necessary, you can replace a specified string of characters with other text everywhere the string occurs. Frequent users of word-processing software are familiar with this capability. It can be particularly useful for changing all occurrences of a particular misspelling to the correct spelling.

Whether you want to find the first occurrence of a string or you want to replace it with another string, you start with the same command, /Range Search. 1-2-3 performs the search column-by-column in the defined search range. The following section shows you how to search for a given string, and the subsequent section shows you how to search for a string and replace it with another string.

Searching for the Occurrence of a String

To search a specified range for a particular string in labels and/or formulas, follow these steps:

1. Call up the 1-2-3 menu by pressing /.
2. Select **R**ange by pressing R.
3. Select Search by pressing S.
4. Highlight the range you want to search, and then press Enter.

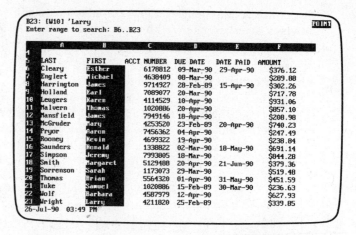

In this example,
highlight the
range B6..B23
and press
⏎Enter.

5. Define the string you want to search for and then press ⏎Enter.
   Note that the search string is not case sensitive; you can enter the
   string in upper- or lowercase characters.

In this example,
to search for all
occurrences of
James in the
highlighted
range, type
james, and then
press ⏎Enter.

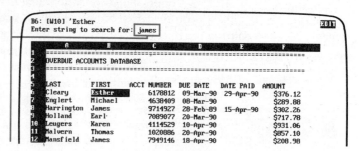

6. Indicate whether to search for **F**ormulas, **L**abels, or **B**oth labels and
   formulas, by pressing F, L, or B, respectively.

To check only
cells that contain
labels, select
Labels by
pressing L.

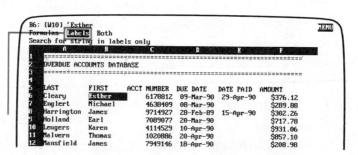

176

7. Select **Find** by pressing F to find a particular string in the range of labels that are selected.

   1-2-3 highlights the first appearance of the string.

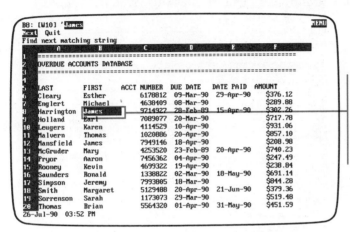

In this example, the first occurrence of James in the search range is highlighted by the cell pointer.

8. To see the next appearance of the string, select **Next** by pressing N.

   The second occurrence of the string, if present, is highlighted by the cell pointer.

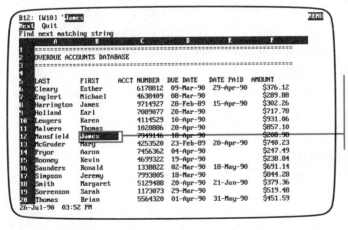

In this example, the next appearance of James in column B is highlighted.

6

9. At each of the successive prompts, select **Next** by pressing $\boxed{N}$ until 1-2-3 finds the last occurrence of your string in the range.

   Note: If you want to end the search before all occurrences of the string have been found, select **Quit** by pressing $\boxed{Q}$.

When 1-2-3 cannot locate another string, an error message is displayed.

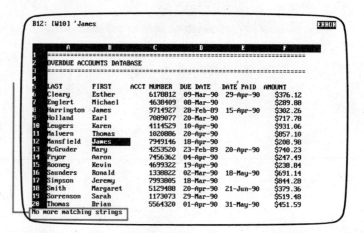

```
B12: [W10] 'James                                                    ERROR

          A           B        C        D          E         F
1  ==============================================================
2  OVERDUE ACCOUNTS DATABASE
3  ==============================================================
4
5  LAST        FIRST    ACCT NUMBER DUE DATE  DATE PAID  AMOUNT
6  Cleary      Esther      6170812  09-Mar-90 29-Apr-90  $376.12
7  Englert     Michael     4638409  08-Mar-90            $289.88
8  Harrington  James       9714927  28-Feb-89 15-Apr-90  $302.26
9  Holland     Earl        7089077  20-Mar-90            $717.78
10 Leugers     Karen       4114529  10-Apr-90            $931.06
11 Malvern     Thomas      1020806  20-Apr-90            $857.10
12 Mansfield   James       7949146  18-Apr-90            $208.98
13 McGruder    Mary        4253520  23-Feb-89 20-Apr-90  $740.23
14 Pryor       Aaron       7456362  04-Apr-90            $247.49
15 Rooney      Kevin       4699322  19-Apr-90            $238.84
16 Saunders    Ronald      1338822  02-Mar-90 18-May-90  $691.14
17 Simpson     Jeremy      7993805  18-Mar-90            $844.28
18 Smith       Margaret    5129488  20-Apr-90 21-Jun-90  $379.36
19 Sorrenson   Sarah       1173073  29-Mar-90            $519.48
20 Thomas      Brian       5564320  01-Apr-90 31-May-90  $451.59
No more matching strings
```

10. Press $\boxed{\text{←Enter}}$ or $\boxed{\text{Esc}}$ to return to READY mode.

Replacing One String with Another String

To replace a string in the worksheet with another specified string, you follow a procedure similar to that which finds a string within a range. You must, however, supply the string of characters that will replace the existing string.

To search a range for a particular string and replace that string with another string, follow these steps:

1. Call up the 1-2-3 menu by pressing $\boxed{/}$.
2. Select **Range** by pressing $\boxed{R}$.
3. Select **Search** by pressing $\boxed{S}$.
4. Highlight the range you want to search, and then press $\boxed{\text{←Enter}}$.

178

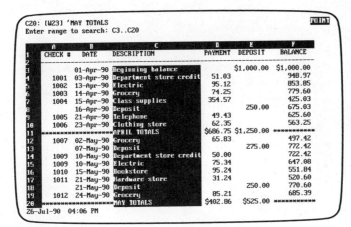

In this example, highlight the range C3..C20 and press ⏎Enter.

5. Define the string you want to search for, and then press ⏎Enter. Note that the search string is not case sensitive.

6

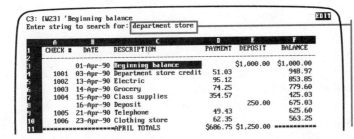

To search for De-partment store in the high-lighted range, type **department store**, and then press ⏎Enter.

6. Indicate whether to search for **F**ormulas, **L**abels, or **B**oth labels and formulas by pressing F, L, or B, respectively.

   If you need to correct a large range of formulas by changing a recurring cell reference, select Formulas. For this example, select Labels by pressing L.

7. Select **R**eplace by pressing R to replace occurrences of the specified string with another string.

8. Define the string that will be used to replace occurrences of the specified search string, and then press ⏎Enter. Note that this string is case sensitive; your use of uppercase and lowercase characters in your definition will be copied to the replacement string.

179

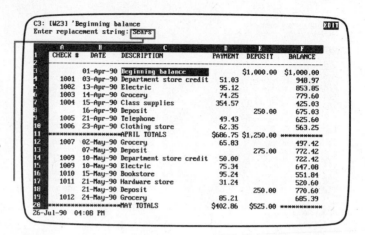

In this example, to replace the occurrences of *Department store* with *Sears*, type **Sears** and press ⏎Enter.

1-2-3 highlights the first occurrence of the search string and provides a menu with four options: **All**, **Replace**, **Next**, and **Quit**.

9. Select one of the four options.

All replaces *every* matching string with the new string.

Replace completes the first instance of search and replace, and positions the cell pointer on the second occurrence—again offering you the same four menu options.

Next lets you move the cell pointer to the next occurrence of the search string without making the replacement—allowing you to use **Replace** selectively.

Quit ends the search and returns 1-2-3 to READY mode.

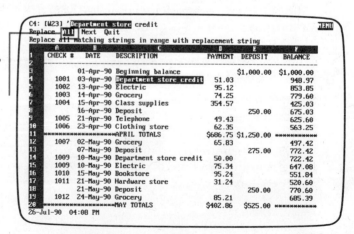

For this example, select **All** by pressing Ⓐ.

6

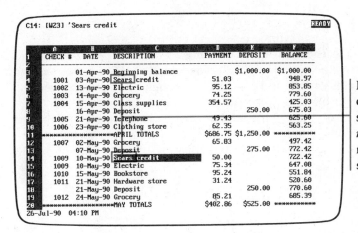

Note how all occurrences of the string *Department store* are replaced with the string *Sears*.

When 1-2-3 cannot locate another appearance of the string after you select Replace or Next, an error message is displayed. Press Enter or Esc to return to READY mode.

Tips for Using the Search-and-Replace Feature

Remember the following tips when using 1-2-3's search-and-replace feature:

- If you confine your search to a given range, you can accelerate the search, and you're less likely to accidentally replace strings you want to be left undisturbed.

- The search string can consist of more than a single word. In fact, the string can be as long as 240 characters and can contain many words.

- The string you are searching for is not case sensitive. 1-2-3 will find any string that matches the characters you type, regardless of whether you type the string in uppercase, lowercase, or a combination of these.

- Unlike the search string, the replacement string is case sensitive. The substitution will consist of precisely what you type, in keeping with your use of uppercase and lowercase.

- The /Range Search command will not search hidden columns. The command can be used, however, to search individual cells that have been formatted with the /Range Format Hidden command.

181

Summary

In this chapter, you learned that when building a worksheet, you can use the /Move command to relocate cells and cell ranges, and the /Copy command to duplicate the contents of cells and cell ranges throughout the worksheet. By specifying relative, absolute, or mixed addressing, you can control cell references for formulas you use in your worksheets. You also learned that 1-2-3 provides a search-and-replace feature (not available in versions prior to Release 2.2) that allows you to find and/or replace specified strings of data in your worksheets.

Specifically, you learned the following key information about 1-2-3:

- The /Move command allows you to move the contents of one or more cells to any location in the worksheet. The data that is moved appears only in the new location.

- The /Copy command enables you to copy information to other parts of the worksheet in four different ways. Once copied, the data appears in both locations.

- The End key, in combination with the arrow keys, can be used with the /Move and /Copy commands to move or copy large ranges of data.

- Two types of cell addresses that are helpful when copying formulas are relative and absolute cell addresses. Combinations of relative and absolute cell addresses are called mixed cell addresses. Dollar signs are used to indicate absolute and mixed cell addresses.

- When creating or modifying relative, absolute, and mixed cell addresses, the Abs (F4) key can be used to toggle between the different types of cell references.

- The /Range Trans command copies data from columns into rows, and rows into columns.

- The /Range Value command copies a range of formulas to their equivalent values in another (or the same) range in the worksheet.

- The /Range Search command finds a specified string of data in a range. This string can also be replaced with a new string.

The next chapter covers some of 1-2-3's built-in functions. Functions are used in formulas to perform complex calculations. A few of the categories of functions that are discussed include mathematical, financial and accounting, and string functions.

Using Functions

In addition to the worksheet formulas you can create, you can take advantage of a variety of ready-made formulas provided by 1-2-3. These built-in formulas— called *functions*—enable you to take advantage of 1-2-3's analytical capability, and are helpful when used with business, engineering, scientific, and statistical applications. Many of these powerful functions can be used even in the simplest of worksheets. You can use functions by themselves, in your own formulas, or in macros and advanced macro command programs to calculate results and solve problems.

1-2-3 provides 92 functions in the following categories:

- Mathematical and trigonometric
- Date and time
- Financial
- Statistical
- Database
- Logical
- String
- Special

Key Terms in This Chapter

Functions 1-2-3's built-in formulas that perform many different types of calculations.

Arguments Inputs needed by most functions in order to perform their calculations.

Syntax The format of a specific function.

This chapter first describes the basic steps for using 1-2-3 functions, and then covers each of these categories in more detail. Although all 1-2-3 functions are listed and briefly described within tables, only the most commonly used 1-2-3 functions are discussed in detail in separate sections of this chapter. Refer to Que's *Using 1-2-3 Release 2.2*, Special Edition, for comprehensive coverage of each of 1-2-3's functions.

Entering a 1-2-3 Function

If you have not yet reviewed Chapter 3, you should study the section of that chapter which introduces functions before you continue with this chapter. There you learn about the eight categories of functions that this chapter covers, as well as about the steps used to enter a specific function.

This chapter does not include numbered steps for entering each function because all functions are entered with the same procedure. To enter a 1-2-3 function into a worksheet, follow this general four-step process:

1. Type @ to tell 1-2-3 that you want to enter a function.
2. Type the function name.
3. Type within parentheses any inputs, or arguments, that the function needs.
4. Press Enter.

An example of a function is @AVG. If you type the function **@AVG(1,2,3)**, 1-2-3 returns the calculated result 2, which is the average of the three arguments—the numbers 1, 2, and 3.

Some functions do not require arguments. For example, the mathematical function @PI returns the value of π; and the mathematical function @RAND produces a random number between zero and one.

Using Mathematical and Trigonometric Functions

1-2-3's nine mathematical functions and eight trigonometric functions are useful in engineering and scientific applications. However, these functions are also convenient tools you can use to perform a variety of standard arithmetic operations, such as rounding values or calculating square roots.

Table 7.1 lists the mathematical and trigonometric functions, their arguments, and the operations they perform. The sections that follow cover the @INT and @ROUND mathematical functions in detail.

Table 7.1
Mathematical and Trigonometric Functions

Function	Description
@ABS(*number* or *cell_reference*)	Computes the absolute value of the argument.
@ACOS(*angle*)	Calculates the arccosine, given an angle in radians.
@ASIN(*angle*)	Calculates the arcsine, given an angle in radians.
@ATAN(*angle*)	Calculates the arctangent, given an angle in radians.
@ATAN2(*number1*, *number2*)	Calculates the four-quadrant arctangent.
@COS(*angle*)	Calculates the cosine, given an angle in radians.
@EXP(*number* or *cell_reference*)	Computes the number *e* raised to the power of the argument.
@INT(*number* or *cell_reference*)	Returns the integer portion of a number.

7

185

Table 7.1—(continued)

Function	Description
@LN(*number* or *cell_reference*)	Calculates the natural logarithm of a number.
@LOG(*number* or *cell_reference*)	Calculates the common, or base 10, logarithm of a number.
@MOD(*number,divisor*)	Computes the remainder of a division operation.
@PI	Returns the value of π.
@RAND	Generates a random number between 0 and 1.
@ROUND(*number* or *cell_reference,precision*)	Rounds a number to a specified precision.
@SIN(*angle*)	Calculates the sine, given an angle in radians.
@SQRT(*number* or *cell_reference*)	Computes the positive square root of a number.
@TAN(*angle*)	Calculates the tangent, given an angle in radians.

Computing Integers with @INT

The @INT function converts a decimal number into an integer, or whole number. @INT creates an integer by truncating, or removing, the decimal portion of a number (without rounding). @INT uses the following format, or syntax:

@INT(*number* or *cell_reference*)

@INT has one argument, which can be either a numeric value or a cell reference to a numeric value. The result of applying @INT to the values 3.1, 4.5, and 5.9 yields integer values of 3, 4, and 5, respectively.

@INT is useful for computations in which the decimal portion of a number is irrelevant or insignificant. Suppose, for example, that you have $1,000 to invest in XYZ company and that shares of XYZ sell for $17 each. You divide 1,000 by 17 to compute the total number of shares that can be purchased.

186

Because you cannot purchase a fractional share, you can use @INT to truncate the decimal portion.

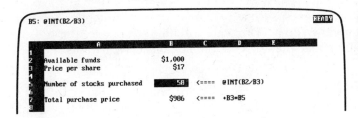

The @INT function calculates the number of shares that can be purchased.

Rounding Numbers with @ROUND

The @ROUND function rounds values to the precision you specify. The function uses two arguments: the value you want to round, and the precision you want to use in the rounding. @ROUND uses the following syntax:

@ROUND(*number* or *cell_reference,precision*)

The first argument can be a numeric value or a cell reference to a numeric value. The *precision* argument determines the number of decimal places and can be a numeric value between −100 and +100. You use positive precision values to specify positions to the right of the decimal place and negative values to specify positions to the left of the decimal place. A precision value of 0 rounds decimal values to the nearest integer.

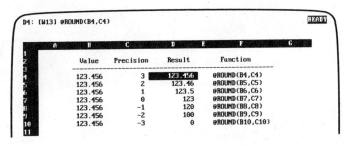

The @ROUND function rounds values to a specified precision.

Note: The @ROUND function and the /**R**ange Format command perform differently. @ROUND actually changes the contents of a cell; /**R**ange Format alters only how the cell's contents are displayed.

Using Date and Time Functions

The 11 date and time functions enable you to convert dates, such as November 26, 1989, and times, such as 6:00 p.m., to serial numbers. You can then use the serial numbers to perform date and time arithmetic. These functions are valuable tools when dates and times affect calculations and logic in your worksheets.

The date and time functions available in 1-2-3 are summarized in table 7.2. The sections that follow review examples of the @DATE, @DATEVALUE, and @NOW functions.

Table 7.2
Date and Time Functions

Function	Description
@DATE(*year,month,day*)	Calculates the serial number of the specified date.
@DATEVALUE(*date_string*)	Converts a date expressed as a string into a serial number.
@DAY(*date_number*)	Extracts the day number from a serial number.
@HOUR(*time_number*)	Extracts the hour number from a serial number.
@MINUTE(*time_number*)	Extracts the minute number from a serial number.
@MONTH(*date_number*)	Extracts the month number from a serial number.
@NOW	Calculates the serial date and time from the current system date and time.
@SECOND(*time_number*)	Extracts the seconds from a serial number.
@TIME(*hour,minutes,seconds*)	Calculates the serial number of the specified time.
@TIMEVALUE(*time_string*)	Converts a time expressed as a string into a serial number.
@YEAR(*date_number*)	Extracts the year number from a serial number.

188

Converting Date Values to Serial Numbers with @DATE

The first step in using dates in arithmetic operations is to convert the dates to serial numbers, which you can then use in arithmetic operations and sorting. Probably the most frequently used date function is @DATE. This function converts any date into a serial number that can be used in calculations and displayed as a date in 1-2-3. @DATE uses the following syntax:

@DATE(*year,month,day*)

You use numbers to identify a year, month, or day. For example, you enter the date November 26, 1989, into the @DATE function as @DATE(89,11,26). The serial number that results is 32838.

1-2-3's internal calendar begins with the serial number 1, which represents January 1, 1900. A single day is represented by an increment of 1; therefore, 1-2-3 represents January 2, 1900, as 2. To display that serial number as a text date, format the cell with the /Range Format Date command.

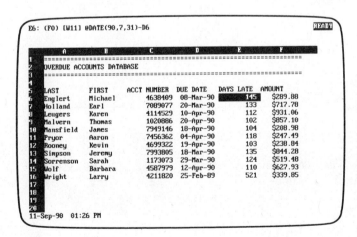

The @DATE function used to calculate the number of days a bill is overdue as of July 31, 1990.

Note: The numbers you enter to represent the year, month, and day need to comprise a valid date; otherwise, 1-2-3 returns ERR. For example, 1-2-3 is programmed so that you can specify February 29 only during leap years, and you never can specify February 30 or 31.

Converting Date Strings to Serial Numbers with @DATEVALUE

@DATEVALUE computes the serial number for a date text string typed into a referenced cell. The text string must use one of the date formats recognized by 1-2-3. @DATEVALUE requires the following syntax:

@DATEVALUE(*date_string*)

If 1-2-3 cannot recognize the format used for the argument, the function results in ERR. After you have entered the function, use the /Range Format Date command to display the serial date number as a text date.

The @DATEVALUE function converts date strings entered as text into serial date numbers, which can then be formatted as 1-2-3 dates.

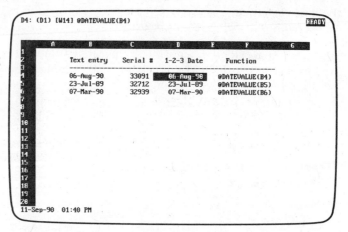

Finding the Current Date and Time with @NOW

The @NOW function displays as a serial number both the current system date and the current system time. The numbers to the left of the decimal point specify the date, while the numbers to the right of the decimal point indicate the time. This function, which requires no arguments, provides a convenient tool for adding dates to worksheets and reports.

After you have entered the @NOW function, use the /Range Format Date command to display the serial date number as a text date or time.

190

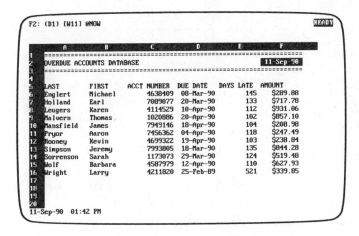

```
F2: (D1) [W11] @NOW                                      READY

        A        B        C         D         E        F
1  ===================================================================
2  OVERDUE ACCOUNTS DATABASE                          11-Sep-90
3  ===================================================================
4
5  LAST     FIRST    ACCT NUMBER  DUE DATE  DAYS LATE  AMOUNT
6  Englert  Michael    4638409    08-Mar-90    145     $289.88
7  Holland  Earl       7089077    20-Mar-90    133     $717.78
8  Leugers  Karen      4114529    10-Apr-90    112     $931.06
9  Malvern  Thomas     1020886    20-Apr-90    102     $857.10
10 Mansfield James      7949146    18-Apr-90    104     $208.98
11 Pryor    Aaron      7456362    04-Apr-90    118     $247.49
12 Rooney   Kevin      4699322    19-Apr-90    103     $238.84
13 Simpson  Jeremy     7993805    18-Mar-90    135     $844.28
14 Sorrenson Sarah     1173073    29-Mar-90    124     $519.48
15 Wolf     Barbara    4587979    12-Apr-90    110     $627.93
16 Wright   Larry      4211820    25-Feb-89    521     $339.85
17
18
19
20
11-Sep-90  01:42 PM
```

The @NOW function, formatted as a date, inserts the current date in a worksheet.

Using Financial Functions

The 11 financial functions enable you to perform a variety of business-related calculations. These calculations include discounting cash flows, computing loan amortization, calculating depreciation, and analyzing the return on investments. This set of functions helps you perform investment analysis and accounting, or budgeting for depreciable assets.

Table 7.3 summarizes the financial functions available in 1-2-3. The sections that follow describe the @PMT, @PV, and @FV functions in greater detail.

Table 7.3
Financial Functions

Function	Description
@CTERM(*interest,future_value, present_value*)	Calculates the number of periods required for a present value amount to grow to a future value amount given a periodic interest rate.
@DDB(*cost,salvage,life, period*)	Calculates depreciation using the double-declining balance method.
@FV(*payments,interest,term*)	Calculates the future value of a series of equal payments compounded at the periodic interest rate.

7

Table 7.3—(continued)

Function	Description
@IRR(*estimate,range*)	Calculates the internal rate of return on an investment.
@NPV(*interest,range*)	Calculates the present value of a series of future cash flows at equal time intervals when the payments are discounted by the periodic interest rate.
@PMT(*principal,interest, term*)	Calculates the loan payment amount.
@PV(*payments,interest,term*)	Calculates the present value of a series of future cash flows of equal payments discounted by the periodic interest rate.
@RATE(*future_value, present_value,term*)	Calculates the periodic rate required to increase the present-value amount to the future-value amount in a specified length of time.
@SLN(*cost,salvage,life*)	Calculates straight-line depreciation for one period.
@SYD(*cost,salvage,life, period*)	Calculates sum-of-the-years' digits depreciation for a specified period.
@TERM(*payments,interest, future_value*)	Calculates the number of payment periods necessary to accumulate the future value, when payments are compounded at the periodic interest rate.

Calculating Loan Payment Amounts with @PMT

You use the @PMT function to calculate the periodic payments necessary to pay the principal on a loan with a given interest rate and time period. Therefore, to use @PMT, you need to know the total loan amount (principal), periodic interest rate, and term, as shown in the following syntax:

@PMT(*principal,interest,term*)

The interest rate and the term must be expressed as the same units of time. For example, if you make monthly payments, you should use the annual interest rate divided by 12, and the term should be the number of months you will be making payments. @PMT assumes that payments are to be made at the end of each period.

The @PMT function can be used to calculate the monthly car payment on a $12,000 car loan. The loan is repaid over 48 months, and the monthly loan rate is 1 percent—12 percent divided by 12 periods per year.

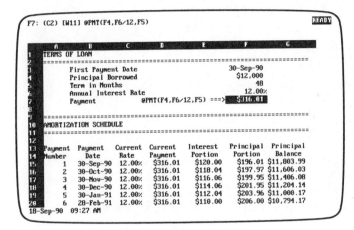

The @PMT function calculates loan payments.

Calculating Present and Future Values with @PV and @FV

@PV calculates the present value of a series of future cash flows of equal payments discounted by the periodic interest rate. The interest rate and the term must be expressed as the same units of time. The @PV function uses the following syntax:

@PV(*payments,interest,term*)

One example of using @PV is to determine whether to receive contest winnings immediately in one lump sum or as a specified amount to be received annually.

193

The @FV function calculates what a current amount will grow to based on a specified interest rate and the number of years. Again, the interest rate and the term must be expressed as the same units of time. @FV uses the following syntax:

@FV(*payments,interest,term*)

You can use @FV to calculate the future value of a savings account that is used solely for making equal automatic deposits on a monthly basis. Simply specify the amount of deduction per month (payments), the monthly interest rate, and the specified number of months (term).

Using Statistical Functions

A set of seven statistical functions enable you to perform all the standard statistical calculations on data in your worksheet or in a 1-2-3 database. You can find minimum and maximum values, calculate averages, and compute standard deviations and variances.

Table 7.4 lists the functions, their arguments, and the statistical operations they perform. The sections that follow cover the @AVG, @COUNT, @MAX, and @MIN statistical functions. The @SUM function, probably the most commonly used 1-2-3 function, is illustrated in the functions section of Chapter 3.

Table 7.4
Statistical Functions

Function	Description
@AVG(*list*)	Calculates the arithmetic mean of a list of values.
@COUNT(*list*)	Counts the number of cells that contain entries.
@MAX(*list*)	Returns the maximum value in a list of values.
@MIN(*list*)	Returns the minimum value in a list of values.
@STD(*list*)	Calculates the population standard deviation of a list of values.
@SUM(*list*)	Sums a list of values.
@VAR(*list*)	Calculates the population variance of a list of values.

Note: The statistical functions perform differently when you specify cells as ranges instead of individually. When you specify a range of cells, 1-2-3 ignores empty cells within the specified range. When you specify cells individually, however, 1-2-3 takes empty cells into consideration for the particular functions mentioned. When you specify cells, keep in mind also that 1-2-3 treats cells containing labels as zeros. This is the case when the cell is included as part of a range or when you specify the cell individually.

Computing the Arithmetic Mean with @AVG

To manually calculate the average of a set of values, you add all the values and then divide the sum by the number of values. Essentially, the @AVG function produces the same result as if you divided @SUM(*list*) by @COUNT(*list*). The @AVG function is a helpful tool for calculating the commonly used arithmetic mean, or average. Use the following syntax for this function:

@AVG(*list*)

The *list* argument can contain any combination of values, cell addresses, single and multiple ranges, and range names.

The @AVG function can be used to calculate the mean price per share of an imaginary company. The function's argument includes the list of stock prices to be averaged. Any empty cells in the list are ignored in the average calculation.

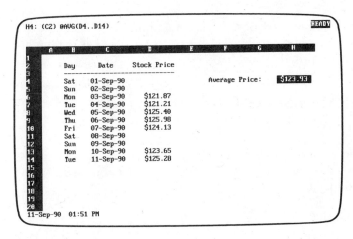

The @AVG function calculates the average price per share of stock.

195

Counting Cell Entries with @COUNT

The @COUNT function totals the number of cells that contain entries of any kind, including labels, label-prefix characters, or the values ERR and NA. Use the following syntax for @COUNT:

@COUNT(*list*)

The *list* argument can contain any combination of values, cell addresses, single and multiple ranges, and range names. For example, you can use @COUNT to show the number of share prices included in the @AVG calculation of the prior example.

The @COUNT function calculates the number of prices per share used in the average calculation.

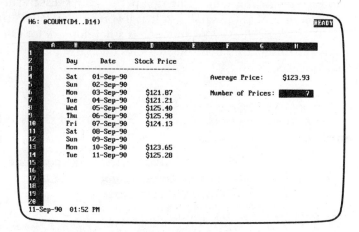

Note: Be sure to include only ranges as the argument in the @COUNT function. If you specify an individual cell, 1-2-3 counts that cell as if it has an entry even if the cell is empty.

Finding Maximum and Minimum Values with @MAX and @MIN

The @MAX function finds the largest value included in the *list* argument; the @MIN function finds the smallest value included in the *list* argument. These functions use the following syntax:

@MAX(*list*)
@MIN(*list*)

196

The @MAX and @MIN functions can help you find the highest and the lowest prices in the stock prices example. Although the example shows only seven values, the true power of these functions is most evident when your list consists of several dozen or several hundred items.

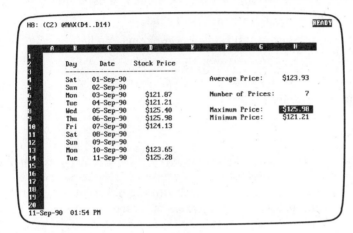

The highlighted @MAX function shows the highest price per share. The @MIN function (just below the highlighted cell) displays the lowest stock price in the list.

Using Database Functions

1-2-3's database functions are similar to the statistical functions, but have been modified for use with database fields. Like other functions, the database functions perform in one simple statement calculations that may otherwise require several statements. This efficiency and ease of application make these functions excellent tools for manipulating 1-2-3 databases. The database functions are described in table 7.5.

The general syntax of each of these functions is as follows:

@DSUM(*input_range,offset,criteria_range*)

The *input range* and *criteria range* are the same as those used by the /Data Query command. The *input range* specifies the database or the part of a database to be searched, and the *criteria range* specifies which records are to be selected. The *offset* indicates which field to select from the database records; the offset value must be either zero or a positive integer. A value of zero indicates the first column in the database, a one indicates the second column, and so on.

197

Table 7.5
Database Functions

Function	Description
@DAVG	Calculates the arithmetic mean of items in a list.
@DCOUNT	Counts the number of entries in a list.
@DMAX	Returns the maximum value among items in a list.
@DMIN	Returns the minimum value among items in a list.
@DSTD	Calculates the standard deviation of items in a list.
@DSUM	Sums the values of items in a list.
@DVAR	Computes the variance of items in a list.

Suppose that you want to compute database statistics of the average interest rates offered by money market funds for a given week. 1-2-3's database functions allow you to find the count, sum, mean (average), variance, standard deviation, maximum, and minimum rates of return.

Database functions are used here with a money market database.

```
B14: [W7] @DCOUNT(A3..B10,1,D4..D5)                              READY

              A              B     C     D         E        F
 1  MONEY MARKET DATABASE (7 DAYS AVERAGE YIELD)
 2
 3  NAME                    WEEK 1      Criteria Range
 4  Alliance Group            7.7       WEEK 1
 5  Kemper Money Funds        7.7       +WEEK 1>7
 6  Paine Webber Cash         7.9
 7  Prudential Bache          7.4
 8  Shearson T-Fund           8.2
 9  Summit Cash Reserves      7.3
10  Value Line Cash Fund      7.7
11
12  Database statistics               Function
13  --------------------------        -----------------------
14  Count              7              @DCOUNT(A3..B10,1,D4..D5)
15  Sum               53.9            @DSUM(A3..B10,1,D4..D5)
16  Average            7.7            @DAVG(A3..B10,1,D4..D5)
17  Variance        0.0771            @DVAR(A3..B10,1,D4..D5)
18  Std Dev         0.2777            @DSTD(A3..B10,1,D4..D5)
19  Maximum            8.2            @DMAX(A3..B10,1,D4..D5)
20  Minimum            7.3            @DMIN(A3..B10,1,D4..D5)
13-Sep-90  10:14 AM
```

As displayed in the control panel, the input range is A3..B10, the offset of 1 indicates column B, and the criteria range is D4..D5. In the lower part of the

198

example, the database functions are located in column B (shown in text format in column D).

Using Logical Functions

Each of 1-2-3's nine logical functions enables you to test whether a condition is true or false. Many of these functions operate in a similar manner—by returning a 1 if the test is true or a 0 if the test is false. These logical tests are important for creating decision-making functions; the results of these functions depend on conditions elsewhere in the worksheet.

The nine logical functions that 1-2-3 provides are summarized in table 7.6. In the text that follows, the @IF, @TRUE, and @FALSE logical functions are described in more detail.

Table 7.6
Logical Functions

Function	Description
@FALSE	Returns the logical value 0, for false.
@IF(*condition,true,false*)	Tests a condition and returns one result if the condition is true and another result if the condition is false.
@ISAAF(*name*)	Tests for a defined add-in program.
@ISAPP(*name*)	Tests for an attached add-in program.
@ISERR(*cell_reference*)	Tests whether the argument results in ERR.
@ISNA(*cell_reference*)	Tests whether the argument results in NA.
@ISNUMBER(*cell_reference*)	Tests whether the argument is a number.
@ISSTRING(*cell_reference*)	Tests whether the argument is a string.
@TRUE	Returns the logical value 1, for true.

7

Creating Conditional Tests with @IF

The @IF function represents a powerful tool—one you can use both to manipulate text within your worksheets and to affect calculations. For example, you can use an @IF statement to test the condition "Is the inventory on-hand below 1,000 units?" and then return one value or label if the answer to the question is true, or another value or label if the answer is false. The @IF function uses the following syntax:

@IF(*condition,true,false*)

The @IF function can use six operators when testing conditions. The following list shows the operators and their corresponding descriptions:

>   Greater than

<   Less than

=   Equal to

>=   Greater than or equal to

<=   Less than or equal to

<>   Not equal to

In addition, you can perform more complex conditional tests by using @IF functions with logical operators that enable you to test multiple conditions in one @IF function. These complex operators and their descriptions are summarized in the following list:

#AND#   Tests two conditions, both of which must be true in order for the entire test to be true.

#NOT#   Tests that a condition is *not* true.

#OR#   Tests two conditions; if either condition is true, the entire test condition is true.

The @IF function can be used to check whether a specified cell's content is between 4 and 10, whether a cell contains a specified text string, and whether a 1-2-3 date falls before or after the current date. The results of these tests depend on whether the condition evaluates as true or false.

7

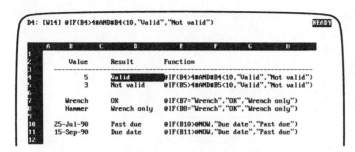

```
D4: [W14] @IF(B4>4#AND#B4<10,"Valid","Not valid")          READY

    A     B          C            D          E        F        G      H
 1
 2
 3       Value      Result       Function
         -------------------------------------------------------------
 4        5         Valid        @IF(B4>4#AND#B4<10,"Valid","Not valid")
 5        3         Not valid    @IF(B5>4#AND#B5<10,"Valid","Not valid")
 6
 7       Wrench     OK           @IF(B7="Wrench","OK","Wrench only")
 8       Hammer     Wrench only  @IF(B8="Wrench","OK","Wrench only")
 9
10       25-Jul-90  Past due     @IF(B10>@NOW,"Due date","Past due")
11       15-Sep-90  Due date     @IF(B11>@NOW,"Due date","Past due")
12
```

Examples of the @IF function test for specified values or labels.

Checking for Errors with @TRUE and @FALSE

You use the @TRUE and @FALSE functions to check for errors. Neither function requires arguments, but each is useful for providing documentation for formulas and advanced macro commands. The @TRUE function always returns the value 1—the logical value for true. The @FALSE function always returns the value 0—the logical value for false. These functions are commonly used in combination with functions requiring a logical value, such as the following @IF formula:

  @IF(B4>4#AND#B4<10,@TRUE,@FALSE)

This formula, similar to the formulas used in the previous example, returns the value of 1 (true) if cell B4 contains a value between 4 and 10; otherwise, a 0 (false) is returned.

Using String Functions

Another set of 1-2-3 functions includes the 19 string functions, which manipulate text. You can use string functions to repeat text characters (a handy trick for creating worksheet and row boundaries and visual borders), to convert letters in a string to uppercase or lowercase, to change strings into numbers, and to change numbers into strings. String functions also are important when you prepare 1-2-3 data to be used in other programs, such as word processing programs.

Included with the string functions are a few special functions for working with the Lotus International Character Set (LICS). The complete set of LICS characters, listed in the 1-2-3 documentation, includes everything from the copyright sign (©) to the lowercase *e* with the grave accent (è).

7

201

Table 7.7 summarizes the string functions available in 1-2-3. The sections that follow discuss the @LOWER, @UPPER, @PROPER, and @REPEAT string functions in more detail.

Table 7.7
String Functions

Function	Description
@CHAR(*number*)	Converts a code number into the corresponding LICS character.
@CLEAN(*string*)	Removes nonprintable characters from the specified string.
@CODE(*string*)	Returns the LICS code that corresponds to the first character of the specified string.
@EXACT(*string1, string2*)	Returns 1 (true) if arguments are exact matches; otherwise, returns 0 (false).
@FIND(*search_string, string, start_number*)	Locates the start position of one string within another string.
@LEFT(*string, number*)	Extracts the leftmost specified number of characters from the string.
@LENGTH(*string*)	Returns the number of characters in the string.
@LOWER(*string*)	Converts all characters in the string to lowercase.
@MID(*string, start_ number, number*)	Extracts a specified number of characters from the middle of another string, beginning at the specified starting position.
@N(*range*)	Returns as a value the contents of the cell in the upper left corner of a range.
@PROPER(*string*)	Converts the first character in each word of the string to uppercase, and the remaining characters in each word to lowercase.
@REPEAT(*string, number*)	Duplicates the string the specified number of times in a cell.
@REPLACE(*original_ string, start_number, number, new_string*)	Replaces a number of characters in the original string with new string characters, starting at the character identified by the start position.

7

Table 7.7—(continued)

Function	Description
@RIGHT(*string, number*)	Extracts the rightmost specified number of characters from the string.
@S(*range*)	Returns as a label the contents of the cell in the upper left corner of a range.
@STRING(*number, decimal_places*)	Converts a value to a string with the specified number of decimal places.
@TRIM(*string*)	Removes blank spaces from the string.
@UPPER(*string*)	Converts all characters in the string to uppercase.
@VALUE(*string*)	Converts the string to a value.

Strings are labels or portions of labels. Strings used within functions consist of characters enclosed in quotation marks, such as "Total". Some functions produce strings, but other functions produce numeric results. If a function's result is not of the data type you need, use the @STRING and @VALUE functions to convert a numeric value to a string, or a string to a numeric value.

Converting the Case of Strings with @LOWER, @UPPER, and @PROPER

1-2-3 offers three different functions for converting the case of a string value. The @LOWER and @UPPER functions convert all characters in the referenced string to lowercase or uppercase, respectively. The @PROPER function converts characters in the string to proper capitalization—with the first letter in uppercase and all remaining letters in lowercase. The general syntax of these functions is as follows:

@LOWER(*string*)
@UPPER(*string*)
@PROPER(*string*)

These three functions work with strings or references to strings. If a cell contains a number or is empty, 1-2-3 returns ERR for these functions.

7

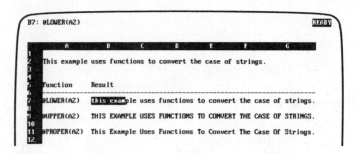

These functions convert the case of alphanumeric strings.

The text versions of the formulas appear in column A, and the formulas and their results are in column B.

You can use @LOWER, @UPPER, or @PROPER to modify the contents of a database so that all entries in a field appear with the same capitalization. This technique produces reports with a consistent appearance. To ensure that data with different capitalization is sorted correctly, create a column, using one of these functions that references the data, and then sort on this new column.

Repeating Strings with @REPEAT

The @REPEAT function repeats a string a specified number of times, much as the backslash (\) repeats strings to fill a single cell. But @REPEAT has some distinct advantages over the backslash. With @REPEAT, you can repeat the string the precise number of times you want. If the result is wider than the cell width, the result is displayed in empty adjacent cells to the right. @REPEAT uses the following syntax:

@REPEAT(*string,number*)

The *number* argument indicates the number of times you want to repeat a string in a cell. For example, if you want to repeat the string -**- 4 times, you can enter the following function:

@REPEAT("-**-",4)

The resulting string will appear as -**--**--**--**-.

204

Using Special Functions

1-2-3 provides a set of 11 special functions. You use these special tools to perform a variety of tasks. For example, 2 special functions return up to 10 different characteristics of a cell. Other special functions count the number of rows or columns in a range, enable you to trap worksheet errors, and use specified keys in the functions' arguments to look up values in tables or lists.

Table 7.8 lists 1-2-3's special functions. The sections that follow discuss the @ERR, @NA, @HLOOKUP, and @VLOOKUP commands.

Table 7.8
Special Functions

Function	Description
@@(*location*)	Returns the contents of the cell referenced in the specified location.
@CELL(*attribute,range*)	Returns an attribute of the cell in the upper left corner of the range.
@CELLPOINTER(*attribute*)	Returns an attribute of the current cell.
@CHOOSE(*offset,list*)	Locates in a list the entry specified by the offset number.
@COLS(*range*)	Counts the number of columns in a range.
@ERR	Displays ERR in the cell.
@HLOOKUP(*key,range, row_offset*)	Locates the number in a table and returns a value from that row of the range.
@INDEX(*range,column_offset, row_offset*)	Returns the contents of a cell specified by the intersection of a row and column within a range.
@NA	Displays NA in the cell.
@ROWS(*range*)	Counts the number of rows in a range.
@VLOOKUP(*key,range, column_offset*)	Locates the number in a lookup table and returns a value from that column of the range.

7

Trapping Errors with @ERR and @NA

When you create 1-2-3 applications, you may want to use @ERR or @NA to distinguish certain cell entries. Suppose, for example, that you are creating a checkbook-balancing worksheet in which checks with dollar amounts less than or equal to zero are unacceptable. One way to indicate that these checks are unacceptable is to use @ERR to signal that fact. You can use the following version of the @IF function:

    @IF(B9<=0,@ERR,B9)

This statement says, "If the amount in cell B9 is less than or equal to zero, then display ERR in that cell; otherwise, display the amount."

The @NA function can be used with a database containing inventory items to fill empty cells (or cells containing zeros) in a Number of Items column with NA. The @IF function can be used in this example also, as follows:

    @IF(C4=0,@NA,C4)

This statement says, "If the value in cell C4 is equal to zero, display NA in that cell; otherwise display the value."

Finding Table Entries with @HLOOKUP and @VLOOKUP

The @HLOOKUP and @VLOOKUP functions retrieve a string or value from a table, based on a specified key used to find the information. The operation and format of the two functions are essentially the same except that @HLOOKUP searches horizontal tables and @VLOOKUP searches vertical tables. These functions use the following syntax:

    @HLOOKUP(*key,range,row_offset*)
    @VLOOKUP(*key,range,column_offset*)

The *key* argument is the string or value that indicates the column (@HLOOKUP) or row (@VLOOKUP) to be searched. The key strings or values belong in the first column or row; numeric keys must be in ascending order for the functions to work properly. The range argument is the area that makes up the entire lookup table. The offset argument specifies from which row (@HLOOKUP) or column (@VLOOKUP) the data is to be retrieved. The offset

7

argument is always a number, ranging from 0 to the highest number of columns or rows in the lookup table.

The @HLOOKUP and @VLOOKUP functions are useful for finding any type of value you would have to look up manually in a table, such as a tax amount, shipping zones, or interest charges.

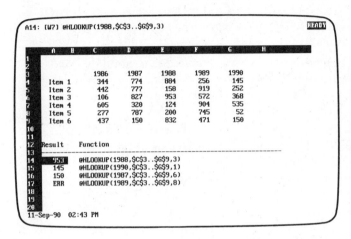

The @HLOOKUP function retrieves values from a table.

Summary

This chapter described the functions that 1-2-3 provides to make formula and worksheet construction easier and, usually, more error-free. After you become accustomed to using these functions, you can use them regularly in your worksheets. The tables of this chapter can be used as a reference for the types of functions available, their syntax, and the types of arguments they require.

Specifically, you learned the following key information about 1-2-3:

- 1-2-3 includes 92 built-in functions for use with 8 different types of applications. These functions perform a variety of powerful calculations that save the user much time when building worksheets.

- 1-2-3 functions are entered by typing the @ symbol, followed by the function name and any required arguments within parentheses. Press Enter to complete the process.

207

- The mathematical and trigonometric functions perform standard arithmetic operations, such as computing the integer with @INT and rounding numbers with @ROUND.

- The date and time functions convert dates and times to serial numbers, which can then be formatted as dates and used in sorting and arithmetic calculations. Examples include @DATE and @DATEVALUE, which convert date values and date strings to serial numbers; and the @NOW function, which can be used to datestamp a worksheet or report.

- The financial functions calculate cash flows, loans, annuities, and asset depreciation. The @PMT function calculates loan payments, while the @PV and @FV functions calculate present and future values, respectively.

- The statistical functions perform standard statistical calculations on lists. For example, @AVG calculates the average of values in a list, @COUNT counts the total number of entries in a list, and @MAX and @MIN find the maximum and minimum values in a list, respectively.

- The database functions are similar to the statistical functions, but are used to perform calculations and queries on databases.

- The logical functions test whether a condition is true or false. The @IF function returns a different value or label depending on the outcome of a specified condition. The @TRUE and @FALSE functions can be used in conditional tests to automatically display a 1 (true) or a 0 (false).

- The string functions, which include the LICS (Lotus International Character Set) functions, can be used to manipulate text. For example, the @LOWER, @UPPER, and @PROPER functions can be used to convert the case of a specified label. The @REPEAT function repeats a string a specified number of times.

- The special functions are used to perform a variety of worksheet tasks. The @ERR and @NA functions trap errors or distinguish certain cell entries. The @HLOOKUP and @VLOOKUP functions return values from a specified row and column of a table.

In the next chapter, you learn how to print reports created in 1-2-3. The various options available for enhancing reports are also discussed.

Printing Reports

1-2-3 is a powerful tool for developing information presented in a column-and-row format. You can enter and edit your worksheet and database files on-screen as well as store the input on disk. To make good use of your data, however, you often need it in printed form—such as a target production schedule, a summary report to your supervisor, or a detailed reorder list to central stores.

Using 1-2-3's /Print command, you can access different options to meet your printing needs. You can elect to write directly from 1-2-3 to the printer by using the /Print Printer command sequence. Or you can use the alternative /Print File *filename* sequence to create a print file on disk. Later, you can produce a printout of the file from within 1-2-3 or from DOS, or you can incorporate the file into a word processing file.

You can use the add-in program Allways (available only with 1-2-3 Release 2.2) to take advantage of presentation-quality printing features not found in the standard 1-2-3 /Print commands. Allways is the subject of the next chapter.

Key Terms in This Chapter

Print defaults	Preset, standard specifications for a 1-2-3 print job.
Borders	One or more rows and/or columns of data and/or labels that are repeated on a multiple-page report.
Header	Information displayed on one line at the top of a page. A header may include a date and a page number.
Footer	Information displayed on one line at the bottom of a page. A footer may include a date and a page number.

To make this chapter effective for learning the basics of printing, and not just a complex series of options, several things are assumed: (1) that you have not modified 1-2-3's preset printing defaults; (2) that you need to produce reports on 8 1/2-by-11-inch paper; and (3) that you want to use basic report-enhancement techniques such as hiding columns and rows, adding headers and footers, and repeating column and row headings. If you want to modify 1-2-3's default settings, consult Que's *Using 1-2-3 Release 2.2*, Special Edition.

8

Selecting /Print Printer or /Print File

Every print command in 1-2-3 starts from the /**Print** option of the main menu.

To begin a /**Print** command, you must select either **Printer** or **File**.

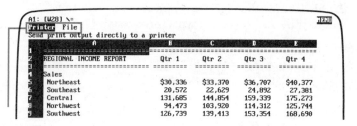

To print directly to a printer, select **Printer**. To create a print file on disk, choose the **File** option; later you can print the file from within 1-2-3 or incorporate it into a word processing file.

If you choose **File**, respond to the prompt for a print-file name by typing a name that is up to eight characters long. A file extension is not necessary because 1-2-3 will automatically assign the PRN (print file) extension.

You can incorporate a PRN file back into a 1-2-3 worksheet by using the /File Import command. The file, however, will not be the same as your original worksheet file because imported PRN files are long labels. You can view a PRN file by using the DOS command TYPE.

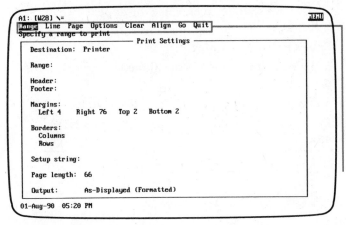

After you select either **Printer** or **File**, the second line of the control panel displays the main Print menu.

A Print Settings sheet is displayed whenever you choose /**Print Printer** or /**Print File**. (The settings sheet is not shown in versions prior to Release 2.2.) To see the worksheet instead of the settings sheet, press the Window (F6) key. Every time you press F6, the screen switches from one type of screen presentation to the other.

In any /**Print** command sequence, you start with /**Print**, branch to either **Printer** or **File** *filename*, and proceed to a common main Print menu. Table 8.1 gives you an overview of the various options on the main Print menu. Regardless of which branch you select, you must choose **Range** and specify a range to print, select **Go**, and then select **Quit** to return to the worksheet. All other selections are optional.

Table 8.1
Options on the Main Print Menu

Menu selection	Description
Range	Indicates what section of the worksheet is to be printed or saved to disk as a print file.
Line	Adjusts the paper line-by-line in the printer.
Page	Adjusts the paper page-by-page in the printer.
Options	Establishes settings to enhance the appearance of the printout.
Clear	Erases previous settings.
Align	Signals that the printer is positioned at the top of the print page.
Go	Starts printing to the printer or a disk file.
Quit	Exits the Print menu and returns 1-2-3 to READY mode.

Printing Draft-Quality Reports

8

Printing doesn't have to be an arduous process. With 1-2-3 you can print quick reports by issuing a few simple commands. In this section, you learn a variety of printing techniques. Specifically, you learn to print a full screen of data, to print a draft-quality report of one page or less, and to print a multipage report with borders.

Printing a Full Screen of Data

Before you print any portion of a 1-2-3 worksheet, decide whether the output must be suitable for distribution or whether all you need is a copy of the screen's contents. If a copy of what you see on-screen is sufficient, send the data to the printer by pressing Shift-PrtSc, or by pressing Print Screen on an enhanced keyboard.

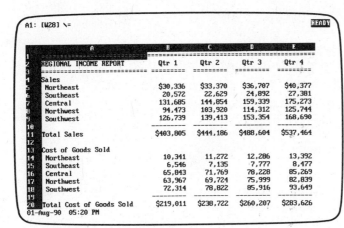

```
A1: [W28] \=                                              READY

         A                  B         C         D         E
1  ================================================================
2  REGIONAL INCOME REPORT    Qtr 1     Qtr 2     Qtr 3     Qtr 4
3  ================================================================
4  Sales
5    Northeast             $30,336   $33,370   $36,707   $40,377
6    Southeast              20,572    22,629    24,892    27,381
7    Central               131,685   144,854   159,339   175,273
8    Northwest              94,473   103,920   114,312   125,744
9    Southwest             126,739   139,413   153,354   168,690
10                        ---------  --------- --------- ---------
11 Total Sales            $403,805  $444,186  $488,604  $537,464
12
13 Cost of Goods Sold
14   Northeast              10,341    11,272    12,286    13,392
15   Southeast               6,546     7,135     7,777     8,477
16   Central                65,843    71,769    78,228    85,269
17   Northwest              63,967    69,724    75,999    82,839
18   Southwest              72,314    78,822    85,916    93,649
19                        ---------  --------- --------- ---------
20 Total Cost of Goods Sold $219,011 $238,722 $260,207 $283,626
01-Aug-90  05:20 PM
```

Suppose that you want a quick printout of the portion of the worksheet you see on-screen.

```
A1: [W28] \=                                              READY

         A                  B         C         D         E
1  ================================================================
2  REGIONAL INCOME REPORT    Qtr 1     Qtr 2     Qtr 3     Qtr 4
3  ================================================================
4  Sales
5    Northeast             $30,336   $33,370   $36,707   $40,377
6    Southeast              20,572    22,629    24,892    27,381
7    Central               131,685   144,854   159,339   175,273
8    Northwest              94,473   103,920   114,312   125,744
9    Southwest             126,739   139,413   153,354   168,690
10                        ---------  --------- --------- ---------
11 Total Sales            $403,805  $444,186  $488,604  $537,464
12
13 Cost of Goods Sold
14   Northeast              10,341    11,272    12,286    13,392
15   Southeast               6,546     7,135     7,777     8,477
16   Central                65,843    71,769    78,228    85,269
17   Northwest              63,967    69,724    75,999    82,839
18   Southwest              72,314    78,822    85,916    93,649
19                        ---------  --------- --------- ---------
20 Total Cost of Goods Sold $219,011 $238,722 $260,207 $283,626
03-Aug-90  09:05 AM                              NUM
```

Press Shift-PrtSc (Print Screen on an enhanced keyboard) to begin printing.

The resulting printout captures everything on the screen, including contents of the highlighted cell and the mode indicator.

A "snapshot" printout may be adequate for some interoffice memos and, because the printout captures the date and time display, for documenting worksheet construction.

8

213

Printing a One-Page Report

If you don't change any of the default print settings, and you haven't entered other print settings during the current worksheet session, printing one page or less involves only a few steps:

1. Choose to print to the printer or file.
2. Highlight the range to be printed.
3. Choose the command to begin printing.

Two other steps may be necessary if another person uses your copy of 1-2-3, and either changes the default settings or enters new settings in the Print menu. First, you can check the default settings by selecting /**Worksheet Global Default Status**. A quick review of the top left section of the Global Status screen will show you whether the printer and page layout settings are the ones you need. Second, you can clear any settings that may have been entered by another user by selecting /**Print Printer Clear All** (covered in a later section of this chapter).

If you are certain that all default settings are correct and no other settings have been entered into the Print commands, you can print a draft-quality report of one page or less by completing the following steps:

1. Check that your printer is on-line and that your paper is positioned properly.
2. Call up the 1-2-3 menu by pressing ⌊/⌋.
3. Select **Print** by pressing ⌊P⌋.
4. Select **Printer** by pressing ⌊P⌋.

1-2-3 displays a Print Settings sheet along with the main Print menu.

```
A1: [W28] \=                                                    MENU
Range Line Page Options Clear Align Go Quit
Specify a range to print
                    ─────────── Print Settings ───────────
  Destination:  Printer

  Range:

  Header:
  Footer:

  Margins:
    Left 4     Right 76    Top 2    Bottom 2

  Borders:
    Columns
    Rows

  Setup string:

  Page length:  66

  Output:       As-Displayed (Formatted)

01-Aug-90  05:22 PM
```

214

(Note that the settings sheet is not displayed in versions prior to Release 2.2.) If you want to see the worksheet instead of the settings sheet, press `F6`.

5. Select **R**ange by pressing `R` to select a range to be printed from the worksheet.

6. Indicate what part of the worksheet you want to print by high-lighting the area; then press `↵Enter`.

   You can use the `PgUp`, `PgDn`, and `End` keys to designate ranges when you print. If you want to designate a range that includes the *entire* active area of the worksheet, move the cell pointer to the top left corner of the active area by pressing `Home`. Then anchor the range by pressing `.` and move the cell pointer to the lower right corner of the active area by pressing the `End` `Home` key combination.

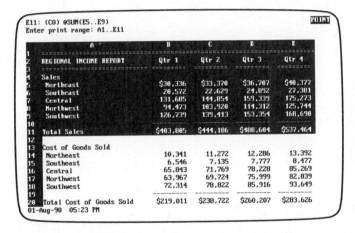

In this example, highlight the range A1..E11 as the range to be printed; then press `↵Enter`.

7. After you highlight the exact range you want to print, select **A**lign by pressing `A`.

   Choosing **A**lign ensures that printing will begin at the top of all successive pages after the first. Before printing, always make sure that your printer paper is correctly positioned.

8. To begin printing, select **G**o by pressing `G`.

The Go option
on the main Print
menu sends your
worksheet data
to the printer.

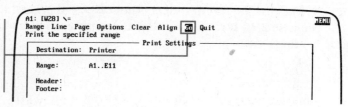

9. After printing is completed, select **Page** by pressing Ⓟ to advance
to the top of the next page.

10. Select **Quit** by pressing Ⓠ.

This is an ex-
ample of a draft-
quality report of
less than one
page, printed
with the default
settings.

```
===================================================================================
REGIONAL INCOME REPORT          Qtr 1      Qtr 2      Qtr 3      Qtr 4
===================================================================================
Sales
  Northeast                   $30,336    $33,370    $36,707    $40,377
  Southeast                    20,572     22,629     24,892     27,381
  Central                     131,685    144,854    159,339    175,273
  Northwest                    94,473    103,920    114,312    125,744
  Southwest                   126,739    139,413    153,354    168,690
                             ---------  ---------  ---------  ---------
Total Sales                  $403,805   $444,186   $488,604   $537,464
```

8

If you accidentally press Enter after you have already used the Go option, the file will print a second time. If this occurs, you can stop printing by pressing Ctrl-Break.

Even if the area of your worksheet has more rows and columns than can be printed on one page, you still can use the basic steps for printing reports on one page or less. Setting the print range so that a new page begins exactly where you want it to begin can sometimes be a bit tricky. Also, if you want to print a section of a large worksheet, you may need to use the /**Print Printer Options Borders** command so that certain labels are repeated on each page. This command is discussed in the following section.

Printing Two or More Pages with Borders

If you want information to be printed on pages correctly, remember that 1-2-3 treats numeric and text data differently when splitting data from one page to the next. Numbers are printed completely because they can span only one cell. Text, however, such as long labels that lie across several cells, may be split in awkward places from one page to the next.

When printing two or more pages, you can repeat certain columns or rows on each printed page. In 1-2-3, the repeated columns and rows are called *borders*.

To repeat column and/or row borders on each page when printing, follow these steps:

1. Call up the 1-2-3 menu by pressing ⌊/⌋.

2. Select **Print** by pressing ⌊P⌋.

3. Select **Printer** by pressing ⌊P⌋.

4. Select **Options** by pressing ⌊O⌋.

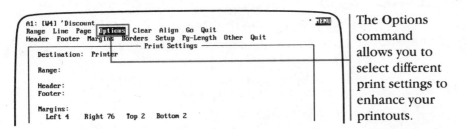

The **Options** command allows you to select different print settings to enhance your printouts.

8

217

5. Select **B**orders by pressing Ⓑ.

The Borders com-
mand enables
you to select row
and/or column
borders to repeat
on each page of
the printout.

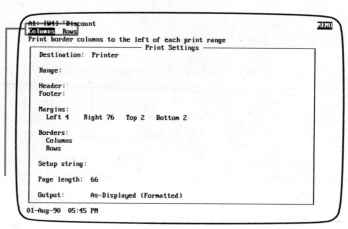

1-2-3 asks
whether the
labels are located
down one or
more columns or
across one or
more rows.

6. Select either **C**olumns by pressing Ⓒ or **R**ows by pressing Ⓡ.

Suppose that you want to print a report on two or more pages and
repeat labels displayed in a column. To do this, select Columns
after choosing Options Borders. To print a report on two or more
pages and repeat labels that are displayed across a row, select **R**ows
after choosing Options Borders.

In this example, select Columns by pressing Ⓒ.

After you choose Columns, the prompt `Enter range for
border columns:` appears.

7. Indicate which rows or columns you want printed on each page by
highlighting the rows or columns; then press `⏎Enter`.

218

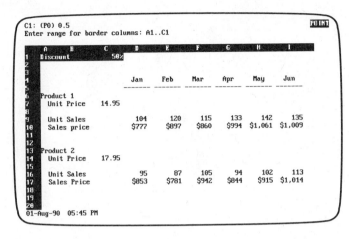

In this example, highlight the range A1..C1 (for columns A through C to appear as a border) and press ⏎Enter .

8. To return to the main Print menu, select **Q**uit by pressing Q .

9. To choose the range to print, select **R**ange by pressing R .

10. Highlight the desired print range, *excluding* those columns or rows you entered using the **O**ptions **B**orders command from the Print menu; then press ⏎Enter .

    Note: You should *not* include the borders you want repeated on each page in your actual print range. 1-2-3 automatically prints the borders on every page of the printout. If you *do* include the borders in the print range, 1-2-3 will print them *twice* on each page.

8

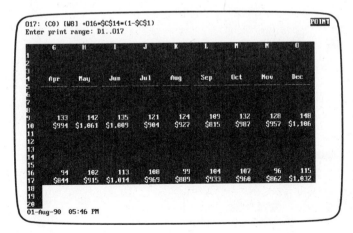

In this example, highlight the range to print as D1..O17 and press ⏎Enter . Note that this range does not include the columns just specified as borders.

219

11. Select **Align** by pressing A.

12. Select **Go** by pressing G.

13. After printing is completed, select **Page** by pressing P to advance to the top of the next page.

14. Select **Quit** by pressing Q.

This is the first page of a two-page report that has column borders repeated on each page.

```
Discount          50%

                         Jan      Feb      Mar      Apr      May      Jun
                        -------  -------  -------  -------  -------  -------
Product 1
   Unit Price   14.95

   Unit Sales            104      120      115      133      142      135
   Sales price          $777     $897     $860     $994   $1,061   $1,009

Product 2
   Unit Price   17.95

   Unit Sales             95       87      105       94      102      113
   Sales Price          $853     $781     $942     $844     $915   $1,014
```

8

220

```
Discount          50%

                   Jul      Aug      Sep      Oct      Nov      Dec
                 -------  -------  -------  -------  -------  -------
Product 1
  Unit Price    14.95

  Unit Sales       121      124      109      132      128      148
  Sales price     $904     $927     $815     $987     $957   $1,106


Product 2
  Unit Price    17.95

  Unit Sales       108       99      104      107       96      115
  Sales Price     $969     $889     $933     $960     $862   $1,032
```

This is the second page of the report with borders.

8

Excluding Segments within a Designated Print Range

Because the /**Print** commands require that you specify a range to print, you can print only rectangular blocks from the worksheet. Nevertheless, you can suppress the display of cell contents within the range. You can hide entire rows or columns, or you can remove from view a segment that spans only part of a row or a column. Whether you want to hide a column (or range) of sensitive financial information or want to compress the worksheet so that the most important data fits on a one-page report, you can use 1-2-3 to prevent certain data from printing.

Excluding Columns

As you learned in Chapter 5, you can use 1-2-3's /Worksheet Column Hide command to mark columns you don't want to display on-screen. If these marked columns are included in a print range, they will not appear on the printout as long as the /Print Printer Options Other setting is As-Displayed (discussed in a later section of this chapter).

To print a worksheet range and exclude one or more columns within that range, follow these steps:

1. Call up the 1-2-3 menu by pressing /.
2. Select **Worksheet** by pressing W.
3. Select **Column** by pressing C.
4. Select **Hide** by pressing H.
5. When the prompt `Specify column to hide:` appears, highlight the column or columns you want to hide; then press Enter.

8

In this example, move the cell pointer to column E (the column to be hidden) and press Enter.

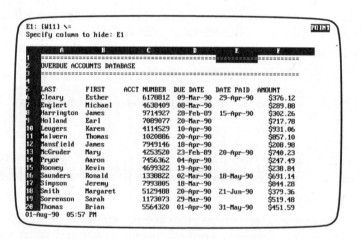

6. To begin printing the range with the hidden column, first call up the 1-2-3 menu by pressing ⟨/⟩.

7. Select **P**rint by pressing ⟨P⟩.

8. Select **P**rinter by pressing ⟨P⟩.

9. To assign the range to print, select **R**ange by pressing ⟨R⟩.

10. Highlight the range you want to print; then press ⟨⏎Enter⟩.

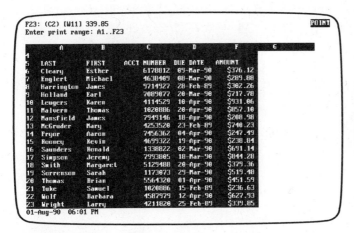

In this example, highlight the range to print as A1..F23 and press ⟨⏎Enter⟩.

11. Select **A**lign by pressing ⟨A⟩.

12. To begin printing, select **G**o by pressing ⟨G⟩.

13. After printing is completed, select **P**age by pressing ⟨P⟩ to advance to the top of the next page.

14. Select **Q**uit by pressing ⟨Q⟩.

8

The printed report excludes the information from the hidden column.

```
===============================================================
OVERDUE ACCOUNTS DATABASE
===============================================================

LAST         FIRST      ACCT NUMBER  DUE DATE    AMOUNT
Cleary       Esther        6178812   09-Mar-90   $376.12
Englert      Michael       4638409   08-Mar-90   $289.88
Harrington   James         9714927   28-Feb-89   $302.26
Holland      Earl          7089077   20-Mar-90   $717.78
Leugers      Karen         4114529   10-Apr-90   $931.06
Malvern      Thomas        1020886   20-Apr-90   $857.10
Mansfield    James         7949146   18-Apr-90   $208.98
McGruder     Mary          4253520   23-Feb-89   $740.23
Pryor        Aaron         7456362   04-Apr-90   $247.49
Rooney       Kevin         4699322   19-Apr-90   $238.84
Saunders     Ronald        1338822   02-Mar-90   $691.14
Simpson      Jeremy        7993805   18-Mar-90   $844.28
Smith        Margaret      5129488   20-Apr-90   $379.36
Sorrenson    Sarah         1173073   29-Mar-90   $519.48
Thomas       Brian         5564320   01-Apr-90   $451.59
Tuke         Samuel        1020886   15-Feb-89   $236.63
Wolf         Barbara       4587979   12-Apr-90   $627.93
Wright       Larry         4211820   25-Feb-89   $339.85
```

Note: To restore hidden columns, select /**Worksheet Column Display**. When the hidden columns (marked with an asterisk) reappear on-screen, you can specify which column or columns to display.

Excluding Rows

To prevent specific rows of the worksheet from printing, you must mark these rows with a symbol for nonprinting. You enter the symbol for nonprinting by typing two vertical bars (¦¦) in the first column of the print range in each row to be excluded.

Only one of the vertical bars appears on-screen, and neither vertical bar appears on the printout. If the row you want to exclude contains data in the first column of the print range, you must insert a new column in which to place the vertical bars. The column with the vertical bars must be the first column of the print range. To avoid alignment problems when inserting a new column for the vertical bars, you can use /Worksheet Column Hide to suppress printing of that column after the print range has already been specified.

To print a worksheet range and suppress one or more rows within that range, follow these steps:

1. Highlight the row to be suppressed from the printout—in the first column of the print range.

   Note: If the first cells in the rows to be marked for omission already contain data, use the /Worksheet Insert Column command to insert a new blank column into your worksheet at column A.

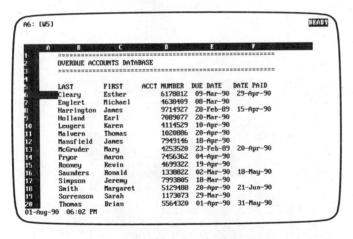

Highlight row 6, which is the first row to be suppressed from the printout.

2. Type ⊡⊡, the symbol for nonprinting, and press ⏎Enter.

8

225

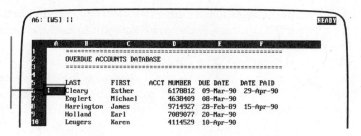

The symbol for nonprinting appears as a single bar in the worksheet.

3. Repeat steps 1 and 2 until all rows to be suppressed from the printout have been marked with two vertical bars.

4. To select the range to print, call up the 1-2-3 menu by pressing ⌨/.

5. Select **P**rint by pressing ⌨P.

6. Select **P**rinter by pressing ⌨P.

7. Select **R**ange by pressing ⌨R.

8. Highlight the range you want to print and press ⌨Enter. You *must* include the column with the vertical bars as the *first* column in the print range.

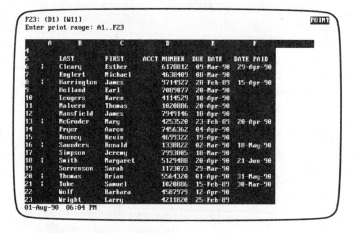

In this example, highlight the range to print as A1..F23 and press ⌨Enter.

9. If you have inserted a new column for the vertical bars, hide the column to avoid alignment problems in your printout. To do this, select **Q**uit from the Print menu, highlight the new column, select /**W**orksheet **C**olumn **H**ide, and press ⌨Enter. Then select /**P**rint **P**rinter to access the Print menu again, and continue with the next step.

226

In this example, you must hide column A before printing to avoid alignment problems. 1-2-3 will still suppress the marked rows, even though the symbols for nonprinting are not visible on-screen.

10. Select **Align** by pressing Ⓐ.

11. To begin printing, select **Go** by pressing Ⓖ.

12. After printing is completed, select **Page** by pressing Ⓟ.

13. Select **Quit** by pressing Ⓠ.

```
===========================================================
OVERDUE ACCOUNTS DATABASE
===========================================================

LAST         FIRST      ACCT NUMBER  DUE DATE   DATE PAID  AMOUNT
Englert      Michael         4638409 08-Mar-90             $289.88
Holland      Earl            7089077 20-Mar-90             $717.78
Leugers      Karen           4114529 10-Apr-90             $931.06
Malvern      Thomas          1020886 20-Apr-90             $857.10
Mansfield    James           7949146 18-Apr-90             $208.98
Pryor        Aaron           7456362 04-Apr-90             $247.49
Rooney       Kevin           4699322 19-Apr-90             $238.84
Simpson      Jeremy          7993805 18-Mar-90             $844.28
Sorrenson    Sarah           1173073 29-Mar-90             $519.48
Wolf         Barbara         4587979 12-Apr-90             $627.93
Wright       Larry           4211820 25-Feb-89             $339.85
```

Rows marked with two vertical bars in the first column of the print range do not appear in the printed output.

8

227

To restore the worksheet after you finish printing, remove the vertical bars from the leftmost cells of the marked rows. If a column was inserted for the vertical bars, display the column again, if necessary, with /Worksheet Column Display, and then delete the column with /Worksheet Column Delete.

Excluding Ranges

If you want to hide only part of a row or column, or an area that partially spans one or more rows and columns, use the /Range Format Hidden command to mark the range.

To exclude a worksheet range from a printout, follow these steps:

1. Call up the 1-2-3 menu by pressing ⧸.
2. Select **Range** by pressing ⓡ.
3. Select **Format** by pressing ⓕ.
4. Select **Hidden** by pressing ⓗ.
5. Specify the range you want to hide by highlighting the range and pressing ⏎Enter.

In this example, highlight the range to hide as A6..B23 and press ⏎Enter.

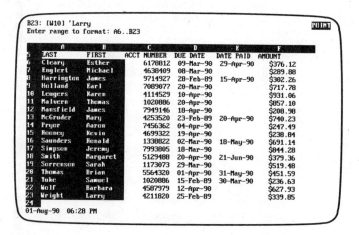

6. To select the range to print, call up the 1-2-3 menu by pressing ⧸.
7. Select **Print** by pressing ⓟ.
8. Select **Printer** by pressing ⓟ.
9. Select **Range** by pressing ⓡ.

228

10. Highlight the range you want to print and press ⏎Enter. Be sure to include the hidden range within the range to be printed.

11. Select **A**lign by pressing Ⓐ.

12. To begin printing, select **G**o by pressing Ⓖ.

13. After printing is completed, select **P**age by pressing Ⓟ.

14. Select **Q**uit by pressing Ⓠ.

```
===============================================================
OVERDUE ACCOUNTS DATABASE
===============================================================

LAST        FIRST      ACCT NUMBER  DUE DATE   DATE PAID  AMOUNT
                            6178812  09-Mar-90  29-Apr-90  $376.12
                            4638409  08-Mar-90             $289.88
                            9714927  28-Feb-89  15-Apr-90  $302.26
                            7089077  20-Mar-90             $717.78
                            4114529  10-Apr-90             $931.06
                            1020886  20-Apr-90             $857.10
                            7949146  18-Apr-90             $208.98
                            4253520  23-Feb-89  20-Apr-90  $740.23
                            7456362  04-Apr-90             $247.49
                            4699322  19-Apr-90             $238.84
                            1338822  02-Mar-90  18-May-90  $691.14
                            7993805  18-Mar-90             $844.28
                            5129488  20-Apr-90  21-Jun-90  $379.36
                            1173073  29-Mar-90             $519.48
                            5564320  01-Apr-90  31-May-90  $451.59
                            1020886  15-Feb-89  30-Mar-90  $236.63
                            4587979  12-Apr-90             $627.93
                            4211820  25-Feb-89             $339.85
```

The range that was hidden with /**R**ange **F**ormat **H**ide is suppressed from the printout.

8

After you finish printing, restore the hidden range to the global format with the /**R**ange **F**ormat **R**eset command.

If you find yourself repeating print operations (hiding the same columns, suppressing and then restoring the same documentation, and so forth), remember that you can save time and minimize frustration by developing and using print macros. Chapter 14 explains the basics about macros; for more detailed information, see Chapters 13 and 14 of *Using 1-2-3 Release 2.2*, Special Edition.

Controlling Paper Movement

With 1-2-3, if you print a one-page report containing fewer lines than the default page length, the printer will *not* automatically advance the paper to the top of the next page. Instead, the next print operation will begin wherever the preceding operation ended. Similarly, if you print a report with more than one page (containing more lines than the default page length), 1-2-3 will automatically insert page breaks in the document between pages, but the paper will not advance to the top of the next page after 1-2-3 has printed the last page.

You can control movement of the paper in your printer from within 1-2-3. You can specify the "top" of a page in any paper position, advance the paper by line or by page, and insert page breaks exactly where you want them.

Using the Line, Page, and Align Options

If you are using continuous-feed paper, position the paper so that the print head is at the top of the page, and then turn on the printer. If your printer is already on, turn it off and then on again. Do not advance the paper manually once the printer is on. Because 1-2-3 coordinates a line counter with the current page-length setting, any lines you advance manually are not counted, and page breaks will crop up in strange places.

You control the movement of the paper in your printer with the Line, **Page**, and Align options.

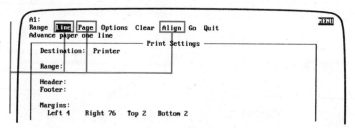

The **Line** option of the Print menu advances the paper one line at a time, and the **Page** option advances the paper one complete page a time. You use the **Align** option to set the beginning of a page.

If you want to advance the paper one line at a time (to separate several small printed ranges that fit on one page, for example), issue the **/Print Printer Line** command. This command sequence will cause the printer to skip a line.

To advance the paper one line at a time, follow these steps:

1. Call up the 1-2-3 menu by pressing /.
2. Select **Print** by pressing P.
3. Select **Printer** by pressing P.
4. Select **Line** by pressing L.

If you want to advance to a new page after printing less than a full page, select **/Print Printer Page**. Whenever you issue this command, the printer will skip to a new page. (Note that the following section shows how you can embed in the print range a page-break symbol that instructs 1-2-3 to advance automatically.)

To advance to a new page after printing less than a full page, follow these steps:

1. Call up the 1-2-3 menu by pressing /.
2. Select **Print** by pressing P.
3. Select **Printer** by pressing P.
4. Select **Page** by pressing P.

Use the **/Print Printer Align** command when the paper perforation and the print head are aligned to establish (or reestablish) correct page breaks. Whenever you begin a print job at the top of a page, always select **Align** before printing.

To align the printer and set the beginning of a page, follow these steps:

1. Call up the 1-2-3 menu by pressing /.
2. Select **Print** by pressing P.
3. Select **Printer** by pressing P.
4. Select **Align** by pressing A.

8

Setting Page Breaks within the Worksheet

As discussed in Chapter 5, page breaks are inserted into the worksheet with the /Worksheet **Page** command. This command should be executed with the cell pointer at the first column of the range to be printed—in the row that should begin the new page. The command automatically inserts a new blank row containing a page-break symbol (|::) in the cell where the cell pointer is located.

An alternative to using /Worksheet **Page** is to add page breaks to your document manually. To do this, insert a blank row into your worksheet where you want a page break, and then type a page-break symbol (|::) into a blank cell in the first column of the print range in that row. The contents of cells in any row marked by the page-break symbol will not print.

When you print the range containing the page-break symbol, 1-2-3 will automatically advance the paper at that point. 1-2-3 will then begin to print the data *after* the page-break symbol on a new page.

Note: Exercise caution when entering page breaks into the worksheet, either manually or with the /Worksheet **Page** command, because you can accidentally delete the wrong row after you finish printing. You can avoid accidents by typing the page-break symbol into the first column in the print range of a row that is already blank in your worksheet. First check to be sure that the row is blank by using the End key and the arrow keys to scan across the row.

8

Enhancing Reports with Print Options

If you are preparing a report for distribution to others, you can add some simple enhancements. For example, you can add headers and footers, or you can change the page layout by adjusting the margins and page length.

Adding Headers and Footers

1-2-3 reserves three lines in a document for a header and an additional three lines for a footer. If specified, headers and footers appear at the top and bottom, respectively, of each page on your printed output. You can either retain the six lines reserved for these options (regardless of whether you use them) or eliminate all six lines by selecting the /Print **Printer** Options **Other** Unformatted command (illustrated later in this chapter).

The **Header** and **Footer** options, accessed from the /Print Printer Options menu, let you specify up to 240 characters of text within one line of your printed output. The header and footer can be positioned at the left, right, or center of the page. The number of characters in the header and footer lines, however, is limited by the size of both the paper and the printed characters. For example, when printing on 8 1/2-by-11-inch paper with 1/2-inch margins and 10 characters per inch type, only 75 characters can be printed in the header and footer.

The header text, which is printed on the first line after any blank top margin lines, is followed by two blank header lines (for spacing). The footer text line is printed above any blank bottom margin lines and below two blank footer lines (for spacing).

Although you can manually enter all features of the text, 1-2-3 provides special characters for controlling page numbers, the current date, and the positioning of text within a header or footer. The following list gives you an overview of the characters that are used to place page numbers and dates in headers, and to set the alignment of the header.

Character	*Function*
#	Automatically prints consecutive page numbers, starting with 1.
@	Automatically prints the current date.
¦	Automatically separates text. Absence of a ¦ symbol left-justifies all text. The first ¦ symbol centers the text that follows. The second ¦ symbol left-justifies remaining text.

To add a header or footer, follow these steps:

1. Call up the 1-2-3 menu by pressing /.
2. Select **Print** by pressing P.
3. Select **Printer** by pressing P.
4. Select **Range** by pressing R. Then highlight the desired print range and press Enter.

   For example, highlight the range A1..E11 and press Enter.
5. Select **Options** by pressing O.
6. Select **Header** by pressing H or select **Footer** by pressing F.

For example, se-
lect **Header** by
pressing $\boxed{\text{H}}$ to
add a header to
the report.

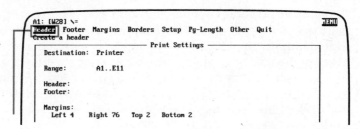

7. When the prompt `Enter header:` or `Enter footer:` appears, type the text and/or codes for date and page number; then press $\boxed{\text{↵Enter}}$.

For example,
type the text
**@¦NATIONAL
MICRO¦#** and
press $\boxed{\text{↵Enter}}$.

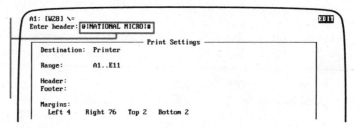

8

@ ¦NATIONAL MICRO¦

The $\boxed{\text{@}}$ sign tells 1-2-3
to include the date in
your header (or footer).
Make sure that your
computer is set to the
correct date.

The $\boxed{\text{¦}}$ symbol tells
1-2-3 how to align the
different items within
the header (or footer)
line.

The $\boxed{\text{#}}$ symbol tells
1-2-3 to print a page
number.

8. To return to the main Print menu, select **Quit** by pressing $\boxed{\text{Q}}$.

9. Select **Align** by pressing $\boxed{\text{A}}$ to signal the top of the page to the printer (if necessary).

10. Select **Go** by pressing $\boxed{\text{G}}$.

11. After printing is completed, select **Page** by pressing $\boxed{\text{P}}$.

12. Select Quit by pressing $\boxed{\text{Q}}$.

```
03-Aug-90              NATIONAL MICRO                    1

================================================================
REGIONAL INCOME REPORT     Qtr 1     Qtr 2     Qtr 3     Qtr 4
================================================================
Sales
  Northeast              $30,336   $33,370   $36,707   $40,377
  Southeast               20,572    22,629    24,892    27,381
  Central                131,685   144,854   159,339   175,273
  Northwest               94,473   103,920   114,312   125,744
  Southwest              126,739   139,413   153,354   168,690
                        --------- --------- --------- ---------
  Total Sales           $403,805  $444,186  $488,604  $537,464
```

The header
appears at the top
of the printed
report.

1-2-3, to a limited extent, can insert the contents of a cell into a header or footer (this feature is not available in versions prior to Release 2.2). When the prompt to enter a header or footer appears, use the backslash character (\) followed by a cell address or existing range name. Your printed output will contain that cell's contents in the header or footer. You cannot, however, use this capability effectively along with the segmentation of a header or footer into left, center, and right portions.

Note the effect of using an address in the following header lines. Each entry is typed after the prompt Enter header:.

8

235

Entry	Result
\A1	Prints the contents of cell A1 left-justified.
¦\A1	Prints the string \a1 (not the contents of cell A1) centered within the header.
@¦\A1	Prints the date left-justified and the string \a1 (not the contents of cell A1) centered.
\A3..A6	Prints the contents of cell A3 only, not the range A3..A6.
\SALES	Prints the contents of the range named SALES, if it exists; otherwise, prints nothing in the header.

Whenever the print range exceeds one single page, the header is reproduced on each succeeding page, and the page number increases by one. If you have used the special page-number character (#) and want to print your report a second time before you leave the Print menu, reset the page counter and set the top of the form by selecting **Align** before you choose **Go**.

If you have specified a header line, but the centered or right-justified text doesn't print, make sure that the right-margin setting (discussed in the next section) is appropriate for the current type size and paper width. To change the header, repeat the sequence to establish the text, press Esc to remove the display of the existing header from the control panel, and press Enter. (You can delete a header or footer without removing other specified options.)

To print a footer on the last page of a report (or on a single-page report), you must use the **Page** command at the end of the printing session. If you select the **Quit** command from the main Print menu without issuing the **Page** command, this final footer will not print. You can, however, reissue the **/Print Printer** command and select **Page**; in this case, the footer will still print.

Changing the Page Layout

Before you change the page layout defaults, be aware of the current settings. 1-2-3 initially assumes 8 1/2-by-11-inch paper and a printer output of 6 lines per inch; the default length of a page is 66 lines. 1-2-3 reserves 2 lines at the top and bottom of each page for the top and bottom margins. Also, 1-2-3 automatically reserves 3 lines at the top and 3 lines at the bottom for headers and footers (1 line for the header or footer, and 2 lines for spacing before or after the main text).

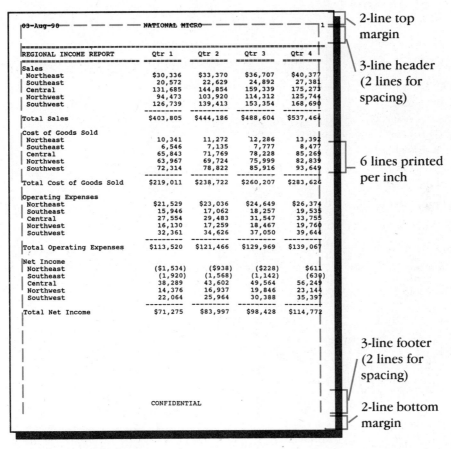

2-line top margin

3-line header (2 lines for spacing)

6 lines printed per inch

3-line footer (2 lines for spacing)

2-line bottom margin

8 1/2-by-11-inch paper

If you want to check the default settings for margins and page length, select /Worksheet Global Default Status.

8

237

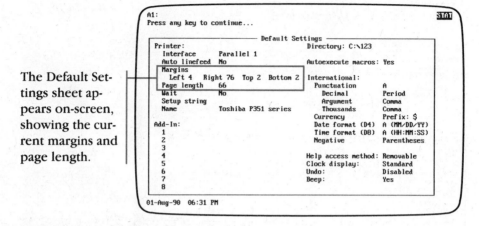

The Default Settings sheet appears on-screen, showing the current margins and page length.

Note: This screen will appear slightly different in versions of 1-2-3 prior to Release 2.2.

To change the page layout of the current worksheet, follow these steps:

1. Call up the 1-2-3 menu by pressing ⌐/⌐.
2. Select **Print** by pressing ⌐P⌐.
3. Select **Printer** by pressing ⌐P⌐.
4. Select **Options** by pressing ⌐O⌐.
5. To change the margins, select **Margins** by pressing ⌐M⌐.

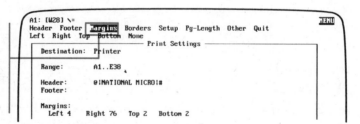

The **Margins** option allows you to modify the size of the margins in the printed report.

6. Select **Left**, **Right**, **Top**, **Bottom**, or **None** from the Margins menu by pressing ⌐L⌐, ⌐R⌐, ⌐T⌐, ⌐B⌐, or ⌐N⌐, respectively.
7. In response to the prompt to enter the margin, type a value within the indicated range and press ⌐↵Enter⌐.

When you select **Left**, you are asked to enter a new left margin setting from the values 0 through 240 (characters). To change the right margin, select **Right** and enter a value from 0 through 240 at the `Enter Right Margin:` prompt. For the top and bottom margins, select **Top** or **Bottom** and enter a margin specification from 0 through 32 (lines).

Be sure that you set left and right margins that are consistent with the width of your paper and the printer's established pitch (characters per inch). The right margin must be greater than the left margin. And make sure that settings for the top and bottom margins are consistent with the paper's length and the established number of lines per inch. The options and messages shown in table 8.2 are involved when you change margin settings.

Table 8.2
Options for Changing Margin Settings

Option	Message (or description)
Left	`Enter Left Margin (0..240):xx`
Right	`Enter Right Margin (0..240):xx`
Top	`Enter Top Margin (0..32):xx`
Bottom	`Enter Bottom Margin (0..32):xx`
None	Sets left, top, and bottom margins to 0; sets right margin to 240

The xx at the end of each line denotes the current setting, which you can change. Notice that the **None** option of the Margins menu resets the left, top, and bottom margins to zero, and the right margin to 240.

To maximize the output on every printed page of a large worksheet, you can use the **/Print Printer Options Other Unformatted** command, which ignores margins, headers, and footers. This command is covered in this chapter's section "Preparing Output for Other Programs." You can also use setup strings that condense print and increase the number of lines per inch.

Printing a Listing of Cell Contents

You can spend hours developing and debugging a model worksheet and additional time entering and verifying data. You should safeguard your work by making backup copies of your important files on disk, and also by printing a listing of the cell contents of important worksheets. Be aware, however, that this print job can eat up lots of time (and paper) if you have a large worksheet.

You can produce printed documentation of cell contents by selecting **/Print Printer Options Other**, and then selecting either **Cell-Formulas** or **As-Displayed**. The two options are related. Choosing **Cell-Formulas** produces a listing with one cell per line showing the cell format, the width of the cell (if different from the default), the cell-protection status, and the contents of cells (including any formulas) in the print range. With **As-Displayed**, the data prints as it appears—showing the cell format, cell width, and protection status—but the contents of the cells are printed as they appear on-screen rather than as formulas.

To print a cell-by-cell listing of the contents of a particular range, follow these steps:

1. Call up the 1-2-3 menu by pressing $\boxed{/}$.
2. Select **Print** by pressing $\boxed{P}$.
3. Select **Printer** by pressing $\boxed{P}$.
4. Select **Options** by pressing $\boxed{O}$.
5. Select **Other** by pressing $\boxed{O}$.
6. Select **Cell-Formulas** by pressing $\boxed{C}$ to print a listing of formulas in cells; or select **As-Displayed** by pressing $\boxed{A}$ to print the range as it appears on-screen.

In this example, select Cell-Formulas by pressing $\boxed{C}$.

```
A1: [W28] \=                                                    MENU
As-Displayed  Cell-Formulas  Formatted  Unformatted
List entries, one per line
                                    Print Settings
     Destination:  Printer

     Range:        A1..E38

     Header:       @!NATIONAL MICRO!#
     Footer:

     Margins:
        Left 4     Right 76    Top 2   Bottom 2

     Borders:
        Columns
        Rows

     Setup string:

     Page length:  66

     Output:       As-Displayed (Formatted)

01-Aug-90  06:34 PM
```

8

7. To return to the main Print menu, select **Q**uit by pressing Q .

8. Select **R**ange by pressing R , highlight the range of cells you want printed, and then press ↵Enter .

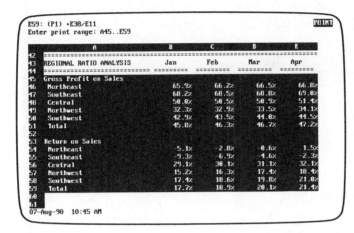

In this example, highlight the range A45..E59 as the range to print and press ↵Enter .

9. Select **A**lign by pressing A .

10. Select **G**o by pressing G .

11. After printing is completed, select **P**age by pressing P .

12. Select **Q**uit by pressing Q .

Each entry in the resulting printout is listed in the following format.

Each entry begins with the location of the cell.

The printed entry ends with the actual contents of the cell, in this case a formula.

$$C47: \ (P1) \ [W11] \ (C6-C15)/C6$$

If the format of the cell is different from the default global format, 1-2-3 prints within parentheses a notation for the cell's format. For example, (P1) indicates that the cell was formatted (with a /**R**ange Format command) as **P**ercent with 1 decimal place.

If the column width of the cell is different from the default global column width, 1-2-3 indicates within square brackets the column width. For example, [W11] indicates that the column is set specifically to be 11 characters wide.

241

1-2-3 prints the
contents of each
cell, moving hori-
zontally across
each row of the
print range.

```
A45: [W28] 'Gross Profit on Sales
A46: [W28] ' Northeast
B46: (P1) (B5-B14)/B5
C46: (P1) [W11] (C5-C14)/C5
D46: (P1) [W11] (D5-D14)/D5
E46: (P1) (E5-E14)/E5
A47: [W28] ' Southeast
B47: (P1) (B6-B15)/B6
C47: (P1) [W11] (C6-C15)/C6
D47: (P1) [W11] (D6-D15)/D6
E47: (P1) (E6-E15)/E6
A48: [W28] ' Central
B48: (P1) (B7-B16)/B7
C48: (P1) [W11] (C7-C16)/C7
D48: (P1) [W11] (D7-D16)/D7
E48: (P1) (E7-E16)/E7
A49: [W28] ' Northwest
B49: (P1) (B8-B17)/B8
C49: (P1) [W11] (C8-C17)/C8
D49: (P1) [W11] (D8-D17)/D8
E49: (P1) (E8-E17)/E8
A50: [W28] ' Southwest
B50: (P1) (B9-B18)/B9
C50: (P1) [W11] (C9-C18)/C9
D50: (P1) [W11] (D9-D18)/D9
E50: (P1) (E9-E18)/E9
A51: [W28] ' Total
B51: (P1) (B11-B20)/B11
C51: (P1) [W11] (C11-C20)/C11
D51: (P1) [W11] (D11-D20)/D11
E51: (P1) (E11-E20)/E11
A53: [W28] 'Return on Sales
A54: [W28] ' Northeast
B54: (P1) +B32/B5
C54: (P1) [W11] +C32/C5
D54: (P1) [W11] +D32/D5
E54: (P1) +E32/E5
A55: [W28] ' Southeast
B55: (P1) +B33/B6
C55: (P1) [W11] +C33/C6
D55: (P1) [W11] +D33/D6
E55: (P1) +E33/E6
A56: [W28] ' Central
B56: (P1) +B34/B7
C56: (P1) [W11] +C34/C7
D56: (P1) [W11] +D34/D7
E56: (P1) +E34/E7
A57: [W28] ' Northwest
B57: (P1) +B35/B8
C57: (P1) [W11] +C35/C8
D57: (P1) [W11] +D35/D8
E57: (P1) +E35/E8
A58: [W28] ' Southwest
B58: (P1) +B36/B9
C58: (P1) [W11] +C36/C9
```

If the cell has been unprotected with the /**R**ange Unprot command, an
uppercase U will appear following the cell format. Cells that are protected
with /**R**ange **P**rot will not have the U or any other character(s) present in this
location.

Clearing the Print Options

When you select **P**rint options, the settings you specify are automatically
saved with the worksheet when you select /**F**ile **S**ave. Saving the settings with

the worksheet for a future print job is a good practice, rather than clearing them after each printing. Minor changes can then be made to the existing settings quickly.

At times, however, you would benefit by clearing all or some of the print settings; you can do this with the /**Print** **Printer** **Clear** command. For example, you may want to print a report in the same worksheet from which you printed earlier, but specify a different print range. You can use /**Print** **Printer** **Clear** **Range** to eliminate only the range setting, thereby allowing you to select the new range quickly. All other print settings remain intact. The /**Print** **Printer** **Clear** **All** command can prove to be helpful when a report isn't printing properly, and you want to reenter the print settings.

To clear some or all print settings, follow these steps:

1. Call up the 1-2-3 menu by pressing ⌞/⌟.
2. Select **Print** by pressing ⌞P⌟.
3. Select **Printer** by pressing ⌞P⌟.
4. Select **Clear** by pressing ⌞C⌟.

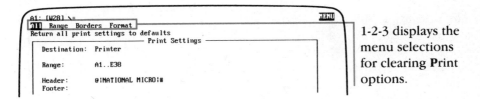

1-2-3 displays the menu selections for clearing **Print** options.

5. Choose the desired selection by pressing ⌞A⌟, ⌞R⌟, ⌞B⌟, or ⌞F⌟. Each selection is described in table 8.3.

Table 8.3
Menu Selections for Clearing the Print Options

Selection	Description
All	Clears every **Print** option, including the print range.
Range	Removes only the previous print-range specification.
Borders	Cancels only **Columns** and **Rows** specified as borders.
Format	Returns **Margins**, **Pg-Length**, and **Setup** string settings to the default settings displayed in the /**Worksheet** **Global** **Default** screen.

243

Preparing Output for Other Programs

Many word processing and other software packages import ASCII text files. You can maximize your chances of successfully exporting 1-2-3 files to other programs if you select several **P**rint command sequences that eliminate unwanted specifications for page layout and page breaks. The primary command you use during this procedure is /**P**rint **F**ile **O**ptions **O**ther **U**nformatted. This section shows you how to use this command to create a PRN file that can be imported into another program.

To prepare output for other programs, follow these steps:

1. Call up the 1-2-3 menu by pressing ⌿ .
2. Select **P**rint by pressing P .
3. Select **F**ile by pressing F to print to a disk rather than to a printer.
4. Specify a file name with up to eight characters to direct output to a PRN file rather than to a printer; then press ⏎Enter .

In this example, type **a:\salesrpt** and press ⏎Enter to direct the output to a PRN file named SALESRPT on drive A.

```
A1: [W28] \=                                                   EDIT
Enter name of text file: a:\salesrpt
                    A              B        C        D        E
1  ==========================================================
2  REGIONAL INCOME REPORT       Qtr 1    Qtr 2    Qtr 3    Qtr 4
3  ==========================================================
4  Sales
5     Northeast               $30,336  $33,370  $36,707  $40,377
6     Southeast                20,572   22,629   24,892   27,381
7     Central                 131,685  144,854  159,339  175,273
8     Northwest                94,473  103,920  114,312  125,744
9     Southwest               126,739  139,413  153,354  168,690
```

5. Select **R**ange by pressing R , and specify the range you want to send to the PRN file; then press ⏎Enter .

In this example, select **R**ange, highlight the range A1..E11, and press ⏎Enter .

```
E11: (C0) @SUM(E5..E9)                                         POINT
Enter print range: A1..E11
                    A              B        C        D        E
1
2  REGIONAL INCOME REPORT       Qtr 1    Qtr 2    Qtr 3    Qtr 4
3
4  Sales
5     Northeast               $30,336  $33,370  $36,707  $40,377
6     Southeast                20,572   22,629   24,892   27,381
7     Central                 131,685  144,854  159,339  175,273
8     Northwest                94,473  103,920  114,312  125,744
9     Southwest               126,739  139,413  153,354  168,690
10
11 Total Sales               $403,805 $444,186 $488,604 $537,464
12
13 Cost of Goods Sold
14    Northeast                10,341   11,272   12,286   13,392
15    Southeast                 6,546    7,135    7,777    8,477
16    Central                  65,843   71,769   78,228   85,269
17    Northwest                63,967   69,724   75,999   82,839
18    Southwest                72,314   78,822   85,916   93,649
19
20 Total Cost of Goods Sold  $219,011 $238,722 $260,207 $283,626
01-Aug-90  06:54 PM
```

6. Select **Options** by pressing ⃝O.

7. Select **Other** by pressing ⃝O.

8. Select **Unformatted** by pressing ⃝U.

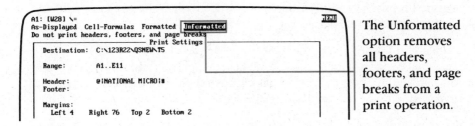

The Unformatted option removes all headers, footers, and page breaks from a print operation.

9. Select **Quit** by pressing ⃝Q to return to the main Print menu.

10. To create the PRN file on disk, select **Go** by pressing ⃝G.

    Note: The **Align** and **Page** commands are not necessary when creating a PRN file, because no printer paper is being used for this command.

11. To return to READY mode, select **Quit** by pressing ⃝Q.

12. Follow the instructions in your word processing or other software package to import the specially prepared 1-2-3 disk files.

8

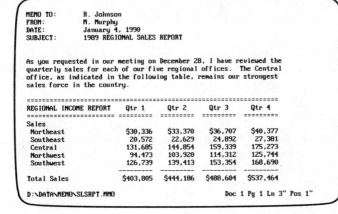

In this example, the PRN file just created has been imported into WordPerfect, a word processing package.

Summary

This chapter showed you how to print reports by selecting the /Print command from 1-2-3's main menu. You can use the /Print Printer command to print a report to a printer, or the /Print File command to create a PRN file on disk that you or someone else can print later.

You learned how to print a document of one page or less, to add borders to a multipage report, and to hide worksheet segments within the print range. You also learned how to control paper movement with the Line, Page, and Align options; and how to create page breaks within a worksheet.

The chapter indicated ways to enhance printouts. You can add headers and footers that can include the date and a page number. You can also change the layout of a page by adjusting the margins and the page length.

Specifically, you learned the following key information about 1-2-3:

- The /Print Printer command allows you to print reports on a printer, while the /Print File *filename* command allows you to "print" a range to a file that can be imported within other software packages.

- To print the current information as it is shown on-screen, press Shift-PrtSc, or press Print Screen if you have an enhanced keyboard.

- The /Print Printer Options Borders command enables you to print specified rows and/or columns on each page of a printed report.

- When you are printing reports, you can hide specific rows, columns, or ranges. Columns are hidden by selecting /Worksheet Column Hide after a print range has been specified; rows are hidden by entering the symbol for nonprinting—two vertical bars (¦¦)—in the first cell of the row; ranges are hidden with the command /Range Format Hidden.

- The /Print Printer Line command advances the paper one line in the printer, and the /Print Printer Page command advances the paper to the top of the next page.

8

■ The /Print **Printer Align** command ensures that printing will begin at the top of all succeeding pages after the first. Before printing, always make sure that your printer paper is correctly positioned.

■ The /Print **Printer Options Other Cell-Formulas** command prints a cell-by-cell listing of a specified range. The listing includes the cell's location, format, width, protection status, and contents (including formulas). The /Print **Printer Options Other As-Displayed** command prints cell contents as they appear on-screen.

■ The /Print **Printer Clear** command clears some or all of a worksheet's print settings. /Print **Printer Clear Range** clears only the specified print range, while /Print **Printer Clear All** clears all settings, including the print range, borders, margins, and other settings.

■ The /Print **File Options Other Unformatted** command allows extra lines to print on the page by eliminating margins and page breaks from the printout.

The next chapter shows you how to use the Allways add-in program to enhance the appearance of your printed output. Among other things, you will learn how to incorporate different sizes and styles of typefaces, shading, outlining, and grids.

8

247

Printing with Allways

In recent years computer hardware and software have become more and more sophisticated. Desktop publishing is now a major segment of the software market. Packages such as Aldus PageMaker and Ventura Publisher have become vital tools in the publishing efforts of many companies. People like the flexibility these packages offer in preparing reports, and they like to avoid the inevitable delays in dealing with printing and publishing companies.

1-2-3 offers many options through its /Print commands. Some features, however, such as shading, selective underlining, and various typefaces and sizes, either are not available or require an unwieldy set of commands.

Allways, a popular spreadsheet publishing package in its own right, is included with Release 2.2 of 1-2-3. If you are using a version of 1-2-3 prior to Release 2.2, you can purchase Allways as a separate package to be used with 1-2-3. Although Allways is not a full-featured desktop publishing package like PageMaker and Ventura Publisher, it can enhance the printing of your worksheets and produce professional-looking reports of presentation quality.

Comparing reports printed with 1-2-3 and Allways

Attaching and invoking Allways

Selecting from a variety of fonts

Using light, dark, and solid shading

Using underlining and boldface

Using lines to outline cells or create grid lines

Changing the size of the image on-screen

Combining graphs with worksheets

Key Terms in This Chapter

Typeface	The design of a character set, such as Times or Triumvirate.
Font	A character set displaying a particular size and style of typeface, such as 12-point Times.
Point size	The size of a particular font. One point is equal to 1/72 of an inch; therefore, 12-point Times is approximately 1/6 of an inch high.
Soft fonts	Fonts provided with the Allways program. These include various sizes and styles of Courier, Times, and Triumvirate.
Accelerator keys	Key combinations that allow you to quickly format an Allways report. For example, Alt-S allows you to shade a range of cells.

With Allways, you can use a variety of typefaces and graphic elements to enhance your reports. For example, you can choose different letter designs (typefaces) and sizes of type; add boldface and underlining to the contents of cells; use light, dark, or solid shading to accentuate portions of the worksheet; and surround individual cells or ranges of cells with lines. You can also include grid lines that outline every cell of the worksheet with lightly dotted lines, giving the appearance of ledger paper. In addition, Allways allows you to adjust the height of rows and the width of columns in small increments to "fine-tune" the appearance of the printout. You can even combine graphs with worksheet data and print them together on one page.

Comparing Reports Printed with 1-2-3 and Allways

If you compare a worksheet printed with the 1-2-3 /Print commands and one printed with Allways, you see a dramatic difference.

9

250

```
REGIONAL INCOME REPORT


                          Qtr 1       Qtr 2       Qtr 3       Qtr 4
SALES
 Northeast               $30,336     $33,370     $36,707     $40,377
 Southeast                20,572      22,629      24,892      27,381
 Central                 131,685     144,854     159,339     175,273
 Northwest                94,473     103,920     114,312     125,744
 Southwest               126,739     139,413     153,354     168,690
                        ---------   ---------   ---------   ---------
Total Sales             $403,805    $444,186    $488,604    $537,464

Cost of Goods Sold
 Northeast                10,341      11,272      12,286      13,392
 Southeast                 6,546       7,135       7,777       8,477
 Central                  65,843      71,769      78,228      85,269
 Northwest                63,967      69,724      75,999      82,839
 Southwest                72,314      78,822      85,916      93,649
                        ---------   ---------   ---------   ---------
Total Cost of Goods Sold $219,011    $238,722    $260,207    $283,626
```

This report was printed using 1-2-3's /Print Printer command.

REGIONAL INCOME REPORT

	Qtr 1	Qtr 2	Qtr 3	Qtr 4
SALES				
Northeast	$30,336	$33,370	$36,707	$40,377
Southeast	20,572	22,629	24,892	27,381
Central	131,685	144,854	159,339	175,273
Northwest	94,473	103,920	114,312	125,744
Southwest	126,739	139,413	153,354	168,690
Total Sales	$403,805	$444,186	$488,604	$537,464
Cost of Goods Sold				
Northeast	10,341	11,272	12,286	13,392
Southeast	6,546	7,135	7,777	8,477
Central	65,843	71,769	78,228	85,269
Northwest	63,967	69,724	75,999	82,839
Southwest	72,314	78,822	85,916	93,649
Total Cost of Goods Sold	$219,011	$238,722	$260,207	$283,626

This report was enhanced and printed using Allways.

9

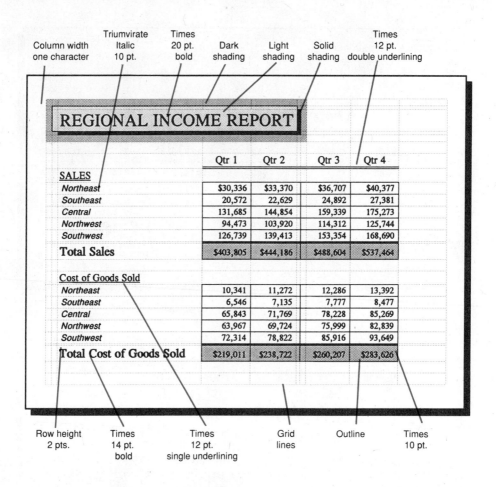

Column width one character — Triumvirate Italic 10 pt. — Times 20 pt. bold — Dark shading — Light shading — Solid shading — Times 12 pt. double underlining

REGIONAL INCOME REPORT

	Qtr 1	Qtr 2	Qtr 3	Qtr 4
SALES				
Northeast	$30,336	$33,370	$36,707	$40,377
Southeast	20,572	22,629	24,892	27,381
Central	131,685	144,854	159,339	175,273
Northwest	94,473	103,920	114,312	125,744
Southwest	126,739	139,413	153,354	168,690
Total Sales	$403,805	$444,186	$488,604	$537,464
Cost of Goods Sold				
Northeast	10,341	11,272	12,286	13,392
Southeast	6,546	7,135	7,777	8,477
Central	65,843	71,769	78,228	85,269
Northwest	63,967	69,724	75,999	82,839
Southwest	72,314	78,822	85,916	93,649
Total Cost of Goods Sold	$219,011	$238,722	$260,207	$283,626

Row height 2 pts. — Times 14 pt. bold — Times 12 pt. single underlining — Grid lines — Outline — Times 10 pt.

These are examples of some of the fonts and graphic elements you can use with Allways.

Attaching and Invoking Allways

Allways is an add-in package—software designed to be used with 1-2-3. You do not access its features directly through the standard 1-2-3 commands. To use it, you must first attach the software, which makes the add-in available for use. Then you must invoke the add-in, which lets you access its commands. An add-in package does not interfere with the operation of 1-2-3; you can switch back and forth between the two without fear of destroying your data. Allways does, however, require a portion of main memory (RAM) for its use. If you are working with an extremely large worksheet, insufficient memory may prevent you from attaching Allways or may limit your freedom to expand the worksheet.

Attaching Allways

There are two ways to attach Allways:

- *Automatically*, by using the command sequence /Worksheet Global Default Other Add-In Set. This sequence of commands ensures that whenever you start using 1-2-3, Allways is automatically attached (available for use). In addition, this command also gives you the option of having Allways automatically invoked (ready for use) when you start 1-2-3. Issue this command once, being sure to use /Worksheet Global Default Update to record the operation on your system. Allways is then available for you to invoke whenever you use 1-2-3.

- *Each time you want to use the program*. If you are concerned about the additional memory Allways requires, and you do not want it attached at all times, use the /Add-In Attach command whenever you need Allways.

With either method, you are prompted to assign an Alt-key sequence for invoking Allways. You can select Alt-F7, Alt-F8, Alt-F9, or No-key. The No-key option means that you invoke Allways in a two-step operation: first, press Alt-F10; then select Allways from a list of attached programs. If you make an Alt-key assignment, you can invoke Allways simply by pressing Alt along with the function key you chose.

To attach Allways using the first method so that the add-in is automatically available every time you use 1-2-3, follow these steps:

1. Call up the 1-2-3 menu by pressing ⌘/⌘.
2. Select **Worksheet** by pressing ⌘W⌘.
3. Select **Global** by pressing ⌘G⌘.
4. Select **Default** by pressing ⌘D⌘.
5. Select **Other** by pressing ⌘O⌘.
6. Select **Add-In** by pressing ⌘A⌘.
7. Select **Set** by pressing ⌘S⌘.

9

253

8. Select a number for Allways by typing one of the numbers from 1 to 8. (You may have up to eight add-ins).

For example, type ⬜1 to assign Allways to the first add-in setting.

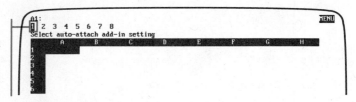

A list of add-in programs that can be attached automatically is displayed.

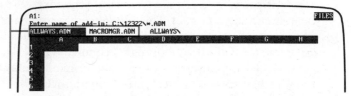

9. Highlight ALLWAYS.ADN and press ⬐Enter.

10. Indicate the key to use to invoke Allways. You can select **No-Key**, **Alt-F7**, **Alt-F8**, or **Alt-F9**, by pressing ⬜N, ⬜7, ⬜8, or ⬜9, respectively.

For example, press ⬜7 to assign Alt-F7 as the key combination to invoke Allways.

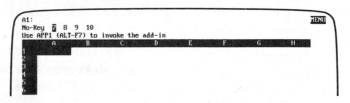

Note: Although the **10** option for assigning Alt-F10 to Allways also appears on this menu, you should select one of the other four options, because the Alt-F10 key combination is sometimes used for other purposes.

11. Select **Yes** by pressing ⬜Y to have Allways invoked automatically whenever you start 1-2-3.

Or

Select **No** by pressing ⬜N if you do not want Allways invoked automatically when you start 1-2-3.

Note: Only one add-in program can be automatically invoked when you start 1-2-3.

The Allways logo appears on-screen momentarily, followed by a menu.

254

12. Select **Q**uit by pressing Q to return to the Global Default menu.

13. Select **U**pdate by pressing U to save the default setting in a configuration file.

14. To return to READY mode, select **Q**uit by pressing Q.

To attach Allways using the second method, which you must repeat once during each 1-2-3 session, follow these steps:

1. Call up the 1-2-3 menu by pressing /.

2. Select **A**dd-In by pressing A.

3. Select **A**ttach by pressing A.

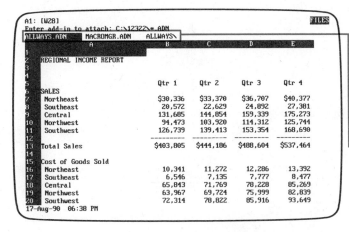

A list of add-in programs you can attach is displayed.

4. Highlight ALLWAYS.ADN and press ↵Enter.

5. Indicate the key to use to invoke Allways. You can select **N**o-Key, Alt-F7, Alt-F8, or Alt-F9, by pressing N, 7, 8, or 9, respectively.

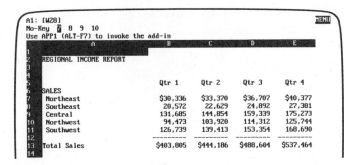

For example, press 7 to assign Alt-F7 as the key combination to invoke Allways.

255

Note: Although the **10** option for assigning Alt-F10 to Allways also appears on this menu, you should select one of the other four options, because the Alt-F10 key combination is sometimes used for other purposes.

The Allways logo appears on-screen momentarily, followed by the Add-In menu.

6. To return to READY mode, select **Quit** by pressing Q.

Invoking Allways

To invoke Allways so that you can use it during your current 1-2-3 session, press the Alt-key combination you selected when attaching Allways, and the Allways screen will appear.

Otherwise, if you chose the **No-Key** option when attaching Allways, follow these steps.

1. Call up the 1-2-3 menu by pressing /.
2. Select **Add-In** by pressing A.
3. Select **Invoke** by pressing I.
4. Highlight ALLWAYS and press ↵Enter.

The ALLWAYS add-in is high-lighted.

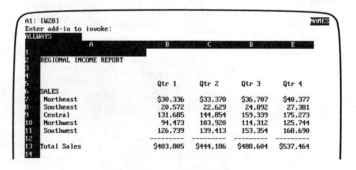

256

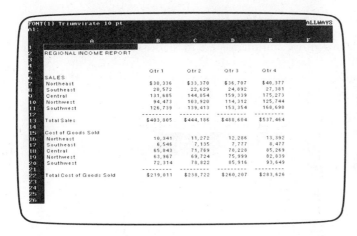

The Allways screen appears— displaying the worksheet with a different typeface than 1-2-3 normally displays.

You can return to 1-2-3 at any time by pressing the Esc key or selecting **Q**uit from the Allways main menu.

Understanding How 1-2-3 and Allways Work Together

Both 1-2-3 and Allways use similar screens and menu systems. The Allways commands are executed in the same manner as 1-2-3; the slash (/) key calls up the Allways main menu.

While using Allways to format reports, you go back and forth between the programs, and any changes that are made to the 1-2-3 worksheet also appear in the Allways version. Format changes that are made within Allways, however, do not affect the 1-2-3 worksheet. All formatting that is executed within Allways is saved in a separate file—having the same name as the worksheet file (but with an ALL extension). This file is created and saved when you select /**F**ile **S**ave within 1-2-3.

The section that follows discusses the commands that are available in the Allways main menu. The subsequent section explains how to specify cell ranges in Allways.

9

257

Using the Allways Menu

When you use Allways, more commands are available to you than you have with the standard 1-2-3 /Print commands. Fortunately, you use Allways commands the same way you use 1-2-3 commands—by pressing the slash (/) key and choosing the command through a menu system.

The Allways main menu is displayed by pressing slash (/).

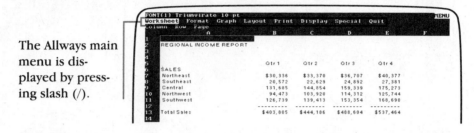

Each of the commands on the Allways main menu is described in table 9.1.

Table 9.1
Selections on the Allways Main Menu

Selection	Description
Worksheet	Changes the height of rows and the width of columns, and installs page breaks either at columns or rows.
Format	Contains most of the commands controlling the worksheet's appearance—font selection, bold, underline, lines, and shading.
Graph	Lets you select, place, enhance, or remove graphs.
Layout	Lets you control headers, footers, titles, margins, and borders.
Print	Sets the print range, configures the printer, and prints the worksheet.
Display	Controls the appearance of the worksheet on the screen by varying the size of the text.
Special	Copies or moves formats from one range to another.
Quit	Returns you to 1-2-3.

9

Specifying Cell Ranges in Allways

Many Allways commands require you to specify a range. Some commands initially anchor the range for you and some do not. You can tell whether Allways has initially anchored a range by looking for the ANC indicator at the bottom of the screen.

If the ANC indicator does not appear and you want to highlight a range, move the cell pointer to the top left cell of the range and anchor it by pressing the period (.) key. To unanchor a range, press either Esc or Backspace.

To point to a multicell range in POINT mode, use any of the direction keys to extend the highlighting over the desired range, and then press Enter. As with 1-2-3, you can choose to type the actual cell addresses in response to the range prompt rather than point to the range in POINT mode.

To prespecify an Allways range that you can invoke when prompted for a range, move the cell pointer to the first cell of the range, press the period (.) key, and extend the range with the arrow keys. Then press slash (/) to bring up the Allways command menu. From this menu, you can choose any series of commands. The preselected range applies to all commands until you change the range specification (by prespecifying or supplying a new range). Prespecifying a range saves time when you want a series of commands to apply to the same range.

Selecting from a Variety of Fonts

9

One of the best features of Allways is its capability of printing different fonts—that is, particular sizes and styles of a typeface—in a single worksheet. With Allways, you can incorporate as many as eight fonts into the printout of a single worksheet in order to improve its appearance and draw attention to its contents.

Allways provides accelerator keys, or predefined key combinations, that allow you to format a worksheet with Allways more rapidly. After you are familiar with the Allways commands, you can begin using the accelerator keys. The accelerator keys are discussed later in this section.

Selecting fonts is fairly easy; use the Allways command /Format Font to display a list of available fonts you can use. All your worksheet entries are originally presented in 10-point Triumvirate. The font used in a cell appears in the first line of the control panel when that cell is highlighted.

Regardless of the type of printer you use, Allways allows you to print many different sizes of Times, Triumvirate, and Courier—both in regular print and in italic.

Times 6 Point
Times 8 Point
Times 10 Point
Times 12 Point
Times 14 Point
Times 17 Point
Times 20 Point
Times 24 Point

Triumvirate 6 Point
Triumvirate 8 Point
Triumvirate 10 Point
Triumvirate 12 Point
Triumvirate 14 Point
Triumvirate 17 Point
Triumvirate 20 Point
Triumvirate 24 Point

Courier 6 Point
Courier 8 Point
Courier 10 Point
Courier 12 Point
Courier 14 Point
Courier 17 Point
Courier 20 Point
Courier 24 Point

9

Times Italic 6 Point

Times Italic 8 Point

Times Italic 10 Point

Times Italic 12 Point

Times Italic 14 Point

Times Italic 17 Point

Times Italic 20 Point

Times Italic 24 Point

Triumvirate Italic 6 Point

Triumvirate Italic 8 Point

Triumvirate Italic 10 Point

Triumvirate Italic 12 Point

Triumvirate Italic 14 Point

Triumvirate Italic 17 Point

Triumvirate Italic 20 Point

Triumvirate Italic 24 Point

Courier Italic 6 Point

Courier Italic 8 Point

Courier Italic 10 Point

Courier Italic 12 Point

Courier Italic 14 Point

Courier Italic 17 Point

Courier Italic 20 Point

Courier Italic 24 Point

9

The term *point* refers to the size of type; 12-point type refers to letters that are one-sixth of an inch high; 24-point type is one-third of an inch high. You can select as many as 8 alternative fonts for a single worksheet and indicate where you want the fonts to be displayed. If you want to change cells in widely spaced parts of the worksheet, you use the /Format Font Use command repeatedly, much as you do when using the /Range Format command in 1-2-3.

You can change the font for a particular range in the worksheet with the /Format Font Use command. If you want to change a particular font to a different font in the entire worksheet, you can do so with the /Format Font Replace command.

Changing the Font for a Range of the Worksheet

You can use the /Format Font Use command to change the font for a selected range of cells. Follow these steps:

1. As in 1-2-3, call up the Allways main menu by pressing ⌨/.
2. Select Format by pressing ⌨F.

A menu of various formatting options is displayed.

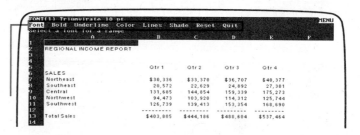

3. Select Font by pressing ⌨F.

   1-2-3 displays a list of the eight default fonts from which you can choose.

4. Use ⌨↑ and ⌨↓ to highlight the desired font.

In this example, 20-point Times is highlighted.

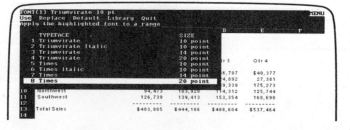

262

5. Select Use by pressing ⎡U⎤.

6. Indicate the range where you want the replacement to be made by highlighting the range (just as you would in 1-2-3) and pressing ⎡↵Enter⎤.

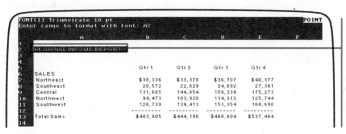

Highlight cell A2 by pressing ⎡Esc⎤ to unanchor (free) the cell pointer, press ⎡↓⎤, and then press ⎡↵Enter⎤.

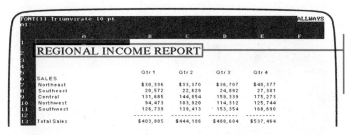

The result of changing the font of cell A2 is shown on-screen.

9

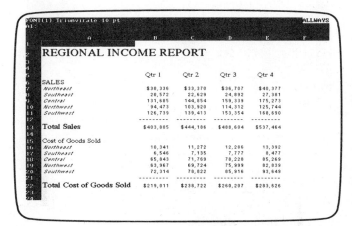

This screen shows the result of using the Allways /Format Font Use command in other ranges throughout the worksheet.

263

When you install Allways, normally just after you install 1-2-3 (see Appendix A of this book), you indicate the kind of printer(s) you are using with your computer. Printers vary in their capability to print certain type styles and degrees of resolution (detail); the list of fonts available when you use /Format Font is keyed to your printer. In addition to Times, Courier, and Triumvirate, your printer may give you the capability of printing the typefaces Pica, Letter Gothic, or Palantino. Italic printing is available with many of the typefaces.

Choosing Alternative Fonts for the Entire Worksheet

If you want to replace all occurrences of one font with another, regardless of where they occur in the worksheet, use the command sequence /Format Font Replace. This command lists the fonts from which you can choose.

In this work-sheet, all nu-meric data is displayed in the default font, 10-point Triumvirate.

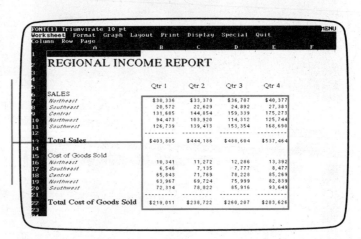

The text of this report was formatted with different fonts. You can change the default font used for the numeric data with a single procedure.

To change one font used throughout the worksheet to a different one, follow these steps:

1. Call up the Allways menu by pressing ⟨/⟩.
2. Select **Format** by pressing ⟨F⟩.

9

3. Select **F**ont by pressing ⬚F .

4. Use ⬚↑ and ⬚↓ to highlight the font you want to change.

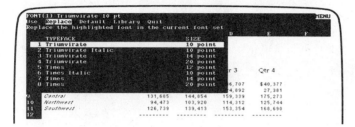

For this example, highlight 10-point Triumvirate to change the default font.

5. Select **R**eplace by pressing ⬚R .

   A box is displayed showing you all the available typefaces.

6. Select the new typeface by highlighting it and pressing ⬚◄Enter .

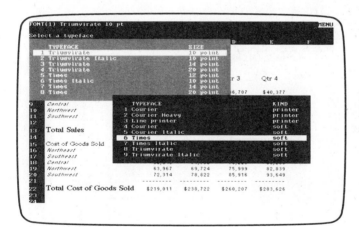

In this example, highlight Times and press ⬚◄Enter .

The term *soft* listed under K I N D (of typeface) refers to typefaces not normally available with your printer; they come in a variety of sizes. Typefaces identified as *printer* are available in standard printer sizes only.

Another (smaller) box is displayed—showing you the available point sizes for the new font you selected.

7. Highlight the desired point size and press ⬚◄Enter .

265

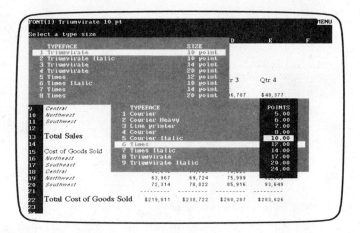

In this example, the desired point size of 10 is highlighted; press ⏎Enter to select this size.

8. Select **Quit** by pressing Q to return to the worksheet.

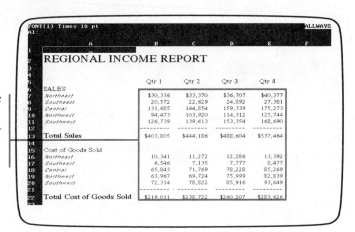

All cells that were in 10-point Triumvirate are now displayed in 10-point Times.

The group of font selections is limited to 8. That is, in any worksheet, you can use as many as 8 different fonts. The list of available fonts is larger, however. The printer you select when you install Allways determines the number of fonts from which you can select.

After experimenting with Allways, you may decide that a particular group of fonts is one you would like to use often. Allways lets you store a group of font selections in a file so that you can have access to those fonts later.

9

Use /Format Font Replace to build the group of font selections. Then use /Format Font Library Save to preserve these changes in a file. Whenever you want to retrieve one of these groups of fonts, use the /Format Font Library Retrieve command.

You can also establish a default font for Allways. That font is used automatically whenever you use Allways with a worksheet for the first time. Use the command /Format Font Default to establish the current setting or to recall the previous default.

Using Shading

For greater variety and visual interest in printing your worksheet, you can use light, dark, or solid shading. If you pick light or dark shading, Allways uses a series of dots, spaced sparsely or densely, to print light or dark gray on the worksheet. If you choose solid shading, Allways completely blackens the part of the worksheet you have specified.

To use any of the shading options, begin with the /Format Shade command. Then pick the style of shading and, at the prompt, highlight the range of cells to be affected.

Using Light and Dark Shading

If you use light or dark shading on cells with data, the contents will remain visible through the shading. To shade an area of the worksheet with light or dark shading, you use the /Format Shade Light or /Format Shade Dark command, respectively.

To highlight or accent portions of a worksheet with light or dark shading, follow these steps:

1. Call up the Allways menu by pressing ⃞/.
2. Select Format by pressing ⃞F.
3. Select Shade by pressing ⃞S.
4. If you want light shading, select Light by pressing ⃞L.

   Or

   If you want dark shading, select Dark by pressing ⃞D.

9

267

In this example, select **Light** for light shading by pressing ⎣L⎦.

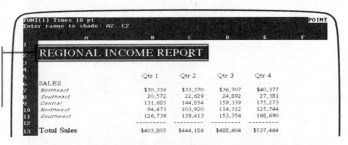

5. Highlight the range you want to shade and press ⎣⏎Enter⎦.

In this example, highlight the range A2..C2 and press ⎣⏎Enter⎦.

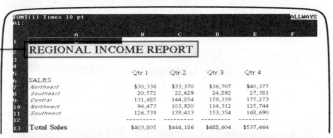

The result of the shading is shown on-screen.

This screen shows dark shading added to the ranges B13..E13 and B22..E22 with the Allways /Format Shade Dark command.

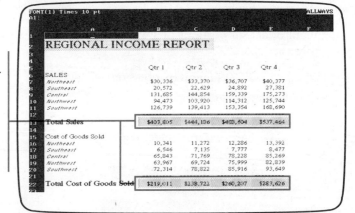

9

268

Using Solid Shading

Use solid shading to blacken a part of the worksheet. When you want to create a thick dark line, select the /Format Shade Solid command to create the effect; then use the /Worksheet Row Set-Height command to shrink the height of the row to the thickness of a heavy line.

Solid shading completely covers any cell contents in the selected worksheet range on-screen. When you use solid shading, however, you may need to remove the cell contents of the shaded ranges from the 1-2-3 worksheet before printing. Otherwise, the cell contents of solid-shaded ranges may appear on the printout above or below the shading—especially when row heights are altered.

To add solid shading to create bold, thick lines, follow these steps:

1. Call up the Allways menu by pressing /.
2. Select Format by pressing F.
3. Select Shade by pressing S.
4. Select Solid by pressing S.
5. Highlight the range you want to shade and press ↵Enter.

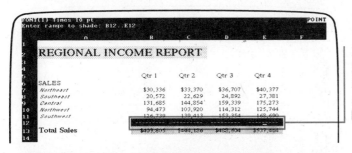

In this example, highlight the range B12..E12 and press ↵Enter.

9

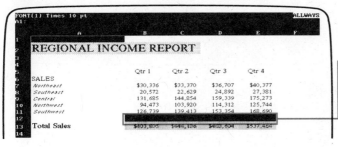

The result of solid shading is shown on-screen.

To change the height of the row where the solid shading occurs, follow these steps:

1. Move the cell pointer to any cell in the row whose height will be adjusted. For this example, move to cell B12.

2. Call up the Allways menu by pressing ⌿.

3. Select **W**orksheet by pressing Ⓦ.

4. Select **R**ow by pressing Ⓡ.

5. Select **S**et-Height by pressing Ⓢ.

6. At the prompt `Enter row height:`, use ⬆ to shorten the height of the row and see this change displayed on-screen; then press ⏎Enter.

In this example, use ⬆ until a 2 is displayed in the control panel; then press ⏎Enter.

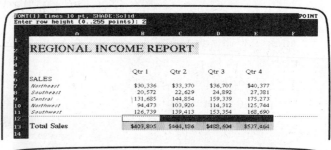

The row height in this example has been set to 2 (the default is 13).

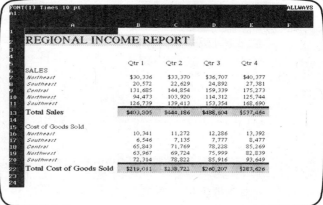

The same procedure has also been used for the range B21..E21. Notice the mostly hidden row indicators for rows 12 and 21 on the left side of the worksheet.

The /Format Shade Solid and /Worksheet Row Set-Height commands can be used together for other effects as well. When you use them along a row of cells beneath a title enclosed in a box, and along the left or right side of the box, you create a three-dimensional effect that makes the title box appear to stand out with a shadow behind it.

Creating three-dimensional effects takes a bit of practice. You probably need to insert some rows or columns, and you have to experiment with changing the height of rows and the width of columns. The final printout of the example (at the end of this chapter) shows a shadow box incorporated with the title of the report.

Removing Existing Shading

You remove existing shading by using the command /Format Shade Clear, and then indicating the range from which shading is to be removed.

To remove existing shading, follow these steps:

1. Call up the Allways menu by pressing `/`.
2. Select Format by pressing `F`.
3. Select Shade by pressing `S`.
4. Select Clear by pressing `C`.
5. Highlight the range from which you want to remove shading and press `↵Enter`.

9

Using Underlining and Boldface

You can use Allways to add underlining and boldface to cell entries. The /Format Underline and /Format Bold commands, discussed in the sections that follow, are useful for emphasizing important areas of the worksheet and increasing the visual impact of printed reports.

Using Underlining

Two styles of underlining are available in Allways: single and double. Unlike the limited underlining available in 1-2-3, which merely repeats the minus sign or equal sign in a separate cell, Allways gives you the kind of solid underlining you can create on paper with a pencil and ruler. Use the /Format Underline command to pick the type of underlining you want, and then, at the prompt, highlight the range of cells to be underlined.

To create a single underline, follow these steps:

1. Call up the Allways menu by pressing ⌨/.

2. Select Format by pressing ⌨F.

3. Select Underline by pressing ⌨U.

4. Select Single by pressing ⌨S.

5. Highlight the range to underline and press ⌨⏎Enter.

In this example, highlight cell A6, and then press ⌨⏎Enter.

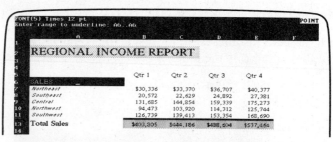

The result of single underlining is shown on-screen. The same procedure is used to create the single under-line in cell A15.

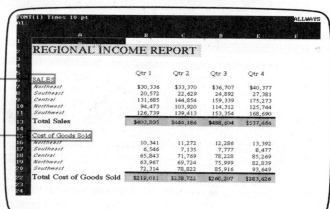

To create a double underline, follow these steps:

1. Call up the Allways menu by pressing ⌨/.

2. Select Format by pressing ⌨F.

3. Select Underline by pressing ⌨U.

272

4. Select **D**ouble by pressing D.

5. Highlight the range to underline, and then press ↵Enter.

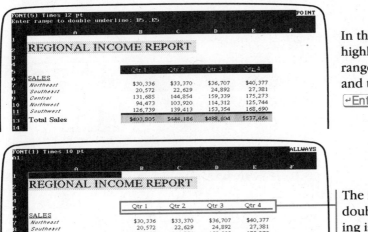

In this example, highlight the range B5..E5, and then press ↵Enter.

The result of double underlining is shown on-screen.

Note that double underlining affects entire cells, whereas single underlining affects only the text within the cell.

To remove existing single and double underlining, use the command /**F**ormat Underline Clear.

9

Using Boldface

You may want to make the contents of some cells darker than other cells for emphasis. In 1-2-3, you can use setup strings to indicate bold printing, but you can select only entire rows or the whole worksheet. With Allways, you can choose any cell or range of cells you want to appear darker. When you use light or dark shading in cells with data, you can see the contents more clearly if the characters are bold. Use the /**F**ormat **B**old command to select bold characters. Then, at the prompt, highlight the range of cells to be boldface.

To create boldface characters, follow these steps:

1. Call up the Allways menu by pressing /.

2. Select **Format** by pressing F.

3. Select **Bold** by pressing B.

4. Select **Set** by pressing S.

5. Highlight the range where you want boldface type to appear, and then press ↵Enter.

In this example, highlight cell A13, and then press ↵Enter.

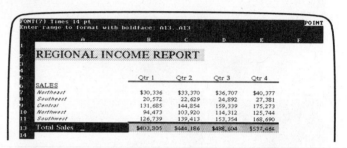

The result of selecting boldface type is shown on-screen. This procedure is used also to create the boldface type in cell A22.

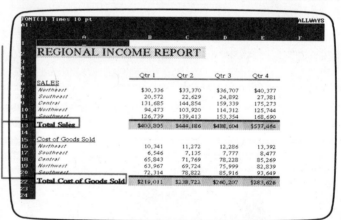

Using Lines To Outline Cells or Create Grid Lines

With Allways, you have a variety of ways to use lines to enclose or separate parts of the worksheet. The options for outlining particular cells are accessed with the /Format Lines command. If you want to show the boundaries of all cells on the worksheet, you can add grid lines by using the /Layout Options Grid command.

Outlining Cells

When you select /Format Lines, you see these options: **Outline**, **Left**, **Right**, **Top**, **Bottom**, **All**, and **Clear**. Usually, you will surround all cells in a given range by selecting **All** or draw lines around the perimeter of a range by choosing **Outline**. If you want to put a single cell in a box, you can use either **/Format Lines Outline** or **/Format Lines All**. A shaded range will be more clearly defined if you surround it by using **/Format Lines Outline**. Remove existing lines with **/Format Lines Clear**; you are prompted for the kinds of lines you want cleared.

To draw lines on all sides of the cells in a range, follow these steps:

1. Call up the Allways menu by pressing ⌨/.
2. Select Format by pressing ⌨F.
3. Select Lines by pressing ⌨L.
4. Select All by pressing ⌨A.
5. Highlight the range of cells that you want to contain lines around each cell, and then press ⌨Enter.

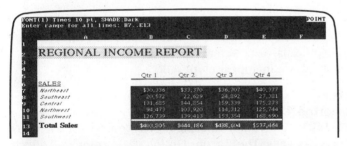

In this example, highlight the range B7..E13 and press ⌨Enter.

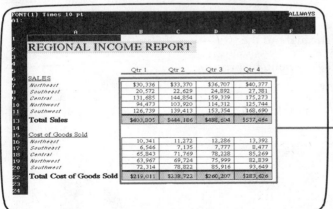

This screen shows the result of drawing lines around all sides of each cell in the range B7..E13 as well as the range B16..E22.

To draw lines on the perimeter (outline) of the cells in a range, follow these steps:

1. Call up the Allways menu by pressing /.
2. Select Format by pressing F.
2. Select Lines by pressing L.
3. Select Outline by pressing O.
4. Highlight the range of cells to be outlined, and then press ↵Enter.

In this example, only cells A2..C2, containing the report title, are outlined.

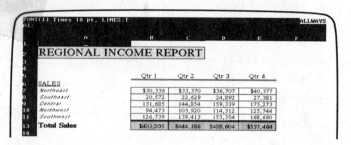

Creating Grid Lines

You can surround every cell in the worksheet with lines if you pick /Format Lines All and highlight all cells. Although this process will display cell boundaries clearly, the result can appear cluttered.

A better way to see cell boundaries without letting the lines dominate the text is to use the command /Layout Options Grid. This command draws lightly dotted lines for all column and row separations. You cannot use grid lines for a selected range of cells. The /Layout Options Grid command affects the entire worksheet.

To create grid lines throughout the worksheet, follow these steps:

1. Call up the Allways menu by pressing /.
2. Select Layout by pressing L.
3. Select Options by pressing O.

276

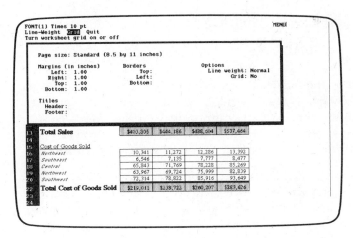

A box appears on-screen displaying the current layout settings.

4. Select **Grid** by pressing G.

5. Select **Yes** by pressing Y if you want the grid lines to print in your printed report; otherwise, select **No** by pressing N.

6. To exit, select **Quit** twice by pressing Q Q, or press Esc twice.

Grid lines surround all cells in the worksheet except for those where labels extend across cell boundaries.

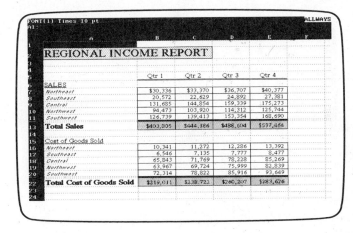

Here, because the text in cell A2 extends through cell C2, grid lines surround (but do not separate) the range A2..C2.

9

Changing the Size of the Image On-Screen

By magnifying or shrinking the display of your worksheet on-screen, you get an idea of how the worksheet is going to look when you eventually print it. With the /Display Zoom command, you can shrink the image on-screen so that characters are as small as 60 percent of their usual size, or you can magnify images so that characters expand up to 140 percent of normal size.

The /Display Zoom command has no effect on printed output. The command may, however, help you to see small fonts more easily on-screen if you pick one of the larger settings. You may be able to visualize an entire page if you choose one of the smaller options.

To change the size of the image on-screen, follow these steps:

1. Call up the Allways menu by pressing ⌷/ .
2. Select Display by pressing ⌷D .

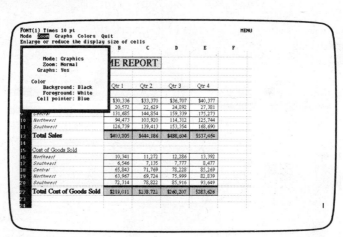

The box that appears on-screen shows the current display settings. The default Zoom size is Normal.

9

3. Select Zoom by pressing ⌷Z .
4. Select the size you want from among the following options: **Tiny, Small, Normal, Large,** or **Huge.**
5. Select **Quit** by pressing ⌷Q to return to a modified screen size.

By altering the font selection and using /Display Zoom, you can produce a wide variety of screen images.

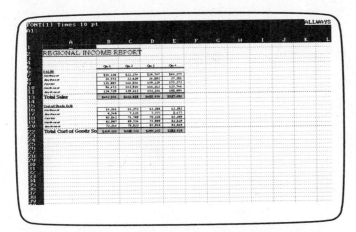

The **Tiny** option displays the image on-screen at 60 percent of normal size.

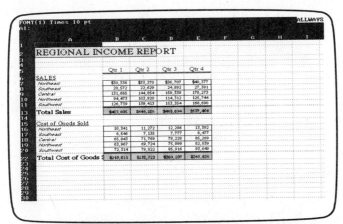

The **Small** option displays the image on-screen at 84 percent of normal size.

9

	Qtr 1	Qtr 2	Qtr 3	Qtr 4
REGIONAL INCOME REPORT				
SALES				
Northeast	$30,336	$33,370	$36,707	$40,377
Southeast	20,572	22,629	24,892	27,381
Central	131,685	144,854	159,339	175,273
Northwest	94,473	103,920	114,312	125,744
Southwest	126,739	139,413	153,354	168,690
Total Sales	$403,805	$444,186	$488,604	$537,464
Cost of Goods Sold				
Northeast	10,341	11,272	12,286	13,392
Southeast	6,546	7,135	7,777	8,477
Central	65,843	71,769	78,228	85,269
Northwest	63,967	69,724	75,999	82,839
Southwest	72,314	78,822	85,916	93,649

The **Large** option displays the image on-screen at 120 percent of normal size.

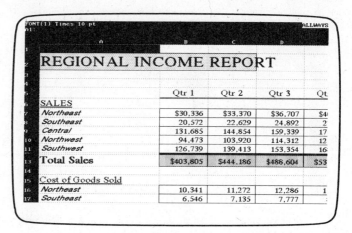

The **Huge** option displays the image on-screen at 140 percent of normal size.

Using the Allways Accelerator Keys

The accelerator keys, provided with the Allways program, give you the option of executing frequently used Allways commands with a reduced number of keystrokes. These shortcuts simply combine the Alt key with a letter or number to automate the formatting tasks. A few of the accelerator keys cycle through two or more options when pressed repeatedly. For example, the Alt-S accelerator key combination alternates between light, dark, solid, and no shading when repeated. You use an accelerator key combination by holding down the Alt key while pressing a letter or number for the desired operation. Table 9.2 shows the accelerator keys as well as the alternate commands that perform the same function within Allways.

Table 9.2
Allways Accelerator Keys for Quick Formatting

Keys	Description/Options	Alternate Command
Alt-B	Boldface (**Set**, **Clear**)	/Format Bold
Alt-G	Grid lines (**On**, **Off**)	/Layout Options Grid
Alt-L	Lines (**Outline**, **All**, **None**)	/Format Lines
Alt-S	Shading (**Light**, **Dark**, **Solid**, **None**)	/Format Shade
Alt-U	Underline (**Single**, **Double**, **None**)	/Format Underline
Alt-1 through Alt-8	Set fonts 1 through 8	/Format Font Use

9

Combining Graphs with Worksheets

A graph can give your worksheet greater visual impact and emphasize the data in the worksheet. Creating graphs is the subject of Chapter 11, and printing graphs with PrintGraph is covered in Chapter 12. In Release 2.2, you can combine graphs with a worksheet only by using Allways.

Printing a graph in 1-2-3 is time-consuming and difficult. You must leave the worksheet with the /Quit Yes command and access the PrintGraph program. Alteration of the graph at this point is limited to changing its size and shape, not its contents. You have no capability of combining a graph and its associated worksheet either on-screen or on paper.

With Allways, you have more flexibility in graph preparation and alteration. You can integrate the presentation of a worksheet and a graph, both on the screen and on paper. You can also position the graph in any location, and you can give it a range whose shape does not necessarily conform to the original range's height-to-width ratio.

The graphs you use for these purposes must come from files created with the 1-2-3 command /Graph Save. These are PIC files, which you can print using the PrintGraph commands.

When you combine graphs and worksheets with Allways, you use the Allways /Graph Add command for each graph you want to include. You have the option of viewing the actual graph on-screen with your worksheet, or you can display just cross-hatching that covers the graph area. The Allways command /Display Graphs lets you view graphs on-screen.

To combine a graph with a worksheet, follow these steps:

1. Place the cell pointer where you want the upper left corner of your graph positioned.

   Note: Graphs in Allways are transparent; if you position your graph so that it overlaps cells containing data, information in those cells will appear as though it were part of the graph.

2. Call up the Allways menu by pressing ⌗/⌗.

3. Select Graph by pressing ⌗G⌗.

4. Select Add by pressing ⌗A⌗.

   A list of PIC files in the current directory is displayed.

5. Select the graph you want by highlighting the graph name and pressing ⌗↵Enter⌗.

9

6. In response to the prompt Enter range for graph:, highlight the range where the graph is to be placed, and then press ↵Enter. Allways will automatically size the graph to fit the specified range. You can alter the graph's dimensions by changing the row heights and/or column widths.

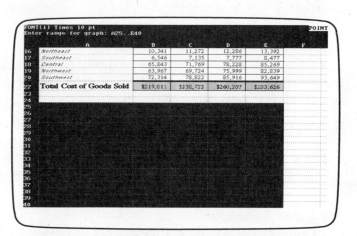

In this example, highlight the range A25..E40 and press ↵Enter.

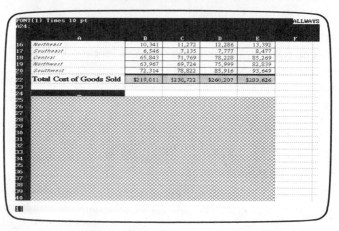

You see only cross-hatching to show what space the graph will take up when you print it.

9

Displaying a graph on-screen while a report is being enhanced requires more time than showing data. Therefore, Allways gives you the option for a quick display so that you have some idea of the placement and size of the graph

282

before you decide to print. If you want to see the actual graph on-screen, choose the command /**Display Graphs Yes** by following these steps:

1. Call up the Allways menu by pressing $\boxed{/}$.

2. Select **Display** by pressing $\boxed{D}$.

3. Select **Graphs** by pressing $\boxed{G}$.

4. To confirm your selection, select **Yes** by pressing $\boxed{Y}$.

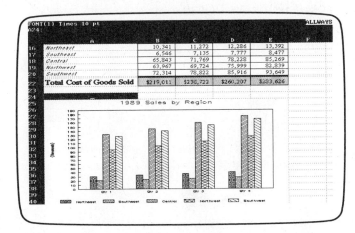

The selected graph appears on-screen.

Allways does not limit you to a single graph, but you must use the /**Graph Add** command for each graph that you want included with your worksheet. Remove a graph from the worksheet by selecting it from a list produced by the command /**Graph Remove**.

Completing the Printing Process

After you finish formatting a report with Allways, you can easily print it with the Allways /**Print Range** command. Before you print, you must specify a print range with the /**Print Range** command; then select **Go** from the Allways Print menu to begin printing. If you choose to print your report at a later time, you can instead select /**Print File** from the Allways menu. /**Print File** creates an encoded file on disk with the ENC extension.

To print a report created with Allways, follow these steps:

1. Call up the Allways menu by pressing ⟨/⟩.
2. Select **Print** by pressing ⟨P⟩.
3. Select **Range** by pressing ⟨R⟩.
4. Select **Set** by pressing ⟨S⟩ to specify the print range, or select **Clear** by pressing ⟨C⟩ to reset the current print range.

   For this example, select **Set** by pressing ⟨S⟩ to specify a print range.
5. Highlight the range you want to print and press ⟨←Enter⟩. Allways displays the print range boundaries and page breaks as dashed lines on-screen.

In this example, highlight the range A1. .E40 and press ⟨←Enter⟩.

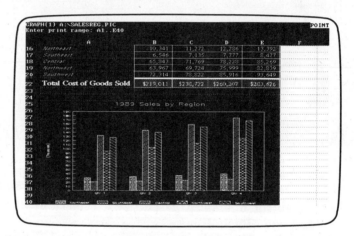

6. To begin printing, select **Go** by pressing ⟨G⟩.

Note: The title of the printed report in the following example does not print exactly as shown on-screen. To correct the problem, the width of column A needs to be increased.

9

284

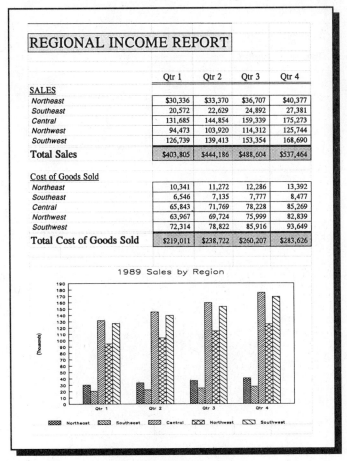

REGIONAL INCOME REPORT

	Qtr 1	Qtr 2	Qtr 3	Qtr 4
SALES				
Northeast	$30,336	$33,370	$36,707	$40,377
Southeast	20,572	22,629	24,892	27,381
Central	131,685	144,854	159,339	175,273
Northwest	94,473	103,920	114,312	125,744
Southwest	126,739	139,413	153,354	168,690
Total Sales	$403,805	$444,186	$488,604	$537,464
Cost of Goods Sold				
Northeast	10,341	11,272	12,286	13,392
Southeast	6,546	7,135	7,777	8,477
Central	65,843	71,769	78,228	85,269
Northwest	63,967	69,724	75,999	82,839
Southwest	72,314	78,822	85,916	93,649
Total Cost of Goods Sold	$219,011	$238,722	$260,207	$283,626

1989 Sales by Region

Northeast   Southeast   Central   Northwest   Southwest

The printout includes the table and associated graph printed on one page.

9

285

This printout shows the effect of removing the grid lines and adding a shadow box to the report title for a more professional appearance.

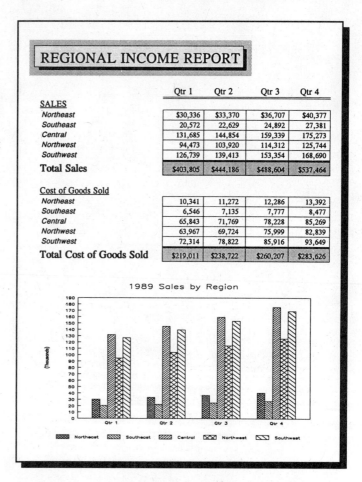

Shadow boxes can be added by using solid shading with adjusted row heights and column widths.

You can use the Allways /Print Settings command to select which pages of a multipage report to print, the page number of the first page, the number of copies to print, and whether to pause the printer for a paper change before printing pages.

The Allways /Print Configuration commands allow you to change the current printer and interface. Depending on your selected printer, other Configuration options may be available, which enable you to select the orientation (portrait or landscape) of your printout, the graphics resolution (level of detail), the specific font cartridge you use, and the paper-feed option.

Summary

This chapter has shown you how to enhance your reports by using the Allways add-in program that accompanies 1-2-3 Release 2.2. You can add boldface, shading, underlining, grids, outlines, and graphs to your printed reports. These enhancements, which appear on-screen while you are formatting the worksheet, let you visualize how the report will appear when printed. Also, you can use different type sizes and styles to emphasize and enhance the text in your report.

Specifically, you learned the following key information about 1-2-3:

- The /Worksheet Global Default Other Add-In Set command ensures that whenever you start using 1-2-3, Allways is automatically attached (available for use).

- As an alternative to the preceding command, the /Add-In Attach and /Add-In Invoke commands can be used to start Allways each time you use the program. This method is useful if you are concerned about the additional memory Allways requires, and you do not need to have it attached at all times.

- To prespecify an Allways range, move the cell pointer to the first cell of the range, press the period (.) key, and extend the range with the arrow keys. Then issue one or more commands which will affect only that range.

- The /Format Font Use command (or Alt-1 through Alt-8) allows you to change the font for a particular range in the worksheet. If you want to use a different default font in the entire worksheet, you can do so with the /Format Font Replace command.

- The /Format Shade Light and /Format Shade Dark commands (or Alt-S) are used to shade an area of the worksheet with light or dark shading, respectively.

9

- The /Format Shade Solid command (or Alt-S) can be used to create a thick dark line. You can use the /Worksheet Row Set-Height command to shrink the height of the row to the thickness of a heavy line.

- The /Format Underline command (or Alt-U) underlines a specified range with single or double underlining. To remove underlining, use the /Format Underline Clear command.

- The /Format Bold command (or Alt-B) enables the characters in a cell or range of cells to appear in boldface.

- The /Format Lines command (or Alt-L) can be used to draw lines around the perimeter of a range, as well as lines on the left, right, top, and/or bottom of a range. To see cell boundaries without letting the lines dominate the text, use the command /Layout Options Grid (or Alt-G).

- The /Display Zoom command can shrink or magnify images on the screen so that characters appear much smaller or larger than normal size. This command does not affect the printed output.

- The accelerator keys provided with Allways execute commonly used commands with a reduced number of keystrokes. These shortcuts combine the Alt key with a letter or number to automate common formatting tasks.

- The /Graph Add command combines graphs with worksheets. The /Display Graphs command lets you view graphs on-screen. Remove a graph from the worksheet by selecting it from a list produced by the /Graph Remove command.

- The /Print Range command allows you to select the range to be printed from Allways. The Go option on the Allways Print menu prints the specified Allways range to the printer.

The next chapter covers some useful file management techniques. You will learn how to protect files with passwords, save and retrieve parts of files, and link cells between worksheets. You will also learn how to list and delete files, change the drive and directory, and import files from other programs into 1-2-3.

288

Managing Files

In Chapter 3, you learned some of the basic file management tasks. You learned to name, save, and retrieve files. In this chapter, some of the other valuable procedures for managing files are covered. For example, you learn how to protect files with passwords so that the files cannot be accessed by unauthorized users. Each password you assign can be easily changed or deleted only by those who know the current password.

This chapter also covers how to save and retrieve parts of files. You learn how to extract a section of data from one worksheet to its own worksheet as well as how to combine parts of several files into one master file. The latter capability is useful for consolidating data from similar worksheets. Individual cells can contain formulas that reference information in another worksheet on disk. These linked cells are automatically updated when a file containing the links is retrieved.

You will also learn to list different types of files on-screen, change the default drive and directory (either permanently or temporarily for only the current 1-2-3 session), delete worksheet and other 1-2-3 files, and import files from outside programs into 1-2-3 using 1-2-3's Translate utility.

Protecting files with passwords

Saving and retrieving partial files

Linking cells between files

Listing different types of files

Specifying a drive and directory

Deleting files

Importing files into 1-2-3

> ## Key Terms in This Chapter
>
> *Password*   A string of up to 15 characters that can be used to limit access to worksheet files.
>
> *File linking*   A 1-2-3 feature that allows you to use formulas in the current worksheet to refer to values in other worksheets.
>
> *ASCII file*   A text (or print) file, created in another program, that can be imported into a 1-2-3 worksheet with the /File Import command.
>
> *Template*   An empty master file that is useful when combining files. A template normally contains the same labels as the worksheets to be combined, but the area containing the specific data values remains blank.

Protecting Files with Passwords

You can protect your files by using 1-2-3's password protection system. When saving files, you can specify passwords that would prevent access to the protected files by unauthorized users. The protected files can be retrieved only by those who know the password for a particular file. This feature is particularly useful for confidential information such as sales and payroll data.

Creating a Password

You can create a password with the /File Save command so that your file can be retrieved only by entering the exact password.

To assign a password to a worksheet, follow these steps when saving a file:

1. Call up the 1-2-3 menu by pressing (/).
2. Select File by pressing (F).
3. Select Save by pressing (S).
4. When the prompt Enter name of file to save: appears, type the file name, leave a space, type (P), and press (↵Enter).

290

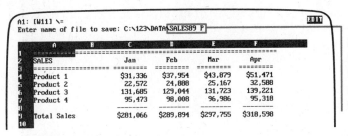

In this example, the name of the file that will be assigned a password is SALES89.

5. When the prompt `Enter password:` appears, type your password and press `⏎Enter`.

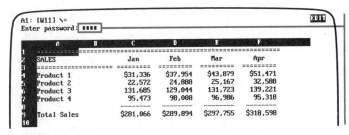

The password never appears on-screen; it is always "hidden" by boxes that are displayed as you type.

6. When the prompt `Verify password:` appears, type the password once more and press `⏎Enter`.

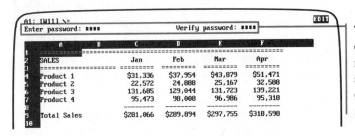

The first and second passwords must match exactly (including case) or they will not be accepted.

At this point, the file has been saved with the new password. Only those who know the password will be able to retrieve the file at another time.

1-2-3 will accept any character in a password, which can be as many as 15 characters long. You need to be careful, however, because 1-2-3 will accept the password only in the exact uppercase or lowercase letters you entered. For example, if you entered **pdfund** as your password, 1-2-3 will not retrieve the file if you type **PDFUND**, **PDfund,** or any other combination of uppercase and lowercase letters. Be sure to remember your password.

Retrieving a Password Protected File

Use the /File **R**etrieve command and type the password to open a protected file. To retrieve a file protected with a password, follow these steps:

1. Call up the 1-2-3 menu by pressing $\boxed{/}$.
2. Select File by pressing $\boxed{F}$.
3. Select **R**etrieve by pressing $\boxed{R}$.
4. Select the file to retrieve by highlighting or typing the file name, and then pressing $\boxed{\leftarrow\text{Enter}}$.
5. When the prompt `Enter password:` appears, type your password exactly as you did when you created it; then press $\boxed{\leftarrow\text{Enter}}$.

The password is
hidden by boxes
as you type.

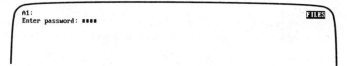

If you enter the password correctly, the worksheet appears. If you enter the wrong password, however, the words `Incorrect password` appear in the screen's lower left corner, and the mode indicator flashes `ERROR`. Press Esc or Enter to return to a blank worksheet.

10

Deleting a Password

You can delete a password by retrieving the file with the password you want to delete. Then, when you are ready to save the file, you select the /File **S**ave command and erase the `[PASSWORD PROTECTED]` message.

To delete password protection from a file, follow these steps:

1. Call up the 1-2-3 menu by pressing $\boxed{/}$.

2. Select **File** by pressing F.

3. Select **Save** by pressing S.

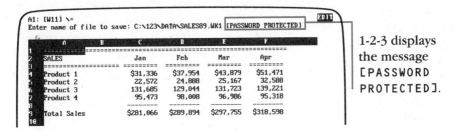

A1: [W11] \=
Enter name of file to save: C:\123\DATA\SALES89.WK1 [PASSWORD PROTECTED]

	A	B	C	D	E	F
1						
2	SALES		Jan	Feb	Mar	Apr
3						
4	Product 1		$31,336	$37,954	$43,879	$51,471
5	Product 2		22,572	24,888	25,167	32,588
6	Product 3		131,685	129,044	131,723	139,221
7	Product 4		95,473	98,008	96,986	95,318
8						
9	Total Sales		$281,066	$289,894	$297,755	$318,598
10						

1-2-3 displays the message [PASSWORD PROTECTED].

4. When the prompt Enter name of file to save: appears, erase [PASSWORD PROTECTED] by pressing ◄Backspace or Esc.

5. Press ◄Enter to save the file without the password.

Changing a Password

To change a password, you delete the existing password and enter a new one. The first part of the procedure is the same as you use to delete a password, and the last part is the same as you use to create a new password.

To change a password, follow these steps:

1. Call up the 1-2-3 menu by pressing /.

2. Select **File** by pressing F.

3. Select **Save** by pressing S.

4. When the prompt Enter name of file to save: appears, erase [PASSWORD PROTECTED] by pressing ◄Backspace or Esc.

5. Type the file name, leave a space, type P, and press ◄Enter.

6. When the prompt Enter password: appears, type the password and press ◄Enter.

7. At the prompt Verify password:, type the password once more and press ◄Enter.

After you complete these steps, the file is saved with the new password.

10

293

Saving and Retrieving Partial Files

Sometimes you may want to store only part of a worksheet (a range of cells, for instance) in a separate file on disk. For example, you can use the /File Xtract command to extract payments from an expense report or revenues from an income statement. One of the best uses for an extract is to break up worksheet files that are too large to be stored on a single disk.

Conversely, you may have several worksheets with similar information. Suppose that you own a store in which each department is its own profit center. At the end of the month, you may want to retrieve a partial file from each department's worksheet and combine the files to get the overall picture of the store's profit and loss. You can use the /File Combine command to perform this operation.

Extracting Data

With the /File Xtract command, you can save part of the worksheet file—either the formulas existing in a range of cells or the current values of the formulas in the range, depending on the option you select. Both options (Formulas and Values) create a separate worksheet file that you can reload into 1-2-3 with the /File Retrieve command.

The /File Xtract command requires that you specify the portion of the worksheet you want to save. The range to be saved can be as small as a cell or as large as the entire worksheet.

To copy a part of your worksheet to a separate file, follow these steps:

1. Call up the 1-2-3 menu by pressing [/]
2. Select File by pressing [F]
3. Select Xtract by pressing [X]
4. To extract data and preserve any formulas in the extract range, select Formulas by pressing [F]

   Or

   To extract data and convert formulas to values, select Values by pressing [V]

10

294

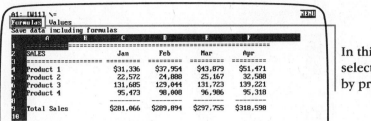

In this example,
select Formulas
by pressing F.

5. When the prompt Enter name of file to extract to:
appears, type a file name for the file to hold the extracted data and
press Enter.

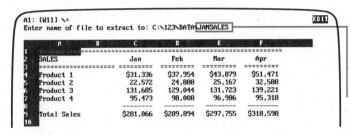

In this
example, type
JANSALES and
press Enter.

6. When the prompt Enter extract range: appears, highlight
the range you want to extract and press Enter.

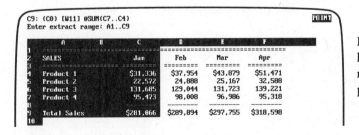

In this example,
highlight the
range A1..C9 and
press Enter.

10

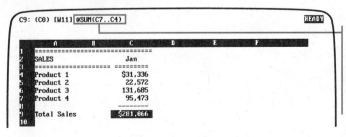

The formula in
cell C9 (dis-
played in the
control panel) is
retained in the
new file.

295

In this example, /File **X**tract Values is selected, and the formula in C9 is converted to a value.

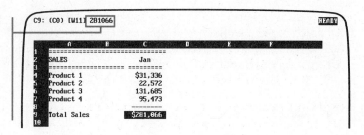

If you choose to save only the current values with /File **X**tract Values, remember that the resulting worksheet file will contain numbers but no formulas. The /File **X**tract Formulas command preserves any formulas that are in the extract range. This option can be particularly useful if your worksheet is too large to fit on one disk, because you can split the file across two disks and still preserve the formulas you need. Make sure, however, that all formulas in the range to be extracted refer only to cells in that same range; otherwise the created file will have formulas referring to blank cells. Use /File **X**tract Values to avoid this problem.

When you select the /File **X**tract Values command, you can "lock" the current values in a worksheet. Think of this process as taking a snapshot of the current worksheet. You can then reload the new, values-only file into the worksheet to easily perform operations that do not require formulas (such as printing and graphing). Before using /File **X**tract Values, however, you should be sure to press Calc (F9) if the CALC indicator appears at the bottom of the screen. Then, you can be sure that the correct formula values will be extracted.

10 Combining Files

Another file management task you may need to perform is copying certain ranges of cells from other worksheets and placing them into strategic spots in the current worksheet. For example, if you work in the sales department of a large firm, you may want to combine quarterly sales information by region into one consolidated worksheet.

A simple technique for accomplishing this kind of consolidation is to start with and keep a copy of an empty master file, or *template*. A template can contain exactly the same labels as the worksheets to be combined, but the area containing the specific data values remains blank. You should have a template ready when the time to perform a consolidation occurs. When you start with a blank template, you can copy the first quarterly sales worksheet onto the template, leaving the original copy of that worksheet untouched. Copying a range of cells can be helpful also when you want to combine divisional data into a single consolidated worksheet.

The command used to combine data from different files is /**F**ile **C**ombine. The **C**opy option of this command copies the worksheet or range to be combined on top of the current worksheet. The **A**dd option adds the values from the combined worksheet or range to the values in the current worksheet. And the **S**ubtract option decreases the values in the current worksheet by the values in the combined worksheet or range.

To combine data from different files, follow these steps:

1. Retrieve the blank template file into which you want to combine files with /**F**ile **R**etrieve.

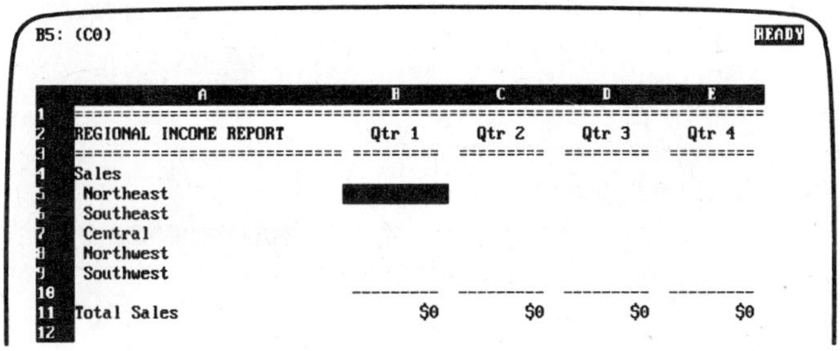

In this example, because the range B5..E9 is blank, all the formulas in row 11 evaluate to zero.

2. Position the cell pointer on the first cell of the range to receive the combined data.
3. Call up the 1-2-3 menu by pressing /.
4. Select **F**ile by pressing F.
5. Select **C**ombine by pressing C.
6. Select **C**opy by pressing C if you want to copy a worksheet or range from another file on top of the existing worksheet, starting at the location of the cell pointer.

   Or

   Select **A**dd by pressing A to add the incoming values in a worksheet or range to the values in the existing worksheet or range, starting at the location of the cell pointer.

Or

Select Subtract by pressing $\boxed{S}$ to decrease the existing values in a worksheet or range by the values in an incoming worksheet or range, starting at the location of the cell pointer.

In this example, select Copy by pressing $\boxed{C}$.

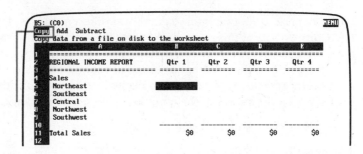

7. If you want to copy an entire incoming file, choose Entire-File by pressing $\boxed{E}$.

   Or

   If you want to copy a specific range from an incoming file, choose Named/Specified Range by pressing $\boxed{N}$.

In this example, select Named /Specified Range by pressing $\boxed{N}$.

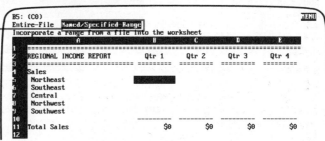

8. If you chose Entire-File in step 7, continue with step 9.

   Or

   If you chose Named/Specified Range in step 7, type the range name or location of the incoming range and press $\boxed{\text{⏎Enter}}$.

10

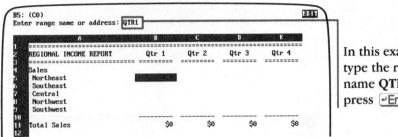

In this example, type the range name **QTR1** and press [Enter].

9. When the prompt `Enter name of file to combine:` appears, indicate the name of the file containing the data to be combined and press [Enter].

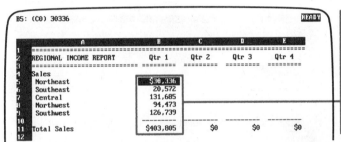

The first quarter data is copied to the range B5..B9 in the blank template. The formula in cell B11 is automatically updated.

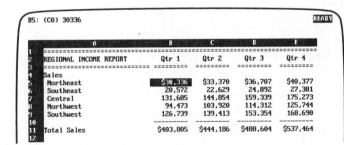

Once you have combined data for all quarters, the result is a filled-in version of the template. The formulas in row 11 display values.

10

The Copy option of /File Combine pulls in an entire worksheet or named range and causes the new contents to write over the corresponding cells in the current worksheet. Cells in the current worksheet that correspond to blank cells in the file or range being combined are not affected. (Note the important distinction here between blank cells and cells containing a space in the file or range to be combined.)

In this example, the **Add** option was selected. The values in the center worksheet (the worksheet to be combined) were added to the values in the corresponding cells of the top worksheet (the current worksheet) to create a worksheet of combined values.

```
B5: (C0) 30336
                  A              B          C          D          E
1 ============================================================================
2 REGIONAL INCOME REPORT-1989   Qtr 1      Qtr 2      Qtr 3      Qtr 4
3 ============================================================================
4 Sales
5   Northeast               $30,336    $33,370    $36,707    $40,377
6   Southeast                20,572     22,629     24,892     27,381
7   Central                 131,685    144,854    159,339    175,273
8   Northwest                94,473    103,920    114,312    125,744
9   Southwest               126,739    139,413    153,354    168,690
10                         ---------  ---------  ---------  ---------
```

```
B5: (C0) 27578
                  A              B          C          D          E
1 ============================================================================
2 REGIONAL INCOME REPORT-1988   Qtr 1      Qtr 2      Qtr 3      Qtr 4
3 ============================================================================
4 Sales
5   Northeast               $27,578    $30,336    $33,370    $36,707
6   Southeast               $18,702    $20,572    $22,629    $24,892
7   Central                $119,714   $131,685   $144,854   $159,339
8   Northwest               $85,885    $94,473   $103,920   $114,312
9   Southwest              $115,217   $126,739   $139,413   $153,354
```

```
B5: (C0) 57914
                  A              B          C          D          E
1 ============================================================================
2 REGIONAL INCOME REPORT        Qtr 1      Qtr 2      Qtr 3      Qtr 4
3 ============================================================================
4 Sales
5   Northeast               $57,914    $63,706    $70,076    $77,084
6   Southeast               $39,274    $43,201    $47,521     52,273
7   Central                $251,399   $276,539   $304,192    334,612
8   Northwest              $180,358   $198,393   $218,233    240,056
9   Southwest              $241,956   $266,152   $292,767    322,044
10                         ---------  ---------  ---------  ---------
11 Total Sales: 1988 and 1989 $770,900   $847,991   $932,790 $1,026,069
12
```

Add pulls in the values from an entire worksheet or a named range and adds these values to the corresponding cells in the current worksheet. The **Add** command affects only cells in the worksheet that are blank or that contain numeric values. In the current worksheet, cells that contain formulas or labels are unchanged. In the file being combined, cells that contain labels or string formulas are not added.

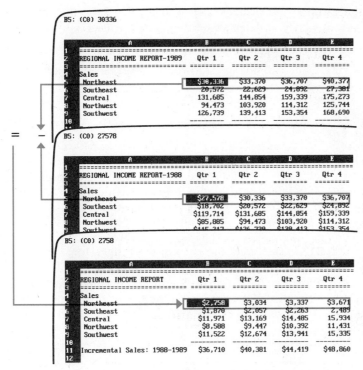

In this example, the Subtract option was selected. The values in the center worksheet (the worksheet to be combined) were subtracted from the values in the corresponding cells in the top worksheet (the current worksheet) to create a worksheet of combined values.

Subtract pulls in an entire worksheet or a named range and subtracts the values from the corresponding cells in the current worksheet. When an existing cell is blank, the incoming value is subtracted from zero. Like **Add**, **Subtract** affects only cells in the worksheet that are blank or that contain numeric values. In the current worksheet, cells containing formulas or labels are unaffected. In the worksheet being combined, cells that contain labels or string formulas are not subtracted.

Linking Cells between Files

1-2-3 allows you to use formulas to link a cell in one worksheet to a cell in another (this feature is not provided with versions prior to Release 2.2). The cell that receives the information is called the *target* cell, and the one that sends the information is the *source* cell. Once this link is established for a given cell in a worksheet and the worksheet is saved with /**File Save**, the linked formulas are automatically updated when the file is retrieved.

The /**File Combine** command must be used every time you want to copy information from file to file. The cell linkage feature, however, is automatic and requires no active use of commands.

Establishing a Link

Linking is performed within the target cell, using a special kind of formula. The formula begins with a plus sign (+), followed by two less-than symbols (<<), the name of the sending file (including the directory name if the file is not in the current directory), then two greater-than symbols (>>), and finally the address or range name of the source cell.

The entry +<<MIAMI>>B17 in cell B8 of the current worksheet, for example, means that B8 is to contain the data found in cell B17 of the file MIAMI.WK1 in the current directory. When this cell entry is complete, data copying occurs at once. For the link to become permanent and automatic (occurring with every subsequent /**File Retrieve**), use the /**File Save** command on the current worksheet.

The income statement worksheet for the Miami region contains a source cell—B17.

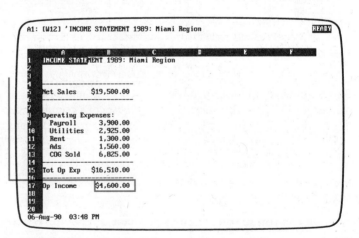

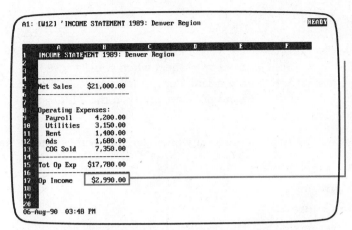

The income statement for the Denver region also contains a source cell—B17 (in a separate file).

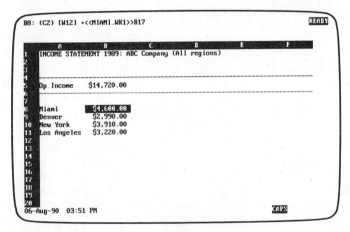

The target file, the income statement worksheet for all regions, uses information that exists in the Miami and Denver files (as well as the files for New York and Los Angeles).

10

Cell B8 is linked to cell B17 of a file named MIAMI.WK1, and cell B9 is linked to cell B17 of a file named DENVER.WK1. The remaining two data cells in the target file are also linked to their respective worksheets. Whenever the target file is retrieved, cells B8 through B11 are updated automatically with information from the source files.

When a cell that serves as a source cell is altered, its contents are not immediately copied to the target cell or cells to which it is linked. In fact, a source cell may go through many changes and its file can be saved many times, yet the target cell might not reflect any of these interim values. The contents of the target cell are updated only upon retrieval of the file containing the target cell.

303

Listing Linked Files

The command /File List Linked will provide a listing of all files that are linked (contribute values) to the current worksheet when you retrieve it or when you use the command /File Admin Link-Refresh (discussed in the next section). The /File List Linked command does not give you the addresses of either the target cell or source cells.

To list the files that are linked to the current worksheet, follow these steps:

1. Call up the 1-2-3 menu by pressing Ⓛ.
2. Select File by pressing Ⓕ.
3. Select List by pressing Ⓛ.
4. Select Linked by pressing Ⓛ. The resulting screen lists all other files that have links to the current file.

In this example, four files are linked to the current file.

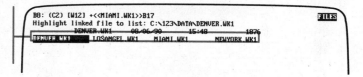

```
B8: (C2) [W12] +<<MIAMI.WK1>>B17                                    FILES
Highlight linked file to list: C:\123\DATA\DENVER.WK1
              DENVER.WK1    08/06/90    15:48        1876
DENVER.WK1        LOSANGEL.WK1    MIAMI.WK1        NEWYORK.WK1
```

Refreshing Links

If you are using Release 2.2 in a network or multiuser environment, others may be altering files that contain source cells for the worksheet you are using. In this case, you may want periodic updating of your target cells. Use the /File Admin Link-Refresh command to update all target cells in the current worksheet to reflect the current contents of the source cells.

To refresh the cells linked to the current worksheet, follow these steps:

1. Call up the 1-2-3 menu by pressing Ⓛ.
2. Select File by pressing Ⓕ.
3. Select Admin by pressing Ⓐ.
4. Select Link-Refresh by pressing Ⓛ.

10

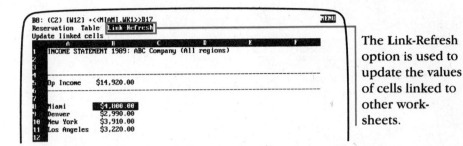

The Link-Refresh option is used to update the values of cells linked to other worksheets.

Listing Different Types of Files

1-2-3 can list all the names of a certain type of file on the current drive and directory with the /File List command. When you list files, you can specify whether you want to list worksheet, print, or graph files; any types of files; or linked files.

To display a list of files on the current drive and directory, follow these steps:

1. Call up the 1-2-3 menu by pressing ⃞/⃞.

2. Select **File** by pressing ⃞F⃞.

3. Select **List** by pressing ⃞L⃞.

4. Select the type of file you want to list: **Worksheet, Print, Graph, Other,** or **Linked.**

   To list only worksheet files (files with a WK1 or WKS extension), choose **Worksheet** by pressing ⃞W⃞.

   To list only print files (files with a PRN extension), choose **Print** by pressing ⃞P⃞.

   To list only graph files (files with a PIC extension), choose **Graph** by pressing ⃞G⃞.

   To list all types of files (files with any extension), choose **Other** by pressing ⃞O⃞.

   To list only files linked to the current worksheet, choose **Linked** by pressing ⃞L⃞.

After you choose an option, the list of files is displayed.

10

In this example, all WK1 files in the current directory are displayed after Worksheet is selected.

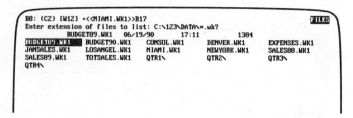

```
B8: (C2) [W12] +<<MIAMI.WK1>>B17                                    FILES
Enter extension of files to list: C:\123\DATA\*.wk?
          BUDGET89.WK1   06/19/90        17:11          1384
BUDGET89.WK1   BUDGET90.WK1   CONSOL.WK1    DENVER.WK1    EXPENSES.WK1
JANSALES.WK1   LOSANGEL.WK1   MIAMI.WK1     NEWYORK.WK1   SALES88.WK1
SALES89.WK1    TOTSALES.WK1   QTR1\         QTR2\         QTR3\
QTR4\
```

Specifying a Drive and Directory

You use the /Worksheet Global Default Directory or the /File Directory commands to change the drive and directory. After installing 1-2-3, the default directory is the directory containing the 1-2-3 program files. /Worksheet Global Default Directory can change the default drive and directory to one that contains your data files. /File Directory, on the other hand, changes the drive and directory temporarily for only the current worksheet session.

To change the default directory, follow these steps:

1. Call up the 1-2-3 menu by pressing /.
2. Select Worksheet by pressing W.
3. Select Global by pressing G.
4. Select Default by pressing D.
5. Select Directory by pressing D. The current default directory is displayed.

10

In this example, C:\123 is the default directory.

```
A1:                                                           EDIT
Enter default directory: C:\123
                        ─── Default Settings ───
   Printer:                          Directory: C:\123
     Interface       Parallel 1
     Auto linefeed   No              Autoexecute macros: Yes
     Margins
       Left 4  Right 76  Top 2  Bottom 2  International:
     Page length     66              Punctuation       A
     Wait            No                Decimal         Period
     Setup string                      Argument        Comma
     Name            Toshiba P351 series  Thousands     Comma
                                         Currency      Prefix: $
   Add-In:                           Date format (D4)  A (MM/DD/YY)
     1                               Time format (D8)  A (HH:MM:SS)
     2                                 Negative        Parentheses
     3
     4                               Help access method: Removable
     5                               Clock display:    Standard
     6                               Undo:             Disabled
     7                               Beep:             Yes
     8
   06-Aug-90  04:06 PM
```

306

6. Press (Esc) or use (*Backspace) to clear the current default directory; then type the new default directory name and press (*Enter). Remember to precede the directory name with the drive letter.

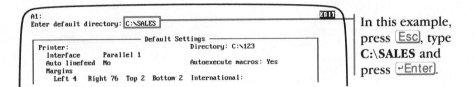

In this example, press (Esc), type **C:\SALES** and press (*Enter).

7. Select **Update** by pressing (U).

   This command updates a program file that allows 1-2-3 to use the new default directory in future sessions.

8. Select **Quit** by pressing (Q) to return to READY mode.

With a hard disk, you can use the default directory setting to your advantage. As in the preceding example, you could set the default directory to C:\DATA. When you want to retrieve a file, 1-2-3 displays all the subdirectories and files within the C:\DATA directory. After you've chosen the proper directory, 1-2-3 again displays the subdirectories and files stored in that directory so that you can make a choice. Setting the default directory this way will save time if you use worksheets in different subdirectories.

If you are working with files in a different directory than the one you normally use, you can change the directory temporarily with the /**File Directory** command. This command overrides the default directory for the current session only.

To change the current directory, follow these steps:

1. Call up the 1-2-3 menu by pressing (/).
2. Select **File** by pressing (F).
3. Select **Directory** by pressing (D). The current directory is displayed.

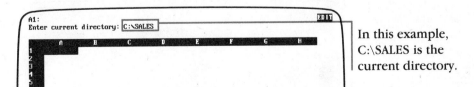

In this example, C:\SALES is the current directory.

10

307

4. Begin typing the new directory name and press ⏎Enter (the current directory name will automatically clear when you start typing). Remember to precede the directory name with the drive letter.

In this example, type **C:\EXPENSES** and press ⏎Enter.

The directory is changed for the current session only. The next time you access 1-2-3, the default directory again becomes the current directory.

Deleting Files

When you save files to a diskette, you may sometimes find that the diskette is full. To alert you, 1-2-3 displays the message Disk full in the screen's lower left corner, and the mode indicator flashes ERROR. You can then either swap diskettes or delete one or more of the files occupying space on the diskette.

You have two ways to delete stored files in 1-2-3: by using the /File Erase command within 1-2-3, or by accessing DOS with the /System command and erasing the file at the DOS level with the ERASE or DEL (delete) command.

To delete a file from within 1-2-3, follow these steps:

1. Call up the 1-2-3 menu by pressing ⁄.
2. Select File by pressing F.
3. Select Erase by pressing E.
4. Select the type of file you want to erase: **Worksheet, Print, Graph,** or **Other.**

To erase a worksheet file (a file with a WK1 extension), choose Worksheet by pressing W.

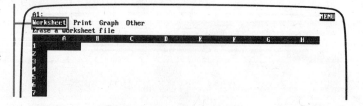

10

308

To erase a print file (a file with a PRN extension), choose **Print** by pressing Ⓟ.

To erase a graph file (a file with a PIC extension), choose **Graph** by pressing Ⓖ.

To erase any type of file, choose **Other** by pressing Ⓞ.

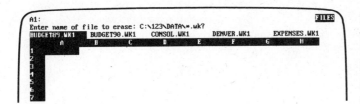

Depending on your choice, 1-2-3 displays files with the appropriate extensions.

5. You can press F3 (Name) to display a full-screen listing of files.

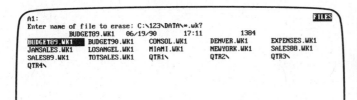

In this example, all worksheet files are displayed in a full-screen listing.

6. Highlight the file you want to erase, or type its name; then press ↵Enter.

You can use the wild-card characters described in Chapter 3 to display all the files of a certain type that are to be deleted. These characters are the same familiar wild-card characters used for DOS and other commands throughout 1-2-3. The following list shows some examples of using wild-card characters:

* Matches the remaining characters of a file name. For example, C* matches CHICAGO, CASHFLOW, and CENTERS.

? Matches all characters in a single position in a file name. For example, SALES8? matches SALES88 and SALES89, but not SALES90 or SALES.

10

Be careful when you use the /File Erase command. After you delete a file, you cannot recover it by conventional means. Always double-check before you delete a file.

Importing Files into 1-2-3

A powerful 1-2-3 feature is its capability to transfer data between 1-2-3 and other programs. To perform a transfer, you use the /File Import and /Print File Options Other Unformatted commands (the latter of which was discussed in Chapter 8), and the Translate utility.

Importing ASCII Text Files

Use the /File Import command to copy standard ASCII files to specific locations in the current worksheet. For example, PRN (print) files are standard ASCII text files created to print after the current 1-2-3 session. Other standard ASCII files include those produced by different word processing and BASIC programs. Many programs, for example database and word processing programs, have the capability of producing ASCII files, as does 1-2-3.

To import an ASCII text file into 1-2-3, follow these steps:

1. Call up the 1-2-3 menu by pressing ⌿.
2. Select File by pressing F.
3. Select Import by pressing I.
4. Select Text by pressing T or Numbers by pressing N.

   Generally, you should use the Text option for importing an ASCII file that was created with your word processor.

   Use the Numbers option when you import delimited files, that is, ASCII files that contain separator characters to distinguish items of data.

In this example, select Text by pressing T. 1-2-3 displays all PRN files in the current directory.

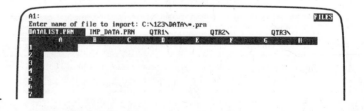

310

5. To display files in a different drive or directory, or with a different extension, type the appropriate drive and directory. Then use wild-card characters (* or ?) and press ⏎Enter to display the desired files.

6. Highlight the name of the text file to be imported and press ⏎Enter. For example, highlight the file name IMP_DATA.PRN and press ⏎Enter.

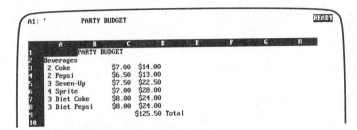

The ASCII text file is imported into 1-2-3.

If you select /**File Import Numbers**, labels and numbers are separated from each other by commas, colons, semicolons, or spaces. Remember that if you import a file with the **Numbers** option, any column headings that aren't enclosed in quotation marks are not imported. Headings that are enclosed in quotation marks are imported as labels.

Importing Files from Other Programs

The Translate utility is used to import files into 1-2-3 from dBASE II, dBASE III, dBASE III Plus, dBASE IV, Multiplan (SYLK), and VisiCalc, and to export 1-2-3 files to dBASE II, dBASE III, dBASE III Plus, dBASE IV, and DIF formats. (Many presentation graphics packages use DIF files.)

This utility provides good communication with dBASE, including dBASE III Plus and dBASE IV (which are not listed on the menu but can be accessed by selecting dBASE III). The Translate utility also provides translation capabilities among all Lotus products, allowing free interchange of work-sheets between 1-2-3 Release 2.2 and Symphony, and earlier releases of 1-2-3.

To use the Translate utility, follow these steps:

1. Select **T**ranslate from the 1-2-3 Access System menu by pressing T.

10

311

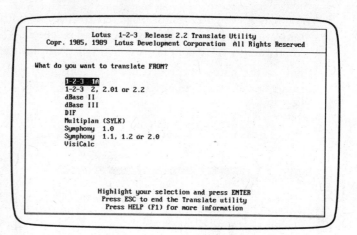

The opening
menu of the
Translate utility
is displayed.

2. Select the format (program) *from* which you want to translate by highlighting your selection and pressing ⏎Enter.

3. Select the format (program) *to* which you want to translate by highlighting your selection and pressing ⏎Enter.

Based on your choice of format, a list of files appears. (As a format choice, for example, you may have chosen *.WK1 for 1-2-3 Release 2.0 or higher, or *.DBF for a dBASE file.)

4. Select the file name to be translated by highlighting the file name and pressing ⏎Enter, or press Esc to edit the subdirectory or file name.

10

In this example,
highlight
EMPFILE.DBF
and press
⏎Enter.

```
          Lotus  1-2-3  Release 2.2 Translate Utility
     Copr. 1985, 1989  Lotus Development Corporation  All Rights Reserved

Translate FROM: dBase III              Translate TO: 1-2-3 2.2

Source file: C:\123\DATA\*.DBF

EMPFILE  DBF   6/19/89  12:00a        666
         EMPFILE  DBF
         SALESDB  DBF




          Highlight the file you want to translate and press ENTER
               Press ESC to edit the source file specification
                    Press HELP (F1) for more information
```

5. Type the name of the file to be created and press ⏎Enter, or simply press ⏎Enter to accept the default file name shown.

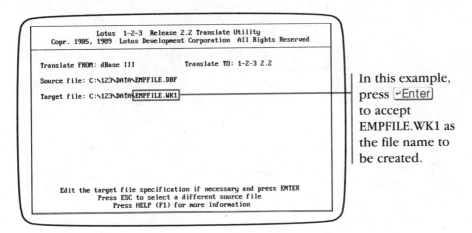

```
              Lotus  1-2-3  Release 2.2 Translate Utility
    Copr. 1985, 1989  Lotus Development Corporation  All Rights Reserved

  Translate FROM: dBase III          Translate TO: 1-2-3 2.2

  Source file: C:\123\DATA\EMPFILE.DBF

  Target file: C:\123\DATA\EMPFILE.WK1




              Edit the target file specification if necessary and press ENTER
                     Press ESC to select a different source file
                     Press HELP (F1) for more information
```

In this example, press ⏎Enter to accept EMPFILE.WK1 as the file name to be created.

6. At the resulting menu, select **Yes** by pressing Y to proceed with the translation.

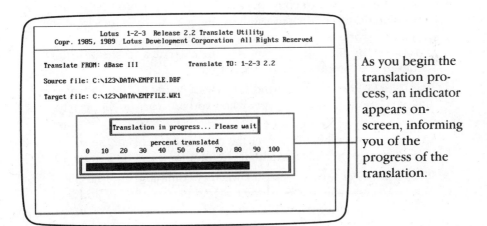

```
              Lotus  1-2-3  Release 2.2 Translate Utility
    Copr. 1985, 1989  Lotus Development Corporation  All Rights Reserved

  Translate FROM: dBase III          Translate TO: 1-2-3 2.2

  Source file: C:\123\DATA\EMPFILE.DBF

  Target file: C:\123\DATA\EMPFILE.WK1


          ┌───────────────────────────────────────┐
          │ Translation in progress... Please wait │
          │                                        │
          │           percent translated          │
          │  0  10  20  30  40  50  60  70  80  90  100 │
          │  ███████████████                       │
          └───────────────────────────────────────┘
```

As you begin the translation process, an indicator appears on-screen, informing you of the progress of the translation.

10

7. When the translation is completed, press Esc twice to reach a menu giving you the option to leave the Translate utility; to exit, select **Yes** by pressing Y.

Summary

Knowing how to manage files is essential for efficient use of 1-2-3. Aside from the basic tasks of naming, saving, and retrieving files you learned in Chapter 3, you sometimes need to perform other file management tasks. This chapter showed you how to protect files with passwords. You also learned how to save partial files when you want to extract or combine portions of a worksheet. You can list and delete files with ease if you know how to specify drives, subdirectories, and file names accurately. You can even import files from other leading software programs.

Specifically, you learned the following key information about 1-2-3:

- You can add passwords to your files with the /File Save command so that your file can be retrieved only by those who know the exact password.

- The /File Xtract command allows you to save part of the worksheet file. You can save either the formulas existing in a range of cells or the current values of the formulas in the range.

- The /File Combine command is used to combine data from different files. You can copy the worksheet or range to be combined on top of the current worksheet, add the values from the combined worksheet or range to the values in the current worksheet, or decrease the values in the current worksheet by the values in the combined worksheet or range.

- The /File List Linked command provides a listing of all files that are linked to the current worksheet when you retrieve the file.

- The /File Admin Link-Refresh command updates all target cells in the current worksheet to reflect the current contents of the source cells. This command is particularly helpful for users on a network.

- The /Worksheet Global Default Directory command and the /File Directory command are used to change the current drive and directory. The latter command affects only the current session of 1-2-3.

- The /File Erase command is used to delete stored files from within 1-2-3. You can also delete files by accessing DOS with the /System command and erasing the file at the DOS level with the ERASE or DEL command.

10

■ The /File Import command allows the transfer of data between 1-2-3 and other programs. This command is commonly used to copy standard ASCII files to specific locations in the current worksheet. The Translate utility, available from the 1-2-3 Access System menu, must be used for this process.

The next chapter will show you how to create graphs within 1-2-3. You will learn about the graph creation process, how to select graph types and data ranges, how to enhance the appearance of a graph, and how to save a graph to disk for later printing.

10

Creating Graphs

Even if 1-2-3 provided only spreadsheet capabilities, the program would be extremely powerful. More information can be quickly assembled and tabulated electronically than can possibly be developed manually. But despite the importance of keeping detailed worksheets that show real or projected data, that information can be worthless if you can't readily understand it.

To help decision-makers who are pressed for time or unable to draw conclusions from countless rows of numeric data, and who may benefit from seeing key figures displayed graphically, 1-2-3 offers graphics capabilities. The program has five types of basic business graphs as well as limited options for enhancing the graphs' appearance. Although 1-2-3 is no match for many stand-alone graphics packages, the strength of its graphics capability lies in its integration with the spreadsheet. Using 1-2-3, you can quickly design and alter graphs as worksheet data changes. This capability means that graphs may be changed almost as fast as 1-2-3 recalculates the data.

An overview of creating a graph

Selecting a graph type

Specifying a data series range

Enhancing the appearance of a graph

Preserving a graph on disk

11

Key Terms in This Chapter

Graph type   The manner in which data is represented graphically.

X-axis   The horizontal bottom edge of a graph.

Y-axis   The vertical left edge of a graph.

Origin   The intersection of the x- and y-axes.

Legend   The description of the shading, color, or symbols assigned to data ranges in line or bar graphs. The legend appears across the bottom of the graph.

Tick marks   The small marks on the axes of a graph, which indicate the increments between the minimum and maximum graph values.

You create graphs with 1-2-3's /Graph commands. Although the program has a number of options, you need to specify only a graph type and a single data range to create a basic graph. After providing the required information, you select the View option of the Graph menu. This command plots the graph to the screen, temporarily replacing the spreadsheet until a key is pressed.

You can perform true graphics "what if" analyses with 1-2-3. In fact, you can use the F10 function key to replot a graph after making changes to the worksheet, without having to redefine the graph with the /Graph commands. This replotting immediately shows the effects of changes on the current graph.

In this chapter, you learn to perform the simple four-step procedure for creating a basic graph, to create five types of graphs from the data on your worksheet, and to enhance your graphs so that they are presentation quality. You will also learn to name and save your graphs in a worksheet file that you can retrieve and modify at any time. In the next chapter, you learn how to use 1-2-3's PrintGraph program to print graphs.

An Overview of Creating a Graph

Before creating your first graph, you must determine whether your hardware supports viewing and printing graphs, whether your 1-2-3 software is correctly installed for graphics, and whether the worksheet on-screen contains data you want to graph. And you should understand which type of graph is best suited for presenting specific numeric data in picture form.

You can use 1-2-3's graphics feature to create and view a graph, store its specifications for later use, and print it. Creating and storing a graph requires only that you have the 1-2-3 software installed on your equipment, that you correctly select options from the Graph menu, and that you save these options with the associated worksheet file.

Hardware Requirements

To view a graph on-screen, you need a graphics monitor or a monitor with a graphics-display adapter. Without this monitor, you can construct and save a 1-2-3 graph, but you must print the graph to view it.

To print a graph, you need a graphics printer supported by 1-2-3 and a separate set of PrintGraph instructions. These instructions are explained in the next chapter.

The Graph Creation Process

To create a 1-2-3 graph, you begin by selecting the **Graph** command from the main menu while the worksheet containing the data you want to graph is displayed.

```
C4: (C0) [W13] 94008                                              MENU
Type  X  A  B  C  D  E  F  Reset  View  Save  Options  Name  Group  Quit
Line  Bar  XY  Stack-Bar  Pie
┌───────────────────────── Graph Settings ─────────────────────────┐
│  Type: Line              Titles: First                            │
│                                  Second                           │
│  X:                              X axis                           │
│  A:                              Y axis                           │
│  B:                                                               │
│  C:                                      Y scale:     X scale:    │
│  D:                              Scaling  Automatic   Automatic   │
│  E:                              Lower                            │
│  F:                              Upper                            │
│                                  Format   (G)         (G)         │
│  Grid: None      Color: No       Indicator Yes        Yes         │
└───────────────────────────────────────────────────────────────────┘
```

Selecting **Graph** from the 1-2-3 main menu produces a Graph Settings sheet and a menu of options for creating graphs.

The Graph Settings sheet (not displayed in versions of 1-2-3 prior to Release 2.2) shows various ranges and options that pertain to the current graph. This sheet remains on-screen while you are using the Graph commands, except when you define the location of data ranges. To see the worksheet while

11

using these commands, press the Window (F6) key. The F6 key toggles the screen display between the worksheet and the settings sheet.

Each option on the Graph main menu is described in table 11.1.

Table 11.1
Selections on the Graph Main Menu

Selection	Description
Type	Provides options for creating five types of graphs: line, bar, XY, stacked-bar, or pie.
X	Specify the range to be used as x-axis labels or values, or labels of pie slices.
A through F	Specify the ranges containing the numeric data to be graphed.
Reset	Clears the current graph settings.
View	Displays a graph on the computer monitor.
Save	Saves a graph in the file format needed for printing the graph with the 1-2-3 PrintGraph program.
Options	Provides choices for labeling, enhancing, or customizing a graph.
Name	Lets you assign a name to one or more graphs and store the graph settings so that you can redisplay the graph(s) whenever you retrieve the worksheet file.
Group	Lets you define a range of contiguous cells to be the X and A through F ranges (not available in versions of 1-2-3 prior to Release 2.2).
Quit	Quits the Graph menu and returns the worksheet to READY mode.

You will use some of these commands every time you create a graph. Other commands (particularly some commands available through **Options**) are used less frequently; you use these commands when you need to enhance or customize your graph or when you want to save your graph in a form that can be printed. If you do not need to enhance, customize, or print the graph, creating a graph that displays nothing more than data points is easy. Only four steps are required to produce a simple graph:

320

1. Select the type of graph (if different from the default type, which is line) by using the /Graph Type command.

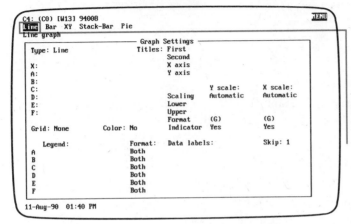

For this example, accept the default of **Line** by pressing ⏎Enter.

2. Indicate the data ranges from your worksheet that you want to graph by selecting one or more of the **A–F** options from the Graph menu.

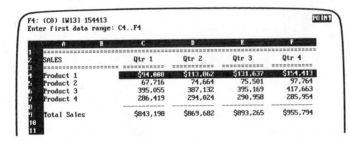

To graph the quarterly sales for Product 1, select **A**. Then highlight the range and press ⏎Enter.

To create a pie graph, use the **A** option to indicate what data range you want to graph, and use the **B** option to set the hatching for each part of the pie graph. To create an XY graph, use the **A–F** options to plot the dependent variables.

3. Use the **X** option from the Graph menu to indicate the data range for labeling the tick marks along the x-axis in a line, bar, or stacked-bar graph; for labeling each part of a pie graph; and for plotting the independent variable in an XY graph.

321

11

For example, select **X**, highlight the labels Qtr 1 through Qtr 4 in row 2, and press ⏎Enter.

```
F2: [W13] ^Qtr 4                                              POINT
Enter x-axis range: C2..F2
         A        B        C        D        E        F
1 ==================================================================
2  SALES                  Qtr 1    Qtr 2    Qtr 3    Qtr 4
3 ==================================================================
4  Product 1            $94,008  $113,862 $131,637 $154,413
5  Product 2             67,716   74,664   75,501   97,764
6  Product 3            395,055  387,132  395,169  417,663
7  Product 4            286,419  294,024  290,958  285,954
8                      --------- -------- -------- --------
9  Total Sales         $843,198 $869,682 $893,265 $955,794
10
11
```

You can also use the /Graph Group command to set all data ranges at once from a contiguous block of cells. By using /Graph Group, you can combine steps 2 and 3 into a one-step operation. This option, not available in versions of 1-2-3 prior to Release 2.2, is described later in the chapter.

4. Display the graph on the screen by selecting the View command from the Graph menu or by pressing [F10] (Graph) when in READY mode. Press [Esc] to return to the worksheet.

The resulting line graph, the default graph type, illustrates the default features for this type of graph.

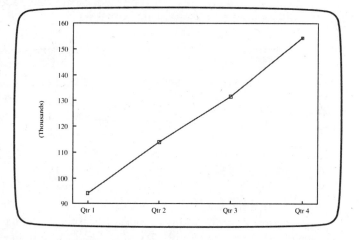

After you have created a basic graph using the preceding four steps, you can choose from among numerous options to change the graph type and add titles, labels, grid lines, and legends. The following line graph, for example, has been enhanced in a number of ways to display the data in presentation-quality form.

322

Because 1-2-3 sets a scale based on minimum and maximum values, the program automatically displays a numeric indicator, such as (Thousands), along the y-axis.

The y-axis measures the amount along the vertical axis.

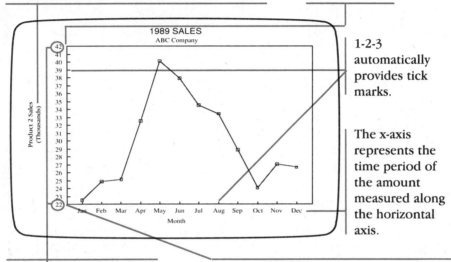

1-2-3 automatically provides tick marks.

The x-axis represents the time period of the amount measured along the horizontal axis.

1-2-3 automatically scales the adjacent numbers on the y-axis, based on the minimum and maximum values of the graphed data.

The origin of the x- and y-axis. Notice that if the origin on the graph is not zero, the upward trend will seem larger than it really is. Use an origin of zero to provide a more accurate picture of the trend.

You learn more about the many ways you can enhance a graph later in this chapter. First, though, you learn the process for creating a basic graph. Specifically, you learn how to select the graph type you need and how to indicate which data from your worksheet you want to appear on the graph.

Selecting a Graph Type

1-2-3's graphic capabilities increase the program's power by giving you a way to represent your data visually. Do you want to see whether there is a trend in the latest sales increase of a particular product? A 1-2-3 graph can show you the answer quickly, when deciphering that type of information from columns of numbers would be difficult. 1-2-3 offers five basic graph types: line, bar, XY, stacked-bar, and pie.

Creating Graphs

11

A line graph is best used for showing numeric data across time.

For example, you can track the sales trend of several products with a line graph.

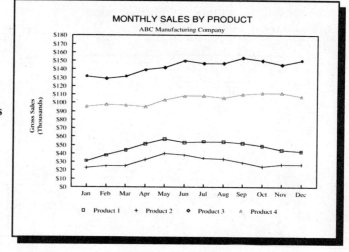

A bar graph, often comparing two or more data items, shows the trend of numeric data across time.

For example, you can track the progress of two or more products with a bar graph.

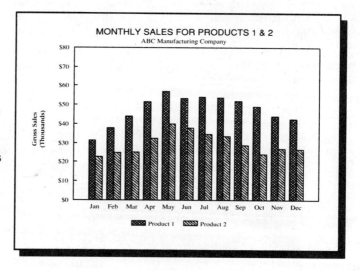

324

An XY graph compares one numeric data series to another across time, to determine whether one set of values (the dependent variable) depends on the other (the independent variable).

11

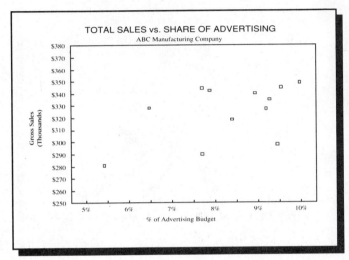

Use an XY graph, for example, to plot total sales and percent of advertising to assess whether sales data appears to depend on the share of advertising.

A stacked-bar graph shows two or more data series that total 100 percent of a specific numeric category. (Do not use this type of graph if your data contains negative numbers.)

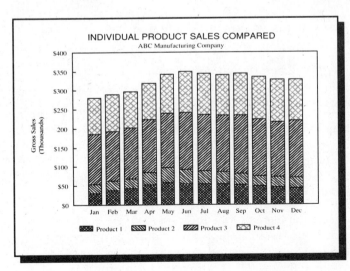

Use a stacked-bar graph, for example, to graph data series for four products (displayed one above the other) to depict the proportion each represents of total product sales throughout the year.

11

A pie graph is used to graph only one data series in which the components total 100 percent of a specific numeric category. (Do not use this type of graph if your data contains negative numbers.)

Use a pie graph, for example, to graph the percentage of total sales by month.

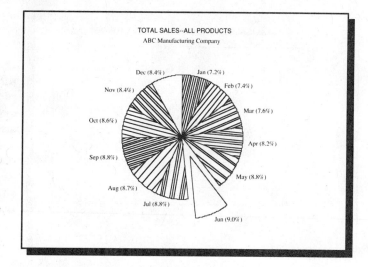

Selecting one of the five available graph types is easy. When you select **Type** from the Graph menu, 1-2-3 displays the following options:

   Line Bar XY Stack-Bar Pie

By selecting one of these options, you set that graph type and automatically return to the Graph menu.

To understand which type will best display specific numeric data, you must know something about plotting points on a graph. Take a few minutes now to review the two basic terms *x-axis* and *y-axis*.

All graphs (except pie graphs) have two axes: the x-axis (the horizontal bottom edge) and the y-axis (the vertical left edge). 1-2-3 automatically provides tick marks for both axes. The program also scales the adjacent numbers on the y-axis, based on the minimum and maximum figures included in the plotted data range(s).

Every point plotted on a graph has a unique location (x,y): *x* represents the time period or the amount measured along the horizontal axis; *y* measures the corresponding amount along the vertical axis. The intersection of the x-axis and the y-axis is called the *origin*. To avoid the misinterpretation of graph results and to make graphs easier to compare, use a zero origin in

11

your graphs. Later in this chapter, you learn how to manually change the upper or lower limits of the scale initially set by 1-2-3.

Of the five 1-2-3 graph types, all but the pie graph display both x- and y-axes. Line, bar, and stacked-bar graphs display numbers (centered on the tick marks) along the y-axis only. The XY graph displays numbers on both axes.

Specifying a Data Series Range

Because more than one type of graph can accomplish the desired presentation, you need to consider what data ranges you want to graph and the relationships among data you want to show. To create a graph, you must specify the range(s) of cells from the current worksheet to be used as data series.

To enter a data series from the main Graph menu, choose from the options **X, A, B, C, D, E, F**, or **Group**.

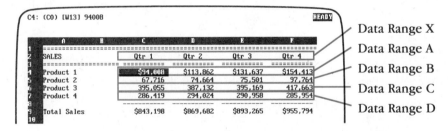

Notice that 1-2-3's menu system does not permit you to type data to be plotted on a graph. Plotting data points is not like typing descriptions, such as titles—a process illustrated later in this chapter.

You have the option of defining each data range on the worksheet separately or defining all the data ranges you want to plot at one time (this option is not available in versions prior to Release 2.2). To define one data range at a time, you use the **X** and **A–F** options from the Graph menu. If all the ranges you want to plot are contiguous (next to each other without any intervening rows or columns), you can use the **Group** option to define all the ranges at once.

Defining One Data Range at a Time

If the ranges you want to plot are located in various parts of the worksheet—that is, the ranges are not all contiguous, you must define one range at a time. You can do so by choosing from among the options **X** and **A–F**.

To specify the data ranges containing x-axis and y-axis data, follow these steps:

1. Call up the 1-2-3 menu by pressing ⌀.
2. Select **Graph** by pressing Ⓖ.
3. Select from the following options the ranges for x- or y-axis data, or labels:

Option	Description
X	Enters the x-axis label range. These are labels such as Jan., Feb., Mar., and so on. Creates labels for pie graph wedges and for line, bar, and stacked-bar graphs.
A	Enters the first y-axis data range. **A** is the only data range used by a pie graph.
B	Enters the second y-axis data range. Identifies pie graph shading values and any slices to be exploded.
C through F	Enters the third through sixth y-axis data ranges.

When you select one of the **X** or **A–F** options, 1-2-3 prompts you for the cell or range of cells containing the data you want to graph. You cannot enter data directly at the prompt.

4. Highlight the data range and press ⏎Enter.

In this example, highlight the **A** range C4..F4 and press ⏎Enter.

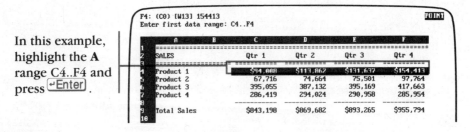

5. To view the graph, select **View** by pressing Ⓥ.

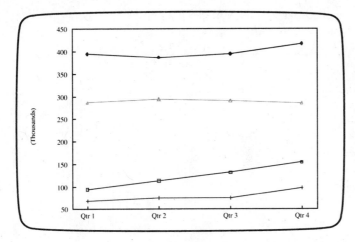

Although this line graph shows four data series, you can enter as many as six data series when you access the Graph menu choices **A** through **F** separately.

You can specify the ranges in any order; the range selected will always correspond with the letter assigned in the selection process. Use the **X** option to plot the time or amount measured along the x-axis. The data points in each data series are marked by a unique symbol.

These six symbols, which correspond to specific data ranges from A through F, are displayed in table 11.2. Shading within bar, stacked-bar, and pie graphs is covered in the following pages.

Table 11.2
Data Range Symbols for Line Graphs

Data Range	Line Graph Symbol
A	□
B	+
C	◇
D	△
E	×
F	▽

11

With bar graphs or stacked-bar graphs, you can also enter as many as six data series when you access separately the Graph menu choices **A–F**.

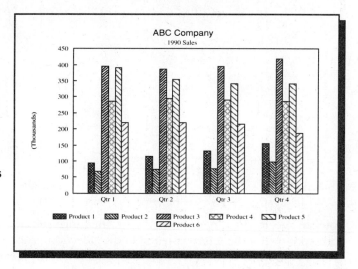

In a bar graph, multiple data ranges appear on the graph from left to right in order of data ranges A through F.

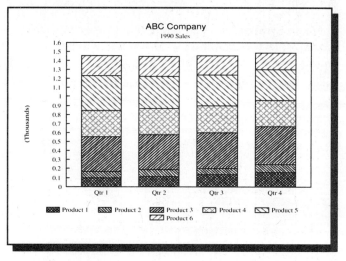

In a stacked-bar graph, multiple data ranges appear on the graph from bottom to top in order of data ranges A through F.

In bar and stacked-bar graphs, the **X** option lets you indicate the time or amount measured along the x-axis. Every data series displayed in monochrome (one color) has unique shading. Data series displayed in color are assigned one of three colors (unless you are using an EGA or VGA monitor, which displays six colors). Refer to table 11.3 for an explanation of the patterns and colors used in bar and stacked-bar graphs. Note that these patterns will appear slightly different in versions of 1-2-3 prior to Release 2.2.

Table 11.3
Data Range Patterns and Colors for Bar Graphs

Data Range	Bar Graph Pattern	Bar Graph Color
A	▨	Red
B	▨	Blue
C	▨	White
D	▨	Red
E	▨	Blue
F	▨	White

```
F4: (C0) [W13] 154413                                    POINT
Enter x-axis range: C4..F4

        A        B        C          D          E          F
   ==============================================================
 1
 2  SALES              Qtr 1      Qtr 2      Qtr 3      Qtr 4
 3  ==============================================================
 4  Product 1          $94,008    $113,062   $131,637   $154,413
 5  Product 2           67,716     74,664     75,501     97,764
 6  Product 3          395,055    387,132    395,169    417,663
 7  Product 4          286,419    294,024    290,958    285,954
 8                    ----------  ---------- ----------  ----------
 9  Total Sales       $843,198   $869,682   $893,265   $955,794
10
11
12  Advertising Expense
13  ------------------
14  Product 1           $5,640     $6,832     $7,898     $9,265
15  Product 2            4,063      2,987      3,775      7,821
16  Product 3           23,703     23,228     23,710     25,060
17  Product 4           17,185     17,641     17,457     17,157
18                    ----------  ---------- ----------  ----------
19                    $50,592    $50,688    $52,841    $59,303
20
11-Aug-90  02:42 PM
```

With XY graphs, to enter the data series being plotted as the independent variable, select **X** from the main Graph menu.

Plot at least one dependent variable (you would usually select **A**). The unique symbols that mark the data points depend on which data series (**A–F**) is selected.

With pie graphs, choose **X** to identify each piece of the pie. Then enter only one data series by selecting **A** from the main Graph menu. Other than the **X** and **A** options, the only other option in the **X** and **A–F** selections you need for creating a pie graph is **B**. By selecting **B**, you can shade and "explode" pieces of the pie.

331

11

To shade pieces of the pie graph, enter a range of numbers from 1 to 8 corresponding to data range A of the graph.

```
F10: [W13] 104                                                    POINT
Enter second data range: C10..F10

       A         B          C          D          E          F
 1  ==================================================================
 2  SALES                  Qtr 1      Qtr 2      Qtr 3      Qtr 4
 3  ==================================================================
 4  Product 1            $94,008   $113,862   $131,637   $154,413
 5  Product 2             67,716     74,664     75,501     97,764
 6  Product 3            395,055    387,132    395,169    417,663
 7  Product 4            286,419    294,024    290,958    285,954
 8                      --------   --------   --------   --------
 9  Total Sales         $843,198   $869,682   $893,265   $955,794
10                             1          2          3        104
11
12  Advertising Expense
13                      --------
14  Product 1             $5,640     $6,832     $7,898     $9,265
15  Product 2              4,063      2,987      3,775      7,821
16  Product 3             23,703     23,228     23,710     25,060
17  Product 4             17,185     17,641     17,457     17,157
18                      --------   --------   --------   --------
19                      $50,592    $50,688    $52,841    $59,303
20
23-Aug-90   08:42 AM
```

To explode a piece of the pie, add 100 to this number. Select **B** from the menu and highlight the range of numbers.

The printed pie graph shows some of the different types of shading and one exploded slice.

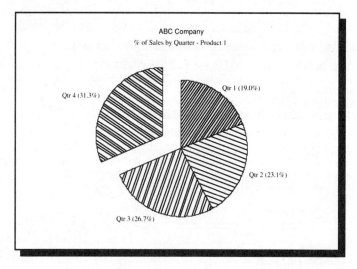

Defining All Data Ranges at Once

If the **X** and the **A–F** ranges are in one contiguous range, you can use the /Graph Group command to define all the ranges at once. The command /Graph Group gives you a quick way to define the **X** and **A–F** ranges without having to specify them individually. For this option to work properly, the

332

cells for the **X** range must be immediately to the left or immediately above the cells of the **A** range. The cells for ranges **B** through **F**, if present, are adjacent one by one to the **A** range. Once you have defined the location of the range, the command prompts you for a "columnwise" or "rowwise" orientation.

To select all the data ranges for a graph, **X** and **A–F**, when data is in adjacent rows and columns are in consecutive order, follow these steps:

1. Call up the 1-2-3 menu by pressing ⌐/⌐.
2. Select **Graph** by pressing Ⓖ.
3. Select **Type** by pressing Ⓣ; then select the type of graph from the selections provided.
4. Select **Group** by pressing Ⓖ.
5. Specify the range that contains **X** and one or more **A** through **F** data ranges, and then press ⌐Enter⌐. The rows or columns must be adjacent and in the order X, A, B, C, and so on.

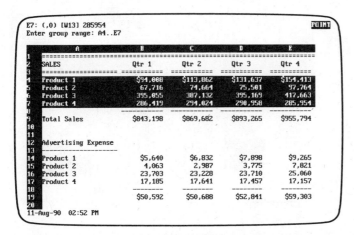

For this example, specify the group range as A4..E7 and press ⌐Enter⌐.

6. Select **Columnwise** by pressing Ⓒ if the data ranges are in columns, or select **Rowwise** by pressing Ⓡ if the data ranges are in rows.

11

For this example, select Column-wise by pressing C.

```
B4: (C0) [W13] 94008                                          MENU
Columnwise  Rowwise
Use columns as data ranges
                              Graph Settings
   Type: Bar                  Titles: First
                                      Second
   X:                                 X axis
   A:                                 Y axis
   B:
   C:                                         Y scale:    X scale:
   D:                                 Scaling Automatic   Automatic
   E:                                 Lower
   F:                                 Upper
                                      Format   (G)         (G)
   Grid: None     Color: No           Indicator Yes        Yes

      Legend:             Format:    Data labels:        Skip: 1
   A                      Both
   B                      Both
   C                      Both
   D                      Both
   E                      Both
   F                      Both

   11-Aug-90  02:53 PM
```

7. Select View by pressing V.

This printed graph shows the result of selecting Column-wise orientation with the /Graph Group command.

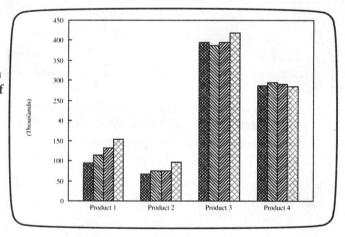

Enhancing the Appearance of a Graph

After you have created a basic graph using the simple four-step procedure described earlier in this chapter, you can improve the appearance of your graphs and produce final-quality output suitable for business presentations. By selecting choices from the Graph Options menu, you can enhance a graph by adding descriptive labels and numbers, and by changing the default graph display items.

334

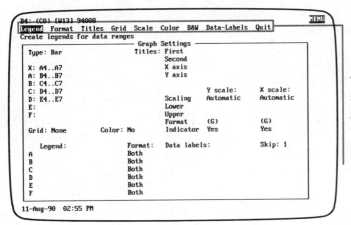

To improve the appearance of a graph, select Options to access the menu shown here.

Each of the selections on the Graph Options menu is described in table 11.4.

Table 11.4
Selections on the Graph Options Menu

Selection	Description
Legend	Lets you specify descriptions to link symbols, shadings, or colors on a line, bar, stacked-bar, or XY graph to specific y-axis data ranges.
Format	Adds lines and/or symbols in a line or XY graph to connect or represent data points.
Titles	Lets you enter titles you want displayed (and printed) at the top of the graph, below the x-axis, and to the left of the y-axis.
Grid	Lets you add horizontal and/or vertical lines within the graph.
Scale	Lets you control the division and format of values along the x-axis or y-axis.
Color	Changes the graph display to color, if available.
B&W	Changes the graph display from color to monochrome.
Data-Labels	Lets you add labels identifying different data points within the graph.
Quit	Returns you to the Graph menu.

11

To add descriptive information to a graph, you can select Legend, Titles, and Data-Labels from the Options menu and the **X** option from the main Graph menu. Data labels appear within the graph. Descriptions entered with the **X** option appear immediately below the x-axis. You can enter as many as four titles: two at the top and one to describe each axis. Legends describing the shadings, colors, or symbols assigned to data ranges in line or bar graphs appear across the bottom of those graphs.

The Group option in the Data-Labels command is similar to the Group option used to define data ranges. If all the ranges you plan to use for data labels are in contiguous rows or columns, define them all at once with the /Graph Options Data-Labels Group command. You also must indicate **Columnwise** or **Rowwise** orientation.

In addition to adding label or number descriptions to the basic graph, you can enhance a graph by changing any of the default graph display items. For example, you can use the /Graph Options Format command to change the connecting lines or symbols in a line or XY graph. You can also use the **Grid** option to display horizontal or vertical grid lines. You can adjust the axes scales with the **Scale** option, and you can adjust the spacing of the labels displayed on the x-axis with the /Graph Options Scale Skip command.

The following sections of this chapter describe and illustrate how you can create basic graphs by using only a few commands. You also learn how to use additional commands from the Graph Options menu to create presentation-quality graphs.

As you add enhancements to your graphs, check the results frequently. Select Quit to leave the Graph Options menu and return to the main Graph menu. Then select View to check the most recent version of the graph. Press any key to exit the graph display and restore the Graph menu to the screen.

To view the current graph while in READY mode, press the Graph (F10) key, which instantly redraws the graph with any updated worksheet data. You can use the Graph (F10) key to "toggle" between the worksheet and the graph.

Using the Titles Option

If you select /Graph Options Titles, the following options are displayed in the control panel:

First Second X-Axis Y-Axis

You can enter one or two centered titles at the top of the graph, a title below the x-axis, and a title to the left of the y-axis.

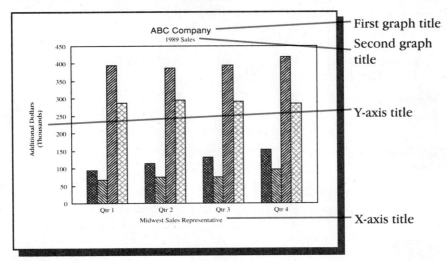

If you enter two titles at the top of the graph, both will be the same size on-screen. On the printed graph, however, the title you enter by selecting **First** will be twice the size of any other title specified. You can enter titles by typing a new description, by specifying a range name, or by referencing the cell location of a label or a number already in the worksheet. Although all titles appear on-screen in the same print style, when you print the graph, you can select one font (such as italic) for the top title and another font for other titles and labels.

To add titles to a graph (after you have chosen the graph type and entered data ranges), complete the following steps:

1. Call up the 1-2-3 menu by pressing ⃞/.
2. Select **Graph** by pressing ⃞G.
3. Select **Options** by pressing ⃞O.
4. Select **Titles** by pressing ⃞T.
5. From the Titles menu, choose from four options: **First**, **Second**, **X-axis**, or **Y-axis**.

   Note: If you choose to have more than one title on the graph, you must first select **Titles** again to access the Titles menu.

11

To display a title
on the top line of
a graph, select
First by pressing
⎡F⎤, type the title,
and press
⎡↵Enter⎤.

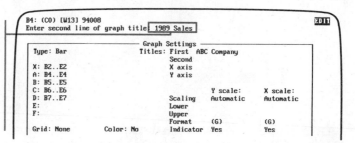

To display a title
on the second
line of a graph,
select **Second** by
pressing ⎡S⎤, type
the title, and
press ⎡↵Enter⎤.

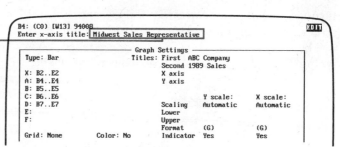

To display a title
below the x-axis,
select **X-Axis** by
pressing ⎡X⎤, type
the title, and
press ⎡↵Enter⎤.

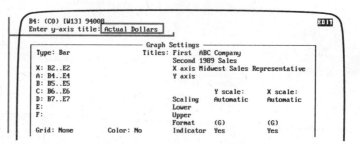

To display a title
to the left of the
y-axis, select **Y-
Axis** by pressing
⎡Y⎤, type the title,
and press
⎡↵Enter⎤.

B4: (C0) [W13] 94008   EDIT
Enter y-axis title: Actual Dollars

                    ┌─── Graph Settings ───
Type: Bar   Titles: First ABC Company
                                       Second 1989 Sales
X: B2..E2   X axis Midwest Sales Representative
A: B4..E4   Y axis
B: B5..E5
C: B6..E6   Y scale: X scale:
D: B7..E7   Scaling   Automatic   Automatic
E: Lower
F: Upper
                               Format (G)   (G)
Grid: None   Color: No   Indicator Yes   Yes

338

11

Note: The **X-Axis** and **Y-Axis** titles do not apply when you construct a pie graph.

6. To view the graph with titles displayed, select **Quit** by pressing Q; then select **View** by pressing V.

To edit a title, use the command sequence that you used for creating the title, **/Graph Options Titles**. The existing text, cell reference, or range name will appear in the control panel, ready for editing. To modify a title, use the left- and right-arrow keys, the Backspace key, or the Esc key. If you want to eliminate a title entirely, press Esc and then press Enter.

Entering Labels within a Graph

After you have graphed a data series, you can enter values or labels to explain each point plotted on a bar, line, or XY graph. For example, you can label points on a line graph illustrating sales figures with the specific values for each point.

To add labels to be displayed within a graph, follow these steps:

1. Call up the 1-2-3 menu by pressing /.

2. Select **Graph** by pressing G.

3. Select **Options** by pressing O.

4. Select **Data-Labels** by pressing D.

5. Specify the data series (**A**, **B**, **C**, **D**, **E**, **F**, or **Group**) to which the data labels apply.

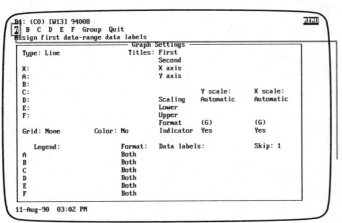

In a line graph that includes only one data range, choose **A** to assign labels to the range.

11

6. Enter the range containing the text or values you want to use as labels for the graph and press ⏎Enter.

To label data points in the sales graph, highlight the range containing the sales figures and press ⏎Enter.

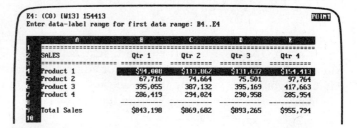

Note: Instead of typing the labels (as you typed the titles), you must specify each data-label range by pointing to an existing range in the worksheet, providing cell coordinates, or specifying a previously determined range name.

7. Indicate the location of the data labels by selecting from the menu options: **Center, Left, Above, Right,** and **Below.** You may need to experiment with two or more positions for data labels to determine which position is best for your graph.

8. To view the graph with data labels displayed, select **Quit** twice by pressing QQ; then select **View** by pressing V.

This graph shows the result of choosing the **Above** option for the location of data labels.

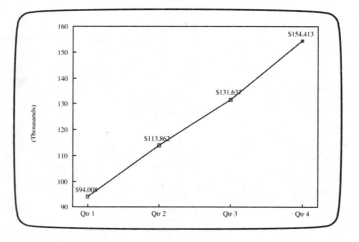

340

11

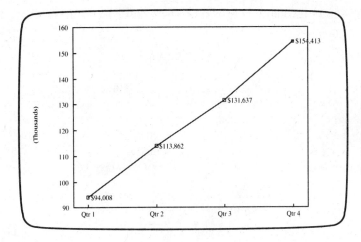

This graph shows the result of choosing the **Right** option for the location of data labels.

If you graph more than one data series, attach the data labels to the data series with the largest figures. Then select **Above** to position the data labels above the data points plotted. To enter text or numbers as the plotted points, use the **Center** option with line graphs that display **Neither** lines nor symbols.

To edit either the range or position of the data label, use the same command sequence you used to create the data label. Edit the current range or specify a different position.

To eliminate data labels that have been specified, you must issue the command you used to specify the data labels, and highlight or type the address of a blank cell or the name of a blank range in the worksheet.

Using the Legend Option

Whenever a graph contains more than one set of data, you need to be able to distinguish between those sets. If you are using a color monitor and select **Color** from the main Graph menu, 1-2-3 differentiates data series with color. If the main Graph menu's default option **B&W** (monochrome) is in effect, the data series in line and XY graphs are marked with special symbols.

If you intend to print the graph on a black-and-white printer, even if you have a color monitor, choose **B&W** before saving the graph. A graph saved

11

under the Color option will print all ranges on a black-and-white printer as solid blocks of black.

You might pick a data series (**A**, **B**, **C**, **D**, **E**, **F**, or Group) because you want certain symbols or shadings, or to avoid using certain combinations of symbols or shadings. For example, if you enter only two data items in a line graph and use data ranges **D** and **F**, you will have difficulty distinguishing between the two assigned symbols—one pointing up and the other pointing down. On the other hand, pairing the **A** range (widely spaced crosshatches) with the **D** range (narrowly spaced crosshatches extending in the opposite direction) on a bar graph produces a distinctly different display.

To provide explanatory text for data that is represented by symbols or shadings, use the /Graph Options Legend command to display legends below the x-axis. To add a legend to your graph, follow these steps:

1. Call up the 1-2-3 menu by pressing ⃞/.
2. Select **Graph** by pressing ⃞G.
3. Select **Options** by pressing ⃞O.
4. Select **Legend** by pressing ⃞L.
5. Select **A** to specify the legend for the first data range.
6. When the prompt `Enter legend for first data range:` appears, type ⃞\; then type the cell address containing the label and press ⃞Enter, or simply type the label and press ⃞Enter.

For this example, type \A4 and press ⃞Enter.

7. Repeat steps 4 through 6 for each data range contained in your graph.
8. To view the graph with a legend displayed, select **Quit** by pressing ⃞Q; then select **View** by pressing ⃞V.

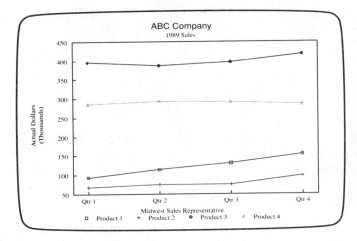

After you have entered all legends and then viewed the graph, the legends appear below the x-axis. As shown, different data ranges in line and XY graphs are distinguished by symbols.

You can use the command /**Graph** **O**ptions **L**egend **R**ange to select the legend in one step if the text to appear in the legend is in adjacent cells in the worksheet. In the previous example, you would type or highlight the range A4..A7 and press Enter (after the /**Graph** **O**ptions **L**egend **R**ange command).

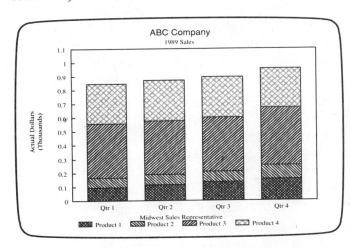

The legends for the different data ranges in bar and stacked-bar graphs are marked with unique shadings.

If you want to edit a legend, use the same command sequence you used to create it. The existing text, cell reference, or range name will appear in the control panel, ready for you to edit. To eliminate a legend, press Esc and then press Enter. You cannot use the **L**egend option for pie graphs, which can have only one data series.

11

As with the /Graph Group command and the /Graph Options Data-Labels command, the Legend option lets you define the placement of all legends at once. Because this range is one-dimensional, you are not prompted for row or column orientation.

Specifying Connecting Lines or Symbols

A few choices on the Options menu do not apply to all graphs. For example, Titles (x- and y-axis), Legend, and Data-Labels are not applicable to pie graphs. The Format option, which is used to display connecting lines and/or symbols on a line-type graph, is appropriate for only two types of graphs: line and XY (a form of line graph).

To add connecting lines and/or symbols for line and XY graphs, follow these steps:

1. Call up the 1-2-3 menu by pressing ⟨/⟩.
2. Select Graph by pressing ⟨G⟩.
3. Select Options by pressing ⟨O⟩.
4. Select Format by pressing ⟨F⟩.

    1-2-3 displays a menu with these options:

    Graph **A B C D E F** Quit

5. Assign lines and/or symbols to the whole graph (Graph), or assign lines and/or symbols to individual data ranges (**A–F**).
6. Select from among the four selections on the displayed menu: Lines, Symbols, Both, or Neither.

Select Lines by pressing ⟨L⟩ if you want data points connected by lines alone.

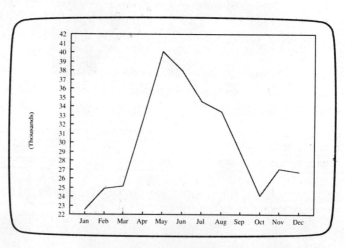

344

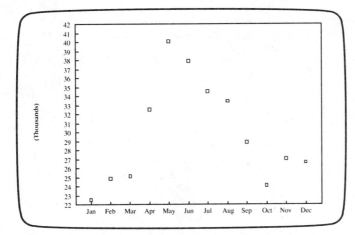

Select **Symbols** by pressing [S] to display symbols only.

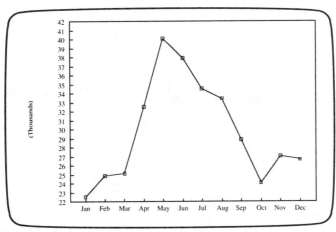

Select **Both** by pressing [B] for both lines and symbols. This is the default setting for a line graph.

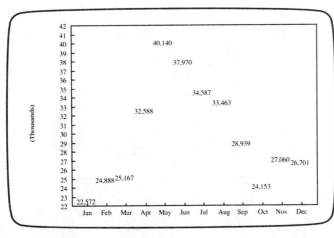

Select **Neither** by pressing [N] if you do not want lines or symbols, but only data labels. Remember that the data labels must be added with the /Graph Options Data-Labels command.

11

7. To view the graph with the specified format, select **Quit** twice by pressing Q Q; then select **View** by pressing V.

To restore the default format setting for the sample line graph, select **/Graph Options Format A Both**. Returning to the main Graph menu and selecting View displays the graph in its original form.

Setting a Background Grid

Ordinarily, you'll use the default background (clear) for your graphs. When 1-2-3 displays a line, bar, stacked-bar, or XY graph, data ranges are displayed without background grids. But sometimes you may want to impose a grid on a graph so that the data-point amounts are easier to read. To display and print line, bar, stacked-bar, or XY graphs with a grid, use the **/Graph Options Grid** command.

To add a grid to your line, bar, stacked-bar, or XY graphs, follow these steps:

1. Call up the 1-2-3 menu by pressing /.
2. Select **Graph** by pressing G.
3. Select **Options** by pressing O.
4. Select **Grid** by pressing G.
5. Select the type of grid you want displayed from the menu options: **Horizontal**, **Vertical**, or **Both**.

Select **Horizontal** by pressing H to display a graph with a horizontal grid. Grid lines are spaced according to the tick marks on the y-axis.

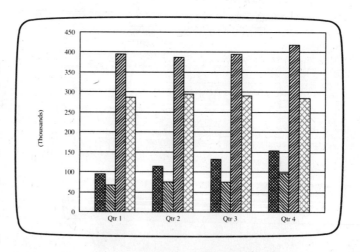

346

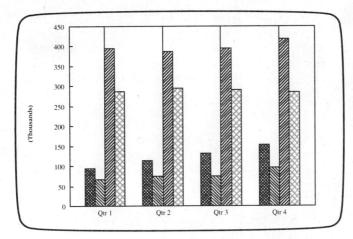

Select **Vertical** by pressing V to display a graph with a vertical grid. Grid lines are spaced according to the tick marks on the x-axis.

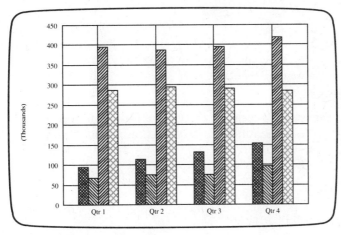

Select **Both** to display a graph with both horizontal and vertical grid lines.

6. To view the graph with grid lines displayed, select **Quit** by pressing Q; then select **View** by pressing V.

Experiment with different grids, repeating the command sequence and specifying other options. Whenever you want to eliminate a grid display, select **/Graph Options Grid Clear**.

Note: You cannot add grids to pie graphs.

11

Changing Axis Scale Settings

You can use the /Graph Options Scale command to alter three distinct
default settings associated with the values displayed along a graph's x- and
y-axes. These settings let you change the upper and lower limits of the y-axis
scale, change the format of y-axis values, and suppress the y-axis scale
indicator. In addition, you can use this option to change the number of
labels displayed along the x-axis.

Note: In the screens depicted throughout this section, the Window (F6) key
was used to depict the worksheet instead of the Graph Settings sheet while
using the /Graph commands.

Changing the Upper and Lower Limits of the Y-Axis Scale

When you create a line, XY, bar, or stacked-bar graph, 1-2-3 automatically
sets scale limits displayed on the y-axis, taking into account the smallest and
largest numbers in the data ranges plotted. (For XY graphs only, 1-2-3 also
establishes x-axis scale values.)

You can change the upper and lower scale limits. You cannot, however,
determine the size of the increment between the maximum and minimum
values. (This increment is indicated by tick marks.)

To change the scale of values displayed along the y-axis of a graph, follow
these steps:

1. Call up the 1-2-3 menu by pressing ⍰.
2. Select **Graph** by pressing Ⓖ.
3. Select **Options** by pressing Ⓞ.
4. Select **Scale** by pressing Ⓢ.
5. From the resulting menu, select the **Y-Scale** option by pressing Ⓨ if
   you want to change the y-axis scale on a bar, stacked-bar, line, or
   XY graph.

   Or

   Select the **X-Scale** option by pressing Ⓧ to change the x-axis scale
   on an XY graph.

348

11

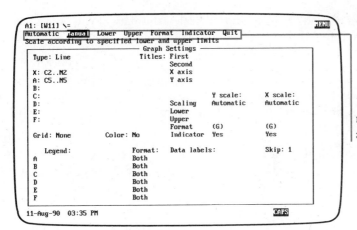

1-2-3 displays the
menu you use to
adjust the scale.

6. Select **Manual** by pressing M to change from 1-2-3's automatic
   scaling to your own scaling. The same menu remains on the screen.

7. Select **Lower** by pressing L to assign the lower value of the scale.
   Type the value to be used as the lower limit and press ↵Enter.

   For example, select **Lower**, and then press ↵Enter to accept the
   default of 0.

8. Select **Upper** by pressing U to assign the upper value of the scale.
   Type the value to be used as the upper limit and press ↵Enter.

   For example, select **Upper**, type **50000,** and press ↵Enter.

9. To view the graph with different y-axis limits, select **Quit** twice by
   pressing Q Q; then select **View** by pressing V.

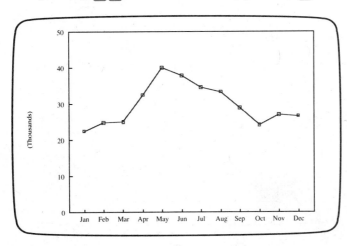

The graph now
appears with the
specified y-axis
lower and upper
limits of 0 and
50,000, respec-
tively.

Creating Graphs

11

You can later select /Graph Options Scale Y-Scale Automatic if you choose to restore the default upper and lower y-axis limits.

If you elect to establish manual limits, remember two basic rules: (1) you must specify both upper and lower settings, and (2) the upper limit must be larger than the lower limit. You can use negative figures for scale values in line and XY graphs, but not in bar, stacked-bar, or pie graphs. The lower limit in a bar or stacked-bar graph is zero.

Select /Graph Options Scale X-Scale only when the graph type is XY. Select Y-Scale for line, XY, bar, and stacked-bar graph types. The Format, Indicator, and Manual scale capabilities are not applicable to pie graphs.

Changing the Format of Y-Axis Values

1-2-3 automatically sets the format of the scale values to General. 1-2-3 does not automatically display dollar signs, commas, and decimal points along the y-axis. To change the format of the values on the y-axis (or x-axis for XY graphs), select the /Graph Options Scale Y-Scale (or X-Scale) Format command. When you choose Format, 1-2-3 displays the same options that are displayed when you use /Range Format or /Worksheet Global Format.

You can change the format to any of the styles available under /Range Format or /Worksheet Global Format. Do not confuse the capability of altering the default format of the scale values with that of bringing in previously formatted worksheet numbers as data labels.

The values formatted as currency on the y-axis scale were produced with the /Graph Options Scale Y-Scale Format Currency command.

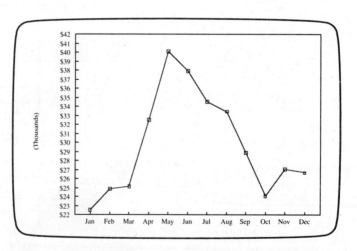

350

Suppressing the Y-Axis or X-Axis Scale Indicator

The scale indicator indicates the magnitude of the values displayed along the y-axis when a line, XY, bar, or stacked-bar graph is created. On an XY graph, an indicator appears also along the x-axis.

Although you cannot change the indicator, you can suppress its display. To understand why you might want to suppress the display of the indicator, imagine a worksheet that contains data with truncated trailing zeros (for example, a sales figure of 94,008,000 that has been entered in the worksheet as 94,008). Graphing the truncated figures will produce the y-axis indicator *Thousands*, but you need *Millions*. In this case, you suppress the display of the indicator entirely and then type an appropriate indicator as part of the y-axis title.

To suppress either the y-axis or x-axis scale indicator, follow these steps:

1. Call up the 1-2-3 menu by pressing /.
2. Select **Graph** by pressing G.
3. Select **Options** by pressing O.
4. Select **Scale** by pressing S.
5. Select the **Y-Scale** option by pressing Y to suppress the y-axis scale indicator on a line, XY, bar, or stacked-bar graph.

   Or

   Select the **X-Scale** option by pressing X to suppress the x-axis scale indicator on an XY graph.
6. Select **Indicator** by pressing I.
7. Select **No** by pressing N to suppress the indicator.
8. To view the graph with the indicator suppressed, select **Quit** twice by pressing Q Q; then select **View** by pressing V.

11

In this example, the y-axis scale indicator has been suppressed.

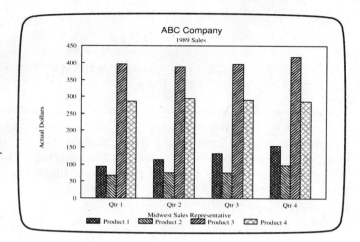

After suppressing the y-axis or x-axis indicator, you can supply your own indicator by using the /Graph Options Titles command, as was done here.

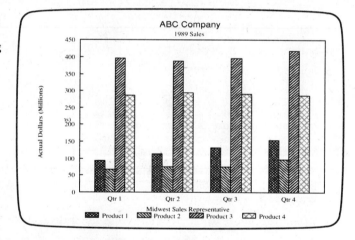

Spacing the Display of X-Axis Labels

You've seen how to use the first two options on the /Graph Options Scale menu. The last option, **Skip**, determines the spacing and number of labels along the x-axis. For example, this command lets you change the x-axis labels from displaying every month to displaying every other month. The default setting of 1 shows every label. If you set the skip factor to 3, every third label is shown.

If the labels are so long that they crowd together or overlap, use this option to improve the appearance of the graph. You will seldom need to set the factor higher than 3 or 4.

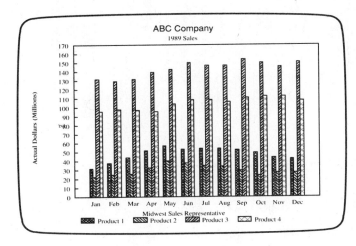

This graph displays labels for every month along the x-axis. The following example shows you how to change the skip factor to display labels for every other month.

To change the spacing of labels displayed along the x-axis, follow these steps:

1. Call up the 1-2-3 menu by pressing ⌐/⌐.
2. Select **Graph** by pressing ⌐G⌐.
3. Select **Options** by pressing ⌐O⌐.
4. Select **Scale** by pressing ⌐S⌐.
5. Select **Skip** by pressing ⌐S⌐.
6. When the prompt `Enter skip factor (1..8192):` appears, type a number and press ⌐↵Enter⌐.

   For example, type ⌐2⌐ and press ⌐↵Enter⌐.
7. To view the graph with the skip factor modified, select **Quit** by pressing ⌐Q⌐; then select **View** by pressing ⌐V⌐.

11

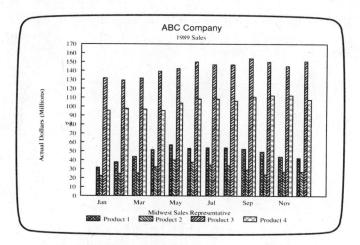

The resulting graph displays labels for every other month along the x-axis, improving the appearance of the graph.

Preserving a Graph on Disk

Although using 1-2-3 to construct a graph from existing data in a worksheet is easy, having to rebuild the graph whenever you want to print or display it on-screen would be tedious. To create a disk file (with the file extension PIC) that can be used only to print the graph, you use the /Graph Save command. To save the graph specifications along with the underlying worksheet, first use the /Graph Name Create command to name the graph, and then save the worksheet to retain the graph settings by using /File Save.

Saving a PIC File for Printing

Suppose that you have constructed a graph you want to store for subsequent printing through the PrintGraph program. (PrintGraph is discussed in the next chapter.) After you verify that the graph type chosen is appropriate for your presentation needs, that the graph data ranges have been specified accurately, and that all desired enhancements have been added, use /Graph Save to create a PIC file on disk.

To save a graph as a PIC file so that you can later print it with the PrintGraph program, follow these steps:

   1. Call up the 1-2-3 menu by pressing ⌐/⌐.

2. Select **Graph** by pressing ⓖ.

3. Select **Save** by pressing Ⓢ.

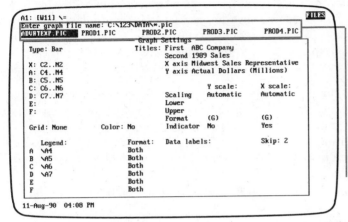

1-2-3 prompts you for a file name and displays (across the top of the screen) a list of the PIC files in the current directory.

4. Type a new file name (as many as eight characters long), or use →
   or ← to highlight a name already listed; then press ↵Enter.

5. If you chose an existing name from the list, select **Replace** by
   pressing Ⓡ to overwrite the old file, or select **Cancel** by pressing
   Ⓒ to avoid overwriting the old file. 1-2-3 automatically adds the
   PIC extension to the file name for you.

After you have saved the graph settings for printing, you can print the graph
with 1-2-3's PrintGraph program, as described in the next chapter.

Remember that /Graph Save stores only an image of the current graph,
locking in all data and enhancements, for the sole purpose of printing it with
the PrintGraph program. When it is time to print, you cannot access this
print file to make changes such as adding a label or editing an underlying
worksheet figure. To be able to modify a graph, you must name the graph
with the /Graph Name Create command and then save the worksheet (before
exiting 1-2-3) with /File Save.

11 Creating Graph Specifications for Reuse

If you want to view on-screen a graph that you created in an earlier graphing session, you must have given the graph a name when you originally constructed the graph. You also must have saved the worksheet, unless the same worksheet is still active. To name a graph, you issue the /Graph Name Create command. Use the /Graph Name options to save the graph along with the underlying worksheet or to retrieve or delete a named graph you have saved.

Only one graph at a time can be the current graph. If you want to save a graph that you have just completed (for subsequent recall to the screen) as well as build a new graph, you must first issue the /Graph Name Create command. The only way to store a graph for later screen display is to issue this command, which instructs 1-2-3 to remember the specifications used to define the current graph. If you do not name a graph and subsequently either reset the graph or change the specifications, you cannot restore the original graph without having to rebuild it.

To store the settings for a graph you created, or to retrieve a graph you have saved, follow these steps:

1. Call up the 1-2-3 menu by pressing ⟨/⟩.
2. Select Graph by pressing ⟨G⟩.
3. Select Name by pressing ⟨N⟩.
4. Select the graph naming activity you want to perform: Create, Use, Delete, Reset, or Table.

   Select Create, by pressing ⟨C⟩, to create a name for the currently defined graph so that you can later access and modify the graph.

   Select Use, by pressing ⟨U⟩, to view a graph whose settings have already been saved with /Graph Name Create. This option allows you to recall any named graph from within the active worksheet.

   Select Delete, by pressing ⟨D⟩, to erase an individual graph name and the settings associated with that graph.

   Select Reset, by pressing ⟨R⟩, to erase all graph names.

   Select Table, by pressing ⟨T⟩, to produce a three-column listing of all graph names, their types (pie, bar, and so on), and titles (the top line of the graph). Note that this option is not available in versions of 1-2-3 prior to Release 2.2. As with the /Range Name Table command, use caution so that the listing does not wipe out existing data that may have been in any of the three columns.

356

11

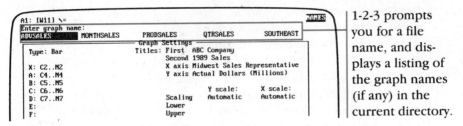

1-2-3 prompts you for a file name, and displays a listing of the graph names (if any) in the current directory.

5. If you selected Create in step 4, type a new name (up to 15 characters in length), and then press ⏎Enter.

Or

If you selected a different option in step 4, use → or ← to highlight in the list the name of the graph you want; then press ⏎Enter.

Note: If you want graph names to be stored with their worksheet, remember to save the worksheet file by using /File Save after creating the names.

Summary

This chapter has shown you how to create graphs. You learned the four basic steps for creating a graph and how to select any one of 1-2-3's five types of graphs: line, XY, bar, stacked-bar, and pie.

You learned, too, how to improve the appearance of graphs by adding titles, data labels, legends, grids, and formatting; assigning connecting lines and symbols; and altering the scaling of the x- and y-axes.

So that you could preserve your work, the chapter showed you how to save and name a special PIC file for printing later with the PrintGraph program, which is described in the next chapter.

Specifically, you learned the following key information about 1-2-3:

- The **Graph** option on the 1-2-3 main menu allows you to create graphs associated with data in the 1-2-3 worksheet.

- The **Graph Settings** sheet (not displayed in versions of 1-2-3 prior to Release 2.2) appears when you select **Graph** from the main menu, and remains on the screen throughout most of the graph creation process (unless you press F6 to display the worksheet instead).

357

■ The /Graph Type command enables you to select from five different types of graphs: Line, Bar, XY, Stack-Bar, and Pie. Which graph type is most appropriate depends on your data and your graphing needs.

■ You can choose the data ranges to be displayed in a graph with the /Graph X and /Graph A through F commands. The /Graph Group command allows you to select all data ranges at once, as long as they form a contiguous block of cells in the worksheet.

■ The /Graph Options command allows you to select from many different options that can be used to enhance the appearance of your graph. You can use this command to add data labels, titles, a legend, and a grid to your graph, as well as change the scale of the axes.

■ The /Graph Save command saves the graph as a PIC file on disk. This file can then be used by the PrintGraph program to print the graph on paper.

■ The /Graph Name command enables you to use existing graph specifications, create a new graph name, delete a graph name, reset all graph names, and display a table of graph names in the worksheet.

■ To modify a graph in a later session of 1-2-3, you must use the /Graph Name Create command and then save the file with /File Save. Otherwise, your graph specifications will be lost, even if a PIC file has been created with /Graph Save.

In the next chapter, you learn how to use PrintGraph to print the graphs you create within 1-2-3.

Printing
Graphs

12

Because the basic 1-2-3 program is not capable of producing printed graphics, Lotus provides with 1-2-3 a separate program called PrintGraph. PrintGraph allows you to create printed or plotted copies of graphs. After you create graphs in 1-2-3, you can save the graphs in files on a disk. The /Graph Save command automatically saves your graph files with a PIC extension. The graph files then can be enhanced and printed with the PrintGraph program. These PIC files are also accessible by the Allways add-in. As you learned in Chapter 9, Allways allows you to combine graphs and worksheet data on a single page for printed output.

The PrintGraph program offers a number of options for additional formatting before a graph is printed. For example, parts of a graph can be assigned different colors, the labels and titles in the graph can be printed in one or several of 11 different fonts (including a script typeface and a block typeface), and the size of the printed graph can be specified. A graph can be printed full-size to occupy an entire printed page, or half-size to fill half of a page; or you can choose a manual option to select a different size. After you have selected the options, the PrintGraph program will print the graph to the specified printer.

Accessing and exiting the PrintGraph program

Understanding the PrintGraph menu

Printing a basic graph

Changing a graph's size, font, and color settings

Setting up your hardware for printing

Controlling printing actions

Saving PrintGraph settings

Previewing a graph

12

> ## Key Terms in This Chapter
>
> *PrintGraph* A separate program, provided with the 1-2-3 software package, that enables you to print graphs that were created with 1-2-3.
>
> *Font* A character set displaying a particular size and style of typeface, such as 12-point Times.
>
> *Previewing a graph* Viewing a selected graph on-screen within the PrintGraph program.

Accessing and Exiting PrintGraph

Once you create a graph within 1-2-3, you need to access the PrintGraph program to print the graph. This is accomplished in several ways: directly from DOS, through the Lotus Access System menu, or by selecting /System from within 1-2-3 (and then using one of the two preceding methods). The following sections cover the different ways to access and exit the PrintGraph program.

Accessing the PrintGraph Program

As you learned in the last chapter, to print a graph within the PrintGraph program, you must first save the graph in 1-2-3 with /Graph Save. So that you can later modify graphs that you create, you must also issue the /Graph Name Create command and save the worksheet with /File Save before you exit 1-2-3.

To access PrintGraph directly from DOS, type **pgraph** at the DOS prompt and press Enter. The PrintGraph program must be in the current directory on a hard disk system; the disk containing the PrintGraph program should be in the active drive on a floppy disk system.

If you use a printer driver other than the default 1-2-3 driver, you must type the name of that driver set (**pgraph hp**, for example) to reach the PrintGraph main menu. However, you are more likely to use PrintGraph immediately after you have created a graph.

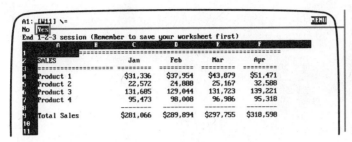

If you originally accessed 1-2-3 by typing **lotus**, select /Quit and then **Yes** to return to the Access System menu.

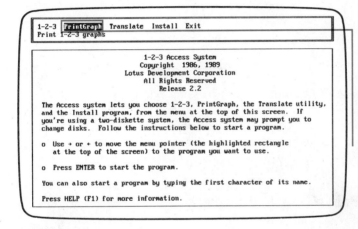

From the Access System menu, select PrintGraph.

If you are using 1-2-3 on a floppy disk system with 5 1/4-inch disks, the program will prompt you to remove the 1-2-3 System disk and insert the PrintGraph disk.

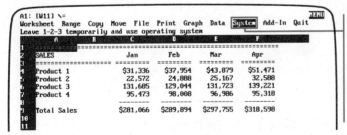

Alternatively, if you have enough memory, you can use PrintGraph after you have issued the /System command.

Then, instead of having to reload 1-2-3 after you leave PrintGraph, you can return directly to 1-2-3 by typing **exit** at the system prompt and pressing Enter.

12

When the opening screen of the PrintGraph program is displayed, you can choose the options you want to set and print your graph.

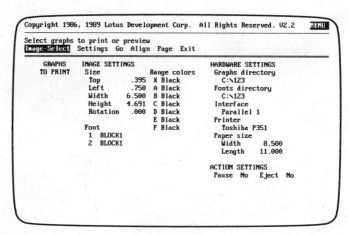

Be careful if you use this last method for accessing PrintGraph, because you must have at least 256K of remaining memory to run PrintGraph and 1-2-3 simultaneously without overwriting your worksheet. Before you use /System, issue the /Worksheet Status command to check remaining conventional memory.

Exiting the PrintGraph Program

To leave the PrintGraph program, select **Exit** from the PrintGraph main menu. Then select **Yes** to verify that you want to end your PrintGraph session.

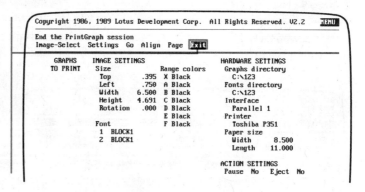

The next screen to appear depends on the method you used to access PrintGraph. If you entered PrintGraph by typing **pgraph** from the DOS prompt, the DOS prompt is restored. If you entered PrintGraph from the 1-2-3 Access System, the Access System menu reappears. Select **Exit** from the Access System menu to restore the DOS prompt.

If you want to enter 1-2-3 after you have exited PrintGraph and restored the DOS prompt, remember how you originally accessed the DOS prompt (before you typed **pgraph**). If you were using 1-2-3 and selected /System to reach the DOS prompt, type **exit** and press Enter to return to the 1-2-3 worksheet. If you were not using 1-2-3 before the PrintGraph session, type **123** or **lotus**, press Enter, and then select **1-2-3** from the Access System menu.

Understanding the PrintGraph Menu

Like 1-2-3, the PrintGraph program is menu-driven. The menu screens not only provide instructions for printing graph (PIC) files, but also information about current print conditions.

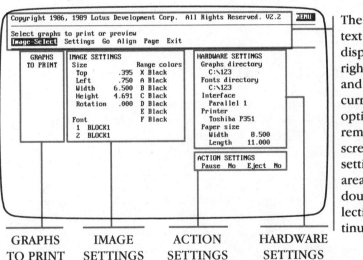

The first three text lines, which display a copyright message and two levels of current menu options, always remain on-screen. In the settings sheet area, below the double line, selections are continually updated.

GRAPHS TO PRINT   IMAGE SETTINGS   ACTION SETTINGS   HARDWARE SETTINGS

Before you begin printing a graph, make sure that you check the settings sheet. The settings displayed in the settings sheet are organized into four areas that are related to either the Image-Select or Settings options of the PrintGraph menu.

A list of graphs that are selected for printing appears under GRAPHS TO PRINT on the left side of the settings sheet. To make changes in the other three settings sheet areas, you first select Settings from the PrintGraph main menu. When you select Settings, a menu of options appears (see table 12.1).

363

12

Table 12.1
Selections on the PrintGraph Settings Menu

Selection	Description
Image	Changes the size, font, and color of the graph; the updated revisions are displayed in the IMAGE SETTINGS area of the settings sheet.
Hardware	Alters the paper size, printer, or disk-drive specifications displayed in the HARDWARE SETTINGS area.
Action	Moves to a new page and pauses while you change specifications for the next graph.
Save	Allows you to save the current settings in a configuration file, to be used when starting PrintGraph.
Reset	Restores the settings to those saved in the configuration file.
Quit	Returns you to the PrintGraph main menu.

Printing a Basic Graph

Printing a graph can be simple if you accept PrintGraph's default print settings. If you have specified the correct hardware configuration, you can produce a half-size, block-style typeface, black-and-white graph on 8 1/2-by-11-inch continuous-feed paper simply by marking a graph for printing and then printing it. Suppose, for example, that you want to print a bar graph with the file name MIDWEST.PIC. Before you begin the printing procedure, make sure that the current printer and interface specifications accurately reflect your hardware, that you're using continuous-feed paper, and that the printer is on-line and the print head is positioned at the page's top. (The sections that follow explain the graph printing process in detail.) Then use the following steps to print the graph with the default settings.

To print a graph using PrintGraph's default settings, follow these steps:

1. Access PrintGraph using one of the methods described earlier.
2. From the PrintGraph main menu, select Image-Select by pressing ⌷ to mark a graph for printing.
3. Move the pointer to the name of the graph(s) you want to print and press the space bar. A # will appear next to the selected graph.

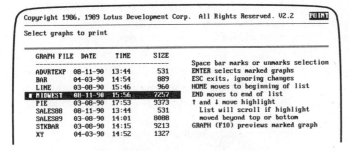

For example, to print the graph file named MIDWEST.PIC, move the pointer to MID-WEST and press the space bar.

4. Press ⏎Enter to select the graph and return to the PrintGraph menu.

5. Select **Align** by pressing Ⓐ to let PrintGraph know that the paper is correctly aligned at the top of the page.

6. Select **G**o by pressing Ⓖ to print the graph.

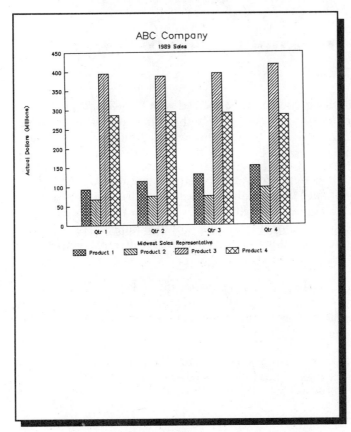

The printed graph is centered upright (zero degrees rotation) on the paper and fills the top half of an 8 1/2-by-11-inch page. The titles are printed in the default BLOCK1 font.

12

Note: A printed graph looks different from its on-screen display. The two titles at the top of the graph in the on-screen version appear to be the same size, but the first title automatically appears larger in a printed graph. Another variation can occur within the y-axis—the tick marks in the on-screen version are occasionally scaled in increments different from that of the printed graph. A third potential difference between an on-screen display and the printed graph is in the legends. In versions of 1-2-3 prior to Release 2.2, legends may spread out so that the first and last items in the legends are not printed. You can solve the problem by reducing the amount of text in each legend.

If you want to enhance this default graph, you can do so by using any or all of PrintGraph's many special features. These special capabilities (which are not available in the main 1-2-3 program) include the enlargement, reduction, and rotation of graph printouts and the use of different colors and fonts. These enhancement options are described in the sections that follow.

Changing the Appearance of the Printed Graph

You can enhance a basic graph you have created with PrintGraph's default settings in a number of ways. You can change the appearance of the printed graph by adjusting its size and orientation, by selecting different fonts, and by choosing alternate colors.

When you select **Settings Image** from the PrintGraph menu, 1-2-3 provides the options Size, **Font**, and **Range-Colors** (as well as **Quit**). Use these options to change the size of a graph, to specify one or two print typefaces on a single graph, and to select colors for the different data ranges. The settings for these options are displayed in the middle of the PrintGraph settings sheet under IMAGE SETTINGS.

Suppose, for example, that you want to enhance the MIDWEST graph that was printed with the default settings. This time, you want to print the image on its side so that it fills the entire sheet of paper, and you want to print the titles in different fonts.

To illustrate what happens if you use PrintGraph's size and font options with the same hardware settings you used for the basic graph created earlier in the chapter, follow these steps:

    1. From the PrintGraph main menu, select **Image-Select** by pressing Ⓘ.

366

12

2. To select the graph you want to enhance, highlight the name of the graph you want to print (MIDWEST for this example), press the space bar (unless the # character already appears next to the desired graph name), and press ⏎Enter.

3. To access the menu from which you can make print enhancements, first select Settings by pressing S.

4. Then select Image by pressing I.

5. To change the size of the graph, select Size by pressing S.

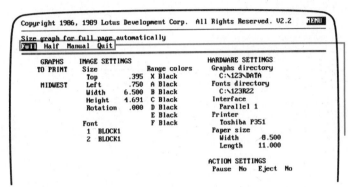

The PrintGraph options for changing the size of a graph are displayed.

6. Select Full by pressing F.

7. Select Quit by pressing Q to return to the Image menu.

8. To change the font for the graph's first title, select Font 1, move the pointer to the font you want, press the space bar, and then press ⏎Enter.

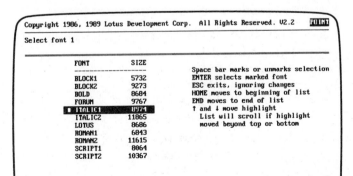

For this example, select Font 1, highlight ITALIC1, press the space bar, and then press ⏎Enter.

12

9. To change the font for the graph's second title, select **Font 2**, and then move the pointer to the font you want (ROMAN1 for this example), press the space bar, and then press ⏎Enter.

10. Select **Quit** twice by pressing Q Q to return to the main menu.

11. Select **Align** by pressing A.

12. To begin printing, select **Go** by pressing G.

The resulting graph is printed on its side (90 degrees rotation) and almost fills an 8 1/2-by-11-inch page. The top center title is printed in the Italic font; the other titles are printed in the Roman font.

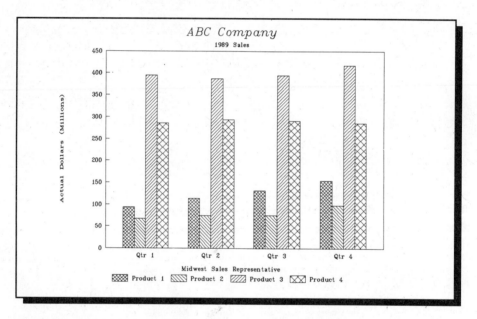

Note: Each of the enhancements made to the MIDWEST graph in the preceding example is discussed in more detail in the sections that follow. You will learn more specifically how to adjust the size and orientation of a graph, how to select fonts, and how to choose colors.

12

Adjusting the Size and Orientation

The **Settings Image Size** command allows you to adjust the size and orientation of printed graphs. You determine the size of the graph by selecting **Full** for full-page graphs, or **Half** for 1/2-page graphs. You may also select **Manual**, which allows you to specify your own width and height, set the graph's position on the page by specifying the top and left margins, and rotate the graph a specified number of degrees on the page.

The **Width** option, available after you select **Manual**, refers to the horizontal graph dimension produced on a page. In a zero-rotation graph, the ratio of x-axis size (width) to y-axis size is 1.385 to 1.

The **Full** option automatically determines a combination of the width, height, top, left, and rotation settings to produce a graph that fills an 8 1/2-by-11-inch page. The top of this horizontal graph (90 degrees rotation) lies along the left edge of the paper.

Suppose, for example, that you want to print a full-page graph on an 8 1/2-by-11-inch page, follow these steps:

1. From the PrintGraph main menu, select **Settings** by pressing ⑤.
2. Select **Image** by pressing ①.
3. Select **Size** by pressing ⑤.
4. Select **Full** by pressing ⑤.
5. Select **Quit** three times by pressing ⑥⑥⑥ to return to the PrintGraph main menu.
6. To print the graph (if already selected), select **Align** by pressing Ⓐ and **Go** by pressing ⑥.

The printed graph appears sideways, using a full page of paper.

If you want to change any or all of the size settings, select **Manual** from the Settings Image Size menu. Then select one or more of the following options:

    Top Left Width Height Rotation Quit

To change the location of a graph, change the margin settings. If you want to center a half-size graph at the top of 11-by-14-inch paper, for example, specify a different left margin by selecting **Settings Image Size Manual Left** and typing **3.5** as the revised number of inches. When you press Enter, the updated left-margin specification is displayed in the settings sheet.

Determine the appropriate number of inches by working from the default values. You know that a half-size graph is centered automatically on an 8 1/2-inch page and that changing to paper 14 inches wide will add 5 1/2 inches to the width. Add half of the increase (2.75 inches) to the default left margin (0.75 inches) to calculate the total number of inches (3.5) for the new dimension.

When you change the **Width** and **Height** settings, be sure to maintain the basic x- to y-axis ratio of approximately 1.385 to 1. For example, suppose that you want to produce an upright (zero-rotation) graph that is only 3 inches high. You know that the x-axis dimension should exceed the y-axis dimension and that, at zero rotation, the x-axis is the width. Multiply the desired height of 3 inches by 1.385 to calculate the proportionate width (4.155 inches) of the graph.

Be sure that the combined dimensions (margin, width, and height) do not exceed the size of the paper. If a graph exceeds the paper's physical bounds, 1-2-3 prints as much of the graph as possible and then truncates the rest.

Although you can set rotation anywhere between 0 and 360 degrees, you will use three settings (0, 90, or 270) for most graphs. Use 0 degrees to print an upright graph. Use 90 degrees to position the graph's center titles along the left edge of the paper. Use 270 degrees to position the graph's center titles along the right edge of the paper.

Selecting Fonts

You can use different fonts in a printed graph. For example, you can print a graph's top center title in one type style (Font 1), and then select a different font (Font 2) for the remaining titles, data-labels, x-axis labels, and legends. If you want to use only one print style, your **Font 1** choice will be used for all descriptions.

You can use the **Font** option from the PrintGraph Settings Image menu to specify a font used on the graph. You can choose from among several different fonts. The default font is BLOCK1.

To select one or two fonts to be used on a printed graph, follow these steps:

1. From the PrintGraph main menu, select **Settings** by pressing ⓢ.
2. Select **Image** by pressing ⓘ.
3. Select **Font** by pressing Ⓕ.
4. Select **1** by pressing ① to change the font of the top center title only, or select **2** to change the font of all remaining graph text.
5. From the list of fonts that appears, highlight the desired font name and press the space bar to mark the font; then press ↵Enter.

    The number after the font name indicates the darkness (density) of the printed characters. If you choose BLOCK2, for example, the printed characters will be the same typeface, but darker than those produced by choosing BLOCK1.

6. Repeat steps 3 through 5 if you want to change the font for all graph text.
7. Select **Quit** twice by pressing ⓆⓆ to return to the PrintGraph main menu.
8. To print the graph (if already selected), select **Align** by pressing Ⓐ and then **Go** by pressing Ⓖ.

Note that the italic and script fonts may be difficult to read, especially on half-size graphs produced on a printer that is not letter-quality. Before you print a final graph in darker density, you should first print the graph at the lower density so that you can determine whether the font settings are correct.

Choosing Colors

If you have a color printer, you can use PrintGraph to assign colors to all parts of a graph.

To print a graph with different colors on a color printer, follow these steps:

1. From the PrintGraph main menu, select **Settings** by pressing ⓢ.
2. Select **Image** by pressing ⓘ.
3. Select **Range-Colors** by pressing Ⓡ.

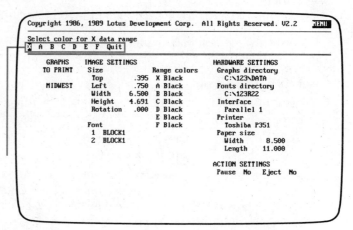

The ranges X and A through F are displayed in a menu.

4. Select the range for which you want to specify a color by pressing [X], [A], [B], [C], [D], [E], or [F].

5. From the resulting menu of colors, highlight the desired color for the specified range and press [⏎Enter].

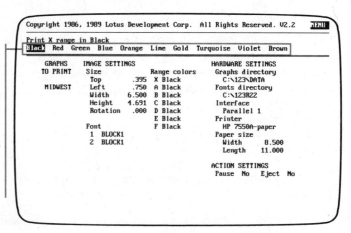

The number of colors displayed depends on the capabilities of the current printer (named in the hardware settings area of the PrintGraph settings sheet).

If your printer does not support color printing, only the **Black** option will appear.

6. Repeat steps 3 through 5 if you want to change the color for additional ranges.

7. Select **Q**uit twice by pressing Q Q to return to the PrintGraph main menu.

8. To print the graph (if already selected) select **A**lign by pressing A and then **G**o by pressing G.

For all graph types except the pie graph, use the **X** option to assign a single color to the edges of the graph, titles, any background grid, and all displayed options other than legends and data labels. Use the **A**, **B**, **C**, **D**, **E**, and **F** options to assign a different color to every data range used. The same color set for an individual data range is used also for any data label or legend assigned to that data range.

You use a different method to determine the print colors for a pie graph. Because you create a pie graph by using only data in the **A** range, and because each wedge of the pie is assigned a **B**-range shading code, you must use the appropriate shading codes to determine which colors will print. You must associate each shading code with the following Settings Image Range-Colors menu options:

Range-Colors option	B-range shading code
X	1 (or 101)
A	2 (or 102)
B	3 (or 103)
C	4 (or 104)
D	5 (or 105)
E	6 (or 106)
F	7 (or 107)

For example, if 4 (or 104) is the shading code assigned to one or more cells in the **B** range, the wedges associated with that code will print in the color assigned to the **C** option in the PrintGraph Settings Image Range-Colors menu. Similarly, 5 (or 105) assigned to a **B** range cell in the worksheet will print in the color assigned to the **D** option within PrintGraph.

In a pie graph, the color assigned to the **X** data range is used for printing labels and titles. The color of the pie border is determined by the color selected for the **A** data range. To improve the graph's appearance, set both the **X** and **A** data ranges to a dark color, such as **Black** or **Blue**.

12

12

If you know that you will print a specific graph in color, select /Graph Options Color within 1-2-3 before you store that graph as a PIC file with the /Graph Save command. If you store the graph in black and white and then print it in color, both the crosshatches and the colors assigned to the ranges will print.

Setting Up Your Hardware for Printing

There is more to printing than just inserting a sheet of paper in a printer and pressing a key. Although the printing process is governed to some extent by your hardware and software, most of the initial decisions are up to you. You need to make decisions about the disk drives containing the print files, the printer type and name, and the size of the paper. The hardware settings are displayed in the settings sheet's rightmost column.

When you select Settings Hardware, this menu appears.

```
Copyright 1986, 1989 Lotus Development Corp.  All Rights Reserved. V2.2    MENU
Specify directory containing graphs
Graphs-Directory  Fonts-Directory  Interface  Printer  Size-Paper  Quit

        GRAPHS    IMAGE SETTINGS                     HARDWARE SETTINGS
        TO PRINT  Size              Range colors     Graphs directory
                  Top        .395   X Black            C:\123\DATA
        MIDWEST   Left       .750   A Black          Fonts directory
                  Width     6.500   B Black            C:\123R22
                  Height    4.691   C Black          Interface
                  Rotation   .000   D Black            Parallel 1
                                    E Black          Printer
                  Font              F Black            Toshiba P351
                  1  BLOCK1                          Paper size
                  2  BLOCK1                            Width     8.500
                                                       Length   11.000

                                                   ACTION SETTINGS
                                                     Pause  No   Eject  No
```

The Graphs-Directory and Fonts-Directory options pertain to disk-drive specifications; Interface and Printer determine the current printer name and type; and Size-Paper permits you to specify the paper width and length in inches. Each of these options is explained in more detail in table 12.2.

Table 12.2
Selections on the Hardware Settings Menu

Selection	Description
Graphs-Directory	Allows you to change the directory that PrintGraph searches for graphs.
Fonts-Directory	Allows you to specify the directory containing PrintGraph's font files.
Interface	Helps you specify the printer or plotter that you use to print the graphs. The Interface option sets the connection type to a graphics printer.
Printer	Establishes a connection to a specific type of printer.
Size-Paper	Allows you to set the size of paper you are using to produce the printed graph. (The default is 8 1/2-by-11-inches.)

Controlling Printing Actions

In addition to specifying hardware settings, you can control printing actions by indicating certain settings before you start the printing process. In particular, you can make the printer pause between graphs and you can decide whether you want the paper ejected after each graph. These action settings are displayed in the settings sheet's rightmost column.

Pausing the Printer between Graphs

If you have selected more than one PIC file for a single print operation, you can make the printer pause between printing the specified graphs. If you are using a manual sheet-feed printer, for example, you can pause to change the paper. Or you may want to stop printing temporarily so that you change the hardware settings in order to direct the output to a different printer. You cannot change the font, color, or size options during the pause.

12

To pause the printer between graphs when printing multiple graphs, follow these steps:

    1. From the PrintGraph main menu, select **Settings** by pressing Ⓢ.

    2. Select **Action** by pressing Ⓐ.

A menu of options for controlling printing actions is displayed.

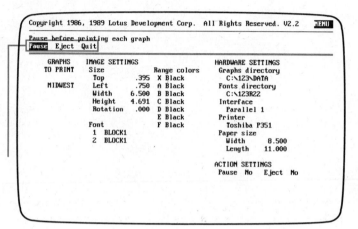

```
Copyright 1986, 1989 Lotus Development Corp. All Rights Reserved. V2.2    MENU

Pause before printing each graph
Pause  Eject  Quit

      GRAPHS   IMAGE SETTINGS                        HARDWARE SETTINGS
     TO PRINT  Size                Range colors       Graphs directory
               Top          .395   X Black              C:\123\DATA
      MIDWEST  Left         .750   A Black           Fonts directory
               Width       6.500   B Black              C:\123R22
               Height      4.691   C Black           Interface
               Rotation     .000   D Black              Parallel 1
                                   E Black           Printer
               Font                F Black              Toshiba P351
                1  BLOCK1                            Paper size
                2  BLOCK1                               Width      8.500
                                                        Length    11.000

                                                     ACTION SETTINGS
                                                        Pause  No   Eject  No
```

    3. Select **Pause** by pressing Ⓟ.

    4. Select **Yes** by pressing Ⓨ.

    5. Select **Quit** twice by pressing ⓆⓆ to return to the PrintGraph main menu.

    6. To print the graph (if already selected), select **Align** by pressing Ⓐ and then **Go** by pressing Ⓖ.

To restore the default setting so that all currently specified graphs will print nonstop, choose **Settings Action Pause No** from the PrintGraph main menu.

After each graph has been printed, the printer will pause and beep. To resume printing, press the space bar.

Ejecting the Paper To Start a New Page

The other Settings Action option applies to "batching" several graphs in one print operation. When you select **Settings Action Eject Yes**, continuous-feed paper advances to the top of a new page before the next graph is printed. Use the alternative default setting, **Settings Action Eject No**, to print two (or more) half-size (or smaller) graphs on a single page.

376

To eject (or advance) the paper after printing each graph, follow these steps:

1. From the PrintGraph main menu, select **Settings** by pressing Ⓢ.
2. Select **Action** by pressing Ⓐ.
3. Select **Eject** by pressing Ⓔ.
4. Select **Yes** by pressing Ⓨ.
5. Select **Quit** twice by pressing ⓆⓆ to return to the PrintGraph main menu.
6. To print the graph (if already selected), select **Align** by pressing Ⓐ and then **Go** by pressing Ⓖ.

Do not confuse the **Settings Action Eject Yes** command sequence with the PrintGraph main menu's **Page** command. Both commands advance the paper to the top of a new page. The **Settings Action Eject Yes** command is more appropriate when you use a single **Go** command to print multiple graphs; the paper advances automatically after each graph has been printed. Select **Page** from the PrintGraph menu, on the other hand, when you want to advance the paper one page at a time before or after a printing session, or when you want to print a single graph at a time.

Completing the Print Cycle

After you create a graph and specify which options you want to use when printing, you can save the PrintGraph settings (if you want to use them again later), preview the graph on-screen (optional), and print the graph.

Saving PrintGraph Settings

After you establish the current **Image**, **Hardware**, and **Action** settings, you can select **Settings Save** if you want to use these settings in a later PrintGraph session. The current options are then written to a file named PGRAPH.CNF, which is read whenever PrintGraph is loaded.

To save the current PrintGraph settings for use in a later session, follow these steps:

1. From the PrintGraph main menu, select **Settings** by pressing Ⓢ.
2. Select **Save** by pressing Ⓢ.

377

12

The current settings are stored in a file named PGRAPH.CNF, and are used whenever PrintGraph is loaded (until you modify and save the settings again).

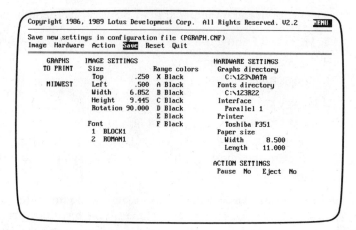

3. Select **Quit** by pressing ⒬ to return to the PrintGraph main menu.

Select Settings **Reset** to restore all **Image**, **Hardware**, and **Action** settings to PrintGraph's default settings or to the options most recently saved. Note, however, that graphs selected to print with the **Image-Select** command are not reset when you issue **Settings Reset**.

Previewing a Graph

Before printing a graph, you may want to first view the graph on-screen—especially when you cannot remember the name of the specific graph you want to print. Instead of returning to 1-2-3, you can view the graph from within PrintGraph just before printing.

To preview a graph from within PrintGraph, follow these steps:

1. From the PrintGraph main menu, select **Image-Select** by pressing ⒤.

   A list of all PIC files in the current **Graphs-Directory** appears on-screen.

2. Highlight the name of the graph you want to view and press Ⓕ⒑ (Graph).

   To verify that the graph shown is the one you want to print, you can use the Graph (F10) key to preview every graph listed.

3. Press any key to remove the graph from the screen.

4. Repeat steps 2 and 3 to view additional graphs on-screen. Then press (Esc) to return to the PrintGraph main menu.

When previewing graphs within PrintGraph, the size, font, and rotation options are not displayed. But the preview does give a good idea of what the printed graph will look like—in some instances, a better idea than you can get with the /Graph View command within 1-2-3.

Selecting and Printing Graphs

Selecting graphs you want to print from the list of PIC files is easy. To mark the files for printing, simply follow the directions that appear on the right side of the screen when you select **Image-Select** from the PrintGraph main menu.

Use the direction keys to position the highlighted bar on the graph you want to select. Then press the space bar to mark the file with a # symbol. The space bar acts as a toggle key; use the same action to remove any unwanted marks. If necessary, continue to mark additional graphs. After you press Enter to accept the currently marked graphs for printing, the updated settings sheet is displayed again, listing all selected graph names under GRAPHS TO PRINT.

The PrintGraph main menu's **Align** option sets the program's built-in top-of-page marker. Regularly selecting **Align** before selecting **Go** is a good practice. The **Page** option advances the paper one page at a time. At the end of a printing session, this useful option advances continuous-feed paper to help you remove the printed output.

To print a graph, select **Go** from the PrintGraph main menu. After you select **Go**, you will see in the screen's menu area messages indicating that picture and font files are loading. Then 1-2-3 will print the graphs. If you want to interrupt the process of printing a graph or series of graphs, press the Ctrl-Break key combination. Then press Esc to access the PrintGraph menu options.

Summary

12

This chapter showed you how to use the PrintGraph program to print graphs created within 1-2-3. You learned how to access and exit PrintGraph, and also how to print a basic graph in four simple steps. Then you learned how to enhance the appearance of a printed graph by adjusting the size and orientation of the graph, selecting different fonts for the text of the graph, and choosing colors for the titles and data ranges.

You were also shown how to set up your hardware to allow printing of graphs, and how to control printing actions such as pausing between graphs and ejecting each graph after it has printed. Finally, you learned how to save your PrintGraph settings, preview a graph before printing, and actually begin the printing process.

Specifically, you learned the following key information about printing graphs created in 1-2-3:

- You can access the PrintGraph program in any of three ways: by typing **pgraph** directly from DOS, by selecting **P**rintGraph from the Access System menu, or by selecting /System from 1-2-3 and then accessing PrintGraph (if you want to return to 1-2-3 after printing the graph).

- To leave the PrintGraph program, select **E**xit from the PrintGraph main menu. If you enter 1-2-3 from the Access System menu, you return to that screen. Otherwise, you return to the DOS prompt. If you use the /System command to access PrintGraph, type **exit** at the DOS prompt to return to 1-2-3.

- The PrintGraph screen consists of three text lines at the top of the screen: a copyright message and two levels of current menu options. The lower area of the screen, which contains the settings sheet, displays the results of option selections. This settings sheet is composed of four areas: GRAPHS TO PRINT, IMAGE SETTINGS, HARDWARE SETTINGS, and ACTION SETTINGS.

- The **I**mage-Select option of the PrintGraph main menu allows you to select which graphs from the current directory are to be printed. You also use this option to preview a graph on-screen before it is printed.

- The **Settings Image** command is used to change the size and orientation (rotation) of the printed graph. This command is also used to select different fonts and colors to be displayed in a graph.

- The **Settings Hardware** command allows you to change the directories where PrintGraph looks to find your graph files and the font program files. You also use this command to select or change the printer or plotter used to print the graphs, and change the paper size from the default of 8 1/2 inches by 11 inches.

- The **Settings Action** command enables you to cause the printer to pause in between graphs, and to eject or advance the paper after each printed graph.

- The **Settings Save** command is used to save any **Image, Hardware,** or **Action** settings you change so that you can use these settings in other PrintGraph sessions. **Settings Reset** returns the PrintGraph settings to the default, or to the settings most recently saved.

- The **Align** and **Go** options on the PrintGraph main menu allow you to tell PrintGraph that the paper is properly aligned in the printer, and to begin printing, respectively. The **Page** option on the main menu is used to advance the paper in the printer to the top of the next page before or after printing.

The next chapter shows you how to begin using the database features of 1-2-3 to manage your data. You will learn how to build and modify a database, and how to sort and search for database records.

12

381

Managing Data

In addition to the electronic spreadsheet and business graphics, 1-2-3 provides a third element: data management. 1-2-3's database feature is fast, easy to access, and relatively simple to use.

The database's speed results from a reduction in the time required to transfer data to and from disks. By doing all the work inside the worksheet, 1-2-3 saves the time required for input and output to disk (the way many database programs function).

The 1-2-3 database is easily accessed because Lotus Development Corporation has made the entire database visible from the worksheet. You can view the contents of the whole database by using worksheet windows and direction keys to scroll through the database.

The relative ease of use is a result of integrating data management with the program's spreadsheet and graphics functions. The procedures for adding, modifying, and deleting items in a database are the same as those you have already seen for manipulating cells or groups of cells within a worksheet. And creating graphs from ranges in a database is as easy as creating them in a worksheet.

Planning and building a database

Modifying a database

Sorting database records

Searching for and listing particular records

13

Key Terms in This Chapter

Database	A collection of data organized so that you can list, sort, or search its contents.
Field	One information item, such as an address or a name.
Record	A collection of associated fields. In 1-2-3, a record is a row of cells within a database.
Key field	A column (or field) to which you attach precedence when the database is sorted.
Input range	The range of the database on which database operations are performed.
Output range	The range to which data is copied when extracted from the database.
Criteria range	The range of the database in which you enter criteria on which a search is conducted.

What Is a Database?

A database is a collection of data organized so that you can list, sort, or search its contents. The list of data may contain any kind of information, from addresses to tax-deductible expenditures. A Rolodex is one form of a database, as are an address book and a file cabinet full of employee records.

384

In 1-2-3, the word *database* means a range of cells that spans at least one column and more than one row. This definition, however, does not distinguish between a database and any other range of cells on a worksheet. Because a database is actually a list, its manner of organization sets it apart from ordinary cells. Just as a list must be organized to be useful, a database must also be arranged in a manner that makes the information easy to access.

The smallest unit in a database is a *field*, or single data item. For example, if you were to develop an information database of customer accounts that are overdue, you might include the following fields of information:

Customer Last Name
Customer First Name
Street
City
State
ZIP Code
Area Code
Telephone Number
Account Number
Payment Due Date
Date Paid
Amount Due

A database *record* is a collection of associated fields. For example, the accumulation of all data about one customer forms one record. In 1-2-3, a *record* is a row of cells within a database, and a *field* is one type of information, such as City.

You must set up a database so that you can access the information it contains. Retrieval of information usually involves relying on key fields. A database *key field* is any field (or column) on which you base a list, sort, or search operation. For example, you can use the ZIP code as a key field to sort the data in the overdue accounts database, and then assign contact representatives to specific geographic areas.

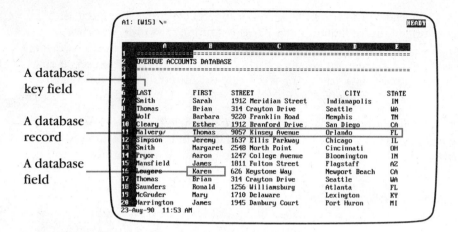

A database key field

A database record

A database field

```
A1: [W15] \=                                                    READY
        A           B           C                  D         E
 1
 2  OVERDUE ACCOUNTS DATABASE
 3
 4
 5
 6  LAST        FIRST       STREET              CITY       STATE
 7  Smith       Sarah       1912 Meridian Street Indianapolis IN
 8  Thomas      Brian       314 Crayton Drive    Seattle      WA
 9  Wolf        Barbara     9220 Franklin Road   Memphis      TN
10  Cleary      Esther      1912 Branford Drive  San Diego    CA
11  Malvern     Thomas      9057 Kinsey Avenue   Orlando      FL
12  Simpson     Jeremy      1637 Ellis Parkway   Chicago      IL
13  Smith       Margaret    2548 North Point     Cincinnati   OH
14  Pryor       Aaron       1247 College Avenue  Bloomington  IN
15  Mansfield   James       1811 Fulton Street   Flagstaff    AZ
16  Leugers     Karen       626 Keystone Way     Newport Beach CA
17  Thomas      Brian       314 Crayton Drive    Seattle      WA
18  Saunders    Ronald      1256 Williamsburg    Atlanta      FL
19  McGruder    Mary        1710 Delaware        Lexington    KY
20  Harrington  James       1945 Danbury Court   Port Huron   MI
    23-Aug-90  11:53 AM
```

The Advantages and Limitations of the 1-2-3 Database

After you have built a database in 1-2-3 (which is no different from building any other worksheet table), you can perform a variety of functions on it. Some of the tasks you will perform on a 1-2-3 database can be accomplished with standard 1-2-3 commands. For example, you can add records and fields using simple worksheet commands such as /Worksheet Insert. Editing data in the database is the same as editing worksheet cells: highlight the cell, press Edit (F2), and make the correction.

You can also sort data. You can sort with both a primary and a secondary key, in ascending or descending order. In addition, you can perform various kinds of mathematical analyses on a field of data over a specified range of records. For example, you can count the number of items in a database that match a set of criteria; compute a mean, variance, or standard deviation; and find the maximum or minimum value in the range. The capability to perform statistical analysis on a database is an advanced feature for database management systems on any microcomputer.

Other database operations specifically require database commands, such as /Data Query Find and /Data Query Unique. Data commands can help you make inquiries and remove duplications from the database. These operations are performed with the /Data Query commands.

You have several options for defining selection criteria with 1-2-3. The criteria range can contain up to 32 cells across the worksheet, with each cell containing multiple criteria. You can use numbers, text, and complex formulas as criteria.

1-2-3 also has a special set of statistical functions that operate only on information stored in the database. Like the /Data Query commands, the statistical functions use criteria to determine on which records they will operate. The database functions include @DCOUNT, @DSUM, @DAVG, @DVAR, @DSTD, @DMAX, and @DMIN.

13

The major disadvantage of 1-2-3's approach to data management is the limitation imposed on the database's size. With some popular database programs, you can get by with loading only portions of your database at once; with 1-2-3, the entire database must be in memory before you can perform any data management operations.

If your computer has 640K of internal memory, you can store only about 1,000 400-byte (character) records or 8,000 50-byte records in a single database. Disk operating system commands and the 1-2-3 program instructions occupy the remaining memory. For large databases, you need to extend the internal memory capacity beyond 640K. If you use floppy disks for external storage of database files, you are limited to files that total approximately 360,000 characters (or 1.2 million characters on a high-density disk). On a hard disk, a database of 8,000 500-byte records occupies 4 million characters, or approximately 4M of disk space.

Understanding the Data Menu

You will use the Data menu for many of 1-2-3's data management tasks. All other options from the 1-2-3 main menu work as well on databases as they do on worksheets. When you select Data from the 1-2-3 main menu, the following options are displayed in the control panel:

   Fill Table Sort Query Distribution Matrix Regression Parse

Each of these options is described in table 13.1.

Table 13.1
Selections on the Data Menu

Selection	Description
Fill	Fills a specified range with values. You can choose the increment by which 1-2-3 increases or decreases successive numbers or dates.
Table	Substitutes different values for a variable used in a formula; often used for "what if" analyses.
Sort	Organizes the database in ascending or descending order based on one or two specified key fields.
Query	Offers different options for performing search operations and manipulating the found data items.
Distribution	Finds how often specific data occurs in a database.
Matrix	Lets you solve systems of simultaneous linear equations and manipulate the resulting solutions.
Regression	Performs multiple regression analysis on X and Y values.
Parse	Separates long labels resulting from /File Import into discrete text and numeric cell entries.

In the Data menu, the Sort and Query (search) options are considered true data management operations. Sort allows you to specify the order in which you want the records of the database organized: by number, by name, or by date, for example. With Query, you can perform a wide range of search operations, allowing you to display quickly a specific record without having to scan a multitude of records.

Planning and Building a Database

Before you begin to create a database in 1-2-3, you should determine the categories (fields) of information you want to include. You can best determine these fields by planning what kind of output you expect to produce from your data. Next, decide which area of the worksheet to use, and then create a database by specifying field names across a row and entering data in cells beneath these names, as you would for any other 1-2-3 application. Entering database contents is simple; the most critical step in creating a database is choosing your fields accurately.

Determining Required Output

1-2-3's data-retrieval techniques rely on finding data by field names. Before you begin typing the kinds of data items you think you may need, write down the output you expect from the database. You also need to consider any source documents already in use that can provide input to the file.

Before you set up the items in your database, be sure to consider how you might look for data in each field. For example, consider how you will look for a particular information item. Will you search by date? By last name? Knowing how you will use your database before you design it will save you a great amount of time that can be lost if you have to later redesign the database.

After you decide on the fields, you need to choose the level of detail needed for each item of information, select the appropriate column width (this can be modified later), and determine whether you will enter the data as a number, label, or date.

Overdue Accounts Database

Item	Column Width	Type of Entry
1. Customer Last Name	15	Label
2. Customer First Name	10	Label
3. Street Address	25	Label
4. City	15	Label
5. State	7	Label
6. ZIP Code	6	Label
7. Area Code	6	Number
8. Telephone Number	11	Label
9. Account Number	10	Number
10. Payment Due Date	11	Date
11. Date Paid	11	Date
12. Amount Due	12	Number

13

Here are some tips for planning various types of fields (columns) in your database:

- For ease in sorting, either put last and first names in separate columns, or put both names in the same cell with the last and first names separated by a comma.

- Some ZIP codes begin with zero, which would not appear in the cell if it were entered as a value. Enter ZIP codes as labels by preceding them with a label prefix.

- Set up a separate area code field apart from your telephone number field if you want to search, sort, or extract records by area code.

- Enter a telephone number as a label. This number must be a label because of the hyphen between the first three and last four digits of a telephone number. A hyphen indicates subtraction in a number entered as a value.

Be sure to plan your database carefully before you establish field names, set column widths and range formats, and enter data. Although modifications may be made after a database is set up, planning will help to reduce the time required for making changes.

Positioning the Database

You can create a database as a new database file or as part of an existing worksheet. If you decide to build a database as part of an existing worksheet, choose a worksheet area where inserting or deleting lines won't affect the worksheet or another database.

If you place a database to the right of a worksheet, inserting and deleting rows may affect the worksheet.

If you place a database directly below a worksheet, inserting and deleting columns may affect the worksheet.

An ideal location for a database is in an area where inserting and deleting rows and columns won't affect other applications above, below, to the right, or to the left of the database.

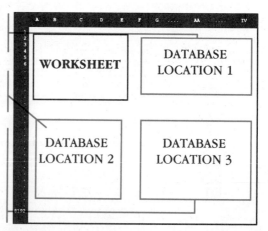

390

Entering Data

After you plan your database and decide which area of the worksheet to use, you can start entering data. Build a database by specifying field names as labels across a row, making sure that each field name is unique and in a separate column.

You can use one or more rows for field names, but 1-2-3 processes only the bottom row; therefore, each field name in the bottom row must be unique. After you enter the field names, enter data in cells as you would for any other 1-2-3 application. Change the column width to fit the information you will enter by using the /Worksheet Column Set-Width command.

To build a 1-2-3 database, follow these general steps:

1. Choose an area for your database.

   For your first database, you should start with a blank worksheet. If you would rather use an existing worksheet, select an area that is out of the way of the data you have entered.

2. Enter the field names across a single row.

   The field names must be labels, even if they are numeric labels. Although you can use more than one row for the field names, 1-2-3 processes only the values that appear in the bottom row. For example, if you have the field name DATE DUE assigned to a column with DATE in row 5 and DUE in row 6, 1-2-3 will reference only DUE as a key field in sort or query operations. Remember that all field names should be unique; any repetition of names can be confusing.

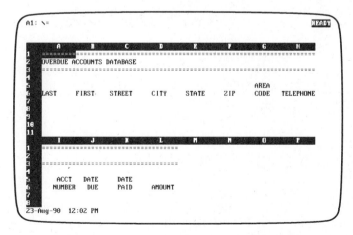

This screen shows all field names in the overdue accounts database, displayed with two windows.

13

391

3. Set the column widths and cell display formats.

Use 1-2-3's /Worksheet Column Set-Width and /Range Format commands to control the width of the columns and the way 1-2-3 displays the data.

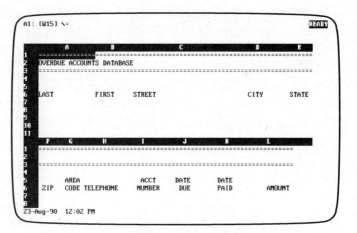

Note that whenever a right-justified column of numeric data is adjacent to a left-justified column of label information, the data looks crowded. You can insert blank columns and adjust the column width of the blank column to change the spacing between fields.

4. Add records to the database.

To enter the first record, move the cell pointer to the row *directly below* the field-names row, and then enter the data across the row in each applicable column (field).

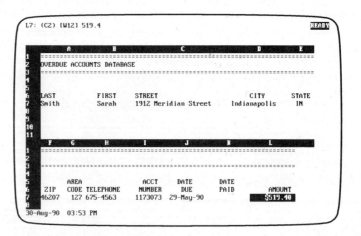

13

Modifying a Database

After you have collected the data for your database and decided which field names and types, column widths, and formats to use, creating a database is easy. Thanks to 1-2-3, maintaining the accuracy of the database contents is also simple. The commands you use to modify a database, which are the same commands used to modify worksheets, are summarized in table 13.2.

13

Table 13.2
Commands for Modifying a Database

Action	Command
Add a record	/Worksheet Insert Row
Add a field	/Worksheet Insert Column
Delete a record	/Worksheet Delete Row
Delete a field	/Worksheet Delete Column
Edit a field	Edit (F2)

The process of modifying fields in a database is the same as that for modifying the contents of cells in any other application. As you know, you change the cell contents either by retyping the cell entry or by using the Edit (F2) key and editing the entry. You will learn more about editing in this chapter's section titled "Editing Records During a Search."

Other 1-2-3 commands, such as those for copying, moving, and formatting cells, are the same for both database and other worksheet applications. For more information about these commands, see Chapters 4 through 6.

Inserting and Deleting Records

To add and delete records in a database, use the 1-2-3 commands for inserting and deleting rows. Because records correspond to rows, you begin inserting one or more records with the /Worksheet Insert Row command. You then fill in the various fields in each row with the appropriate data. To delete one or more rows, you use the /Worksheet Delete Row command.

To insert one or more rows (records) in the database, follow these steps:

1. Call up the 1-2-3 menu by pressing ⟨/⟩.

13

2. Select **W**orksheet by pressing Ⓦ.

3. Select **I**nsert by pressing Ⓘ.

4. Select **R**ow by pressing Ⓡ.

5. When the prompt Enter row insert range: appears,
   highlight (or type the cell address of) the location where you want
   the row (record) inserted; then press ↵Enter.

When you press
Enter, a blank
row appears,
ready for you to
enter a new
record.

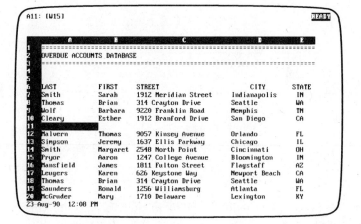

To delete one or more rows (records) from the database, follow these steps:

1. Call up the 1-2-3 menu by pressing Ⓘ.

2. Select **W**orksheet by pressing Ⓦ.

3. Select **D**elete by pressing Ⓓ.

4. Select **R**ow by pressing Ⓡ.

5. When the prompt Enter range of rows to delete:
   appears, highlight (or type the cell address of) the rows (records)
   you want to delete; then press ↵Enter.

394

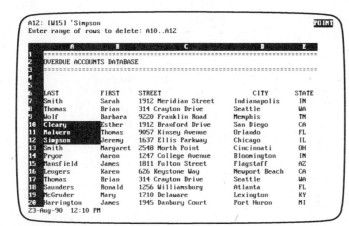

In this example, to delete rows 10 through 12, highlight the rows and press ↵Enter.

13

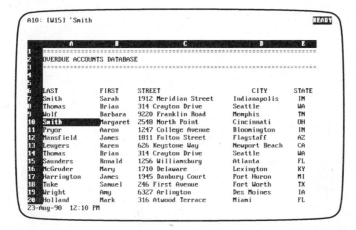

When you press Enter, the records in the highlighted range are deleted.

Because you do not have an opportunity to verify the range before you issue the /**W**orksheet **D**elete **R**ow command, be extremely careful when you specify the records to be deleted. If you want only to remove inactive records, first consider using the /**D**ata **Q**uery **E**xtract command, explained later in this chapter, to store the inactive records in a separate location (or file) before you permanently delete the records.

Inserting and Deleting Fields

To add and delete fields from a database, use the 1-2-3 applications for inserting and deleting columns. To add one or more fields, use the /Worksheet Insert Column command; to delete one or more fields, use the /Worksheet Delete Column command.

To insert one or more new fields (columns) to the database, follow these steps:

1. Call up the 1-2-3 menu by pressing ⃞/⃞.
2. Select **Worksheet** by pressing ⃞W⃞.
3. Select **Insert** by pressing ⃞I⃞.
4. Select **Column** by pressing ⃞C⃞.
5. When the prompt Enter column insert range: appears, highlight (or type the cell address of) the location where you want the column (field) inserted; then press ⏎Enter⃞.

When you press Enter, a blank column appears—ready for you to enter new data.

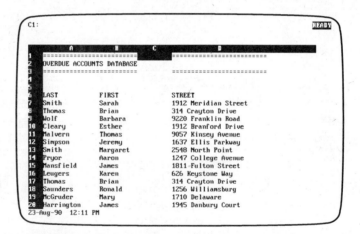

Because maintaining data takes up valuable memory, you can remove seldom-used data fields from the database.

To delete one or more fields (columns) from the database, follow these steps:

1. Call up the 1-2-3 menu by pressing ⃞/⃞.
2. Select **Worksheet** by pressing ⃞W⃞.
3. Select **Delete** by pressing ⃞D⃞.

396

4. Select **C**olumn by pressing Ⓒ.

5. When the `Enter range of columns to delete:` prompt appears, highlight the columns (fields) you want to delete; then press ↵Enter.

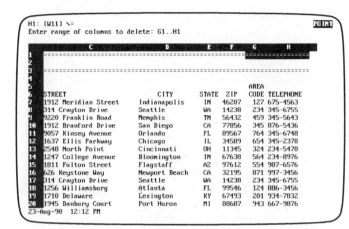

In this example, to delete columns G and H, highlight the columns and press ↵Enter.

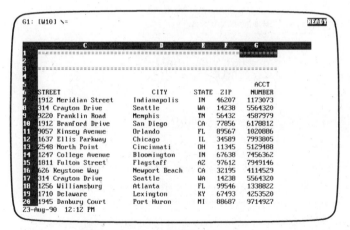

When you press Enter, the fields in the highlighted range are deleted.

Sorting Database Records

Storing data in a database would be meaningless if you were unable to alphabetize the data or sort it numerically. Sorting is an important function of any database. 1-2-3's data management capability lets you change the order of records by sorting them according to the contents of the fields. To sort data, you use the options available when you select /Data Sort:

Data-Range Primary-Key Secondary-Key Reset Go Quit

Each of these options is described in table 13.3.

Table 13.3
Selections on the Data Sort Menu

Selection	Description
Data-Range	Allows you to specify the range on which the sort operation will occur.
Primary-Key	Lets you specify the first item on which the sort is performed.
Secondary-Key	Lets you specify the second item on which the sort is performed.
Reset	Resets the sort options.
Go	Starts the search.
Quit	Exits the Data Sort menu.

Before you issue a /Data Sort command, you should save the database to disk. That way, if the sort procedure does not produce the results you expected, you can restore the file to its original order by retrieving it again.

To sort a database, you use this general procedure:

1. Issue the /Data Sort command.

2. Select Data-Range and designate the range you want to sort.

   This range must be long enough to include all the records to be sorted and wide enough to include all the fields in each record.

   Note: Do not include the field-names row in the data range to be sorted. (If you are unfamiliar with how to designate ranges or how to name them, see Chapter 4.)

   The data range does not necessarily have to include all rows in the database, but must include all fields (columns) in order to maintain the proper contents of each record. If some of the database records already have the organization you want, or if you don't want to sort all the records, you can sort a portion of these records.

3. Specify the key field(s) for the sort, and specify ascending or descending order for each key field.

   Key fields are the columns to which you attach the highest precedence when the database is sorted. The column (or field) with the highest precedence is the **Primary-Key**, and the field with the next highest precedence is the **Secondary-Key**. You must always set a **Primary-Key**; setting the **Secondary-Key** is optional.

4. Select **Go** to perform the sort.

As you choose the various Sort commands, a Sort Settings sheet (not shown in versions of 1-2-3 prior to Release 2.2) will display the current status of the data range, key fields, and sort order. You can remove this settings sheet from the screen by pressing the Window (F6) key.

The One-Key Sort

One of the simplest examples of a database sorted according to a primary key is the white pages of the telephone book. All the records in the white pages are sorted in ascending alphabetical order using the last name as the primary key.

Suppose, for example, that you want to reorder records alphabetically on the LAST name field. To perform a one-key sort operation, follow these steps:

1. Call up the 1-2-3 menu by pressing `/`.
2. Select **Data** by pressing `D`.
3. Select **Sort** by pressing `S`.
4. Select **Data-Range** by pressing `D` to designate the range you want to sort.
5. When the prompt `Enter data range:` appears, highlight (or type) the cell addresses, or enter the range name for the range you want to sort; then press `←Enter`.

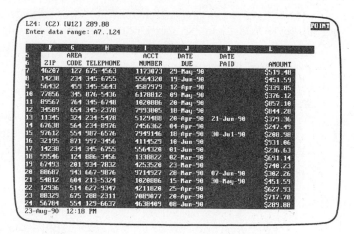

In this example, highlight the range for the entire database, A7..L24 (excluding the field names in row 6); then press ⏎Enter.

6. From the Sort menu, select **P**rimary-Key by pressing Ⓟ.

7. Type or point to any cell in the column containing the primary-key field on which you want to sort; then press ⏎Enter.

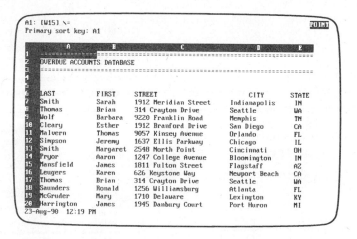

In this example, to sort the database by the LAST (last name) field, highlight any cell in column A; then press ⏎Enter.

8. Type **A** or **D**, and then press ⏎Enter to indicate whether you want your database sorted in ascending or descending order of the selected primary key.

400

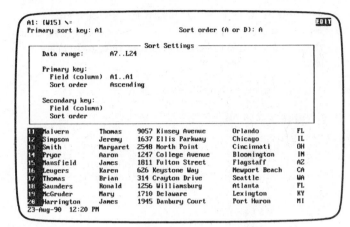

In this example, type **A** and press ⏎Enter to sort the database so that the last names are alphabetized from A to Z.

13

9. When the Sort menu returns, select **Go** by pressing Ⓖ to have 1-2-3 sort the database.

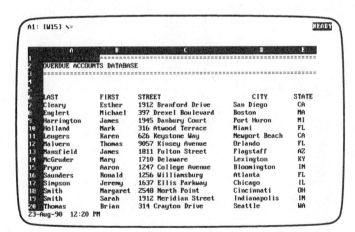

The database now displays the result of the one-key sort on the LAST field.

The Two-Key Sort

A two-key database sort uses both a primary and secondary key. In the yellow pages, records are sorted first according to business type (the primary key) and then by business name (the secondary key). Another example of a two-key sort (first by one key and then by another key within the first sort order) is an addresses database, sorted first by state and then by city within state.

Suppose, for example, that you want to perform a two-key sort on an overdue accounts database. First, you want to sort records according to due date; then, when more than one record has the same due date, you want to sort further according to account number.

To perform a two-key sort operation, follow these steps:

1. Call up the 1-2-3 menu by pressing ⌐/⌐.
2. Select Data by pressing ⌐D⌐.
3. Select Sort by pressing ⌐S⌐.
4. Select Data-Range by pressing ⌐D⌐ to designate the range you want to sort.
5. When the prompt `Enter Data-Range:` appears, highlight (or type) the cell addresses, or enter the range name for the range you want to sort; then press ⌐↵Enter⌐.

   For this example, highlight the range A7..L24 and press ⌐↵Enter⌐.
6. From the Sort menu, select Primary-Key by pressing ⌐P⌐ to indicate the first field on which you want the data sorted.
7. Type or highlight any cell in the column containing the primary-key field on which you want to sort; then press ⌐↵Enter⌐.

In this example, to first sort the database by the DATE DUE column, highlight any cell in column J; then press ⌐↵Enter⌐.

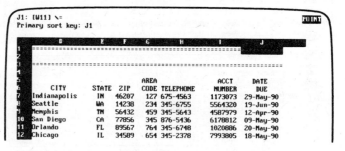

8. Indicate the sort order by typing **A** for ascending or **D** for descending; then press ⌐↵Enter⌐.

   For this example, type **A** and press ⌐↵Enter⌐ to sort the database so that the due dates are arranged from earliest to most recent.
9. Select Secondary-Key by pressing ⌐S⌐ to have the data sorted a second time within the primary sort order.

10. Type or highlight any cell in the column containing the secondary-key field on which you want to sort; then press ⏎Enter .

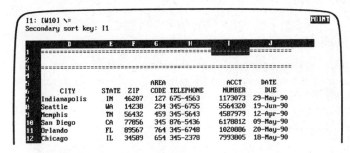

To sort according to ACCT NUMBER after sorting by DUE DATE, highlight any cell in column I and press ⏎Enter .

11. Indicate the sort order by typing **A** for ascending or **D** for descending; then press ⏎Enter .

For this example, type **A** for Ascending; then press ⏎Enter .

12. Select **G**o by pressing G to have 1-2-3 sort the database.

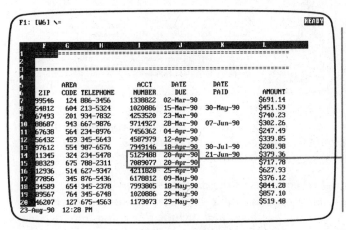

The database now displays the result of the two-key sort on the DATE DUE and ACCT NUMBER fields. Accounts that are due on the same day are sorted according to their account numbers.

Note: Although 1-2-3 seems to limit you to sorting on only two key fields, you actually can sort on any number of key fields by using the program's string capabilities. You can, for example, sort a database by state, by city, and then by county. For more information about using string formulas for database operations, refer to Chapter 12 of *Using 1-2-3 Release 2.2*, Special Edition, published by Que Corporation.

Tips for Sorting Database Records

Here are a few tips to help you sort database records more successfully.

Tip 1: Don't include blank rows in your data range before you sort the database.

If you accidentally include one or more blank rows in your data range, the blank rows will appear at the top of your data range. Therefore, remember to include only rows with data when specifying the data range to be sorted.

Because blanks have precedence over all other characters in a sort, blank rows included in the sort data range appear at the top of the sorted database.

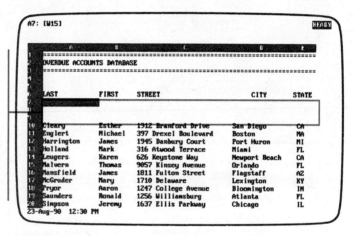

Tip 2: Use the /Worksheet Insert Column and /Data Fill commands to create a "counter" field so that you can easily re-sort the database to its original order if necessary.

After you sort the original contents of the database on any field, you cannot restore the records to their original order. If you add a "counter" column to the database before any sort, however, and include this column in the sort range, you can restore the original order by re-sorting on the counter field. The counter field assigns a number to each record so that you can restore the records to their original order.

To create a "counter" field, follow these steps:

1. Insert a blank column with /Worksheet Insert Column by pressing /W I C. You can reduce the column width of this new column with the /Worksheet Column Set-Width command.

2. Select /Data Fill by pressing ⑦ⒹⒻ.

3. Within the blank column, highlight the rows of your database (or the records you want to sort) where counter numbers should be entered; then press ⏎Enter.

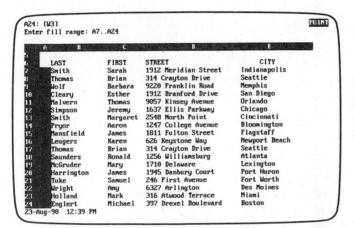

In this example, highlight the range A7..A24 and press ⏎Enter.

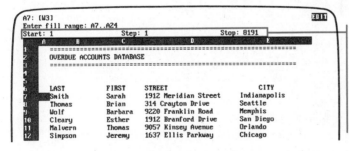

After indicating the /Data Fill range, 1-2-3 prompts you for the Start, Step (increment), and Stop numbers.

4. Type ① and press ⏎Enter for Start, and then type ① and press ⏎Enter for Step. Next, press ⏎Enter to accept the default Stop value.

Note: Although the default Stop value of 8192 is larger than it needs to be, 1-2-3 will use only the numbers necessary to fill the specified range.

13

1-2-3 fills the range with consecutive numbers, beginning with 1 and ending with the number of the last record that was highlighted.

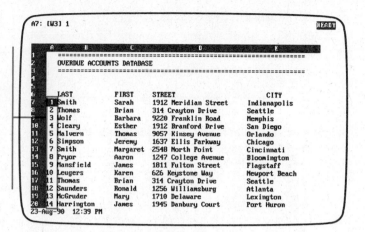

When you sort the database, include the counter column in your data range. To re-sort the database to its original order, use the counter field as your primary-key field.

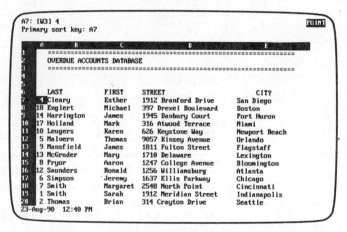

Tip 3: Add new records to the end of the database. Then expand the sort range to include the new records.

You can add a record to an alphabetized name-and-address database without having to insert a row manually and place the new record in the proper position. Simply add the new record to the bottom of the current database, expand the sort data range, and then sort the database again by last name.

Searching for Records

You have learned how to use the /Data Sort command to reorganize information from the database by sorting records according to key fields. In this section of the chapter, you learn how to use /Data Query to search for records and then edit, extract, or delete the records you find.

Looking for records that meet one condition is the simplest form of searching a 1-2-3 database. In an inventory database, for example, you could determine when to reorder items by using a search operation to find any records with an on-hand quantity of fewer than four units. Once you find the information you want, you can extract or copy the found records from the database to another section of the worksheet, separate from the database. For example, you can extract all records with a future purchase order date and print the newly extracted area as a record of pending purchases.

With 1-2-3's search operations, you also have the option of looking for only the first occurrence of a specified field value in order to develop a unique list of field entries. For example, you can search and extract a list of the different units of measure. Then you can delete all inventory records for which quantity on-hand equals zero (if you don't want to reorder these items).

Minimum Search Requirements

The /Data Query command lets you search for and extract data that meets specific criteria. After you choose /Data Query, a menu of nine options is displayed for performing search and extract operations:

Input Criteria Output Find Extract Unique Delete Reset Quit

These options are described in table 13.4.

The first three options specify ranges applicable to the search operation. Input and Criteria, which give the locations of the search area and the search conditions, respectively, must be specified in all Query operations. An output range, specified with the Output option, must be established only when you select a /Data Query command that copies records or parts of records to an area outside the database.

Table 13.4
Selections on the Data Query Menu

Selection	Description
Input	Allows you to specify the location of the search area.
Criteria	Lets you specify the conditions on which the search is based.
Output	Allows you to specify the range where you want the records extracted from the database to be located.
Find	Finds records based on specified criteria.
Extract	Copies from the database the records matching the specified criteria and places them in the output range.
Unique	Eliminates duplicates as records matching the specified criteria are copied to the output range.
Delete	Removes from the input range records that match the specified criteria.
Reset	Resets the input, criteria, and output ranges.
Quit	Returns 1-2-3 to READY mode.

The next four options of the Data Query menu perform a variety of search functions. Find moves down through a database and positions the cell pointer on records that match given criteria. You can enter or change data in the records as you move the cell pointer through them. Extract creates copies, in a specified area of the worksheet, of all or some of the fields in certain records that match given criteria. Unique is similar to Extract, but ignores duplicates as entries are copied to the output range. Delete erases from a database all the records that match the given criteria and shifts the remaining records to fill in the gaps that remain.

The last two options of the Data Query menu, **Reset** and **Quit**, signal the end of the current search operation. **Reset** removes all previous search-related ranges so that you can specify a different search location, condition, and output range (if applicable). **Quit** restores 1-2-3 to READY mode.

Searching for Specific Records

If you want to search for one or a number of specific records that meet certain criteria, you need to use three commands from the Data Query menu: **Input, Criteria,** and **Find.** Suppose, for example, that you want to search a database containing a list of customers with overdue accounts to find a specific customer. The following sections describe the procedure.

Defining the Input Range

The *input range* for the /Data Query command is the range of records you want to search. The specified area does not have to include the entire database. Whether you search all or only part of a database, you *must* include the field-names row in the input range. (In contrast, remember that you do *not* include the field names in a sort operation.) If field names occupy space on more than one row, specify only the bottom row to start the input range. Do not use a blank row or a dashed line to separate the field names from the database records.

Select **/Data Query Input,** and then specify the range by typing or highlighting the range, or by typing an assigned range name. You do not have to specify the range again in later query operations unless the search area changes.

The input range for the database containing a list of overdue accounts includes the entire database and the field names. To define the input range containing the records to be searched, follow these steps:

1. Call up the 1-2-3 menu by pressing $\boxed{/}$.
2. Select **Data** by pressing $\boxed{D}$.
3. Select **Query** by pressing $\boxed{Q}$.

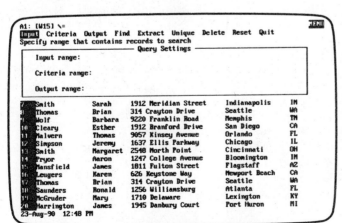

The Query Settings sheet is displayed.

13

4. Select Input by pressing ⟨I⟩.

5. When the prompt `Enter input range:` appears, specify the range by typing or highlighting the range, or by typing an assigned range name; then press ⟨↵Enter⟩.

In this example, highlight the range A6..L24 and press ⟨↵Enter⟩.

```
L24: (C2) [W12] 289.88                                          POINT
Enter input range: A6..L24

      F       G       H            I        J        K         L
                AREA                       ACCT    DATE     DATE
5       ZIP    CODE  TELEPHONE    NUMBER    DUE     PAID      AMOUNT
6
7     46287    127  675-4563     1123673  29-May-90           $519.40
8     14238    234  345-6755     5564320  19-Jun-90           $451.59
9     56432    459  345-5643     4587929  12-Apr-90           $339.85
10    77056    345  876-5436     6178812  09-May-90           $376.12
11    89567    764  345-6748     1020886  20-May-90           $857.10
12    34589    654  345-2378     7993005  18-May-90           $844.28
13    11345    324  234-5478     5129480  20-Apr-90  21-Jun-90 $379.36
14    67638    564  234-8976     7456362  04-Apr-90           $247.49
15    97612    554  987-6576     7949146  18-Apr-90  30-Jul-90 $208.98
16    32195    871  997-3456     4114529  10-Jun-90           $931.86
17    14238    234  345-6755     5564320  01-Jun-90           $236.63
18    99546    124  886-3456     1330822  02-Mar-90           $691.14
19    67493    201  934-7832     4253520  23-Mar-90           $748.23
20    88687    943  667-9876     9714927  28-Mar-90  07-Jun-90 $302.26
21    54812    604  213-5324     1020886  15-Mar-90  30-May-90 $451.59
22    12936    514  627-9347     4211028  25-Apr-90           $627.93
23    88329    675  788-2311     7089877  20-Apr-90           $717.28
24    56704    554  129-6637     4638409  08-Jun-90           $289.88
23-Aug-90   12:49 PM
```

6. To return to READY mode, select Quit by pressing ⟨Q⟩.

As you choose the various **Query** commands, a Query Settings sheet (not shown in versions of 1-2-3 prior to Release 2.2) displays the current status of the input, criteria, and output ranges. You can remove this settings sheet from the screen by pressing the Window (F6) key.

After you have defined the input range, the next step in a data query operation is to define the criteria range. This procedure is covered in the section that follows.

Defining the Criteria Range

To search for data that meets certain conditions, or criteria, you must set up a special range called a *criteria range*, which specifies the criteria on which the search is conducted. After you find an empty area of the worksheet for your criteria range, use the /Data Query Criteria command for specifying the criteria on which 1-2-3 should search.

You can use numbers, labels, or formulas as criteria. A criteria range can be up to 32 columns wide and two or more rows long. The first row must contain the field names of the search criteria, such as STATE in the previous example. The rows below the unique field names contain the actual criteria, such as OH. The field names of the input range and the criteria range must match exactly.

Suppose that in an overdue accounts database, you want to identify all records for customers with the last name Smith. To define the criteria range containing the search conditions, follow these steps:

1. Begin by locating an area of the worksheet where you can enter the criteria on which you want to search the database. Type the label **CRITERIA RANGE** and press ⏎Enter to mark the area.

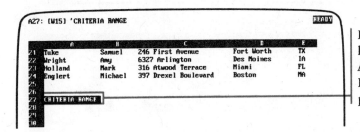

In this example, highlight cell A27, type **CRITE-RIA RANGE**, and press ⏎Enter.

2. Copy the exact field names of your database to the section of the worksheet where you want the criteria range to be located.

   Note: You do not have to include each field name in the criteria range. However, you should copy all field names, because you may choose to enter criteria based on different field names at a later time.

   In this example, copy all field names by issuing the /Copy command and copying from the range A6..L6 to cell A28.

3. Type the search criteria just below a field name and press ⏎Enter.

13

411

In the cell below the LAST field name, type the last name **Smith**, and then press ⏎Enter .

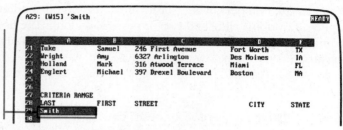

4. Select **/Data Query Criteria** by pressing ⃞/ ⃞D ⃞Q ⃞C .

5. When the prompt Enter criteria range: appears, highlight or type the range of cells containing the field names and specific criteria; then press ⏎Enter .

In this example, highlight the range A28..L29 and press ⏎Enter .

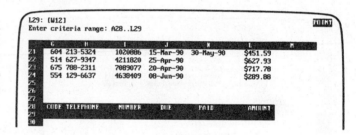

6. To return to READY mode, select **Quit** by pressing ⃞Q .

The next step, which involves searching for (but not copying) the specified records, is covered in the next section.

Finding Records That Meet the Criteria

After you enter the input and criteria ranges, you have completed the minimum requirements for executing a Find or Delete command. Be sure to enter the specific field names above the conditions in the worksheet (in READY mode) before you use the /Data Query Criteria command sequence.

To search for records that meet the criteria you have specified, follow these steps:

1. Call up the 1-2-3 menu by pressing ⃞/ .

2. Select **Data** by pressing ⃞D .

412

3. Select **Query** by pressing Q.
4. Select **Find** by pressing F.

A highlight bar rests on the first record (in the input range) that meets the conditions specified in the criteria range. Notice that the mode indicator changes to FIND during the search.

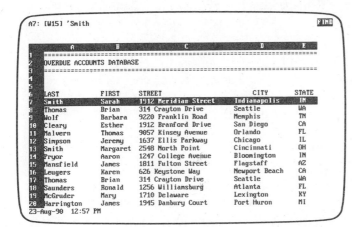

In this example, the highlight bar rests on the first record that includes Smith in the LAST field, in row 7 of the worksheet.

5. Press ↓ to move the highlight bar to the next record that meets the specified criteria. You can continue pressing ↓ until the last record that meets the search conditions has been highlighted.

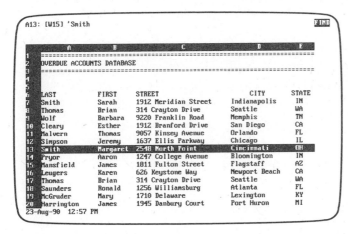

In this example, the highlight bar moves to row 13, the next occurrence of Smith in the LAST field of the database.

413

6. When you want to end the search, press <kbd>⏎Enter</kbd> or <kbd>Esc</kbd> to return to the Data Query menu.

7. To return to READY mode, select **Quit** by pressing <kbd>Q</kbd>.

Use the down- and up-arrow keys to position the highlight bar on the next and previous records that meet the search condition specified in the criteria range. You can use the Home and End keys to position the highlight bar on the first and last records in the database, even if those records do not fit the search criteria.

In FIND mode, you can use the right- and left-arrow keys to move the single-character flashing cursor to different fields in the current highlighted record. Then enter new values or use the Edit (F2) key to update the current values in the field. The next section discusses editing while in FIND mode.

Editing Records During a Search

If you need to change a record while conducting a search, you can switch from FIND to EDIT mode temporarily, edit the record, and then return to searching for other records. Suppose, for example, that you want to update a record in an overdue accounts database. Follow these steps to edit a record during a search:

1. To begin the search operation, select **/Data Query Find** by pressing <kbd>/</kbd><kbd>D</kbd><kbd>Q</kbd><kbd>F</kbd>.

2. In FIND mode, press <kbd>→</kbd> or <kbd>←</kbd> until the blinking cursor is in the cell where you want to edit data.

3. When the blinking cursor is in the cell you want to edit, press <kbd>F2</kbd> to change from FIND to EDIT mode. The cell contents (if any) appear in the control panel.

4. Type new data, or edit existing data by pressing <kbd>F2</kbd> (Edit); then press <kbd>⏎Enter</kbd>.

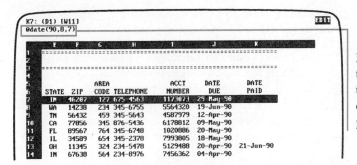

In this example, type new data in the DATE PAID column; then press ⏎Enter.

13

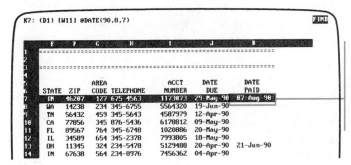

After you edit the record, 1-2-3 returns to FIND mode, and the new or edited data is displayed.

Listing All Specified Records

The Find command has limited use, especially in a large database, because the command must scroll through the entire file if you want to view each record that meets the specified criteria. As an alternative to the Find command, you can use the Extract command to copy to a blank area of the worksheet only those records that meet specified conditions. Before you issue the command, you must define the blank area of the worksheet as an output range. You can view a list of all the extracted records, print the range of the newly extracted records, or even use the /File Xtract command to copy only the extracted record range to a new file on disk.

Defining the Output Range

Choose a blank area in the worksheet as the output range to receive records copied in an extract operation. Designate the range to the right of or below the database. In the first row of the output range, type the names of only

415

13

those fields whose contents you want to extract. You do not have to type these names in the same order as they appear in the database.

The field names in both the criteria and output ranges must match exactly the corresponding field names in the input range. If you enter a database field name incorrectly in the output range—for example, you enter FIRSTNAME instead of FIRST—an extract operation based on that field name will not work. To avoid mismatch errors, use the /Copy command to copy the database field names to the criteria and output ranges.

You can create an open-ended output range by entering only the field-names row as the range. The output range, in this case, can be any size, according to how many records meet the criteria. Or, you can set the exact size of the extract area so that no data located below the area is accidentally overwritten.

To define the output range where records meeting the specified criteria will be copied, follow these steps:

1. Begin by locating an area of the worksheet where you want the records meeting the criteria to be copied. Type the label **OUTPUT RANGE** and press ⏎Enter to mark the area.

2. Copy the exact field names of your database to the section of the worksheet where you want the output range to be located.

   Note: You do not have to extract entire records or maintain the order of field names in the output range. If you do not need to see information for every field in the output range, copy only the desired field names.

In this example, copy all field names by issuing the /Copy command and copying from the range A6..L6 to cell A34.

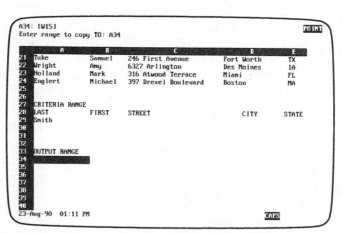

3. Select /Data Query Output by pressing `/` `D` `Q` `O`.

4. When the prompt `Enter output range:` appears, highlight the range where the records should be copied and press `↵Enter`. You can indicate either an unlimited range or a range limited to a specific block of cells.

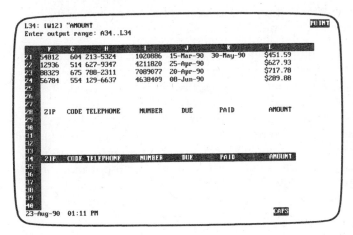

To enter an unlimited output range, highlight only the cells containing field names. In this example, highlight the range A34..L34 and press `↵Enter`.

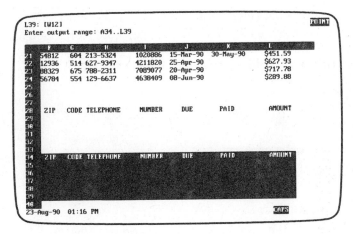

To enter a limited output range, specify additional rows below the field-names row and press `↵Enter`.

5. To return to READY mode, select Quit by pressing `Q`.

13

To create an open-ended extract area that does not limit the number of incoming records, specify as the output range only the row containing the output field names. Keep in mind that an extract operation first removes all existing data from the output range. If you use only the field-names row to specify the output area, all data below that row (down to row 8192) will be destroyed to make room for the unknown number of incoming extracted records. Therefore, ensure that no data is located below the row of field names if you choose an open-ended output range.

To limit the size of the output range, enter the upper left to lower right cell coordinates of the entire output range. The first row in the specified range must contain the field names; the remaining rows must accommodate the maximum number of records you expect to receive from the extract operation. Use this method when you want to retain additional data that is below the extract area. If you do not allow sufficient room in the fixed-length output area, the extract operation will abort, and the message Too many records will be displayed on-screen. Nevertheless, the output area will be filled with as many records as will fit.

Executing the Extract Command

Before you can execute the /Data Query Extract command, you must have already typed the search conditions in the criteria range of the worksheet, copied the output field names to the output range in the worksheet, and specified the input, criteria, and output ranges with the /Data Query commands.

To extract (or copy) to the output range records that meet the specified criteria, follow these steps:

1. Call up the 1-2-3 menu by pressing /.
2. Select Data by pressing D.
3. Select Query by pressing Q.
4. Select Extract by pressing E.

   All records that meet the specified criteria in the criteria range are copied to the output area, in the order of their occurrence in the input range.

```
A34: [W15] 'LAST                                    MENU
Input  Criteria  Output  Find  Extract  Unique  Delete  Reset  Quit
Copy all records that match criteria to output range
                        Query Settings
    Input range:      A6..L24

    Criteria range:   A28..L29

    Output range:     A34..L34

27 CRITERIA RANGE
28 LAST          FIRST     STREET                    CITY        STATE
29 Smith
30
31
32
33 OUTPUT RANGE
34 LAST          FIRST     STREET                    CITY        STATE
35 Smith         Sarah     1912 Meridian Street      Indianapolis   IN
36 Smith         Margaret  2548 North Point          Cincinnati     OH
37
38
39
40
23-Aug-90  01:16 PM                                    CAPS
```

In this example, all records in the LAST field that correspond to the search criteria of Smith have been copied to the output range.

5. To return to READY mode, select **Quit** by pressing Q.

To accelerate what seems to be a time-consuming setup process, you can establish standard input, criteria, and output ranges, and then store the range names for these locations. Keeping in mind the limit of 32 criteria fields, you can establish a single criteria range that encompasses all the key fields on which you might search. By establishing such a range, you save the time needed to respecify a criteria range for each extract on different field names.

When 1-2-3 is in READY mode, you can press the Query (F7) key to repeat the most recent query operation (Extract, in this example) and eliminate the need to select /Data Query Extract after modifying the criteria range. Use the shortcut method only when you do not want to change the locations of the input, criteria, and output ranges.

Copying Extracted Records to a New File

If you want to copy extracted records to their own special file, follow these steps:

1. Call up the 1-2-3 menu by pressing /.
2. Select **File** by pressing F.
3. Select **Xtract** by pressing X.
4. Select either **Formulas** by pressing F or **Values** by pressing V, depending on whether the data contains formulas you want retained in the new file.

419

5. Type the name you want to give to the new file and press ⏎Enter.

6. Highlight the range or type the range address of the records you want to copy to a new file; then press ⏎Enter.

   For example, highlight the range A34..L36 and press ⏎Enter.

A new file is created containing the data from your extract range. To access this file, you must issue the /File Retrieve command and specify the new file name.

Creating More Complex Criteria Ranges

In addition to searching for an "exact match" of a specified label within a field of labels (such as *Smith* within the LAST field), 1-2-3 permits a wide variety of other types of record searches. For example, you can search for an exact match in numeric fields. In addition, you can choose a search criteria that only partially matches the contents of specified fields. You can also include formulas in your search criteria, as well as use multiple criteria that involve searching for specified conditions in more than one field.

Using Wild Cards in Criteria Ranges

Depending on the complexity of your database operations, you may need to be a bit more creative when you are specifying criteria ranges in 1-2-3. For that reason, 1-2-3 allows you to use wild cards and formulas in criteria ranges. The following are some examples that show how you can use wild cards in search operations:

Enter	To find
N?	NC, NJ, and NY
BO?L?	BOWLE, but not BOWL
BO?L*	BOWLE, BOWL, BOLLESON, and BOELING
SAN*	SANTA BARBARA and SAN FRANCISCO
SAN *	SAN FRANCISCO and SAN DIEGO, but not SANTA BARBARA
~N*	Strings (in specified fields) that do not begin with the letter N

13

420

You can use 1-2-3's wild cards for matching labels in database operations. The characters ?, *, and ~ have special meanings when they are used in the criteria range. The ? character instructs 1-2-3 to accept any single character in that specific position; ? can be used only to find fields of the same length. The * character, which tells 1-2-3 to accept any and all characters that follow, can be used on field contents of unequal length meeting the specified criteria. By placing a tilde (~) at the beginning of a search condition, you tell 1-2-3 to accept all values except those that follow.

13

```
E29: [W7] '~IN                                                  MENU
Input  Criteria  Output  Find  Extract  Unique  Delete  Reset  Quit
Copy all records that match criteria to output range
───────────────── Query Settings ─────────────────
   Input range:     A6..L24

   Criteria range:  A28..L29

   Output range:    A34..L34

27 CRITERIA RANGE
28 LAST        FIRST    STREET                   CITY       STATE
29                                                          ~IN
30
31
32
33 OUTPUT RANGE
34 LAST        FIRST    STREET                   CITY       STATE
35 Thomas      Brian    314 Crayton Drive        Seattle    WA
36 Wolf        Barbara  9220 Franklin Road       Memphis    TN
37 Cleary      Esther   1912 Branford Drive      San Diego  CA
38 Malvern     Thomas   9057 Kinsey Avenue       Orlando    FL
39 Simpson     Jeremy   1637 Ellis Parkway       Chicago    IL
40 Smith       Margaret 2548 North Point         Cincinnati OH
23-Aug-90  01:19 PM
```

With ~IN specified in the STATE field of the criteria range, the output range after an Extract includes all records that do not match IN (Indiana).

Use the ? and * wild-card characters when you are unsure of the spelling used in field contents. Be sure that the results of any extract operation that uses a wild card are what you need. And be extremely careful when you use wild cards with a **Delete** command (discussed later in this chapter). If you are not careful, you may remove more records than you intend.

Entering Formulas in Criteria Ranges

To set up formulas that query numeric fields in the database, you can use the following relational (or logical) operators:

>	Greater than
<	Less than
=	Equal to
>=	Greater than or equal to
<=	Less than or equal to
<>	Not equal to

Create a formula that references the first field entry in the numeric column you want to search. 1-2-3 tests the formula on each cell down the column until the program reaches the end of the specified input range. If you want to reference cells outside the input range of the database, use formulas that include absolute cell addressing rather than relative cell addressing.

With the formula +L7>=600 specified in the AMOUNT field of the criteria range, the output range after an Extract includes all records with an amount due greater than or equal to $600.

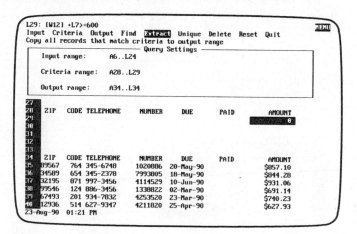

Note: The reference to cell L7 in the formula indicates the location of the first record of the corresponding search field. For example, the first record of the database is in row 7, and the search field is located in column L.

Specifying Multiple Criteria

So far, you have seen how to base a **Find** or **Extract** operation on only one criterion. In this section, you will learn how to use multiple criteria for your queries. When you maintain a criteria range that includes all (or many) field names, you can quickly extract records based on alternative conditions. You also can continue to add more conditions that must be met.

You can set up multiple criteria in which *all* the criteria must be met or in which any *one* criterion must be met. For example, searching a music department's library for sheet music requiring drums *and* trumpets is likely to produce fewer selections than searching for music appropriate for drums *or* trumpets. You can indicate two or more criteria, all of which must be met, by specifying the conditions in separate fields of the criteria row immediately below the field names.

13

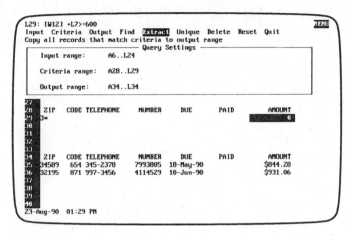

The conditions shown display in the output range (after an **Extract**) all customers with ZIP codes that begin with 3 *and* who owe at least $600.

Using multiple criteria in a single row of the criteria range tells 1-2-3 to "search for the records that meet this *and* that criterion." Notice that the search criteria are listed in a single row immediately below the field-names row.

In contrast, criteria placed on different rows find or extract records based on this field condition *or* that field condition. You can also search on one or more fields using this type of multiple criteria.

Searching a single field for more than one condition is the simplest use of criteria entered on separate rows. For example, you can extract from the overdue accounts database only those records with state abbreviations of IN or TX. To perform this search, under the STATE criteria field, you type one condition immediately below the other. Be sure to use the /Data Query Criteria command to expand the definition of the criteria range to include the additional row.

13

In this example, criteria are entered in separate rows to find all accounts originating in Indiana *or* Texas.

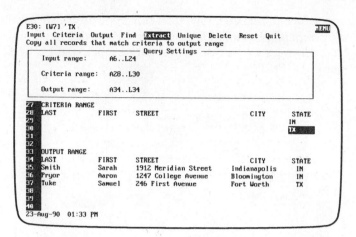

Notice that each condition is listed in a separate row under the field-names row. The result of the Extract is shown in the output range.

You can also specify multiple criteria on different rows with two or more different criteria fields. Building on the preceding example, suppose you want to find the records with the states IN or TX *or* with overdue amounts of at least $600.

Multiple criteria on different rows are used here to find the items that have either IN or TX in the STATE field, *or* have overdue amounts of at least $600.

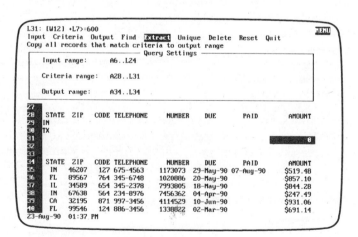

As shown, when the **Extract** command is issued, the records that meet either condition appear in the output range.

If you are careful when you specify conditions, you can mix both multiple fields and multiple rows within the criteria range. Follow the format of placing records that meet *all* criteria at once in a single row immediately below the criteria field-names row, and placing records that meet *any* of the criteria in a separate row below. Because using multiple criteria may sometimes get confusing, a good practice is to test the logic of your criteria on a small sample of records to verify that the results are what you want. Then you can proceed to search all your records according to the multiple criteria.

Using Special Operators

To combine search conditions within a single field, use the special operators #AND# and #OR#. Use the special operator #NOT# to negate a search condition. Use #AND# or #OR# to search on two or more conditions within the same field. For example, suppose that you want to extract from the overdue accounts database all records with the states Indiana (IN) and Texas (TX) in the STATE field, but not California (CA).

You use the #AND#, #OR#, and #NOT# operators to enter (in one field) conditions that can be entered some other way (usually in at least two fields). For example, you can enter the following in a single cell of the STATE field in the criteria range as an alternative criteria entry to entering each condition on a separate line:

```
+E7="IN"#OR#E7="TX"
```

Again, the reference to cell E7 in the formula indicates that you are searching the field located in column E, beginning with the first database record located in row 7. Use #NOT# at the beginning of a condition to negate that condition. For example, you can find all records that do not have CA listed in the STATE field by specifying the criteria #NOT#CA in the criteria range.

Here, the formula condition has been entered in cell E29, as shown in the control panel. The extracted records are displayed in rows 35 through 37.

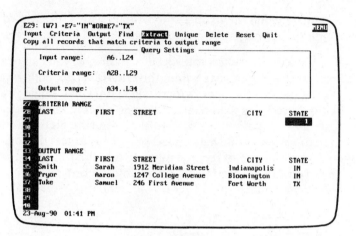

Performing Other Types of Searches

In addition to the Find and Extract commands, you can use the Data Query menu's Unique and Delete commands for performing searches. By issuing the Unique command, you can produce (in the output range) a copy of only the first occurrence of a record that meets the specified criteria. The Delete command allows you to update the contents of your 1-2-3 database by deleting all records that meet the specified criteria. After entering the search conditions, you need to specify only the input and criteria ranges before you issue the Delete command.

Searching for Unique Records

Ordinarily, the Unique command is used to copy into the output area only a small portion of each record that meets the criteria. For example, if you want a list of states represented in the overdue accounts database, set up an output range that includes only the STATE field. To search all records, leave blank the row below the field-names row in the criteria range. Then define the input, criteria, and output ranges and select /Data Query Unique. In the following example, the output range includes only the STATE field, and the row below the field-names row in the criteria range is blank.

To copy to the output range unique records that meet the criteria you have specified, follow these steps:

1. Call up the 1-2-3 menu by pressing ⬜ /.

426

2. Select **Data** by pressing D .

3. Select **Query** by pressing Q .

4. Select **Unique** by pressing U .

All records that meet the specified criteria in the criteria range are copied to the output area, in the same order of their occurrence in the input range.

13

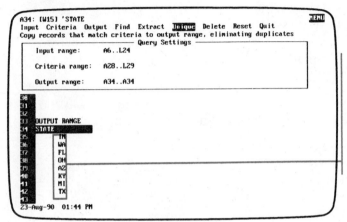

In this example, issuing the Unique command produces a list of the different states represented in the database.

5. To return to READY mode, select **Quit** by pressing Q .

Deleting Specified Records

As you know, you can use the /Worksheet Delete Row command to remove records from a worksheet. An alternative approach is to use the /Data Query Delete command to remove from the database unwanted records matching a specified criteria. Before you select Delete from the Query menu, specify the range of records to be searched (the input range) and the conditions for the deletion (the criteria).

In the following example, the records in the overdue accounts database that have an entry in the DATE PAID column will be deleted from the database. The first row of the DATE PAID column in the criteria range contains the following formula that will produce the desired results:

+K7<>""

To delete from a database records that meet the specified criteria, follow these steps:

1. Call up the 1-2-3 menu by pressing ⃞/.

2. Select **Data** by pressing ⃞D.

3. Select **Query** by pressing ⃞Q.

4. Select **Delete** by pressing ⃞D.

5. Select **Cancel** by pressing ⃞C or select **Delete** by pressing ⃞D to proceed with the command. In this example, select **Delete** by pressing ⃞D. 1-2-3 acts on the **Delete** command without displaying the records that will be deleted.

All records with an entry in the DATE PAID column of the database have been deleted.

```
F1: [W6] \=                                                       MENU
Input  Criteria  Output  Find  Extract  Unique  Delete  Reset  Quit
Delete all records that match criteria
        F      G        H          I        J        K          L
 1
 2      ==================================================================
 3
 4      ==================================================================
 5
        AREA                      ACCT     DATE     DATE
 6      ZIP   CODE TELEPHONE      NUMBER   DUE      PAID            AMOUNT
 7  14238    234  345-6755       5564320  19-Jun-90               $451.59
 8  56432    459  345-5643       4587979  12-Apr-90               $339.85
 9  77856    345  876-5436       6178812  09-May-90               $376.12
10  89567    764  345-6748       1020886  20-May-90               $857.10
11  34589    654  345-2378       7993805  18-May-90               $844.28
12  67638    564  234-8976       7456362  04-Apr-90               $247.49
13  32195    871  997-3456       4114529  10-Jun-90               $931.06
14  14238    234  345-6755       5564320  01-Jun-90               $236.63
15  99546    124  886-3456       1338822  02-Mar-90               $691.14
16  67493    201  934-7832       4253520  23-Mar-90               $740.23
17  12936    514  627-9347       4211820  25-Apr-90               $627.93
18  88329    675  788-2311       7089077  20-Apr-90               $717.78
19  56784    554  129-6637       4638409  08-Jun-90               $289.88
20
23-Aug-90   01:52 PM
```

6. To return to READY mode, select **Quit** by pressing ⃞Q.

Be extremely careful when you issue the **Delete** command. To give you the opportunity to verify that you indeed want to select the **Delete** command, 1-2-3 asks you to select **Cancel** or **Delete**. Choose **Cancel** to abort the **Delete** command. Select **Delete** to verify that you want to execute the delete operation.

Although you are asked to verify that you indeed want to delete records, you won't have the opportunity to view the records that match the criteria you specified. For this reason, use /File Save to make a copy of the database. Or you can use the **Extract** command to copy the records you plan to delete, view them, and then proceed with the delete operation when you are sure that those records should be removed from the database.

428

Summary

Although used frequently for spreadsheet applications, 1-2-3 also is used for many types of database applications. Because a 1-2-3 database is created within the column-row worksheet and uses the same cell pointer and direction keys as are used for other applications, 1-2-3's database feature is generally faster, and easier to access and use than programs whose sole function is data management.

The Data command on 1-2-3's main menu leads to commands for performing common database applications such as sorting data, searching for records that meet specific criteria, and extracting records from the main database. Although fast and easy to use, 1-2-3's sorting capabilities are limited to sorting data on one or two fields. When searching for and extracting records, you must create in the worksheet an *input range* that contains the field names and all records to be searched, and a *criteria range* to specify the search conditions. When extracting records from a 1-2-3 database, you must also indicate the *output range*, where the data will be copied when extracted.

Search conditions in a 1-2-3 database can be text strings or numbers, but can also be much more complicated. More complicated conditions on which to search a 1-2-3 database can include formulas, as well as conditions that involve multiple criteria.

Specifically, you learned the following key information about 1-2-3:

- A database consists of records and fields. In 1-2-3, a record is a row of cells in the database, and a field is one type of information within the record, such as a ZIP code.
- 1-2-3's Data menu contains most of the commands commonly used to manage and manipulate databases. However, other options from the 1-2-3 main menu that are used often with worksheets can also be used to manage databases.
- A database should be planned carefully before it is created by determining which categories, or fields, of information should be included, as well as what type of output is desired.
- An ideal location for a database is an area where inserting and deleting rows and columns won't affect other applications above, below, to the right, or to the left of the database.

13

■ The /Worksheet Insert Row and /Worksheet Delete Row commands can be used to add or delete records (rows) in the database. Similarly, the /Worksheet Insert Column and /Worksheet Delete Column commands can be used to add or delete fields (columns) in the database.

■ The /Data Sort command allows you to change the order of records by sorting them according to the contents of specified key fields. In 1-2-3, you can sort with a primary and secondary key, in ascending or descending order.

■ The /Data Query command is used to set up a database, as well as search a database for records matching a specified criteria. Before starting a search, you must first specify an *input range* and a *criteria range* with the commands /Data Query Input and /Data Query Criteria, respectively. When using the Extract and Unique options of this command, you must also specify an *output range* with the /Data Query Output command.

■ The /Data Query Find command positions the cell pointer on records matching a given criteria. Records can be modified as you move the cell pointer among them.

■ The /Data Query Extract command copies records (or specified portions of records) matching a given criteria to another area of the worksheet.

■ The wild-card characters ?, *, and ~ can be used to allow more complex search operations to be performed. Formulas can also be entered in criteria ranges, as well as multiple criteria involving two or more fields.

■ The /Data Query Unique command also copies records to an output range, but does not copy duplicate entries based on fields specified in the criteria range.

■ The /Data Query Delete command erases from a database the records that match conditions specified in the criteria range. 1-2-3 asks for confirmation before deleting the records.

Now that you have learned about 1-2-3's worksheet, graphics, and data management capabilities, you can go on to the next (and last) chapter, which introduces 1-2-3 macros. Macros allow you to perform simple or complex routine operations with the press of a few keystrokes.

Understanding Macros

In addition to the capabilities available from the commands in 1-2-3's main menu, another feature makes 1-2-3 the most powerful and popular integrated spreadsheet, graphics, and database program available today. 1-2-3 macros and the advanced macro commands allow you to automate and customize your 1-2-3 applications. Macros enable you to reduce tasks requiring multiple keystrokes to a two-keystroke operation. Just press two keys and 1-2-3 does the rest, whether you're formatting a range, creating a graph, or printing a worksheet. You also can control and customize worksheet applications by using 1-2-3's powerful advanced macro commands—50 built-in commands that give you a greater range of control over your 1-2-3 applications.

You can think of simple keystroke macros as the building blocks for advanced macro command programs. When you begin to add advanced macro commands to simple keystroke macros, you can control and automate many of the actions required to build, modify, and update 1-2-3 worksheets. At the most sophisticated level, 1-2-3's advanced macro commands can be used as a full-fledged programming language for developing custom business applications.

Planning macros

Positioning macros in the worksheet

Documenting and naming macros

Using the Learn feature to record keystrokes

Executing macros

Using an automatic macro

Debugging and editing macros

Creating a macro library

14

Key Terms in This Chapter

Macro	A series of stored keystrokes or commands that are carried out by pressing two or more keys.
Program	A list of instructions in a computer programming language, such as 1-2-3's advanced macro commands, which tells the computer what to do.
Advanced macro commands	1-2-3's powerful programming language consisting of more than 50 built-in commands that are not accessible through the 1-2-3 menu system.
Tilde (~)	The symbol used in a macro to indicate the Enter keystroke.
Key names	Representations of keyboard keys used in macros. Key names are enclosed in braces—for example, {EDIT}.
Documented macro or program	A macro or program that contains information explaining each step in the macro or program.
Bug	An error in a macro or program.
Debugging	The process of identifying and fixing errors in a macro or program.

In this chapter, you find an introduction to the concept and application of macros. You also will find some simple keystroke macros, which can be included in your own macro library. For more detailed information on macros and the advanced macro commands, consult Que's *Using 1-2-3 Release 2.2*, Special Edition, or *1-2-3 Macro Library*, 3rd Edition.

What Is a Macro?

A *macro*, in its most basic form, is a collection of stored keystrokes that you can replay at any time to carry out a particular operation. These keystrokes can be commands or simple text and numeric entries. Macros provide an alternative to typing data and commands from the keyboard. Macros, therefore, can save you time by automating frequently performed tasks.

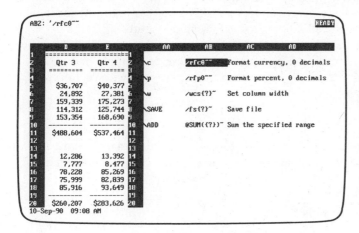

This screen shows five simple keystroke macros in the window on the right. The window on the left displays worksheet data.

By creating a simple macro, for example, you can automate the sequence of seven keystrokes necessary for formatting a cell in Currency format with zero decimal places.

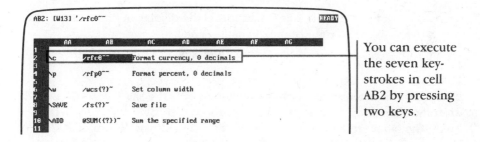

You can execute the seven keystrokes in cell AB2 by pressing two keys.

You can name macros in two different ways. One way is to use the backslash key (\) and a single letter. An Alt-*letter* macro is executed by holding down the Alt key and pressing the letter that identifies the macro. (This is the only method available for use with versions of 1-2-3 prior to Release 2.2.) In Release 2.2, you can name macros by using descriptive names of up to 15 characters in length. Access these macros by pressing Run (Alt-F3). When the list of macro names appears, highlight the one you want to use and press Enter.

14

The Elements of Macros

1-2-3 macros follow a specific format, whether they are simple keystroke macros or macros that perform complex tasks. A macro is nothing more than a specially named text cell. All macros are created by entering into a worksheet cell the keystrokes (or representations of those keystrokes) to be stored. Suppose, for example, that you want to create a simple macro that will format the current cell to appear in Currency format with no decimal places. The macro would look like this:

'/rfc0~~

The following are the macro elements for the formatting macro, along with descriptions of the actions that result when 1-2-3 executes each element:

Macro Element	Action
'	Tells 1-2-3 that the information which follows is a label.
/	Calls up the 1-2-3 menu.
r	Selects **Range**.
f	Selects **Format**.
c	Selects **Currency**.
0	Tells 1-2-3 to suppress the display of digits to the right of the decimal point.
~~	Functions as two Enter keystrokes. (Each tilde acts as one Enter keystroke.)

You enter this macro into the worksheet in exactly the same way you would any other label: by typing a label prefix, followed by the characters in the label. The label prefix (displayed only in the control panel) informs 1-2-3 that what follows should be treated as a label. Every macro that starts with a nontext character (/, \, +, –, or a number) must begin with a label prefix. If this prefix were not used, 1-2-3 would automatically interpret the next character, /, as a command to be executed immediately instead of stored in the cell. Any of the three 1-2-3 label prefixes (', ", or ^) works equally well.

The next four characters in the macro represent the command used to create the desired format. After all, /rfc is simply shorthand for /**Range Format Currency**. The 0 (zero) tells 1-2-3 that you want no digits displayed to the right of the decimal point. If you were entering this command from the keyboard, you would type the 0 in response to a prompt.

434

At the end of the macro are two characters called *tildes*. When used in a macro, a tilde (~) represents the Enter key. In this case, the two tildes signal that the Enter key should be pressed twice—once to accept the number of decimal places, and the second time to select the current cell as the range to format.

Other elements used in macros include range names and cell addresses. Although these two elements can be used interchangeably, you should use range names instead of cell addresses whenever possible. Range names are preferred because if you move data included in specified ranges, or insert or delete rows and columns, the range names adjust automatically, and the macro continues to refer to the correct cells and ranges. Cell references used in macros do not adjust to any changes made in the worksheet and must be modified manually.

The {?} command that is included in some of the macro examples in this chapter is actually a type of advanced macro command. This command is used to pause the macro so that you can type information, such as a file name, from the keyboard. The macro continues executing when you press the Enter key. For example, a macro that sets column widths can include the {?} command to let you type the new column width when the macro pauses. Then you can press Enter to complete execution of the macro.

Characters in macro commands are not case-sensitive; you can use capitalization wherever you want. For readability in this book, however, lowercase letters are used in macros to indicate commands; range names and key names are in uppercase letters.

Macro Key Names and Special Keys

1-2-3 uses symbols besides the tilde (~) to stand for other keystrokes. You can add to the formatting example some key names and special keys that highlight a range of the worksheet just as if you were using /Range Format.

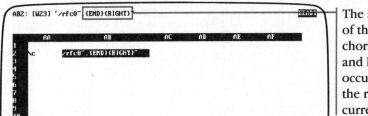

The added part of the macro anchors the range and highlights all occupied cells to the right in the current row.

435

This revised macro is similar to the preceding one, except that the
.{END}{RIGHT} command causes the cell pointer to move. You can use
this version of the macro to format an entire row instead of just one cell.

Once again, notice the apostrophe (') at the beginning of the macro
(displayed in the control panel) and the tilde (~) at the end. Notice also the
phrase .{END}{RIGHT} in the macro. The period (.) anchors the cell
pointer. The {END} key name stands for the End key on the keyboard. The
{RIGHT} key name represents the right-arrow key. This phrase has the same
effect in the macro as these three keys would have if they were pressed in
sequence from the keyboard. The cell pointer moves to the next boundary
between blank and occupied cells in the row.

Representations like these are used to indicate key names and special keys
on the keyboard. In every case, the key name is enclosed in braces. For
example, {UP} represents the up-arrow key, {ESC} stands for the Esc
(Escape) key, and {GRAPH} represents the F10 function key.

Tables 14.1 through 14.4 provide lists of macro key names and special keys
grouped according to their uses: function keys, direction keys, editing keys,
and special keys.

Table 14.1
Macro Key Names for Function Keys

Function Key	Key Name	Action
Help (F1)	{HELP}	Accesses 1-2-3's on-line help system.
Edit (F2)	{EDIT}	Edits the contents of the current cell.
Name (F3)	{NAME}	Displays a list of range names in the current worksheet.
Abs (F4)	{ABS}	Converts a relative reference to absolute, or an absolute reference to relative.
GoTo (F5)	{GOTO}	Jumps the cell pointer to the specified cell address or range name.
Window (F6)	{WINDOW}	Moves the cell pointer to the other side of a split screen. Also turns the display of settings sheets in Release 2.2 on or off (when applicable).
Query (F7)	{QUERY}	Repeats the most recent /Data Query operation.

Table 14.1—(continued)

Direction Key	Key Name	Action
Table (F8)	{TABLE}	Repeats the most recent table operation.
Calc (F9)	{CALC}	Recalculates the worksheet.
Graph (F10)	{GRAPH}	Redraws the current graph on-screen.

Table 14.2
Macro Key Names for Direction Keys

Direction Key	Key Name	Action
Up arrow (↑)	{UP} or {U}	Moves the cell pointer up one row.
Down arrow (↓)	{DOWN} or {D}	Moves the cell pointer down one row.
Left arrow (←)	{LEFT} or {L}	Moves the cell pointer left one column.
Right arrow (→)	{RIGHT} or {R}	Moves the cell pointer right one column.
Shift-Tab or Ctrl-←	{BIGLEFT}	Moves the cell pointer left one screen.
Tab or Ctrl-→	{BIGRIGHT}	Moves the cell pointer right one screen.
PgUp or Page Up	{PGUP}	Moves the cell pointer up one screen.
PgDn or Page Down	{PGDN}	Moves the cell pointer down one screen.
Home	{HOME}	Moves the cell pointer to cell A1 or, if /Worksheet Titles is set, to the top left cell outside the titles area.
End	{END}	Used with {UP}, {DOWN}, {LEFT}, or {RIGHT} to move the cell pointer in the indicated direction to the next boundary between blank cells and cells that hold data. Used with {HOME} to move the cell pointer to the lower right corner of the worksheet.

14

437

Table 14.3
Macro Key Names for Editing Keys

Editing Key	Key Name	Action
Delete or Del	{DELETE} or {DEL}	Used with {EDIT} to delete a single character from a cell entry.
Insert or Ins	{INSERT} or {INS}	Toggles between insert and overtype modes when you are editing a cell.
Esc	{ESCAPE} or {ESC}	Indicates the Esc key.
Backspace	{BACKSPACE} or {BS}	Indicates the Backspace key.

Table 14.4
Macro Key Names for Special Keys

Special Key	Key Name	Action
Enter	~	Indicates the Enter key.
~ (Tilde)	{~}	Causes a tilde to appear in the worksheet.
{ (Open brace)	{{}	Causes an open brace to appear in the worksheet.
} (Close brace)	{}}	Causes a close brace to appear in the worksheet.

Note: A few keys or key combinations do not have a key name to identify them. These include Shift, Caps Lock, Num Lock, Scroll Lock, Print Screen, Compose (Alt-F1), Step (Alt-F2), Run (Alt-F3), and Undo (Alt-F4). None of these keys or key combinations can be represented within macros.

To specify more than one use of a key name, you can include repetition factors inside the braces. For example, you can use the following statements in macros:

Statement	Action
{PGUP 3}	Press the PgUp key three times in a row.
{RIGHT JUMP}	Press the right-arrow key the number of times indicated by the value in the cell named JUMP.

Planning Macros

A simple keystroke macro can be thought of as a substitute for keyboard commands. Because of this, the best way to plan a macro is to step through the series of instructions you intend to include in the macro from the keyboard, one keystroke at a time. Perform this exercise before you start creating the macro. Take notes about each step as you proceed with the commands on-screen, and then translate the keystrokes that you've written down into a macro that conforms to the rules discussed in this chapter.

Stepping through an operation at the keyboard is an easy way to build simple macros. The more experience you have with 1-2-3 commands, the easier it becomes to "think out" the keystrokes you need to use in a macro and enter them directly into the worksheet.

For more complex macros, the best approach is to break them into smaller macros that execute in a series. Each small macro performs one simple operation; the series of simple operations together performs the desired application.

This approach starts with the result of an application. What is the application supposed to do or produce? What form must the results take? If you start with the desired results and work backward, you lower the risk of producing the wrong results with your macro.

Next, consider input. What data is needed? What data is available and in what form? How much work is involved in going from the data to the results?

Finally, look at the process. How do you analyze available data and, using 1-2-3, produce the desired results? How can necessary calculations be divided into a series of tasks, each of which can have a simple macro?

This "divide-and-conquer" method of breaking a complex task into smaller and simpler pieces is the key to successful development of macros and complex worksheets. Although this method entails some initial work, you

14

will be able to detect and correct errors more easily because they will be located in a smaller section of the macro.

Positioning Macros in the Worksheet

In most cases, you should place your macros outside the area that will be occupied by the data on your worksheet. This practice helps you avoid accidentally overwriting or erasing part of a macro as you create your model.

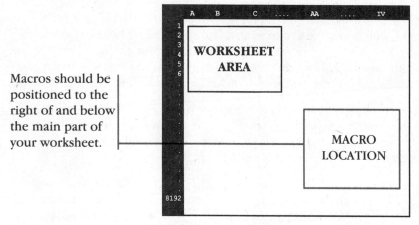

Macros should be positioned to the right of and below the main part of your worksheet.

This positioning lessens the possibility that the macro's range could accidentally be included in worksheet operations. With this placement, deleting rows or columns in the worksheet area will not affect the cells in the macro location.

1-2-3 has no rule that says you must place your macros in the same place in every worksheet. You may, however, want to make a habit of always placing your macros in a certain column, such as column AA. You will then always know where to look in your applications for the macros if they need to be modified. Also, if your worksheets rarely require more than 26 columns, you don't have to worry about overwriting the macro area with the worksheet data. Such positioning of the macros means that deleting rows or columns from the main part of your worksheet will not affect the cells in the macro location. Finally, column AA is close enough to the home screen that you can easily reach the macro area with the Tab key.

In small worksheets, on the other hand, you may want to put your macros in column I. The macros can be reached from the home screen with a single press of the Tab key when all the columns have a width of nine characters.

You can assign the range name MACROS to the area containing the macros. Using a range name allows you to move to the macro area quickly with the GoTo (F5) key.

Documenting Macros

14

Professional programmers usually write programs that are *documented*. This term means that the program contains comments which help to explain each step in the program. In BASIC, these comments are in REM (for REMark) statements. For example, in the following program, the REM statements explain the actions taken by the other statements.

```
10 REM This program adds two numbers
20 REM Enter first number
30 INPUT A
40 REM Enter second number
50 INPUT B
60 REM Add numbers together
70 C=A+B
80 REM Display result
90 Print C
```

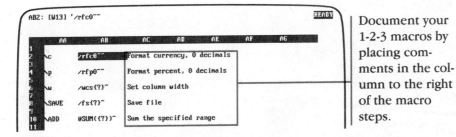

Document your 1-2-3 macros by placing comments in the column to the right of the macro steps.

Including comments in your macros will make them far easier to use. Comments are especially useful when you have created complex macros that are important to the worksheet's overall design. Suppose that you have created a complex macro but have not looked at it for a month. Then you decide that you want to modify the macro. Without built-in comments, you might have a difficult time remembering what each step of the macro does.

Naming Macros

A macro that has been entered in the worksheet as a label (or a series of labels) must be given a name before it can be executed.

Name a macro by using a backslash (\) followed by a single letter (Alt-*letter*) or a descriptive name like a typical range name.

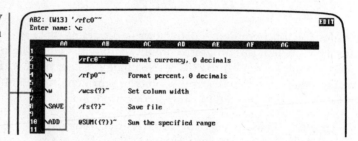

If you choose to use the single-letter naming convention, select a character that in some way helps describe the macro. For example, a macro that formats a range as currency could be named \c.

To assign a name to a macro, follow these steps:

1. Call up the 1-2-3 menu by pressing [/]
2. Select **Range** by pressing [R].
3. Select **Name** by pressing [N].
4. Select **Create** by pressing [C].
5. Type [\] and a single letter, and then press [↵Enter];
   Or
   Type a descriptive name of up to 15 characters and press [↵Enter].
   For this example, type [\][c], and then press [↵Enter].
6. When the prompt `Enter range:` appears, highlight (or type the cell addresses of) the range where the macro commands are stored; then press [↵Enter].

442

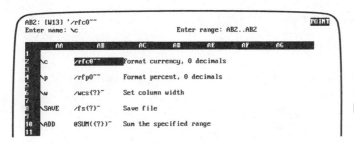

```
AB2: [W13] '/rfc0~~                                                  POINT
Enter name: \c                          Enter range: AB2..AB2

          AA          AB          AC          AD          AE          AF          AG
 1
 2    \c          /rfc0~~       Format currency, 0 decimals
 3
 4    \p          /rfp0~~       Format percent, 0 decimals
 5
 6    \w          /wcs{?}~      Set column width
 7
 8    \SAVE       /fs{?}~       Save file
 9
10    \ADD        @SUM({?})~    Sum the specified range
11
```

In this example, highlight cell AB2 and press ⏎Enter.

This book and the 1-2-3 documentation use a format that places the name of the macro in the cell to the immediate left of the macro's first command. If you follow this format, you can use the command /**R**ange Name Labels **R**ight and specify the range containing the macro names to assign these names to your macros in the adjacent column. This approach works with descriptive and Alt-*letter* macro names and also ensures that you include the name of the macro within the worksheet for easy identification. The /**R**ange Name Labels **R**ight command is also useful for naming several macros at once, rather than naming them individually with /**R**ange Name **C**reate.

The advantage of using a single letter for a macro name is that you can activate the macro more quickly from the keyboard; a disadvantage is that a single-letter name doesn't offer as much flexibility in describing what the macro does. Therefore, remembering the name and purpose of a specific macro may be difficult.

In versions of 1-2-3 prior to Release 2.2, single-letter names are the only names you can use for macros. 1-2-3 Release 2.2, however, allows you to assign descriptive names (up to 15 characters in length) to ranges containing macros. To avoid confusing macro names with other range names, you can also begin descriptive macro names with the backslash (\) character. For example, in this chapter, illustrated macros include one named \SAVE, which can be used to save files, and another named \ADD, which uses the @SUM function to add a specified range of values.

Note: 1-2-3 lets you assign a third type of name to a macro. You can use the name \0 (backslash zero) to create an automatic macro. Automatic macros are discussed later in this chapter.

14

443

Using the Learn Feature To Record Keystrokes

In Release 2.2, 1-2-3 can keep track of every keystroke and command you issue, and then use this information to build a macro. Instead of creating a macro by typing it manually into worksheet cells, you can use the Learn feature to record all keyboard activity for an indefinite period. The macro is built for you as you step through the procedures you want to include.

To use the Learn feature to record keystrokes, first use the /Worksheet Learn Range command to set aside an area in the worksheet where the keystrokes are to be saved. After you designate the range to hold your macro keystrokes, activate recording mode by pressing Learn (Alt-F5). All your commands and keystrokes are stored in the Learn area as you proceed through the operations you want. You can stop recording at any time by pressing Learn (Alt-F5) again. You can resume recording by pressing Learn (Alt-F5) once more.

To record keystrokes for a macro with the Learn feature, follow these steps:

1. Call up the 1-2-3 menu by pressing ⃞/ ⃞.
2. Select **W**orksheet by pressing ⃞W⃞.
3. Select **L**earn by pressing ⃞L⃞.
4. Select **R**ange by pressing ⃞R⃞.
5. When the prompt Enter learn range: appears, highlight a single-column range to hold the keystrokes and press ⃞⏎Enter⃞. Select as many cells as necessary in an area off to the side of your worksheet, and be sure that the area doesn't disturb existing data.

In this example, highlight the range AB1..AB20 and press ⃞⏎Enter⃞. (The macro names can later be added to the appropriate cells in column AA.)

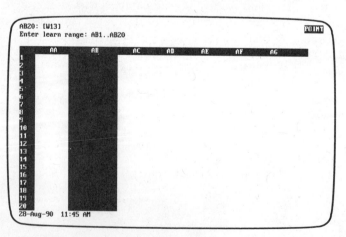

14

444

6. Move the cell pointer to the worksheet area and press Alt F5 (Learn) to begin recording keystrokes.

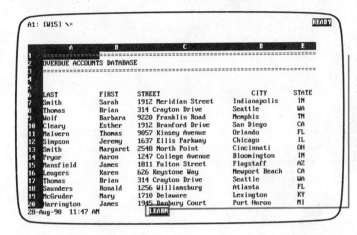

The LEARN indicator, which tells you that your keystrokes are being recorded, appears at the bottom of the screen.

7. Manually type all commands and keystrokes necessary to create your macro.

For example, you can build a macro that automatically sorts a database. After you record the keystrokes, your database will be sorted, and the Learn range will contain your keystrokes for future use.

8. Press Alt F5 (Learn) to stop recording keystrokes.

To see what you have recorded, move the cell pointer to the Learn range.

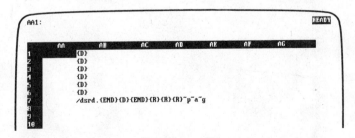

The recorded keystrokes and commands look like a macro you could have typed manually.

Note: If you move to the Learn range without having first deactivated LEARN mode, you will see many directional key names ({L},{D},{R}, and {U}) at the end of the Learn range.

445

As shown, repetitious cell-pointer movement can make your macro much longer than it would be had you typed it manually. A series of pressing the down-arrow key six times is recorded as the following:

{D}
{D}
{D}
{D}
{D}
{D}

This series of keystrokes can be written more simply in a single cell as {DOWN 6} or {D 6}. You can edit the Learn range to consolidate directional key names, but you are not required to. A later section of this chapter describes how to edit your macros.

1-2-3 records the activity of special keys in macro notation. For example, if one of the keys you press while in LEARN mode is the Window (F6) key, the Learn range will contain the macro key name {WINDOW}.

If the size of your Learn range is insufficient to hold the keystrokes being accumulated during LEARN mode, you hear a beep, and the recording activity stops. To continue, simply use the /Worksheet **Learn Range** command again to expand the Learn range downward. Press Learn (Alt-F5) when you're ready to continue recording.

When you are satisfied that the recorded activity represents what you want the macro to do, assign a name, such as \SORT, to the first cell of the macro.

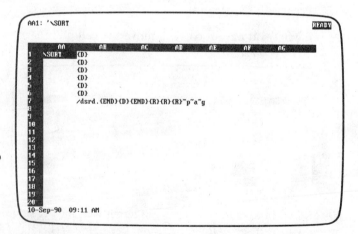

446

Note: When naming macros, you need to name only the *first* cell of the macro, rather than the entire macro range.

At first, you may find using the Learn feature awkward; the Learn range can quickly be filled with irrelevant directional key names and other unwanted commands. If that happens, you can erase the entire contents of the Learn range with the command /Worksheet Learn Erase, and then resume recording with an empty Learn range.

Executing Macros

14

Alt-*letter* macros named with a backslash and a single letter are the simplest to run. If necessary, move the cell pointer to the appropriate position before you execute the macro. For example, when using a macro to format the current cell, you must move the cell pointer to the cell to be formatted before running the macro.

To execute an Alt-*letter* macro, follow these steps:

1. Press and hold down the Alt key.
2. Press the letter in the macro name.
3. Release both keys.

For example, if the macro is named \a, you invoke it by pressing Alt-A. The \ symbol in the name represents the Alt key. Pressing Alt-A plays back the keystrokes that are recorded in the macro.

When a macro is identified with a longer descriptive name, you cannot execute the macro quite as easily. You must first press Run (Alt-F3) to display a list of range names, highlight the macro name, and then press Enter. The list of names you see when you press Run (Alt-F3) will include range names as well as macro names. To simplify your search for macro names, begin them with a backslash.

To execute a macro with a descriptive name, follow these steps:

1. Press Alt F3 (Run).

The screen displays up to five names. If you don't see the name of the macro you want to run, press F3 (Name) again to display a full-screen listing of names.

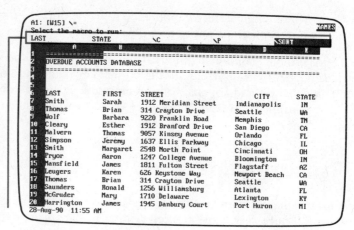

2. Highlight the name of the macro you want to execute and press ↵Enter.

As soon as the command to execute a macro is issued, the macro starts to run. If you have no special instructions built into the macro (such as a pause) and if no bugs are present, the macro continues to run until it is finished. You will be amazed at its speed. The commands are issued faster than you can see them.

Many macro keystrokes or commands can be stored in a single cell. Some that are especially long, or that include special commands, must be split into two or more cells. When 1-2-3 starts executing a macro, the program begins with the first cell and continues in the first cell until all the keystrokes stored there are executed. Next, 1-2-3 moves down one cell to continue execution. If the next cell is blank, the program stops. If that cell contains more macro commands, however, 1-2-3 continues reading down the column until encountering the first blank cell.

Using an Automatic Macro

1-2-3 allows you to create an *automatic macro* that will execute automatically when the worksheet is loaded. This macro is created just like any other; the only difference is its name. The macro that you want to execute automatically must have the name \0 (backslash zero). Only one automatic macro can be used in a single worksheet.

448

For example, you can use an automatic macro to position the cell pointer at the upper left corner of a range named DATABASE each time you access the worksheet file. The macro can then redefine the range DATABASE by anchoring the cell pointer and moving it to the right and down to include all contiguous cells.

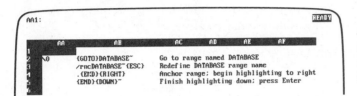

An automatic (\0) macro is executed when a file is retrieved.

14

Pressing the Alt key is not required to start the macro in this case. The macro is executed as soon as you retrieve the worksheet.

Note that automatic macros cannot be executed by the Alt-0 key combination. If you need to be able to execute the macro from the keyboard, you can use Run (Alt-F3) or you can assign the \0 macro an additional name, such as \a. You then have two identical macros on your system: one that executes automatically, and one that can be executed from the keyboard. This tip is especially useful when testing new automatic macros.

Debugging and Editing Macros

Almost no program works perfectly the first time. In nearly every case, errors cause programs to malfunction. Programmers call these problems *bugs*. The process of eliminating bugs is referred to as *debugging* the program.

Like programs written in other programming languages, 1-2-3 macros usually need to be debugged before they can be used. 1-2-3 has a useful feature— STEP mode—that helps make debugging much simpler. When 1-2-3 is in STEP mode, macros are executed one step at a time. 1-2-3 literally pauses between keystrokes stored in the macro. Using this feature means that you can follow along step by step with the macro as it executes.

When an error is discovered, you must get out of the macro and return 1-2-3 to READY mode by pressing Esc one or more times. Then you can start editing the macro.

Common Errors in Macros

Like all computer programs, macros are literal creatures. They have no capability to discern an error in the code. For example, you recognize immediately that {GOTI} is a misspelling of {GOTO}. But a macro cannot make this distinction. The macro tries to interpret the misspelled word and, being unable to, delivers an error message. Here are three reminders to help you avoid some of the most common macro errors:

- Verify all syntax and spelling in your macros.
- Include all required tildes (~) to represent Enter keystrokes in macros.
- Use range names in macros whenever possible to avoid problems with incorrect cell references. Cell references in macros are always absolute—they never change when modifications are made to the worksheet.

If a macro is not working correctly, you can use two 1-2-3 features to help you correct worksheet and/or macro errors. Use the Undo (Alt-F4) feature to "undo" damage to the worksheet created by the faulty execution of a macro. Also, use STEP mode to help pinpoint the location of an error in a macro.

Undoing Macros

The Undo feature (not available in versions of 1-2-3 prior to Release 2.2) offers a significant advantage when debugging macros. When a macro not only doesn't work, but also appears to have caused major problems within the worksheet, press Undo (Alt-F4), and all the steps in the macro will be undone. Remember, the Undo feature restores the worksheet as it was before the last operation. A macro, even though it may contain many steps, is considered one operation.

If you want to undo a macro, make sure that the Undo feature is active before you actually execute the macro. The UNDO indicator should appear at the bottom of the screen. If the macro produces unsatisfactory results, do not perform another operation; use Undo immediately to reverse the effect of the macro.

Note: Certain commands that cannot normally be reversed with Undo (Alt-F4) also cannot be reversed within macros. For example, a macro that

14

includes the /File Save command cannot be reversed. Therefore, you should not rely entirely on Undo when you test macros.

To reverse the results of a macro safely, save the file before you execute a macro. Then, if necessary, you can retrieve the original file after the macro has executed.

Using STEP Mode To Debug Macros

Most programs need to be debugged before they can be used. If you can't locate an error in a macro, your best option is to enter STEP mode and rerun the macro one step at a time. After each step, the macro pauses and waits for you to type any keystroke before continuing. Although any key can be used, you should use the space bar to step through a macro. As you step through the macro, each command appears in the control panel, and the macro code appears in the status line at the bottom of the screen.

To use STEP mode to debug a macro, follow these steps:

1. Press Alt F2 (Step).

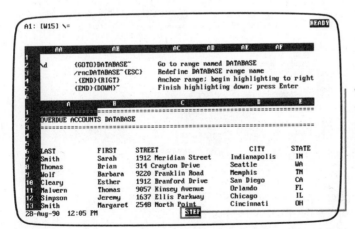

The mode indica-
tor STEP appears
at the bottom of
the screen.

2. Execute the macro by pressing Alt followed by the letter of the macro name, or use Alt F3 to select the macro name and press ⏎Enter.

   The STEP indicator changes to SST as soon as you execute the macro.

451

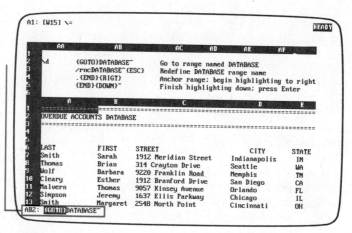

In Release 2.2, the macro code and its associated address appear at the bottom of the screen as you run the macro in STEP mode.

3. Evaluate each step of the macro, pressing the space bar after you have checked each step.

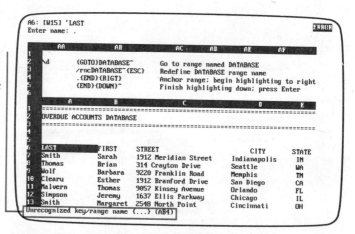

An error message is displayed at the bottom of the screen. In this example, the error is caused by the misspelled key name in cell AB4.

4. When you discover an error, press Ctrl Break, followed by Esc or ↵Enter, to return 1-2-3 to READY mode.

5. When 1-2-3 is in READY mode, edit the macro. You can edit the macro while the STEP indicator is displayed at the bottom of the screen.

6. To exit STEP mode, press Alt F2 (Step).

14

Editing Macros

After you identify an error in a macro, you can correct the error. Fixing an error in a macro is as simple as editing the cell that contains the erroneous code. You don't need to rewrite the entire cell contents. You need only to change the element in error. Although editing a complex macro can be much more challenging than editing a simple one, the concept is exactly the same.

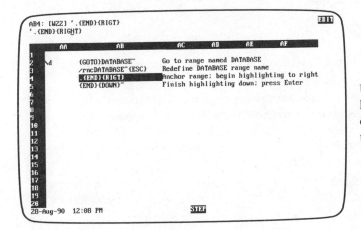

Use the Edit (F2) key to correct the cell that contains the error.

Creating a Macro Library

A macro library is a group of macros that can be used with many different worksheet files. These macros can range from simple keystroke macros to more specialized advanced macro command programs. Macro libraries can save the time necessary to re-create the same macros in different files. After you have created a macro library file, you can copy the macros into the current worksheet.

This section introduces five simple keystroke macros that you can create for use in your own macro library. These macros perform common tasks that would require additional keystrokes (and time) if performed manually. The first three macros described in this section appeared at the beginning of this chapter but were not explained there. Two additional macros are also introduced. All macros in this section will work with prior versions of 1-2-3 as well as Release 2.2.

14

453

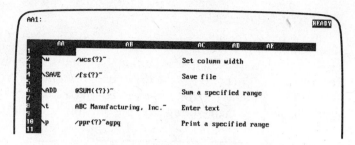

These five simple keystroke macros can be included in a macro library.

14

To create a macros library file, follow these general steps:

1. Start with a blank worksheet, with the cell pointer at the Home position.

2. Begin typing the exact keystrokes displayed in columns A, B, and C. Column A contains the macro names, column B contains the actual macros, and column C contains the documentation for each macro. *Remember to first type a label prefix (such as ') before entering each of the macros in column B.*

3. Use the **/Range Name Labels Right** command to name the macros by specifying the range containing all macro names in column AA and pressing ⏎Enter.

4. Use the **/File Save** command to save the macros in a separate file.

When you are ready to copy the macros in the macro library file to your current worksheet, position the cell pointer where you want the macros located (such as column AA), and then issue the **/File Combine Entire-File** command. Highlight or type the file name containing the macros, and then press Enter.

Execute one of the Alt-*letter* macros (\w, \t, or \p) by pressing the Alt key followed by the letter key assigned to the macro. The macros with a descriptive name (\SAVE or \ADD) by pressing Alt-F3 (Run), selecting the desired macro name, and pressing Return.

The sections that follow provide a brief explanation of the operation of each macro.

A Macro That Sets Column Widths

The \w macro in cell AB2 can be used to change the column width of the current column. Highlight the column whose width you want to change, and then press Alt-W. The macro begins by executing the /Worksheet Column Set-Width command. Then, as a result of the {?} command, the macro pauses for input. Enter the desired character width and press Enter. The adjusted column width is displayed.

You can modify this macro to change the column width of a *range* of columns (in Release 2.2 only) by typing the following in place of the macro in cell B2:

'/wccs{?}~{?}~

This modified macro executes the command /Worksheet Column Column-Range Set-Width and then pauses for you to enter the column range and press Enter. The macro pauses again until you type the column width and press Enter. The range of specified columns is then displayed with the selected column width.

A Macro That Saves a File

The \SAVE macro in cell B4 saves the current file in the current directory on disk. To use this macro, press Run (Alt-F3), select \SAVE from the list of macro and range names, and then press Enter. This macro executes the /File Save command and then pauses for you to enter the desired name. After you type the name of the file and press Enter, 1-2-3 begins to save the file. If the file already exists, select **R**eplace from the resulting menu to continue saving the file.

A Macro That Sums a Specified Range

The \ADD macro in cell B6 uses the @SUM function to add values from a specified range. To use this macro, first highlight the cell to contain the result of the formula. Then press Run (Alt-F3), select \ADD from the list of macro and range names, and then press Enter. The macro pauses for you to highlight a range of cells that you want to sum. After you select the range and press Enter, the formula result is displayed on-screen.

A Macro That Enters Text

The \t macro in cell B8 enters a long text label into the current cell. Press Alt-T to execute the macro, and the specified label is automatically entered

455

into the highlighted cell. This macro is straightforward, but very useful for entering any long label that commonly appears throughout the worksheet.

A Macro That Prints a Specified Range

The \p macro in cell B10 prints a range that you specify directly to the printer and then advances the paper to the top of the next page. To run this macro, press Alt-P. The macro executes the /**P**rint **P**rinter **R**ange command, and then pauses for you to specify the desired print range. After you highlight the range you want to print and press Enter, the command **Align Go Page Quit** (from the Print Printer menu) aligns the paper, prints the range, advances the paper to the top of the page, and returns 1-2-3 to READY mode.

If you normally print the same range from a particular worksheet, you can name this print range (with /**R**ange Name Create) and use this name in place of {?} in the Alt-P macro. For example, to print a range named SALES, use the following macro in place of the macro in cell AB10:

    '/pprSALES~agpq

If you use this form of the print macro, remember to redefine the range named SALES whenever new data is added to the range you want to print.

Summary

This chapter provided the basic information you need to begin creating your own simple keystroke macros—tools you can use to save time, reduce repetition, and automate your worksheet applications. The chapter identified each of the steps necessary to create macros and described ways to document, name, and execute macros. The Learn feature of Release 2.2, which allows you to create macros by recording all keyboard activity, was discussed. You also learned about automatic (\0) macros, as well as about methods to debug and edit your simple keystroke macros.

Specifically, you learned the following key information about 1-2-3:

■ The elements of macros include actual command keystrokes, key names, range names and cell addresses, the tilde (~) to represent the Enter key, and the advanced macro commands.

■ Macro key names, which represent keyboard keys, are enclosed within braces, such as {EDIT}. Key names are available for the function keys, direction keys, editing keys, and special keys.

■ You can specify more than one use of a key name by including repetition factors within the braces separated by a single space, such as {DOWN 5}.

■ Take time to plan your macros. Consider the available input and the desired results. Use the keyboard to proceed through your tasks, while jotting down the keystrokes necessary to create simple macros. More complex macros can be created by breaking them into smaller macros consisting of simple operations.

■ Position macros outside of the main area of your worksheet. So that you can quickly find your macros, place them in the same location in each of your worksheets, such as in column AA.

■ Always document your 1-2-3 macros. An easy way to do this is to include comments in the cells to the right of the macro steps.

■ Macros can be named in two different ways—with a backslash (\) followed by a single letter, or with a descriptive name of up to 15 characters (only in Release 2.2). Use the /Range Name Create or /Range Name Labels Right command to name your macros.

■ The Learn feature of 1-2-3 Release 2.2 lets you create macros automatically by recording your keystrokes and storing them in a specified range. This range must first be defined with the /Worksheet Learn Range command. Then use Learn (Alt-F5) to start and stop recording keystrokes.

■ To execute Alt-*letter* macros, press the Alt key while pressing the letter key assigned to the macro. Macros with descriptive names are executed by pressing Run (Alt-F3), selecting the macro name, and pressing Enter.

■ Automatic (\0) macros execute automatically when a file is retrieved. Only one automatic macro can be used in each worksheet.

■ 1-2-3's STEP mode, accessed by pressing Step (Alt-F2), can be used to find macro errors by proceeding through a macro one step at a time. The Undo feature sometimes can be used to reverse the effect of a macro in Release 2.2 if the macro has caused errors in the worksheet.

14

457

■ Macros can be edited just like any cell entries in the worksheet—by pressing Edit (F2) and correcting each cell containing the error. Rewriting the entire contents of these cells is not necessary.

■ A macro library is a collection of two or more macros that are saved in a separate file and used with several different files. Use the /File Combine Copy Entire-File command to copy a macro library into the current file.

14

Installing 1-2-3 Release 2.2

Before you install 1-2-3 on your computer system, you need to copy the 1-2-3 disks to your hard disk, if you have one, or prepare the 1-2-3 disks for use on a two floppy disk system. Preparing the disks consists of making working copies and copying the DOS COMMAND.COM file to the working disks.

The first matter to consider when you prepare to install 1-2-3 is how to tailor the program to your particular computer system. You will need to let 1-2-3 know what kind of display hardware you have. For example, you must tell the program whether the graphs you create will be displayed on a color monitor or on a single-color monitor (green-on-black, amber-on-black, or white-on-black).

Another consideration is the printer configuration—for both the text printer and the graphics printer or plotter. If your text printer is capable of printing graphs or if you have a separate graphics printer or plotter, you can configure the printer for 1-2-3 graphics. When you run the Install program, 1-2-3 stores all the installation settings, including the configuration settings for your text and graphics printers, in a file called a driver set. If you have special printing needs and use several printers, you will need to configure all your printers for 1-2-3. You also may need to create additional driver sets.

After you decide how you want to tailor 1-2-3 for your system, you can run the Install program to complete the installation for your system. Before you begin working with the newly installed program, you need to prepare data disks for use with 1-2-3.

The 1-2-3 Disks

Release 2.2 of 1-2-3 comes with two sets of disks: twelve 5 1/4-inch disks (five for the Allways software) for use on computers with 5 1/4-inch disk drives; and six 3 1/2-inch microfloppy disks (three for Allways) for computers with 3 1/2-inch disk drives. The programs contained on the two sets of disks are exactly the same, but are divided among the disks differently.

In previous versions of 1-2-3, the System disk contained a hidden copy-protection scheme. Lotus did not copy-protect Release 2.2 in order to allow users to make backup copies of the System disk in case of accidental or careless deletion of files. To use your copy of Release 2.2, however, you must first run a setup program that requires you to enter your name and the name of your company. This process is designed to discourage illegal copying of software by users who have not purchased the package.

Note that in this appendix, the term System disk refers to not only the System disk for 5 1/4-inch disk drives, but also to the System, Help, and PrintGraph disk for computers with 3 1/2-inch disk drives.

The 1-2-3 Disks for Computers with 5 1/4-Inch Disk Drives

The 1-2-3 Release 2.2 package includes 12 floppy disks for computers with 5 1/4-inch disk drives. These include the following:

> System disk
> Help disk
> PrintGraph disk
> Translate disk
> Install disk
> Install Library disk
> Sample Files disk
> Allways Setup disk
> Allways disks (four disks)

460

The most important of these disks, the System disk, contains all the 1-2-3 operations except one: the commands for printing graphs. Printing graphs requires the use of the separate PrintGraph disk (see Chapter 12).

The Help disk contains the on-line help system that you can access while using 1-2-3 by pressing the Help (F1) key.

The Translate disk contains a program that you use to transfer data between 1-2-3 and dBASE II, dBASE III, Symphony, Multiplan, earlier releases of 1-2-3, DIF, and VisiCalc.

The Install and Install Library disks contain programs for installation and the library of drivers you use to set up 1-2-3 for your system. With the Install program, you can tailor 1-2-3 to your computer system. Drivers are programs that 1-2-3 uses to control your hardware. For example, you install a different drive to control a color monitor than you install to control a monochrome monitor.

The Sample Files disk contains files to use in conjunction with 1-2-3's 160-page tutorial, included in the 1-2-3 documentation. In Release 2.2, this disk replaces the on-line tutorial available in earlier versions of 1-2-3.

The Allways Setup disk contains the setup files necessary to install the Allways publishing add-in program on your computer.

The four remaining Allways disks contain font files for printing different typefaces and styles, and driver files to correspond with the various printers you can use with the software. These disks are labeled Allways Disk 2, Allways Disk 3, and so on.

The 1-2-3 Disks for Computers with 3 1/2-Inch Disk Drives

The 1-2-3 Release 2.2 package includes six microfloppy disks for computers with 3 1/2-inch disk drives. These include the following:

    System, Help, and PrintGraph disk
    Translate and Sample Files disk
    Install and Install Library disk
    Allways Setup disk
    Allways disks (two disks)

A

The System disk contains all the 1-2-3 operations, including the commands for printing graphs. Although you can run 1-2-3 entirely from the System disk, you wouldn't do this if you have a hard disk; instead you would install 1-2-3 on the hard disk. If your computer does not have a hard disk, however, this grouping of programs on the System disk helps you avoid having to swap disks.

The Translate and Sample Files disk contains a program that you use to transfer data between 1-2-3 and dBASE II, dBASE III, Symphony, Multiplan, earlier releases of 1-2-3, DIF, and VisiCalc. The sample files on this disk are used in conjunction with 1-2-3's 160-page tutorial, included in the 1-2-3 documentation. In Release 2.2, this disk replaces the on-line tutorial available in earlier versions of 1-2-3.

The Install and Install Library disk contains the Install program, which you use to tailor 1-2-3 to your computer system. This disk also contains the library of drivers you use with the Install program to set up 1-2-3 for your system. Drivers, briefly, are programs that 1-2-3 uses to control your hardware. For example, the driver that controls a color monitor is different than the one that controls a monochrome monitor. This grouping of the Install program with the library of drivers allows you to complete installation from one disk.

The Allways Setup disk contains the setup files necessary to install the Allways publishing add-in program on your computer.

The two remaining Allways disks contain font files for printing different typefaces and styles, and driver files to correspond with the various printers you can use with the software. These disks are labeled Allways Disk 2 and Allways Disk 3.

Initializing 1-2-3

In Release 2.2, before you can install 1-2-3 on either a hard disk or a floppy disk system, you must first initialize 1-2-3, a short process that requires you to record your name and your company's name on the System disk. The following instructions assume that you have a hard disk which contains DOS and that drive C is the current drive.

Follow these steps to initialize 1-2-3:

1. Make sure that your computer is turned on, the 1-2-3 System disk is in drive A, and the DOS C> prompt is on-screen.

2. Type **A:** and press ⏎Enter.

3. Type **INIT** and press ⏎Enter.

4. Press ⏎Enter again to advance beyond the copyright screen; then read the information explaining the installation process.

5. Press ⏎Enter after you finish reading the screen.

6. Respond to the remaining prompts that ask you to enter your name and the name of your company by typing your response and pressing ⏎Enter. (Use your name for the company name if this software is licensed to you.)

After you confirm that these entries are correct and you terminate the initialization process, this information is permanently recorded on the System disk. You cannot change this information. These entries will be copied to a hard disk if you proceed with installation of 1-2-3 on a hard disk system. If you are going to use 1-2-3 on a floppy disk system, you will use this System disk whenever you start 1-2-3. In either case, the name and company entries will always appear at start-up time when you use 1-2-3.

Copying the 1-2-3 Disks to a Hard Disk

Even if you are installing 1-2-3 on a hard disk system, you should make backup copies of the master disks. You need to copy each master disk onto a blank formatted disk. For more information about formatting and copying disks, see Que's *Using DOS* or *MS-DOS User's Guide*, Special Edition. After you make backup copies of your master disks, you can go on to install 1-2-3 on your hard disk.

The following steps are required to copy the 1-2-3 disks onto your hard disk so that all the 1-2-3 programs can be started from the hard disk. If your computer does not have a hard disk, skip to the following section, "Installing 1-2-3 on a Two Floppy Disk System." The instructions that follow assume that your hard disk is formatted, that DOS is installed on the hard disk, and that drive C is the current drive.

A

463

To copy the 1-2-3 disks to a hard disk, follow these steps:

1. Start your computer; if the C> prompt does not appear, type **C:** and press ⏎Enter.
2. Create a subdirectory to hold the 1-2-3 files. To create a subdirectory of the current directory (the root directory), use the DOS MD (Make Directory) command. For example, type **MD \123** and press ⏎Enter to create a subdirectory named 123.
3. Make this subdirectory the current directory. In this case, type **CD \123** and press ⏎Enter.
4. Starting with the System disk, copy the contents of each 1-2-3 master disk onto the hard disk, following this procedure:
   a. Place, in turn, each master disk in drive A.
   b. Type **COPY A:*.* /V** and press ⏎Enter. The /V will verify the copy. (DOS recognizes that you want the files copied to the current directory—C:\123.)
   c. When copying is complete, remove the master disk from drive A.
5. Repeat step 4 for all remaining disks except for the Allways disks.

Installing 1-2-3 on a Two Floppy Disk System

Preparing to install 1-2-3 for a two floppy (5 1/4-inch) or a two microfloppy (3 1/2-inch) disk system is a fairly easy procedure and a necessary part of configuring the program to your system. Without this step, the 1-2-3 program will run, but you will not be able to use your printer with 1-2-3 or display graphs on-screen.

If you have a system with two floppy or two microfloppy disk drives, the general procedure for preparing and then using the disks that come with 1-2-3 consists of making working copies of the 1-2-3 disks (as described in the following section) and then adding the COMMAND.COM file to the disks you will use to run the 1-2-3 programs.

Note: Make working copies of all disks except for the Allways disks. Also be sure to add the COMMAND.COM file to all disks except the Install disk.

Making Working Copies of the 1-2-3 Disks

You should make working copies of all the 1-2-3 disks if you work with a two floppy or two microfloppy disk system. You frequently will need to use all the 1-2-3 disks; therefore, you should work with working copies of the master disks and store the masters in a safe place. If you damage any of the working disks in any way, you can use the master disks to make replacement copies.

Before making working copies, you should become familiar with your computer's disk operating system. For specific explanations of formatting disks and copying files, refer to Que's books *Using DOS* or *MS-DOS User's Guide*, Special Edition, or check your system's manual.

For computers with 5 1/4-inch disk drives, follow these steps to create working copies of the 1-2-3 disks:

A

1. Format seven blank disks, using the DOS FORMAT command.
2. Label the seven blank disks as follows:

    Working Copy: System

    Working Copy: Help

    Working Copy: PrintGraph

    Working Copy: Translate

    Working Copy: Install

    Working Copy: Install Library

    Working Copy: Sample Files

3. Copy each 1-2-3 master disk onto the appropriate formatted blank disk as follows:

    a. Place a master disk in drive A and the appropriate formatted blank disk in drive B.

    b. At any DOS prompt, type **COPY A:*.* B:** /V and press ⏎Enter . The **/V** will verify the copy. (Lotus suggests using the COPY command instead of the DISKCOPY command.)

    c. After all files have been copied from the master disk onto the formatted disk, remove the master disk from drive A and the working copy from drive B.

4. Repeat step 3 for each of the six remaining disks.

For computers with 3 1/2-inch disk drives, follow these steps to make working copies of the 1-2-3 disks:

1. Format three blank disks, using the DOS FORMAT command.
2. Label the three blank disks as follows:

   Working Copy: System, Help, and PrintGraph

   Working Copy: Translate and Sample Files

   Working Copy: Install and Install Library

3. Copy each 1-2-3 master disk onto the appropriate formatted blank disk as follows:

   a. Place a master disk in drive A and the appropriate formatted blank disk in drive B.

   b. At any DOS prompt, type **COPY A:*.* B:** /V and press ⏎Enter. The /V will verify the copy. (Lotus suggests using the COPY command instead of the DISKCOPY command.)

   c. After all files have been copied from the master disk onto the formatted disk, remove the master disk from drive A and the working copy from drive B.

4. Repeat step 3 for each of the two remaining disks.

Adding COMMAND.COM to the Working 1-2-3 Disks

For a two floppy or a two microfloppy disk system, Lotus suggests that you copy the COMMAND.COM file from your DOS disk to all working 1-2-3 disks, except the Install disk. If you try to exit 1-2-3 when drive A contains a disk that does not hold the COMMAND.COM file, the message Insert disk with COMMAND.COM in drive A and strike any key when ready appears on-screen. By having COMMAND.COM on your 1-2-3 disks, you avoid this problem.

To copy COMMAND.COM onto each of your working 1-2-3 disks, proceed as follows. With the DOS A> prompt on-screen and your DOS disk in drive A:

1. Place one of the 1-2-3 working disks in drive B. Make sure that no write-protect tab is on the disk.
2. Type the command **COPY A:COMMAND.COM B:** /V and press ⏎Enter

466

3. Remove the disk from drive B.

4. Repeat steps 1 through 3 for each of the disks except for the Install disk(s).

Put all the master disks in a safe place, and keep your working disks available. You will need your working copy of the System disk each time you load 1-2-3.

Installing Driver Programs

Installing driver programs is the next step in tailoring the 1-2-3 disks to your particular system. Each driver is a separate program that resides on the Install Library disk.

The driver files store information about your computer system, such as information about the display(s), printer(s), and plotters. You can create one or many driver files, depending on your needs. For example, suppose that you want to run 1-2-3 on an IBM PC that is capable of displaying graphics in color and also run 1-2-3 on a COMPAQ that displays graphics and text in one color. By creating two separate driver files, you can run 1-2-3 on both computers whenever you like.

When you make your driver selection, carefully review the options. Whether your system can display graphs and text at the same time and in color depends on a number of factors: the type of monitor(s) you will use; the type of video adapter card(s) your computer has (whether the monitor will produce only text or also graphics and color); and the number of colors that are displayed.

Some equipment selections enable you to view text and graphics on-screen, but only at different times (One-Monitor mode). An IBM color monitor with a color/graphics card, for example, will display both graphs and text in color, but not at the same time. On the other hand, some dual-monitor combinations enable you to view color graphs on one screen and text on the other at the same time (Two-Monitor mode).

Before you run the Install program, prepare a list of your equipment. When you run Install, you will first need to indicate to 1-2-3 what display hardware you have. For example, a color/graphics card uses graphics control characters

A

to display graphs, but a monochrome adapter displays regular green-on-black, amber-on-black, or white-on-black text.

Second, you will need to specify what kind of text printer(s) you have. You can specify more than one printer at installation and then select the current one from within 1-2-3.

Third, 1-2-3 will ask you to indicate the graphics printer(s) or plotter(s) you will be using. Again, if you specify several graphics printers during installation, you can later select the current one from within 1-2-3. Note that the same printer can be installed as both the text printer and the graphics printer.

If you do not have a hard disk, keep in mind that multiple drivers take up space on your 1-2-3 disk. If disk space is a problem, keep the list of printers to a minimum, or store your additional driver files on a separate disk. When you want to use another driver, place the system disk containing your usual driver set (123.SET) into drive A and the disk containing your other drivers into drive B. At the A> prompt, type

123 B:*name*.SET

In this command, *name* is the name of the particular driver set you want to use. 1-2-3 will then load onto your computer the specified driver from the disk in drive B.

To select drivers to run 1-2-3 on a hard disk system, follow these steps:

1. Make sure that your current directory is 123 by typing **CD \123** and pressing ⏎Enter at the DOS C> prompt.
2. Type **INSTALL** and press ⏎Enter.
3. When the main Install menu appears, highlight First-Time Installation and press ⏎Enter.
4. Create your driver set by following the step-by-step instructions that appear on your computer screen.

If you are creating only one driver set, use the default driver name 123.SET. If you are creating two or more driver sets, you must name each driver. For example, if you have a graphics plotter, you could name your second driver set PLOT.SET.

468

When you exit the Install program, 1-2-3 automatically saves your driver selections for you.

To select drivers to run 1-2-3 on a two floppy (5 1/4-inch) disk system, follow these steps:

1. Insert the Install disk in drive A.
2. Type **INSTALL** and press (⏎Enter).
3. When 1-2-3 prompts you to do so, replace the disk in drive A with the Install Library disk.
4. When the main Install menu appears, highlight First-Time Installation, and press (⏎Enter).
5. Create your driver set by following the step-by-step instructions that appear on-screen.

If you are creating only one driver set, use the default driver name 123.SET. If you are creating two or more driver sets, you must name each driver. For example, if you have a graphics plotter, you could name your second driver PLOT.SET. Save your driver set(s) on your other disks by following the on-screen directions.

Note: In Release 2.01, if you try to store additional drivers on your System disk, you may get an error message indicating insufficient disk space. Check your documentation for a way to free up space on the System disk.

To select drivers to run 1-2-3 on a two microfloppy (3 1/2-inch) disk system, follow these steps:

1. Insert the Install disk in drive A.
2. Type **INSTALL** and press (⏎Enter).
3. When the main Install menu appears, highlight First-Time Installation, and then press (⏎Enter).
4. Create your driver set by following the step-by-step instructions that appear on-screen.

If you are creating only one driver set, use the default driver name 123.SET. If you are creating two or more driver sets, you must name each driver. For example, if you have a graphics plotter, you could name your second driver PLOT.SET. Save your driver set(s) on your other disks by following the on-screen directions.

A

If you need to make a change or correction to your existing driver set(s), enter the Install program and select the **Change Selected Equipment** option. Then follow the on-screen instructions.

Installing Allways

Your computer must have a hard disk and 512K of RAM if you want to use the add-in program Allways. Before you install Allways, you must have completed installation of 1-2-3.

With the Allways Setup disk in drive A, follow these steps to install Allways:

1. At the DOS C> prompt, type **A:** and press (↵Enter).
2. Type **AWSETUP** and press (↵Enter).
3. Choose First-Time Installation and follow the on-screen directions.

The Allways installation process will determine the type of monitor and printer your system has and will establish a subdirectory named ALLWAYS under the 123 directory on your hard disk. All necessary files will be copied to this subdirectory during installation.

After completion of the Allways installation, you are ready to use 1-2-3 and, whenever you want, to access Allways from 1-2-3. See Chapter 9 for more information on using Allways.

Preparing Data Disks

The final procedure for getting started with 1-2-3 is to prepare data disks for storing your 1-2-3 data files. All disks must be properly formatted, using the DOS FORMAT command, before they can be used. With the 1-2-3 /System command, you can access DOS without exiting 1-2-3 (see Chapter 2). For more information on how to format disks, see *Using DOS* or *MS-DOS User's Guide,* Special Edition; both books are published by Que Corporation.

Summary of 1-2-3 Commands

B

Action	Commands
Cell Pointer Movement	
Move one column to left	←
Move one column to right	→
Move up one row	↑
Move down one row	↓
Move one screen to right	Tab⇥ or Ctrl→
Move one screen to left	⇧Shift Tab⇥ or Ctrl←
Move up one screen	PgUp
Move down one screen	PgDn
Return to cell A1	Home
Move in direction of arrow to next boundary	End-arrow key
Move to specified cell coordinates	F5 (GoTo), type cell address or range name

Summary of 1-2-3 Commands

Action	Commands
Editing	
Align range of labels	/**Range Label**; **Left, Right**, or **Center**; highlight range, ⏎Enter
Align labels in entire worksheet	/**Worksheet Global Label-Prefix**; **Left, Right**, or **Center**
Edit cell contents	F2 (Edit)
Move cursor one position to left	←
Move cursor one position to right	→
Move cursor 5 characters to right	Tab⇄ or Ctrl→
Move cursor 5 characters to left	⇧Shift Tab⇄ or Ctrl←
Move cursor to first character in entry	Home
Move cursor to right of last character in entry	End
Delete character to left of cursor	⌫Backspace
Toggle between insert and overtype modes	Ins
Delete character above cursor	Del
Clear edit line	Esc
Undo last command	Alt F4 (Undo) when Undo feature is enabled
Temporarily disable Undo	/**Worksheet Global Default Other Undo Disable**
Saving and Retrieving Files	
Save file	/**File Save**, highlight file name or type new one, ⏎Enter
Retrieve file	/**File Retrieve**, highlight or type file name, ⏎Enter

B

472

Action	Commands
Ranges	
Designate a range	Type address of upper left cell in range, type one or two periods, type address of lower right cell in range, ⏎Enter
	Or
	In POINT mode, move cell pointer to highlight cells in range, ⏎Enter
	Or
	Type existing range name (or press F3 and highlight range name), ⏎Enter
Assign a name to a multicell range	/**Range Name Create**, type name, ⏎Enter, type cell addresses or highlight range, ⏎Enter
Assign names to a series of one-cell entries with adjacent labels	Position cell pointer on first label to use as a range name; /**Range Name Labels**; **Right, Left, Above,** or **Below**; highlight cells containing labels to use as range names, ⏎Enter
Delete a single range name	/**Range Name Delete**, highlight or type range name, ⏎Enter
Delete all range names in a worksheet	/**Range Name Reset**
Erase a range	/**Range Erase**, highlight range to erase, ⏎Enter
Display at top of screen a list of range names in current worksheet	In POINT mode, press F3 (Name)
Display a full-screen list of range names in current worksheet	In POINT mode, press F3 (Name) twice.
Create a range name table	Move cell pointer to worksheet location that will display upper left corner of table, /**Range Name Table**, ⏎Enter

B

473

Action	*Commands*
Move cell pointer to a named range	[F5] (GoTo), [F3] (Name), highlight name, [↵Enter]
Change format of a cell or range of cells	/Range Format; select format—Fixed, Sci, Currency, , (Comma), General, +/−, Percent, Date, Text, or Hidden; if prompted, enter number of decimal places or accept default number, [↵Enter]; highlight range to format, [↵Enter].
Return format of range to global default setting	/Range Format Reset; highlight range to reset, [↵Enter].
Set format for date and time, currency symbols, negative values, and punctuation	/Worksheet Global Default Other International

Building a Worksheet

Action	*Commands*
Set formats that affect entire worksheet	/Worksheet Global
Erase the worksheet	/Worksheet Erase Yes
Set width of single column	/Worksheet Column Set-Width, type width or use left- or right-arrow keys to expand or shrink column, [↵Enter]
Reset single column to default width	/Worksheet Column Reset-Width
Set widths of all columns at once	/Worksheet Global Column-Width, type width or use left- or right-arrow keys to expand or shrink column, [↵Enter]
Set widths of contiguous columns	/Worksheet Column Column-Range Set-Width; highlight column range, [↵Enter]; type width, or use left- or right-arrow keys to expand or shrink columns, [↵Enter]
Reset contiguous columns to default width	/Worksheet Column Column-Range Reset-Width
Split the screen	Position cell pointer at location for split; /Worksheet Window; Horizontal or Vertical; [↵Enter]

B

474

Action	Commands
Return to single window	**/Worksheet Window Clear**
Freeze titles on the screen	Position cell pointer below and to the right of rows and/or columns to freeze; **/Worksheet Titles; Both, Horizontal, or Vertical**
Unlock frozen titles	**/Worksheet Titles Clear**
Insert columns and rows	Position cell pointer where column(s) or row(s) should be inserted; **/Worksheet Insert; Column or Row**; highlight range to insert multiple columns or rows, ⏎Enter
Delete columns and rows	Position cell pointer in first column or row to be deleted; **/Worksheet Delete; Column or Row**; highlight range of column(s) or row(s) to be deleted, ⏎Enter
Hide columns	**/Worksheet Column Hide**, highlight column range to be hidden, ⏎Enter
Redisplay hidden columns	**/Worksheet Column Display**, specify columns to redisplay, ⏎Enter
Suppress display of zeros	**/Worksheet Global Zero; No or Label**
Redisplay zeros	**/Worksheet Global Zero Yes**
Modify worksheet recalculation settings	**/Worksheet Global Recalculation**
Protect entire worksheet	**/Worksheet Global Protection Enable**
Unprotect entire worksheet	**/Worksheet Global Protection Disable**
Turn off protection in a range	**/Range Unprot**, specify range, ⏎Enter.
Reprotect cells in a range	**/Range Prot** specify range, ⏎Enter.
Restrict movement to a particular range	**/Range Input**, specify range that includes the unprotected cells, ⏎Enter
Check status of global settings	**/Worksheet Status**

B

475

Action	Commands
Enter a page-break character	Position cell pointer in first column at row where new page should begin, /Worksheet Page

Modifying a Worksheet

Action	Commands
Move contents of cells	/Move; specify range to move FROM, ⏎Enter; specify range to move TO, ⏎Enter
Copy contents of cells	/Copy; specify range to copy FROM, ⏎Enter; specify range to copy TO, ⏎Enter
Convert cell addresses to absolute or mixed cell addresses	Highlight cell containing formula, F2 (Edit), move cursor to cell address, F4 (Abs)
Transpose rows and columns	/Range Trans; specify range to copy FROM, ⏎Enter; specify range to copy TO, ⏎Enter
Convert formulas to values	/Range Value; specify range of formulas to copy FROM, ⏎Enter; specify range to copy TO, ⏎Enter
Search for occurrence of string	/Range Search; highlight range, ⏎Enter; define string to search for, ⏎Enter; Formulas, Labels, or Both; Find; Next
Replace one string with another	/Range Search; highlight range, ⏎Enter; define string to search for, ⏎Enter; Formulas, Labels, or Both; Replace, define replacement string, ⏎Enter; All, Replace, Next, or Quit

Functions

Action	Commands
Enter a 1-2-3 function	@, type function name, (, type arguments (if any),), ⏎Enter

476

Action	*Commands*
Printing Reports	
Print directly to a printer	**/Print Printer**
Create a print file on disk	**/Print File**, type filename, ⏎Enter
Print draft of full screen of data	⬆Shift PrtSc or PrtSc
Print one-page report	**/Print Printer Range**, highlight range to be printed, ⏎Enter; **Align, Go, Page; Quit**
Print two or more pages with borders	**/Print Printer Options Borders; Columns** or **Rows**; highlight columns or rows, ⏎Enter; **Quit; Range**, highlight range to be printed, ⏎Enter; **Align, Go, Page; Quit**
Exclude columns within print range	**/Worksheet Column Hide**, highlight column(s), ⏎Enter; **/Print Printer Range**, highlight range to be printed, ⏎Enter; **Align, Go, Page; Quit**
Exclude row within print range	Highlight row to be suppressed in first column of print range, type ⎹⎹, ⏎Enter; **/Print Printer Range**, highlight range to be printed, ⏎Enter; **Align, Go, Page; Quit**
Exclude range from printout	**/Range Format Hidden**, highlight range to be hidden, ⏎Enter; **/Print Printer Range**, highlight range to be printed, ⏎Enter; **Align, Go, Page; Quit**
Advance paper one line at a time	**/Print Printer Line**
Advance to new page after printing less than full page	**/Print Printer Page**
Align printer and set beginning of page	**/Print Printer Align**

B

477

Action	Commands
Insert page break manually	Insert blank row at location for page break, type ⏐:⏐ into blank cell in first column of print range in that row
Add header or footer	**/Print Printer Range**, highlight print range, ⏎Enter; **Options, Header** or **Footer**, type header of footer—including text or codes for date and page number (if used), ⏎Enter; **Quit; Align, Go, Page, Quit**
Change page layout	**/Print Printer Options Margins; Left, Right, Top, Bottom,** or **None**; type a value, ⏎Enter
Print listing of cell contents	**/Print Printer Options Other; Cell-Formulas** or **As-Displayed; Quit; Range**, highlight range to be printed, ⏎Enter; **Align, Go, Page; Quit**
Clear print options	**/Print Printer Clear; All, Range, Borders,** or **Format; Quit**
Prepare output for other programs	**/Print File**, type file name, ⏎Enter; **Range**, specify range, ⏎Enter; **Options Other Unformatted; Quit; Go; Quit**; follow instructions in other software program

Printing with Allways

Action	Commands
Attach Allways automatically	**/Worksheet Global Default Other Add-In Set**; select number (**1–8**); highlight ALLWAYS.ADN, ⏎Enter; select key to invoke Allways (**No-Key, 7, 8,** or **9**), **Yes; Quit; Update; Quit**
Attach Allways each time it will be used	**/Add-In Attach**; highlight ALLWAYS.ADN, ⏎Enter; select key to invoke Allways, (**No-Key, 7, 8,** or **9**); **Quit**

B

478

Action	*Commands*
Invoke Allways	Press Alt-key combination (Alt-7, Alt-8, or Alt-9); or, if No-Key was selected, /Add-In Invoke, highlight ALLWAYS, `↵Enter`
Prespecify a cell range	Move cell pointer to first cell of range, press period (.), extend range with arrow keys
Change font for particular range	/Format Font, highlight font, Use, highlight range, `↵Enter`; or `Alt` `1` through `Alt` `8`
Choose alternative font for entire worksheet	/Format Font, highlight existing font, Replace; highlight new typeface, `↵Enter`; highlight point size, `↵Enter`; Quit
Shade area of worksheet	/Format Shade, Light or Dark, highlight range, `↵Enter`; or `Alt` `S`
Create a thick line	/Format Shade Solid, highlight range, `↵Enter`; or `Alt` `S`. Then /Worksheet Row Set-Height, use `↑` to decrease row height, `↵Enter`
Remove existing shading	/Format Shade Clear, highlight range, `↵Enter`; or `Alt` `S`
Create underline	/Format Underline, Single or Double, highlight range, `↵Enter`; or `Alt` `U`
Remove existing underline	/Format Underline Clear, highlight range, `↵Enter`; or `Alt` `U`
Create boldface characters	/Format Bold Set, highlight range, `↵Enter`; or `Alt` `B`
Remove existing boldface	/Format Bold Clear, highlight range, `↵Enter`; or `Alt` `B`
Outline each cell in range of cells	/Format Lines All, highlight range, `↵Enter`; or `Alt` `L`
Outline perimeter of range of cells	/Format Lines Outline, highlight range, `↵Enter`; or `Alt` `L`

B

Action	Commands
Create grid lines	/**Layout O**ptions **G**rid **Y**es, **Q**uit, **Q**uit; or (Alt)(G)
Change size of image on-screen	/**Display Z**oom, **T**iny, **S**mall, **N**ormal, **L**arge, or **H**uge; **Q**uit; or (F4) and (Alt)(F4)
Combine graph with worksheet	Position cell pointer at location for graph, /**Graph Add**, highlight graph name, (↵Enter); highlight range for graph, (↵Enter)
View graph on-screen	/**Display Graphs Y**es; **Q**uit
Remove graph from worksheet	/**Graph Remove**, specify graph name, (↵Enter)
Print a report with Allways	/**Print Range Set**, highlight range, (↵Enter), **Go**; **Q**uit

Managing Files

Action	Commands
Create a password	/**File Save**, type file name, leave a space, type **P**, (↵Enter); type password, (↵Enter); type password again, (↵Enter)
Retrieve a password-protected file	/**File Retrieve**, highlight file name, (↵Enter); type password, (↵Enter)
Delete a password	/**File Save**, erase [PASSWORD PROTECTED], by pressing (Esc) or (◆Backspace), (↵Enter)
Change a password	/**File Save**, erase [PASSWORD PROTECTED], by pressing (Esc) or (◆Backspace), type file name, leave a space, type **P**, (↵Enter); type new password, (↵Enter); type new password again, (↵Enter)
Copy partial worksheet to separate file	/**File Xtract**; **F**ormulas or **V**alues; type file name to hold extracted data, (↵Enter); highlight range to be extracted, (↵Enter)

B

480

Action	Commands
Combine files	Position cell pointer on range to receive data; /File Combine; Copy, Add, or Subtract; Entire-File or Named/Specified Range; indicate data file or location of incoming range, ⏎Enter
List linked files	/File List Linked
Refresh links	/File Admin Link-Refresh
List files on current drive and directory	/File List, select file type (Worksheet, Print, Graph, Other, or Linked)
Change default directory	/Worksheet Global Default Directory; Esc or ◆Backspace; type new default directory name, ⏎Enter; Update; Quit
Temporarily change directory	/File Directory, type new directory name, ⏎Enter
Delete a file	/File Erase, select type of file (Worksheet, Print, Graph, or Other); highlight file name, ⏎Enter; Yes
Import ASCII text file into 1-2-3	/File Import; Text or Numbers; highlight name of text file to be imported, ⏎Enter
Use Translate Utility	From 1-2-3 Access System menu, Translate; highlight format of file to be translated, ⏎Enter; highlight format to translate to, ⏎Enter; highlight name of file to be translated, ⏎Enter; type name of file to be created, ⏎Enter; Yes, Esc twice, Yes

B

481

Action	*Commands*
Creating Graphs	
Create a basic graph	Select graph type, specify data ranges, select range for labeling x-axis, display graph on-screen
Select graph type	**/Graph Type**, select type (**Line**, **Bar**, **XY**, **Stack-Bar**, or **Pie**)
Specify a data series range	**/Graph**, choose a range (**A–F**), highlight the range, ⏎Enter
Indicate x-axis data range	**/Graph**, **X**, highlight range, ⏎Enter
Define all data ranges at once	**/Graph**, **Group**; highlight a single range that contains **X** and **A–F** data ranges, ⏎Enter; **Columnwise** or **Rowwise**
Display graph on-screen	**/Graph View**; or F10 (Graph)
Add titles to a graph	**/Graph Options Titles**, choose an option (**First**, **Second**, **X-Axis** or **Y-Axis**)
Enter labels within a graph	**/Graph Options Data-Labels**; specify data series (**A–F** or **Group**); highlight range to be used as labels, ⏎Enter; indicate location of labels (**Center**, **Left**, **Above**, **Right**, or **Below**)
Add a legend to a graph	**/Graph Options Legend**; select range (**A–F**), type \, type cell address containing the label, ⏎Enter; repeat for each label to be included in legend
Add connecting lines and/or symbols	**/Graph Options Format**, assign lines or symbols to whole graph or to individual ranges; **Lines**, **Symbols**, or **Both**
Set background grid	**/Graph Options Grid**, select type of grid (**Horizontal**, **Vertical**, or **Both**)

B

482

Action	Commands
Change upper and lower limits of y-axis scale	/**Graph Options Scale**; **Y**-Scale or **X**-Scale; **Manual**; **Lower**, type value, ↵Enter; **Upper**, type value, ↵Enter
Change format of y-axis values	/**Graph Options Scale**; **Y**-Scale; **Format**
Suppress y-axis or x-axis scale indicator	/**Graph Options Scale**; **Y**-Scale or **X**-Scale; **Indicator**, **No**
Space the display of x-axis labels	/**Graph Options Scale Skip**, type number, ↵Enter
Save a graph on disk as PIC file	/**Graph Save**, type or highlight file name, ↵Enter
Store settings for graph to allow later modification	/**Graph Name**, select graph naming activity (**Create**, **Use**, **Delete**, **Reset**, or **Table**)

Printing Graphs

Action	Commands
Access PrintGraph program from DOS	From DOS prompt, type **pgraph**, ↵Enter
Access PrintGraph program from 1-2-3 Access System menu	From 1-2-3 Access System menu, **PrintGraph**
Access PrintGraph program from 1-2-3 so that you can later return to 1-2-3	/**System**, type **pgraph**, ↵Enter
Exit PrintGraph program	From PrintGraph menu, **Exit**
Print a basic graph	From PrintGraph menu, **Image-Select**; highlight name of graph, press space bar, ↵Enter; **Align**, **Go**
Adjust size and orientation of graph	From PrintGraph menu, **Settings Image Size**; **Full**, **Half**, or **Manual**; **Quit** three times; **Align**, **Go**
Select a different font for a graph	From PrintGraph menu, **Settings Image Font**, **1** or **2**, highlight name of font, press space bar, ↵Enter, **Quit** twice
Choose a different color for a graph	From PrintGraph menu, **Settings Image Range-Colors**; **X** or **A–F**; highlight color, ↵Enter; **Quit** three times

B

483

Action	Commands
Set up hardware for printing a graph	From PrintGraph menu, **Settings Hardware**
Pause printer between graphs	From PrintGraph menu, **Settings Action Pause Yes**; **Quit** twice
Eject paper after printing each graph	From PrintGraph menu, **Settings Action Eject Yes**; **Quit** twice
Save PrintGraph settings	From PrintGraph menu, **Settings Save**
Return PrintGraph settings to defaults	From PrintGraph menu, **Settings Reset**
Preview a graph	From PrintGraph menu, **Image-Select**; highlight graph name; `F10` (Graph)

Managing Data

Build a database	Choose area for database, enter field names across a single row, set column widths and cell display formats, add records
Add a record	**/Worksheet Insert Row**; move cell pointer to location for new record, `↵Enter`; enter data for new record
Delete a record	**/Worksheet Delete Row**; move cell pointer to record to be deleted, `↵Enter`
Add a field	**/Worksheet Insert Column**; move cell pointer to location for new field, `↵Enter`; enter data for new field
Delete a field	**/Worksheet Delete Column**; move cell pointer to field to be deleted, `↵Enter`
Edit a field	Highlight cell to be edited, `F2` (Edit)
Sort a database	**/Data Sort Data-Range**, designate range, `↵Enter` specify key field(s), `↵Enter`, choose ascending or descending order for each key field, `↵Enter`, **Go**

B

484

Action	*Commands*
Perform a one-key sort	/**Data Sort Data-Range,** highlight range, ⏎Enter, **Primary-Key,** point to cell in column containing primary-key field, ⏎Enter, type **A** for ascending or **D** for descending, ⏎Enter, **Go**
Perform a two-key sort	/**Data Sort Data-Range,** highlight range, ⏎Enter, **Primary-Key,** point to cell in column containing primary-key field, ⏎Enter, type **A** for ascending or **D** for descending, ⏎Enter, **Secondary-Key,** point to cell in column containing secondary-key field, ⏎Enter, type **A** for ascending or **D** for descending, ⏎Enter, **Go**
Create a "counter" column	Insert blank column with /**Worksheet Insert Column;** reduce column width of new column with /**Worksheet Column Set-Width;** /**Data Fill,** highlight rows in new column, ⏎Enter, type ⌴1⌴ and press ⏎Enter for Start, type ⌴1⌴ and press ⏎Enter for Step, press ⏎Enter to accept the default Stop value
Define input range	/**Data Query Input;** highlight range, ⏎Enter, **Quit**
Define criteria range	Type the label **CRITERIA RANGE**, ⏎Enter, copy exact field names to section of worksheet where criteria range is to be located; type search criteria just below a field name, ⏎Enter, /**Data Query Criteria,** highlight range, ⏎Enter, **Quit**
Reset input, criteria, and output ranges	/**Data Query Reset**

B

485

Action	Commands
Find records that meet criteria	/**Data Query Find**, press ⬇ to move highlight bar to next record that meets criteria
End a search	⏎Enter or Esc; **Quit**
Edit records during search	/**Data Query Find**, press ➡ or ⬅ until blinking cursor is in cell to be edited; F2 (Edit); modify cell contents, ⏎Enter
Define output range	Type the label **OUTPUT RANGE**, ⏎Enter; copy exact field names to section of worksheet where output range is to be located; /**Data Query Output**, highlight range, ⏎Enter; **Quit**
List all specified records to output range	/**Data Query Extract**; **Quit**
Copy extracted records to new file	/**File Xtract**; **Formulas** or **Values**; type new file name, ⏎Enter; highlight range of records to copy, ⏎Enter
Copy unique records that meet criteria to output range	/**Data Query Unique**; **Quit**
Delete specified records	/**Data Query Delete Delete**; **Quit**

Macros

Action	Commands
Assign an Alt-*letter* name to a macro	/**Range Name Create**; type \ and a single letter, ⏎Enter; highlight first cell in range where macro commands are stored, ⏎Enter
Assign a descriptive name to a macro	/**Range Name Create**; type descriptive name of up to 15 characters, ⏎Enter; highlight first cell in range where macro commands are stored, ⏎Enter

B

Action	Commands
Assign a name to an automatic macro	/**Range Name Create**; type ⟨\⟩⟨0⟩ (backslash zero), ⟨⏎Enter⟩; highlight first cell in range where macro commands are stored, ⟨⏎Enter⟩
Assign names to a group of macros	/**Range Name Labels Right**; highlight names to be assigned to macros; ⟨⏎Enter⟩
Record keystrokes for a macro with the Learn feature	/**Worksheet Learn Range**; highlight single-column range, ⟨⏎Enter⟩; move cell pointer to worksheet location; Alt ⟨F5⟩ (Learn); type all commands and keystrokes to be included in macro; ⟨Alt⟩⟨F5⟩ (Learn) to end
Execute an Alt-*letter* macro	Press ⟨Alt⟩-*letter*
Execute a macro with a descriptive name	⟨Alt⟩⟨F3⟩ (Run), highlight macro name, ⟨⏎Enter⟩
Undo a macro	With Undo feature enabled, press ⟨Alt⟩⟨F4⟩ (Undo)
Use STEP mode to debug a macro	⟨Alt⟩⟨F2⟩ (Step); execute macro; evaluate each step of macro and press space bar after checking each step; when error is found, ⟨Ctrl⟩⟨Break⟩ and ⟨Esc⟩; edit the macro; with ⟨F2⟩ (Edit) ⟨Alt⟩⟨F2⟩ (Step)
Edit a macro	Highlight cell to be modified, ⟨F2⟩ (Edit)

B

Index